GUNSHOT WOUNDS

Practical Aspects of Firearms, Ballistics, and Forensic Techniques

SECOND EDITION

CRC SERIES IN
PRACTICAL ASPECTS OF CRIMINAL
AND FORENSIC INVESTIGATIONS

VERNON J. GEBERTH, BBA, MPS, FBINA *Series Editor*

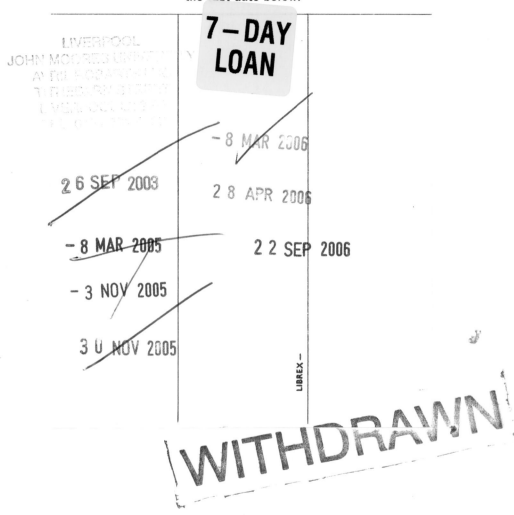

GUNSHOT WOUNDS

Practical Aspects of Firearms, Ballistics, and Forensic Techniques

SECOND EDITION

Vincent J.M. Di Maio

CRC Press

Boca Raton   London   New York   Washington, D.C.

Library of Congress Cataloging-in-Publication Data

Catalog record is available from the Library of Congress

Visit the CRC Press Web site at www.crcpress.com

© 1999 by CRC Press LLC

No claim to original U.S. Government works
International Standard Book Number 0-8493-8163-0
Printed in the United States of America   4 5 6 7 8 9 0
Printed on acid-free paper

To My Parents

Contents

6   Wounds from .22 Caliber Rimfire Weapons   153

7   Wounds from Centerfire Rifles   167

8   Wounds from Shotguns   203

9   Bloody Bodies and Bloody Scenes   253

10   Miscellaneous Weapons and Ammunition   277

Foreword

This Second Edition of *Gunshot Wounds: Practical Aspects of Firearms, Ballistics, and Forensic Techniques*, written by Vincent J. M. Di Maio, M.D. has been greatly expanded to include over 78 new photographs with references and discussions not covered in the original text. Dr. Di Maio has taken his personal observations, experience and research of gunshot wounds and firearms to create an extremely practical hands-on guide.

Guns continue to be the most frequently used weapons in murder and firearms account for more than half of the slayings. Therefore, this Second Edition of *Gunshot Wounds: Practical Aspects of Firearms, Ballistics, and Forensic Techniques*, will continue to be the definitive source and reference for Medical Examiners, forensic pathologists, professional law enforcement officers, forensic crime laboratories, lawyers and others involved in the criminal justice and forensic fields.

In 1985, the First Edition of *Gunshot Wounds: Practical Aspects of Firearms, Ballistics, and Forensic Techniques* written by Vincent J. M. Di Maio, M.D. was published within my *Practical Aspects of Criminal and Forensic Investigations* Series.

At the time of this first publication, I had the opportunity to write the Foreword and stated; "…without a doubt this text was the most comprehensive text on gunshot wounds available today." Little did I know how significant that statement would become. In fact, the First Edition became a benchmark within the forensic community and could only be replaced with this new and augmented Second Edition.

I have known Dr. Di Maio for over twenty years and I consider him to be the nation's foremost authority in the sphere of gunshot wounds and forensic techniques as they relate to firearm injuries. In both my Second and Third Editions of *Practical Homicide Investigation: Tactics, Procedures and Forensic Techniques* I cite the work of Dr. Di Maio.

Dr. Di Maio, who is presently the Chief Medical Examiner of Bexar County, in San Antonio, Texas was previously affiliated with Southwestern Institute of Forensic Sciences in Dallas, Texas. Dr. Di Maio has been able to view gunshot wounds at the same time as the weapons and ammunition used to inflict them. He has also been able to discuss the weapons and ammunition with firearm examiners at the time of autopsy.

This Second Edition of *Gunshot Wounds: Practical Aspects of Firearms, Ballistics, and Forensic Techniques* combines over twenty-five years of medicolegal investigation with practical experience.

The book begins with an excellent presentation regarding firearms and ammunition and acquaints the reader with some basic knowledge of firearms and the terminology used by ballistics and firearm examiners. The text then describes the practical aspects of ballistics, wound ballistics, and the classification of various wounds pertaining to handguns, bang guns, rifles, and shotguns. The Second Edition has been expanded to include new information on the use of DNA and cytology to associate a bullet recovered at the scene to a deceased; rubber and plastic bullets, hangfires, slamfires and wounds due to assault rifles.

In addition, Dr. Di Maio has expanded on a number of topics not discussed in the original edition and has updated and expanded on wound structures and suicide investigation involving firearms. The final chapters deal with autopsy technique and procedure as well as the very pertinent laboratory analysis relating to weapons and gunshot evidence.

Gunshot Wounds: Practical Aspects of Firearms, Ballistics, and Forensic Techniques, Second Edition is written clearly and concisely. The text is accented by numerous photographs that depict exactly what to look for and how to interpret gunshot wounds and evidence. As I have said before; "Without a doubt, this book is the most comprehensive text on gunshot wounds available today.

Vernon J. Geberth, M.S., M.P.S.
Homicide and Forensic Consultant
Retired Homicide Commander
New York City Police Department

Acknowledgment

I wish to thank the following individuals who aided me in the preparation of the second edition of this book: my wife, Theresa, for her encouragement and support; Gloria Delgado for her secretarial assistance; Suzanna Dana, M.D., for proofreading the manuscript; and Rudyard Kipling for pointing out that "Iron — Cold Iron — is master of men all!"

Editor's Note

This textbook is part of a series entitled "Practical Aspects of Criminal and Forensic Investigation." This series was created by Vernon J. Geberth, New York City Police Department Lieutenant Commander (Retired), who is an author, educator, and consultant on homicide and forensic investigations.

This series has been designed to provide contemporary, comprehensive, and pragmatic information to the practitioner involved in criminal and forensic investigations by authors who are nationally recognized experts in their respective fields.

Firearms and Ammunition

"My wife yes; My dog maybe; My gun never!"

Bumper sticker

In order to interpret gunshot wounds, a certain basic knowledge of firearms and ammunition is necessary. This chapter will attempt to present such information.

Small Arms

There are five general categories of small arms: handguns, rifles, shotguns, submachine guns, and machine guns.

Handguns

There are four basic types of handguns:

1. Single-shot pistols
2. Derringers
3. Revolvers
4. Auto-loading pistols (automatics)

Single-shot pistols.   A single-shot pistol has one firing chamber integral with the barrel, which must be loaded manually each time the weapon is to be fired (Figure 1.1A).

Derringers.   They are a variant of single-shot pistols. Derringers are small pocket firearms having multiple barrels, each of which is loaded and fired separately. The traditional derringer has two barrels (Figure 1.1B).

1

Figure 1.1 **(A)** Single-shot pistol; **(B)** derringer.

Revolvers. The revolver is the most common type of handgun in the United States. Revolvers have a revolving cylinder that contains several chambers, each of which holds one cartridge. The cylinder is rotated mechanically so as to align each chamber successively with the barrel and firing pin. The first revolver was produced by Samuel Colt in 1835–1836.

There are three types of revolvers, the most common of which is the "swingout" (Figure 1.2A). On pressing the cylinder latch, normally found on the left side of the frame and pushing the cylinder to the left, the cylinder swings out, exposing the chambers. Each individual chamber is then loaded with a cartridge. The cylinder is then swung back into the frame, engaging the cylinder latch. The weapon is now ready to be fired. After discharge of all the cartridges, the cylinder latch is pressed and the cylinder is swung out.

An ejector rod, affixed to the front of the cylinder, is pressed to the rear, ejecting the fired cases. The cylinder is now ready to be reloaded.

In break-top revolvers, the frame is hinged at the rear such that, on release of a top catch, the barrel and cylinder swing down, exposing the back of the cylinder for loading (Figure 1.2B). The opening action will also eject empty cases from the cylinder. This form of weapon is relatively uncommon in the United States, but is the traditional form of revolver in Great Britain.

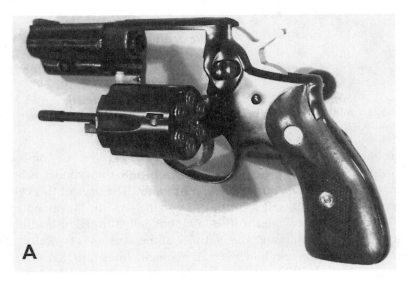

Figure 1.2 (A) A 9-mm revolver, swing-out type, with cylinder swung open exposing chambers; (B) break-top revolver with action open.

Figure 1.3 Solid-frame revolver with loading gate swung open. Arrow points to loading port where individual cartridges are inserted.

The solid-frame revolver is the oldest form of revolver, dating back to Colt's original weapons (Figure 1.3). In this weapon, the cylinder is held in the frame by a central pin, around which it rotates. The back of this cylinder is never exposed completely by either "swinging out" or "breaking open." Each chamber in the cylinder is loaded individually through a loading gate on the right side of the frame. The hammer of the weapon is typically pulled back to half cock, and the cylinder is then manually rotated so that a chamber is aligned with the loading gate. A cartridge is inserted. The cylinder is then manually rotated to the next chamber and a second cartridge is inserted. This procedure is continued until the cylinder is completely filled. After the weapon is discharged, the cylinder has to be manually rotated again and aligned with the loading gate, and each cartridge is ejected through the gate using the ejector rod. This type of construction is most commonly encountered in single-action revolvers and the early model Saturday Night Specials. The latter term, dating back to the turn of the century, refers to a cheap weapon usually of poor construction and does not refer to concealability.

Revolvers may be either single-action or double-action types. In single-action revolvers, the hammer must be cocked manually each time the weapon is to be fired. Cocking the hammer revolves the cylinder, aligning the chamber with the barrel and the firing pin. Pressure applied to the trigger then releases the hammer, discharging the weapon. In double-action revolvers a continuous pressure on the trigger revolves the cylinder, aligns the chamber with the barrel, and cocks and then releases the hammer, firing the weapon. Most double-action revolvers may be fired in a single-action mode. The amount of pressure on a trigger necessary to fire a well-made double-action revolver varies from 12 to 15 lb. If these weapons are cocked and fired in single-action mode, less pressure (2–4 lb) is necessary to fire them. The double-action trigger pull for cheap, poorly made revolvers is usually much greater, while single-action trigger pull may vary from less than a pound to as much as the double-action pull in a well-made revolver.

Many single-action revolvers have a "half-cock" notch in the cocking hammer that lies between the position of "full cock" and "fired." The purpose of the half-cock notch is to catch the hammer if it accidentally slips from the thumb as it is being manually cocked. Many individuals incorrectly consider the half-cock notch a safety position and will carry weapons on "half cock." Dropping a weapon when on half cock may cause the hammer to disengage, fly forward, and discharge the weapon. Some single-action revolvers will fire from the half-cock position if the trigger is pulled. Ruger single-action revolvers equipped with a safety bar do not have a half-cock notch.

The cylinder of a revolver may rotate either clockwise (Colt revolvers) or counterclockwise (Smith & Wesson revolvers). This difference has resulted in a number of deaths among individuals playing Russian roulette, in which an individual loads one chamber of a revolver and spins the cylinder. They then "peek" to locate the cartridge. If it is in any cylinder except the one that will be rotated into firing position on pulling the trigger, the gun is then put to the head and the trigger pulled. If the cartridge is in the lethal chamber, the player makes some excuse to spin the cylinder again. This system of playing Russian roulette is theoretically "safe" if one knows which way the cylinder rotates. A person familiar with playing the game using a Colt revolver may try it with a Smith & Wesson revolver in which the cylinder rotates in the opposite direction and may experience a fatal conclusion to the "game."

Auto-loading pistols (automatics). Auto-loading or automatic pistols make up the fourth category of handguns. The term "automatic pistol" is a misnomer, as this form of pistol is an auto-loader in which the trigger must be pulled for every shot fired. Regardless of the correct terminology, however, these weapons are invariably called "automatics" or just "pistols." These pistols use the forces generated by the fired cartridge to operate the mechanism that extracts and ejects the empty cases, loads the fresh cartridge, and returns the mechanism into position to fire the next round (Figure 1.4). The first commercial automatic pistol was produced in 1893 by Borchardt; this weapon was the predecessor of the Luger.

The cartridges are almost invariably stored in a removable magazine in the grip of the pistol. Some automatic pistols, such as the Intratec Tec 9, and the Mauser M1896, have the magazine in front of the trigger guard. The Calico Auto Pistol uses a 50 or 100 round helical-feed magazine on the top

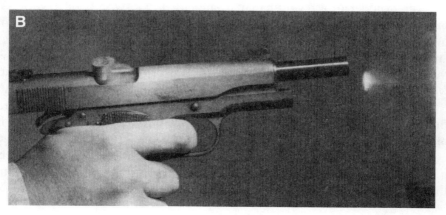

Figure 1.4 (A) The weapon has just been fired. The slide has begun to recoil with the bullet a few inches in front of the muzzle. (B) The slide has recoiled all the way back. The fired cartridge case is being ejected and the gun cocked. The slide will now come forward, chambering a new round.

rear of the frame. The term "clip" is often used synonymously with the term "magazine." In fact, a clip is a device designed to facilitate the loading of a number of cartridges into a magazine, however, most people use the terms interchangeably.

There are five methods of operation of automatic pistols: blow-back, delayed or retarded blow-back, blow-forward, recoil, and gas. Only two of these methods are currently in widespread use: blow-back and recoil. In a blow-back action, the pressure of the gas produced by combustion of the powder forces an unlocked slide to the rear, thus starting the cycle of extraction, ejection, and reloading.

Heckler and Koch P7 pistols are blow-back-operated pistols with a recoil breaking system that delays breech opening (Figure 1.5). On firing the gun, part of the propellant gas is directed through a small vent in the barrel ahead of the chamber into a cylinder beneath the barrel. A piston attached to the slide enters the front end of this cylinder. The gas entering the cylinder acts against the piston, such that as the slide begins to move rearward by virtue of the recoil pressure, the movement of the piston in the cylinder is resisted by the gas pressure, delaying the movement of the slide and delaying the opening of the breech. Another unusual feature of this weapons is that the firing pin is cocked by a squeeze cocker incorporated in the front of the grip (Figure 1.5). On grasping the grip, the fingers depress the squeeze cocker, automatically cocking the gun. If the pressure on the grip is released, the squeeze cocker goes forward uncocking the gun. P7 pistols have fluted firing chambers and polygonal rifling of the barrels (see Chapter 2).

In a recoil-operated automatic pistol, the barrel and the slide are locked together at the moment of firing. As the bullet leaves the barrel, the rearward thrust of the propellant gas on the cartridge case starts the barrel and slide moving to the rear. After a short distance, the barrel is halted, and the locking device is withdrawn from the slide (Figure 1.6). The slide then continues to the rear, ejecting the fired case and starting the reloading cycle.

Traditionally, automatic pistols have had at least one manually operated safety device. Manual safeties are thumb pieces or buttons that are mounted on either the slide or receiver (Figure 1.7). Customarily, on the left side, they are now often ambidextrous or reversible. Putting on the safety locks the firing mechanism (hammer, striker, and sometimes sear) and prevents the weapon from discharging. Less commonly, automatic pistols, e.g., the Colt M1911, are equipped with grip safeties (Figure 1.7), movable pieces mounted in the grip which prevent connection between the trigger and the sear except when the pistol is held firmly in the hand, ready for shooting. The grip safety is held out by springs when at rest. Grasping the grip pushes the piece in and permits connection between the trigger and sear and thus firing of the weapon.

Many of the newer double-action automatic pistols have a thumb piece on either the slide or frame which externally resembles the usual safety lever but is in fact a decocking lever (Figure 1.8A). It may be on the left side, ambidextrous or reversible. When this thumb piece is pushed down, the hammer falls. The weapon will not discharge, however, as the thumb piece locks the firing pin and/or rotates a steel surface between the hammer and the firing pin to prevent contact between the two. In some weapons, the decocking lever now functions as a safety and the weapon will not fire as long as this device is down. Other automatic pistols do not have any manual safety but only a decocking lever, e.g., Sig-Sauer (Figure 1.8B). In such guns, depressing the thumb piece causes the hammer to drop, putting the gun on

Figure 1.5 (**A**) Heckler-Koch P7 9-mm pistol with squeeze cocker constituting front portion of grip; (**B**) Disassembled with piston visible and projecting downward from end of slide.

a double action mode but not putting on a safety. The Glock pistols have neither a manually operated safety nor a decocking lever.

The Sig-Sauers, as well as most of the newer quality automatics, are equipped with a firing pin safety (lock). This internal device locks the firing pin in place preventing forward movement and thus accidental discharge. In order to fire the weapon, the trigger must be pulled back in order to disengage this safety.

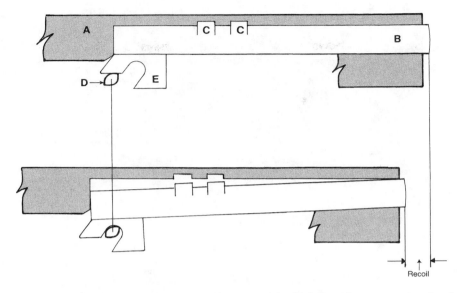

Figure 1.6 Locking action of recoil-operated locked breech automatic pistol. On firing, the slide (**A**) and barrel (**B**), which are locked together by the ribs (**C**), recoil. After a short distance, the barrel is haltered by a bar (**D**) engaging the barrel lug (**E**). The ribs disengage and the slide continues backward to extract and eject the fired cartridge case. The slide then comes forward to chamber a new round and cock the weapon.

Figure 1.7 Left side of Colt .45 automatic pistol with manual safety and grip safety (arrow).

Figure 1.8 **(A)** Beretta with decocking lever/safety mounted on slide **(B)** Sig Sauer P226 with decocking lever (but no safety) on frame above magazine button.

Some pistols have a device that tells whether the chamber contains a cartridge. This may be a protruding pin at the rear of the slide or just protrusion of the extractor. Some automatic pistols have magazine safeties. This device prevents discharge of the weapon when the magazine has been removed from it. In some weapons, it is possible to deactivate or remove this device.

With rare exceptions, currently manufactured revolvers do not have manually operated safety devices. This fact seems to have escaped British writers, who in their detective and action fiction always have their characters putting on and taking off the "safety" of their revolver. Although thumb safeties are not present on modern revolvers, Smith & Wesson did at one time manufacture a model with a grip safety. As regards derringers, they may or may not be equipped with a push-button safety that blocks the fall of the hammer.

Preparing an automatic pistol to fire involves two steps. First, the loaded magazine is inserted into the grip. The slide is grasped, pulled rearward, and released. A spring drives the slide forward, stripping a cartridge from the magazine and loading it into the firing chamber. The weapon is now cocked and ready to be fired. If the weapon has a manually operated safety, the safety may now be applied and the weapon carried in a cocked-and-locked mode. Alternatively, the weapon may be decocked using the decocking switch or by holding the hammer back (usually with the thumb), pressing the trigger and gradually lowering the hammer. In the case of weapons of older design (the Colt M1911, the Browning HiPower), to fire the gun after the hammer is lowered, the hammer must be manually recocked for the first shot. After the first shot, the operating mechanism of the automatic pistol automatically cocks the hammer. Most auto-loading pistols are now equipped with a double-action trigger that will cock and fire the first shot as a result of continuous pressure on the trigger. In these weapons, after the hammer is lowered, in order to fire, one just pulls the trigger. After this, the weapon automatically cocks itself for each succeeding shot. Even in double-action automatic pistols, however, the slide must be pulled back initially to chamber a cartridge.

Some of the newer double-action auto-loading pistols are manufactured in a number of variations. Thus, they can be purchased double action only and with or without safety levers. Browning has a model, the BDM (Browning Double Mode), that has a screw-slotted selector on the left side of the slide. Using it, the trigger and hammer can be set for conventional double/single action or double action only.

The Colt Model 2000 (now discontinued) had a sliding trigger; turning-barrel locking system; polymer frame; slide latch; hammerless striker and automatic internal striker block that is cleared only in the last fraction of trigger movement. It only fires in the double-action mode.

Beretta manufactures auto-loading pistols with a tip-up barrel for first-round loading (Figure 1.9). In this weapon, a loaded magazine is placed in the grip. A latch is depressed on the side of the frame and the barrel tips up exposing the firing chamber. A cartridge can then be inserted directly into the firing chamber. The action is then closed and the weapon is now ready to fire. A round can also be chambered the traditional way by pulling back and releasing the slide.

Following its introduction into the United States, the Glock pistol became involved in controversy when members of the media and some politicians contended it was a "plastic gun" that was not detectible by x-ray or metal detectors. This is, of course, nonsense. While the gun does have a polymer

Figure 1.9   Beretta with tip-up barrel.

frame, the slide, barrel, and internal components are steel. Since then, a number of other pistols with polymer frames have been introduced.

Rifles

A rifle is a firearm with a rifled barrel which is designed to be fired from the shoulder. Barrel length is immaterial in classifying a firearm as a rifle. However, U.S. Federal law requires rifles to have a minimum barrel length of 16 inches. The types of rifles commonly encountered are single-shot, lever-action, bolt-action, pump-action, and auto-loading. A single-shot rifle has one firing chamber integral with the barrel which has to be manually loaded each time the weapon is fired. A lever-action rifle has a lever beneath the grip which is used to open the rifle action, to extract the cartridge case, and, in closing the action, to insert a fresh cartridge in the firing chamber and to cock the gun.

In a bolt-action rifle, a handle projects from a bolt. Pulling back and pushing forward on this projection causes the bolt to extract and eject a cartridge case and then to insert a new cartridge while cocking the gun. The slide-action rifle uses the manual movement of a slide under and parallel to the barrel to open the action, extract and eject a cartridge, load a fresh cartridge, and cock the weapon.

In auto-loading or semi-automatic rifles, the weapon fires, extracts, ejects, reloads, and cocks with each pull of the trigger using the force of gas pressure or recoil to operate the action. After each shot the trigger must be released and then pulled again to repeat the cycle. Auto-loading rifles are commonly but incorrectly called "automatic rifles." A fully automatic rifle is one that, on pulling the trigger and firing the weapon, utilizes the force of gas pressure or recoil to eject the fired case, load the next round, fire it, and then eject it. This cycle is repeated until all the ammunition is used or the trigger is released. Automatic weapons are generally used only by military and police organizations. While it is possible to alter some semi-automatic rifles to deliver automatic fire, unlike the impression given by the media and some politicians, this is not a simple procedure. In fact, such conversions are uncommon. In the United States, deaths due to full-automatic weapons (rifles and submachine guns) are extremely rare. The author has seen only three such deaths in the past 30 years, all of which occurred in the same incident and involved illegal drug dealings and an alleged professional killer. Weapons fired in the full-automatic mode are very difficult to control. In most instances, while the first shot may be on target, subsequent rounds fly high and to the right.

Assault Rifles

The term "assault rifle" refers to a rifle that is: (1) auto-loading, (2) has a large-capacity (20 rounds or more) detachable magazine, (3) is capable of full-automatic fire, and (4) fires an intermediate rifle cartridge. This term has been corrupted by the media and some politicians to include most self-loading weapons. They have also coined the meaningless term "assault pistol" which appears to refer to large, ugly-looking pistols having large-capacity magazines (20 to 40 rounds) or to semi-automatic versions of submachine guns such as the Uzi (Figure 1.10). "Assault pistols" are with rare exception cumbersome, difficult to shoot, inaccurate, and cheaply made. They are usually acquired by individuals with little knowledge of firearms who associate the effectiveness of a weapon with "ugliness."

Weapons that fire pistol ammunition are not by definition assault rifles, nor are self-loading rifles with fixed magazines that were never intended for full-automatic fire. The best example of the latter weapon is the SKS-45 (Figure 1.11). While this weapon is an auto-loader and chambered for an intermediate-power cartridge, it has a fixed ten-round magazine and was never intended for full-automatic fire. The weapon may be altered to accept a 30-round magazine, however.

There is a group of weapons that might be considered "assault rifles" if one eliminates the criteria of full-automatic capability. This would include weapons such as the AKS-47, MAK-90 and Colt AR-15 Sporter and their variants (Figure 1.12). These are semi-automatic versions of the AK-47 and M-16 assault rifles.

Figure 1.10 Intratec Tec 9 often referred to as an "assault pistol," is just a cumbersome, ugly-looking pistol with a large magazine capacity.

One of the common fallacies about assault rifles is that the wounds they produce are more severe than those due to ordinary centerfire rifles. In fact, the wounds are less severe than those produced by virtually all hunting rifles even the Winchester M-94 (introduced in 1894) and its cartridge the .30–30 (introduced in 1895). As we shall see in Chapters 3 and 7, in dealing with rifles, the severity of the wound is determined by the amount of kinetic energy lost by a bullet in the body. The intermediate cartridges used in assault rifles possess significantly less kinetic energy than a regular centerfire rifle cartridge

Figure 1.11   SKS-45.

Figure 1.12   Chinese AKS-47 semi-automatic rifle.

designed for hunting. In addition, since most ammunition used in these weapons is loaded with a full-metal jacketed bullet, the wound is even less severe than one might expect.

Shotguns

A shotgun is a weapon that is intended to be fired from the shoulder; it has a smooth bore and is designed to fire multiple pellets from the barrel. Again, barrel length is immaterial in classifying a firearm as a shotgun, although U.S. federal law requires a minimal barrel length of 18 inches. A shotgun may be classified as a single-shot, over-and-under, double-barrel, bolt-action, lever-action, pump-action, or auto-loading. The over-and under shotgun has two barrels one above the other, and the double-barrel version has its barrels side by side. The two barrels in these weapons are often of different choke.

Submachine Guns/Machine Pistols

A submachine gun or machine pistol is a weapon that is designed to be fired from either the shoulder and/or the hip; is capable of full-automatic fire; has a rifled barrel, and fires pistol ammunition. It is often incorrectly called a "machine gun." Semi-automatic carbines (excluding the M-1 Carbine) are a variation of submachine guns. These are either semi-automatic versions of submachine guns or weapons that have the external appearance of a subma-chine gun. The media has dubbed these "assault pistols." In the case of semi-automatic versions of submachine guns, the internal mechanism is typically so altered that they are essentially a different weapon.

Machine Guns

A machine gun is a weapon that is capable of full-automatic firing and that fires rifle ammunition. It is generally crew-operated, but some forms may be fired by single individuals. Most machine guns have the ammunition fed by belts, although some use magazines.

Caliber Nomenclature for Rifled Weapons

Rifles, handguns, submachine guns, and machine guns have rifled barrels; that is, spiral grooves have been cut the length of the interior or bore of the barrel (Figure 1.13). Rifling consists of these grooves and the metal left between the grooves — the lands.

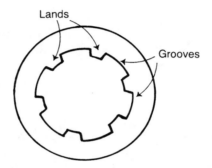

Figure 1.13 Cross-section of barrel showing lands and grooves.

In the United States, the caliber of a rifle or handgun is supposed to be the diameter of the bore, measured from land to land. This measurement represents the diameter of the barrel before the rifling grooves were cut. In reality, however, caliber may be given in terms of bullet, land, or groove diameter. Caliber specifications using the U.S. system are neither accurate nor consistent, i.e., the .303 Savage fires a 0.308-in.-diameter bullet, while the .303 British cartridge has a 0.312-in.-diameter bullet. Both the .30-06 and the .308 Winchester cartridges are loaded with bullets having a diameter of 0.308 in. The "06" in .30-06 refers to the year of adoption of this cartridge. American cartridges that originally used black powder are designated by caliber, the original black powder charge, and, in some cases, bullet weight. Thus, the .45-70-405 cartridge has a 405-gr. bullet, 0.45 in. in diameter, and was originally propelled by 70 grains of black powder. The term "grains" refers to the weight of powder, not the number of granules of powder. A few of the smokeless powder cartridges that came out in the late-nineteenth century also used this method of designation. Thus, the .30-30 cartridge has a 0.308-in.-diameter bullet originally propelled by 30 gr. of smokeless powder.

With the development of newer types of powder, this powder charge is no longer used.

The best example of confusing caliber designation and the one most significant to the forensic pathologist involves the .38 Special and .357 Magnum cartridges. Weapons chambered for these calibers have barrels with the same bore and groove diameters. Bullets loaded in each of these cartridges have identical dimensions. The .357 Magnum revolver chambers and fires all .38 Special ammunition, although a weapon chambered for a .38 Special cartridge cannot ordinarily chamber and should never use the .357 Magnum cartridge. The .357 Magnum cartridge case is, in fact, the .38 Special cartridge case lengthened and loaded with additional propellant. Except for the difference in the length of the cartridge cases, all other physical dimensions are the same for both calibers.

The European system of cartridge designation, which uses the metric system, is more thorough and logical than the U.S. system. It clearly and specifically identifies a cartridge by giving the bullet diameter and the case length in millimeters, as well as by designating the type of cartridge case. Thus, the Russian rimmed-service round becomes the 7.62 × 54 mm R. The 7.62 refers to the diameter of the bullet; 54 mm indicates the length of the cartridge case; and **R** indicates that the round is rimmed. The letters **SR** are used for semi-rimmed cases, **RB** for rebated cartridge cases, and **B** for belted cases. No letter is used to describe rimless cartridge cases. Thus, the .30–06 in the metric designation is the 7.62 × 63 mm.

The term "Magnum," is used to describe a cartridge that is larger and produces higher velocity than standard cartridges. In the case of shotgun ammunition, it may or may not be larger but does contain more shot than the standard shell.

A Wildcat cartridge is a nonstandard cartridge produced by a small company, independent gunsmith, or other individual; it is not available from major ammunition manufacturers.

Ammunition

A small-arms cartridge consists of a cartridge case, a primer, propellant (gunpowder), and a bullet or projectile (Figure 1.14). Blank cartridges are sealed with paper disks instead of a bullet or have a crimped neck. Dummy cartridges have neither a primer nor powder. Some dummy cartridges contain inert granular material that simulates powder.

Cartridge Cases

Cartridge cases are usually made of brass, a composition of 70% copper and 30% zinc. Less commonly, they are made of steel or aluminum. Zinc and

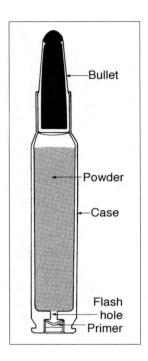

Figure 1.14 Small arms cartridge with bullet, powder, cartridge, case and primer.

plastic materials have been used experimentally. Brass, plastic, and paper are used for shot-shell tubes.

The main function of the cartridge case is to expand and seal the chamber against rearward escape of gases when the cartridge is fired. When a brass cartridge is fired in a weapon, the gas pressure produced by the burning of the propellant expands the case tightly against the walls of the chamber. If the brass is tempered to the correct hardness, it will spring back to approximately its original dimensions and make the case easy to extract. If the brass is too soft, it will not spring back and will make extraction difficult. If the brass is too hard — that is, brittle — it will crack.

There are three general shapes for cartridge cases: straight, bottleneck, and tapered. Almost all pistol cartridges are straight, whereas almost all rifle cartridges are bottle-necked. The bottle-neck design permits more powder to be packed in a shorter, fatter cartridge than would be possible in a straight cartridge, where the lumen is approximately the diameter of the bullet. Cartridges with tapered cases are virtually obsolete.

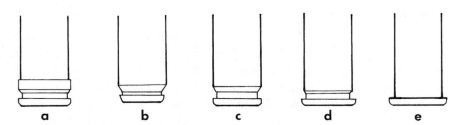

Figure 1.15   Cartridge case head designs: (a) belted; (b) rebated; (c) rimless; (d) semi-rimmed; (e) rimmed.

Cartridge cases are classified into five types according to the configuration of their bases (Figure 1.15):

Rimmed
Semi-rimmed
Rimless
Rebated
Belted

Rimmed cartridge cases have an extractor flange that is larger than the diameter of the cartridge case body. The letter **R** is added after case length numbers in the metric system of caliber designation.

Semi-rimmed cartridge cases have an extractor flange that is larger in diameter than the cartridge case body, but they also have a groove around the case body just in front of the flange. The metric designation for these cartridges is **SR.**

Rimless cartridge cases have an extractor flange whose diameter is the same as that of the cartridge case body and also have a groove around the body of the case in front of the flange. In the metric system of caliber designation, no letter is used for this type of cartridge case.

A rebated cartridge case has an extractor flange that is smaller than the diameter of the case. A groove around the body of the case is present in front of the flange. The metric designation is **RB.**

A belted cartridge case has a pronounced, raised belt encircling the cartridge case body in front of the groove in the body. The diameter of the extractor flange is immaterial. The metric designation is **B.**

Head Stamps

Virtually all cartridge cases have head stamps on their bases (Figure 1.16). The head stamp is a series of letters, numbers, symbols, and/or trade names. They are either imprinted or embossed on a cartridge case head for identification purposes. Civilian cartridges are usually marked with the initials or code of the manufacturer, as well as the caliber. Military cartridges are usually marked with the manufacturer's initials or code plus the last two numerals of the year of manufacture. The caliber may be designated as well. American military Match ammunition has the word "Match" or the letters "NM" (National Match) imprinted on it. Ammunition meeting NATO specifications carries the NATO symbol which is a cross within a circle (Figure 1.16).

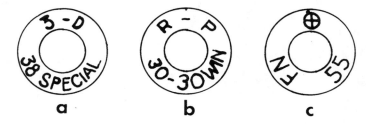

Figure 1.16 Headstamps on centerfire cartridges: (a) .38 Special cartridge manufactured by 3 D; (b) rifle cartridge manufactured by Remington-Peters of caliber .30–30 Winchester; (c) rifle cartridge manufactured by Fabrique Nationale in 1955 with a NATO symbol.

Head stamps are not necessarily reliable indicators of the caliber of the particular cartridge case or the manufacturer because a cartridge case may have been reformed to another caliber. Thus a .308 cartridge case may have been necked down to a .243 cartridge. Commercial concerns that buy large quantities of ammunition may have their name stamped on the cartridge cases rather than the designation of the actual manufacturer.

Ammunition manufactured by Russia and Japan during World War II and some 7.62 × 39 mm ammunition manufactured by the U.S. government during the Vietnam war do not have head stamps. Occasionally, a cartridge case may be seen with a surcharge. These are markings added to the base of the cartridge after the original head stamp has been formed. They are not necessarily applied in the plant that performs the original head stamp operation on the cartridge case, and they may indicate that the cartridge has been reloaded.

Handgun ammunition with a head stamps reading +**P** or +**P**+ indicates that the ammunition is loaded to higher pressures than normal for the particular caliber cartridge.

Primers

Small-arms cartridges are classified as centerfire or rimfire, depending on the location of the primer. In centerfire cartridges, the primer is located in the center of the base of the cartridge case. There are two types of primers for metallic cartridges: Boxer and Berdan. American centerfire rifle and pistol cartridges have Boxer primers (Blazer® ammunition is the exception). A Boxer primer consists of a brass or gilding-metal cup, a pellet containing a sensitive explosive, a paper disk and a brass anvil (Figure 1.17). These component parts are assembled to form a complete primer. The Boxer primer has a single large flash hole in the bottom of the case.

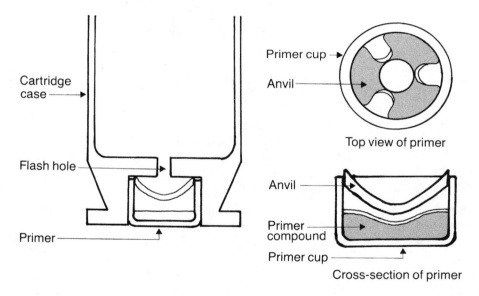

Figure 1.17 Boxer primer.

European metallic cartridges traditionally are loaded with Berdan primers. The Berdan primer differs from the American Boxer primer in that it has no integral anvil. Instead, the anvil is built into the cartridge case and forms a projection in the primer pocket (Figure 1.18). Berdan primers have two flash holes in the primer pocket.

Shot-shell primers are a variant of Boxer primers used in metallic cartridges. The main difference is that the shotshell primer has its own supporting cup — the battery cup — which encloses the anvil, the paper disk, the priming mixture, and the primer cup. This battery cup primer is inserted in the base of the shotgun shell.

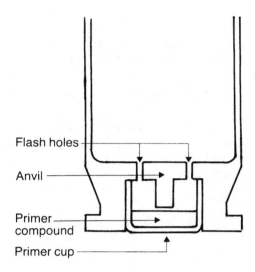

Figure 1.18 Berdan primer.

Primers made for rifles and pistols differ in construction in that the cups of pistol primers are made with thinner metal. The rifle primer also has a mixture that burns with a more intense and sustained flame.

Primers come in five sizes: large rifle, small rifle, large pistol, small pistol, and shotgun. The large primers measure 0.210 in. in diameter; the small 0.175 in. and shotgun primers 0.243. Magnum primers (either rifle or pistol) produce a more intense and sustained flame, which is necessary for better ignition in Magnum cartridges.

When a weapon is fired, the firing pin strikes the center of the primer cup, compressing the primer composition between the cup and anvil and causing the composition to explode. The vents in the anvil allow the flame to pass through the flash hole(s) into the cartridge case and thereby igniting the propellant.

Primer compounds originally were made of fulminate of mercury. On firing, free mercury was released. This amalgamated with the brass of the cartridge case, making it brittle and ruining it for reloading. In addition, storage of ammunition containing mercury primers for long periods of time led to deterioration of the brass because of the mercury. Mercury compounds were then replaced with chlorate compounds. Unfortunately, on firing, these broke down to chloride salts, causing severe rusting of the barrels.

All primers currently manufactured in the U.S. use chemical ingredients that are non-mercuric and noncorrosive. The compounds that are used vary: lead styphnate, barium nitrate, and antimony sulfide are most commonly used. Most centerfire primers of either U.S. or foreign manufacture contain all three compounds. The detection of these compounds constitutes the basis for tests to determine whether an individual has fired a firearm. Blount Industries (CCI), Remington, Federal, and Winchester now manufacture some centerfire pistol ammunition that does not contain lead in the primer.

Rimfire ammunition does not contain a primer assembly. Instead, the primer composition is spun into the rim of the cartridge case with the propellant in intimate contact with this composition (Figure 1.19). On firing, the firing pin strikes the rim of the cartridge case, compressing the primer composition and initiating its detonation. The primer mixture used in .22 rimfire ammunition manufactured by Winchester and CCI contains compounds of lead and barium. Federal ammunition uses compounds of lead, barium, and antimony. Remington rimfire ammunition used to contain only lead compounds, but now uses compounds of lead and barium. Some Mexican manufactured rimfire ammunition uses only lead compounds in the primer.

Propellants

Until the end of the nineteenth century, all cartridges were loaded with black powder. Black powder is a mixture of charcoal, sulfur, and potassium nitrate. These materials were individually ground to a powder, mechanically mixed, ground together, incorporated with the help of moisture and pressed into hard cakes, dried, and then broken down into the desired granulation. In such a mixture, the charcoal is the fuel; the potassium nitrate the oxygen supplier or oxidizer while the sulfur gives the mixture more density and workability and makes it more readily ignitable. When black powder burns properly, it produces 44% of its original weight in gases and 56% in solid residues.[1] These residues appear principally as a dense, white smoke.

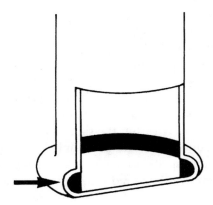

Figure 1.19 Cross-section of base of .22 rimfire cartridge with primer composition in rim of case (arrow).

In 1884, Vieille, a French chemist, first synthesized an effective, practical form of what is now known as smokeless powder.[2] Using alcohol and ether, he reduced nitrocellulose to a gelatinous colloid, which was rolled into sheets and cut into flakes. In 1887, Alfred Nobel developed a slightly different form of smokeless powder.[2] Utilizing nitrocellulose that was not as highly nitrated as that used by Vieille, he colloided it with nitroglycerine and then dried, rolled, and cut it into flakes. These two types of smokeless powder are known as single-base and double-base powders, respectively. The physical configuration of individual powder grains can be disk, flake, or cylinder, whether the powder is single- or double-base.

The next major step in the development of smokeless powder was the introduction of ball powder by Winchester in 1933.[2] In ball powder, the nitrocellulose instead of being colloided is dissolved completely and the resultant lacquer is agitated under conditions to make it form into small balls that constitute the powder grains. By manipulation of the process, the diameter of the balls of powder can be controlled, whereas in an extra operation the balls of powder may be flattened between rollers, thus altering the surface area and thus the burning rate of the powder. True ball powder appears as small, uniform silver-black spheres or ovals having a shiny, reflective surface; flattened ball powder as irregular, flattened chips with a silver-black shiny surface. In most flattened ball powder one can find non-flattened spheres and ovoid grains. Between the extremes of true ball and flattened ball powder is a wide spectrum of physical variations.

Smokeless powder is, theoretically, converted completely into gaseous products. Unlike black powder, it does not leave a significant residue in the bore. Smokeless powders burn at the surface only. Thus, the burning surface decreases continuously as the grains are consumed. This degressive burning, an unfavorable characteristic, can be overcome to a degree by putting a hole in the individual powder grain, with a resultant increase in the surface area as the grain burns. More commonly, chemical coating deterrents are applied to powder grains to slow the burning initially in order to make progressive burning powder. These grains of powder burn slowly at first and then rapidly. The grains of powder may also be coated with graphite to eliminate static electricity and facilitate the flow of powder while the cartridges are loaded. Rather than having a shiny black appearance, uncoated grains of powder are a pale-green color. Powder grains recovered from the skin or clothing after discharge of a gun may not be black, but rather, pale-green or beige due to losing the coating.

The weight of the propellant charge in a cartridge is adjusted for each lot of propellant to give the required muzzle velocity for the weight of the bullet with a chamber pressure within the limits prescribed for the weapon.

Pyrodex, a "synthetic" black powder, was developed to replace black powder in weapons in which only black powder can be used. It was developed for two reasons: first, there is a shortage of black powder and second, there are a number of restrictions in the United States put on the sale and storage of black powder because of its explosive properties. As Pyrodex is a nitrocellulose-based powder, it is considerably safer than black powder and avoids these restrictions. The problem with developing a replacement for black powder is that black powder burns at substantially the same rate whether unconfined or fired in a weapon. Smokeless powder, however, burns slowly when unconfined, requiring about 1000 lb/in.^{2} of pressure to burn consistently. As pressure increases, it burns at an increasing rate, producing pressures that exceed those that can be tolerated by black powder firearms.

Pyrodex has more bulk than black powder, with an equal volume of Pyrodex having about 88% of the weight of black powder. In weapons chambered for black powder, Pyrodex is loaded bulk for bulk with black powder, not by weight. The pressures and velocities generated are, thus, compatible with those achieved with black powder.

Bullets

The bullet is that part of the cartridge that leaves the muzzle of the firearm when it discharges. Bullets were originally lead spheres. These worked satisfactorily with smooth-bore weapons, in which accuracy and long range were not expected. By the early nineteenth century, however, the superiority of the muzzle-loading rifle over the smooth-bore musket was accepted. These rifled weapons had a greater range and considerably more accuracy. The main difficulty, however, was in reloading. To make such a rifle shoot accurately, the bullet had to fit the bore. This qualification made the gun difficult to load and decreased the rate of fire. The bullet had to be forced down the barrel with a mallet. American riflemen developed a more rapid way of loading their rifles. They used a bullet that was slightly under bore diameter. This bullet was wrapped in a greased patch of fabric, and the patch and the spherical bullet were rammed down the barrel together. This step speeded up the rate of loading to some degree, but it did not solve the problem. What was needed was to develop a bullet with a diameter less than the bore which would expand to fit the rifling grooves on firing and also would have a better aerodynamic shape than the ball. The solution was the Minie bullet, developed by Captain Charles Minie of the French Army.[3] It originally consisted of a conical-shaped, hollow-based lead bullet into whose base an iron wedge was inserted. The bullet was smaller in diameter than the bore and could easily be pushed down the bore. On firing, the gases of combustion would drive the wedge into the base of the bullet, expanding the base of the Minie bullet to fit the rifling grooves and to seal the propellant gases behind the bullet. Subsequent research found that the wedge could be eliminated and that the propellant gases working on the hollow base alone were sufficient to flare out the base of the bullet and seal the bore. Soon after the development of the Minie bullet, breech-loading rifled weapons firing metallic cartridges were perfected. Thus, bullets could be made to bore diameter because it was not necessary to force them down the bore during the loading process.

Modern bullets fall into two categories: lead- and metal-jacketed. Lead bullets were traditionally used only in revolvers and .22 rimfire cartridges; metal-jacketed bullets in automatic pistols and in high-velocity rifles. These generalizations, however, are no longer true.

Lead bullets are made out of lead to which antimony and/or tin have been added to increase the hardness of the alloy. These bullets are lubricated with grease or lubricating compound to help prevent leading (lead fouling) of the barrel. Lead bullets generally, but not inevitably, have one or more cannelures, or grooves (Figure 1.20). The Federal Arms Company manufactured a .38 Special bullet that had no cannelures. In bullets with cannelures, the cartridge case neck is crimped into one groove with lubricating material placed in the other grooves. When the bullet is assembled in the cartridge case, the cannelures containing the lubricated material may be on the outside and readily visible or beneath the neck of the cartridge case and not visible.

Some lead bullets are covered by an extremely thin coating of copper or copper alloy. This coating, which both hardens and lubricates the bullet, is called "gilding." It is approximately 0.001 in. in thickness. Copper gilding is used extensively in .22 high-velocity rimfire ammunition. Blount Industries electroplates some of its bullets with a thick, hard coat of copper such that on initial inspection one believes that one is dealing with a completely jacketed bullet. This coating covers the complete external surface of the bullet including the base.

There are four general configurations of lead bullets: roundnose, wadcutter, semi-wadcutter and hollow-point (Figure 1.20). A roundnose lead bullet has a semiblunt, conical shape and a flat or bevelled base. The wadcutter bullet, which resembles a cylinder of lead, has a base that may be either bevelled or hollow. Wadcutter bullets are designed primarily for target use.

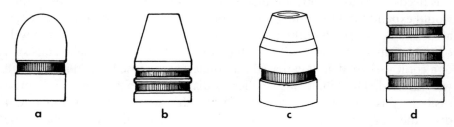

Figure 1.20 Lead bullets: (a) round nose; (b) semi-wadcutter; (c) hollow-point; (d) wadcutter.

The semi-wadcutter configuration is that of a truncated cone with a flat tip and a sharp shoulder of bore diameter at the base of the cone. The lead hollow-point bullet has a semi-wadcutter configuration with a cavity in the nose that is designed to facilitate expansion of the bullet upon impact with the target.

Occasionally, lead bullets with a copper cup crimped to their base may be encountered. This cup is called a "gas check." It protects the bullet base from melting due to the high pressure and temperature of the propellant gases.

Lead bullets ordinarily cannot be used in centerfire rifles, because the bullet would melt or fragment as it was driven down the barrel at high velocity. The bullet emerging from the barrel would be of bore diameter rather than groove diameter, as a result of the lead being stripped from the sides of the bullet. Jacketing is used in high-velocity rifles to prevent this fragmenting or melting. Some handloaders will load cast bullets of a very hard lead alloy in rifle cartridges. However, the powder loadings are reduced so that muzzle velocity usually does not exceed 2000 ft/sec. Such cast bullets may or may not have gas checks.

Jacketed ammunition is used in semi-automatic pistols to prevent leading of the action and barrel as well as jams that would result if a large number of lead bullets were fired. These jams are due to the deposit of small fragments of lead on the ramp and in the action as the bullets are stripped from the magazine and propelled up the ramp into the chamber. Handloaders sometimes use lead bullets in reloading automatic pistol cartridges.

Jacketed bullets have a lead or steel core covered by an outside jacket of gilding metal (copper and zinc), gilding metal-clad steel, cupro-nickel (copper and nickel), or aluminum. Jackets generally range from 0.0165 to 0.030 in. in thickness. Cannelures may be present in the jackets of such bullets to provide a recess into which the mouth of the case may be crimped.

Jacketed bullets may be either full metal-jacketed or partial metal-jacketed. Military ammunition, both rifle and pistol, is loaded with full metal-jacketed bullets. Five different types of bullets are in use by the military. The most common is ball ammunition, which consists of a bullet with a lead or mild steel core covered by a full metal jacket. Armor-piercing ammunition has a hard steel core. A lead base and point filler may also be present. Tracer bullets consist of a full metal jacket, a lead core in the forward position, and tracer composition in the base. In some cartridges the composition is of two types: Tracer Dim and Tracer Bright. The Tracer Dim composition burns first, leaving a very dim or faint flame for a distance from the gun. This is followed by Tracer Bright. Use of the Tracer Dim composition initially prevents revealing the location of the gun. Incendiary bullets contain an incendiary composition. Armor-piercing incendiary bullets consist of the full metal jacket, a steel core, and incendiary material to cause a fire.

Center-fire rifle ammunition used for hunting has always been loaded with partial metal-jacketed bullets. In these bullets, the metal jacket is open at the tip of the bullet to expose the lead core, while usually closed at the base.

Until the 1960s, all ammunition intended for automatic pistols was loaded with full metal-jacketed bullets having a lead core. At this time, partial metal-jacketed ammunition was introduced for use in both auto-loading pistols and revolvers. Most handgun ammunition now used by police organizations is partial metal-jacketed.

The two most common forms of partial metal-jacketed ammunition, whether for rifles or handguns, are the semi-jacketed soft-point and the semi-jacketed hollow-point type. The former style of bullet is most popular for rifles; the latter, for handguns. In some rifle ammunition, the lead tip may be covered by a very light secondary jacket, usually of aluminum, e.g., the Silver-Tip® while others may have an expanding device made of metal or plastic in the tip. The tip of the semi-jacketed soft-point is rounded or pointed in rifles and flattened in a semi-wadcutter configuration in handguns. A varying degree of lead is exposed depending on the bullet design. The jacket at its junction with the exposed lead core may be scalloped or notched to aid in expansion ("mushrooming"). In semi-jacketed hollow-point ammunition the tip of the bullet has a cavity in it. Again, the partial metal jacket may be scalloped or notched to aid expansion or may extend down into the cavity.

Occasionally encountered are full metal-jacketed semi-wadcutter and wadcutter handgun bullets used for target shooting. More common are handgun bullets in which the lead core is fully enclosed by a copper jacket. This bullet, in conjunction with lead-free primers in the cartridge case, is intended for use in indoor firing ranges and is so designed as to reduce lead pollution of the air.

Caseless Ammunition

Caseless ammunition,[4] while it has been tried in civilian weapons, is principally of interest to the military. This ammunition was developed to increase the probability of a bullet hitting a target in combat. Theoretically, a rifle firing short bursts of full-automatic fire at a very high rate of fire has a greater hit probability. The German military determined that, allowing for normal aiming error and assuming no recoil, at a range of 300 m, a circular dispersion of three shots would hit a target. With traditional cartridges and weapons, this is not possible due to recoil. After the first shot, the recoil causes the muzzle of the weapon to rise such that each successive shot is higher and to the right. If, however, the rate of fire was raised to 2000 rds/min, the three rounds would already have left the barrel before the weapon began to recoil. This rate of fire is not possible with conventional ammunition but is with caseless ammunition. As a result of this work, the German's developed the 4.7mm G11 Heckler and Koch rifle and the 4.73 × 33 mm DM11 caseless cartridge. The cartridge weighing 5.2 g, consists of a 8 × 8 × 32.8-mm block of propellant in which a 3.2 g bullet is completely embedded, such that only its tip is visible at the front end of a central hole. The bullet has a steel jacket and lead core. Muzzle velocity is 930 m/s — K.E. 1380 J. The propellant is a moderated high explosive mixed with a binder. At the rear, there is a primer consisting of a small pellet of explosive. A booster charge lies in between the primer and bullet. On ignition, the primer ignites the booster which propels the bullet forward engaging the rifling and acting as a seal for the gas from the propellant. At the same time, the booster ignites the main charge. Since there is no cartridge to be extracted, the weapon only has to load and fire. At full-automatic fire, the rate is approx 600 rds/min; at three shot burst it is 2200 rds/min. The first production weapons were apparently issued to German Special Forces in 1990. The end of the Cold War, the unification of Germany, defense cuts and the availability of large numbers of small arms at cheap prices has apparently led to the demise of this project for the present time.

Flint and Percussion Weapons

Metallic cartridges appeared in the mid-nineteenth century. Prior to this time, weapons were of either flintlock or percussion design. In both types of weapons, a measured amount of black powder was poured down the barrel. This was followed by either a paper or cloth wad and a lead ball — all rammed down the barrel by a ramrod. The ignition system of these weapons was called the "lock." Thus, a weapon consisted of "the lock, stock, and barrel."

The lock of a flintlock consists of a cock (the hammer), a piece of flint attached to the cock, a pan containing loose powder (the primary charge), and a steel right-angle cover hinged over the pan (the batterie or frizzen). After the barrel had been loaded with the powder, wad, and ball, a small amount of loose powder was placed in the pan. The weapon was cocked and the trigger pulled. The cock fell causing the piece of the flint to strike the frizzen. This blow pushed the hinged cover back, exposing the priming powder in the pan. The flint sweeping across the steel frizzen produced sparks that ignited the powder in the pan. The resultant flame jumped from the pan through a small hole in the base of the barrel (the flash hole), into the bore, igniting the main charge and firing the weapon. Occasionally, the powder in the pan would ignite but the flame would fail to ignite the main charge in the barrel. This was a "flash-in-the-pan."

The percussion lock appeared in the early nineteenth century but rapidly became obsolete on introduction of metallic cartridges. In percussion weapons the piece of flint, the pan, and the frizzen are all eliminated. The lock consists of a hammer and a nipple. The latter has a flash hole that connects with the bore. A percussion cap is placed over the nipple after the barrel is loaded with the powder, wad, and ball. The cap was essentially a primer containing fulminate of mercury. To fire, the barrel is loaded, a percussion cap is placed over the nipple, the hammer is cocked, and the trigger is pulled. The falling hammer strikes the percussion cap, detonates it, and sends a jet of flame through the flash hole into the bore igniting the powder.

For most of this century, flintlock and percussion weapons have been only of historical interest. In the past few decades, there has arisen an interest in replica black-powder arms. Numerous weapons of this type have been sold. These range from precise replicas of historical weapons to totally new designs. Most of these weapons are manufactured abroad. They are available as flintlock and percussion muskets, rifles, and shotguns and percussion revolvers. Calibers range from .31 to .75, with bullets varying from round lead balls to Minie bullets.

Percussion revolvers are of particular interest in that they have been involved in some homicides and suicides. These weapons may fire either ball or conical bullets. To load the weapon, the hammer is put on half-cock so that the cylinder may be rotated. Black powder is poured into a chamber of the cylinder from the front. A lead ball having a diameter slightly greater than that of the chamber (0.001 to 0.002 in.) is placed over the powder charge. The cylinder is rotated so that the chamber is positioned underneath the loading rammer and the lever is activated to ram the bullet home (Figure 1.21). Conical bullets have a reduced diameter heel so that the shooter can start them in the chamber with their fingers before the loading rammer is used. After all the chambers are loaded, a percussion cap is put on the nipple at the rear of each chamber. The weapon is now ready to fire.

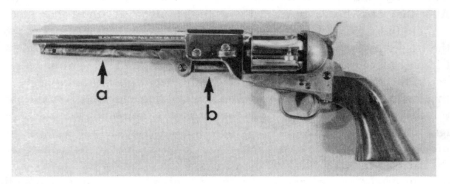

Figure 1.21   Black powder revolver with (a) rammer lever and (b) loading rammer.

References

1. Lowry, E. D. *Interior Ballistics: How a Gun Converts Chemical Energy into Projectile Motion.* Garden City, NY: Doubleday and Co. 1968.

2. *NRA Illustrated Reloading Handbook.* Washington D.C.: National Rifle Association.

3. Butler, D. F. *United States Firearms: The First Century 1776–1875.* New York: Winchester Press, 1971.

4. *Jane's Infantry Weapons,* Jane's Information Group Limited, Sentinel House, Coulsdon, Surrey, U.K. (annual).

General References

Barnes, F. C. *Cartridges of the World,* 8th Edition. Northfield, IL: Digest Books Inc., 1996.

Hogg, I. V. and Weeks, J. *Pistols of the World.* San Rafael, CA: Presidio Press, 1978.

Gun Digest. (annual) Northfield, IL: DBI Books, Inc.

Jones A. (Editor) *Speer Reloading Rifle & Pistol Manual,* Lewiston, ID, 1994.

Sellier K. G. and Kneubuehl B. P. *Wound Ballistics and the Scientific Background.* Elsevier, The Netherlands, 1994.

Small Arms Ammunition, TM 9-1305-200, Department of Army Technical Manual, June 1961.

Wilson, R. K. and Hogg, I. V. *Textbook of Automatic Pistols.* Harrisburg, PA: Stackpole Books, 1975.

The Forensic Aspects of Ballistics

2

Rifles and handguns have rifled barrels, that is, spiral grooves have been cut the length of the interior or bore of the barrel (Figure 2.1). Rifling consists of these grooves and the metal left between the grooves—the lands (see Figure 1.13). The purpose of rifling is to impart a rotational spin to the bullet along its longitudinal axis. This gyroscopic effect stabilizes the bullet's flight through the air, preventing it from tumbling end over end. This spin does not, however, stabilize the bullet after it enters the body due to the greater density of tissue compared to air. The term "twist," as it pertains to rifling, refers to the number of inches or centimeters of bore required for one complete rifling spiral. All modern weapons have a twist which is constant for the entire length of the barrel. Some weapons manufactured in the beginning of the 20th century, had a "gain" twist; in this type of rifling, the rate of twist increases from breech to muzzle.

A different form of rifling for both rifles and handguns was introduced by Heckler and Koch. Instead of the traditional lands and grooves, the bore of the weapon has a rounded rectangular profile (polygonal boring) (Figure 2.2A). Muzzle velocity is allegedly increased 5 to 6%. Ballistic comparison of bullets fired from weapons with polygonal boring may be very difficult. Because of this, when one police department ordered their Glock pistols, they specified that the barrels have the traditional rifling rather than the polygonal rifling that is routinely used in Glocks.

The direction of rifling can be either right (clockwise) or left (counterclockwise). In a specific barrel, the direction of the rifling can easily be determined by examining the upper half of the bore and observing whether the rifling curves to the left (left twist, counterclockwise) or to the right (right twist, clockwise) as it proceeds away from one's view. The direction of the twist is the same whether one views the barrel from the muzzle or breech

Figure 2.1 Cross-section of barrel with traditional rifling; right-hand twist.

end. Among U.S. handgun manufacturers, the Colt Company is the only major concern that consistently uses a left-hand or counterclockwise twist. The Mark III, manufactured by Colt, was a temporary exception to the manufacturer's policy in that for a number of years this weapon was produced with a right-hand twist. A minority of foreign handgun manufacturers and some U.S. manufacturers of cheap weapons also use a left-hand twist. The majority of domestic and foreign handgun manufacturers, however, use a right-hand twist. Polygonal rifling has a right-hand twist.

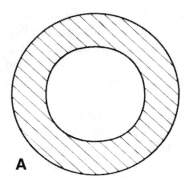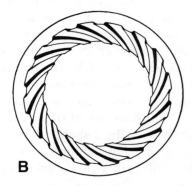

Figure 2.2 (A) Cross-section of barrel showing polygonal rifling. (B) Cross-section of barrel with micro-groove rifling. (From DiMaio, V.J.M. Wounds caused by centerfire rifles. *Clin. Lab. Med.* 3:257–271, 1983. With permission.)

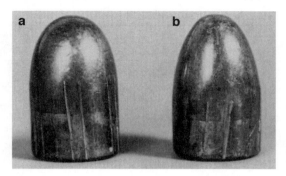

Figure 2.3 Two 9-mm bullets fired from weapons with (a) left twist and (b) right twist to their rifling.

Figure 2.3 shows two bullets, one fired in a weapon with left twist and the other in a weapon with a right twist. Figure 2.4 shows two .45 ACP bullets, one with traditional rifling marks and the other with markings from polygonal rifling.

The number of lands and grooves in a weapon can range from 2 to 22. Most modern weapons have four, five, or six grooves (Table 2.1). Colt handguns traditionally have had six lands and grooves with a left-hand twist, while Smith & Wesson has had five lands and grooves with a right-hand twist. Most centerfire rifles have four or six grooves, with a right-hand twist. Rifle barrels with two grooves were manufactured during World War II for the M-1 Carbine, the .30–06 Springfield rifle, and the British .303 Enfield. A commercial M-1 Carbine manufactured by Universal had a barrel with 12 grooves and a right hand twist. A CDM derringer examined by the author had one barrel with six grooves and the other with twelve. The author has seen handguns of various manufacture, in which the barrel was devoid of rifling do to a mistake in manufacturing.

Figure 2.4 Two .45 ACP bullets: (a) with traditional rifling marks, the other (b) with markings from polygonal rifling.

Table 2.1   Rifling Characteristics of Rifles and Handguns

Caliber	Manufacturer	Direction of Twist	Number of Lands and Grooves
Handguns			
.22 S, L, LR	Colt	L	06
	CDM, Beretta,		
	Hi-Standard, Browning		
	Smith & Wesson, Ruger	R	06
	Rohm	R	08
	Phoenix, Jennings	R	16
.22 Magnum	Colt	L	06
	Ruger, Smith & Wesson	R	06
	Rohm	R	08
.25 ACP	Colt, Astra, Raven, Davis	L	06
	Titan, Beretta, Browning	R	06
7.62 × 25	Former Soviet Bloc	R	04
.32 ACP-.380 ACP	Colt, Davis	L	06
	Browning, Beretta, Lorcin		
	Walther, Sig-Sauer	R	06
.32 S&W, S&W Long	Colt, Clerke	L	06
	Smith & Wesson	R	05
	Rohm, Charter, H & R	R	08
	Arminius	R	06/10
9-mm Makarov	Former Soviet Bloc	R	04
9-mm Parabellum	Smith & Wesson	R	05
	Colt	L	06
	Browning, Smith & Wesson		
	Walther, Taurus, Beretta		
	Glock, Sig-Sauer, H&K		
	Lorcin	R	06
.38 S & W	Colt	L	06
	Smith & Wesson	R	05
	Enfield	R	07
.38 Special	Colt, Miroku	L	06
	Smith & Wesson, Taurus		
	Ruger D.A.	R	05
	Colt MK III, Rossi, Taurus		
	Arminius, Rohm	R	08
	Charter Arms	R	08
	Rohm, Arminius	R	10
.357 Magnum	Colt	L	06
	Smith & Wesson		
	Ruger DA, Taurus	R	05
	Colt MK III, Dan Wesson	R	06

Table 2.1 Rifling Characteristics of Rifles and Handguns (continued)

Caliber	Manufacturer	Direction of Twist	Number of Lands and Grooves
.357 Magnum	Ruger SA/DA	R	06
(continued)	Ruger SA	R	08
.40 S&W	Smith & Wesson Beretta, Glock, Star Taurus, Astra, H&K	L	06
	Ruger	R	06
.41 Magnum	Smith & Wesson	R	05
	Ruger	R	06
.44 Magnum	Smith & Wesson	R	05
	Ruger SA	R	06
	Ruger/Marlin Carbine	R	12
.45 ACP	Colt, Sig	L	06
	Star, Llama, Smith & Wesson	R	06
Centerfire Rifles			
.223	AR-15 (M-16)	R	06
	Ruger Mini-14	R	06
	Heckler and Koch	R	06
	Remington	R	06
.243	All Remington, Browning, Winshester and Savage rifles	R	06
	Mossberg rifles	R	08
.270	Winchester	R	04
	Remington, Savage	R	06
7-mm Mag.		R	06
.30 Carbine	Numerous manufacturers	R	02
		R	04
		R	06
		R	12
.30–06	M 1917	L	05
	Springfield	R	02
		R	04
		R	06
	Winchester M-70	R	04
	Remington	R	06
.30–30	Winchester M-94	R	06
	Marlin 336	R	12
.32 Winchester	Marlin 336	R	04
Special	Winchester 94	L	06

(continues)

Table 2.1   Rifling Characteristics of Rifles and Handguns (continued)

Caliber	Manufacturer	Direction of Twist	Number of Lands and Grooves
.303 British	Lee Enfield	L	05
	No. 1 MK-III	L	02
	No. 4 MK-I	L	05
		L	06
.308	Winchester M-70	R	04
	M 14, H&K 93, Galeil	R	04
	Remington, Savage	R	06
7.62 × 39	AK-47	R	04
Rimfire Rifles			
.22	Winchester	R	04
	Remington	R	05
	Remington	R	06
	Ruger	R	06
	Winchester	R	06
	Mossberg	R	08
	Marlin	R	16
Magnum Rifles			
.22	Winchester	R	06
	Marlin	R	20

Rifles manufactured by Marlin and sold under their own and other names have Micro-Groove® rifling (Figure 2.2B). Micro-Groove® rifling was developed by Marlin in the early 1950s. Instead of 4 to 6 deep rifling grooves, their barrels have 12 to 20 shallow grooves. Marlin rifles can be found in the following calibers: .22 Rimfire, .22 Magnum, .30 Carbine, .357 Magnum, 9-mm Parabellum, .44 Magnum, .45 ACP, .30–30, .35 Remington, .444 Marlin, and .45/70. Weapons chambered for the .22 Short, Long and Long Rifle cartridges have 16 lands and grooves; .22 Magnum 20, and all centerfire rifles 12. All rifling is right-hand twist.

Recovery of a bullet with Micro-Groove® rifling indicates that the individual was shot with a rifle since such rifling is not found in handguns (see Figure 6.2). Jenning's Firearms and Phoenix Arms produce semi-automatic pistols chambered for the .22 LR cartridge that have barrels with 16 lands and grooves with a right twist. Rifling imparted to a bullet fired down such a barrel can be confused with Micro-Groove® rifling. The difference is that Micro-Groove® rifling has extremely narrow lands with grooves twice the width of the lands. In contrast, in Jenning's weapons the lands and grooves have equal widths while the Phoenix pistols have lands that are only slightly narrower compared to the grooves.

Class and Individual Characteristics of Bullets

When a bullet is fired down a rifled barrel, the rifling imparts a number of markings to the bullet that are called "class characteristics." These markings may indicate the make and model of the gun from which the bullet has been fired. They result from the specifications of the rifling, as laid down by the individual manufacturer. These characteristics are:

1. Number of lands and grooves
2. Diameter of lands and grooves
3. Width of lands and grooves
4. Depth of grooves
5. Direction of rifling twist
6. Degree of twist

In addition to these class characteristics, imperfections on the surfaces of the lands and grooves score the bullets, producing individual characteristics. For lead bullets these individual characteristics are more pronounced where the grooves score the bullet. In contrast, for jacketed bullets, the land markings are the most pronounced.[1] These individual characteristics are peculiar to the particular firearm that fired the bullet and not to any others. They are as individual as fingerprints. No two barrels, even those made consecutively by the same tools, will produce the same markings on a bullet. Thus, while the class characteristics may be identical on bullets fired by two different weapons, the individual characteristics will be different. In addition to markings on the bullets, the magazine, firing pin, extractor, ejector, and breech face of a weapon may all impart class and individual markings to a cartridge case or primer.

Comparison of Bullets

When a gun is discharged, the bullet is forced down the barrel by the gases of combustion. Both class and individual characteristics are imparted to the bullet, whether it is lead or jacketed. Because lead is softer, one might postulate that bullet markings on lead bullets are more distinctive than those found on jacketed bullets. In actual practice, markings on the jacketed bullets are usually superior, because the jacket of harder metal is less likely to have the rifling marks wiped off by the target.

In order to recover bullets for ballistic comparison, bullets were traditionally fired into cotton waste. The tumbling of the bullet through this material may cause a wipe-off of some of the finer individual characteristics if the bullet is made of soft lead. This is especially true for the .22 rimfire bullets. Therefore, ballistic laboratories now fire bullets into water traps, in which loss of fine markings does not occur.

The individual characteristics that a barrel imparts to a bullet may be destroyed by rust, corrosion, or the firing of thousands of rounds of jacketed ammunition down a barrel. Accumulation of large quantities of dirt and grease from multiple firings may also alter to some degree markings imparted to a bullet.

If a bullet with a diameter smaller than that intended for the specific weapon is fired down a barrel, the bullet will be unable to follow the rifling sufficiently to produce repetitive markings. Comparisons cannot be made, as it is highly unlikely that two bullets will "slip" down the barrel in the same identical manner.

If the bore of the weapon is severely rusted, it is possible for serially fired bullets to have different markings. These occur because each bullet strips off rust and changes the surface of the grooves and lands.

The material of which the bullet is constructed and the velocity and pressures to which the cartridge is loaded have an effect on bullet markings. Therefore, it is good practice to use the same brand of ammunition as that fired from the suspect's gun when trying to make a comparison. In fact, it is best to use other cartridges taken from the gun or from the same box of ammunition for comparison testing. The reason for these suggestions is that ammunition may vary greatly from one lot to another. The bullets used in one lot may be slightly different in composition from those of another lot. The powder used may be completely different, and the cartridges may be loaded to a higher or lower pressure. Because of all these variables, it is always best to try to obtain ammunition from the same lot as that from which it is to be compared.

Bullets that have been fired from revolvers may show skid marks when examined under the comparison microscope (Figure 2.5); that is, the grooves on the bullet are wider at the nose than at the base. Skidding occurs when the bullet jumps the gap between the cylinder and the barrel and strikes the lands. The bullet resists the attempt of the lands to impart a spin and "skids." Bullets fired from an automatic may show skid marks when the bullet is slightly smaller than the desired diameter for a particular bore. This discrepancy causes the bullet to skid as it enters the rifling before settling down. As a general rule, however, skidding rarely occurs in automatic pistols, as the bullet is in contact with the lands before firing and follows them from the start. The presence of skid marks on an automatic pistol bullet may be of significance, as it may indicate that the bullet was fired in a revolver rather than in an automatic. Revolvers have been designed and manufactured to fire the .25 ACP and the .32 ACP pistol cartridges and have been and are still

Figure 2.5 .38 Special bullet showing "skid marks."

being manufactured for the 9-mm Parabellum and .45 ACP cartridges. Some revolvers have even been chambered for rifle cartridges, e.g., .30 Carbine, etc. Revolvers have been and still are manufactured with the capability of firing different calibers by changing the cylinder, e.g., .38/9-mm, .22LR/.22 Magnum.

Semi-automatic pistols have been chambered for revolver cartridges, e.g., .32 Smith & Wesson Long, .38 Special, .357 Magnum, .44 Magnum etc.; derringers for semi-automatic pistol cartridges (.25 ACP, .32 ACP, 9-mm Parabellum, .45 ACP, etc.), rifle cartridges (.22 Hornet, .223, .30–30, etc.) and shotgun cartridges. Single-shot weapons have been chambered for a host of revolver, pistol, and rifle cartridges. Rifles have been chambered for handgun cartridges. Double-barreled rifles have been produced with one barrel chambered for a rifle cartridge and the other for a shotgun shell.

Shaving one surface of a bullet fired from a revolver is sometimes encountered. This happens because the cylinder of the revolver is improperly aligned with the bore of the barrel (so-called poor indexing) and thus lead is shaved from the bullet as it jumps the gap from the cylinder to barrel. Both cheaply made revolvers and revolvers of quality that are badly worn may cause shaving.

In some cases, a bullet recovered from a body is too mutilated to make a bullet comparison possible. In other cases, the bulk of the bullet exited, and only bullet fragments are recovered. In such cases, it is possible by using semi-quantitative or quantitative compositional analysis to link the recovered bullet to bullets from or known to be fired by a specific gun. Recovered bullet fragments can be linked to a bullet recovered from the scene or to bullets from or known to be fired by a specific gun. Scanning electron microscopy with energy dispersive x-ray (SEM–EDX) is suitable for semi-quantitative and inductively coupled plasma atomic emission spectroscopy for quantitative compositional analysis.

In some instances, bullets may appear distorted when recovered from a body due to the fact that they were fired in weapons not chambered for them. Ward et al. reported two cases, a homicide and a suicide, in which .38 Special wadcutter cartridges were fired in .30–30 rifles.[2] The .38 Special cartridge will chamber and fire in this rifle, though the cases expand and usually burst. The diameter of a .38 Special wadcutter bullet (.358 inches) is significantly greater than that of a .30–30 bullet (.308 inches). On firing, the .38 Special is swaged down to the bore diameter of the rifle resulting in an elongated bullet, the diameter of the bore, with prominent lands and grooves.

Bullets recovered from decomposed bodies may show partial or complete loss of individual rifling striations depending upon the tissue from which the bullet was recovered and the construction of the bullet. In an experiment to determine the effects of decomposition on bullet striations, Smith et al. inserted bullets, of various construction, into different areas of a human body and let it decompose for 66 days.[3] They found:

1. Nylon-clad bullets were uniformly unaffected by decomposition.
2. Aluminum jacketed bullets were mildly affected but there was no loss of striations.
3. Lead bullets from the brain, chest cavity, and abdominal cavity showed mild tarnishing but were matchable while those from fat and muscle showed dissolution and oxidation to the point of impairing a match.
4. Bullets with copper alloy jacketing, including those with nickel-wash, were not matchable except for copper alloy bullets recovered from the chest cavity which were borderline.

Cartridge Cases

Examination of a fired cartridge case may make possible the identification of a weapon in terms of type, make, and model. The presence of magazine markings, the type of breech-block mark, and the size, shape, and location of ejector and extractor marks are important imprints in making such identification. The size, shape, and location of the firing pin on fired rimfire cartridge cases can also be used to determine the make of the weapon. The appearance of the firing pin imprint from centerfire weapons may indicate the make of weapon used. Identification of a weapon as having fired a particular cartridge case can be made by comparing markings on test cartridges with those on the evidence cartridge. Again, it is extremely important that the same brand and preferably the same lot of ammunition be used for tests. In fact, this consistency is more important in cartridge case comparison than in bullet comparison.[1]

Figure 2.6 Markings on rifle cartridge case due to fluted chamber.

In rimfire cartridge cases, the firing pin impression is the most important identifying mark. Extractor, ejector, and breech block marks are less useful.[1]

Occasionally one will encounter a fired cartridge case having a series of parallel longitudinal markings impressed on the case (Figure 2.6).[4] These marks may be either linear areas of swelling or linear deposits of soot. Such markings are a consequence of a fluted chamber. During manufacture, small parallel grooves have been cut into the wall of the chamber permitting powder gases to surround the cartridge case to allow the neck of the cartridge case to "float" on gas, thus aiding extraction. They are found in rifles, pistols, submachine guns, and machineguns. Flute marks may be present only on the neck or shoulder area of cases or along most of its length. The number of grooves may vary from 2 to 18. Heckler-Koch rifles, submachine guns, and pistols typically have fluted chambers. In the HK-4 pistol, there are 3 flutes that are designed to retard cartridge case extraction rather than facilitate it.

Some chambers have annular or helical grooves cut into the walls that retard extraction of cartridge cases by gas expanding the walls of the cases into the grooves. These weapons are relatively rare. Examples are the PRC Type 64 and 77 pistols.

Base Markings

On discharge of a weapon, powder grains may be propelled against the base of the bullet with sufficient force to mark the base. Such markings are most evident in bullets with a lead base, that is, lead bullets or full metal-jacketed

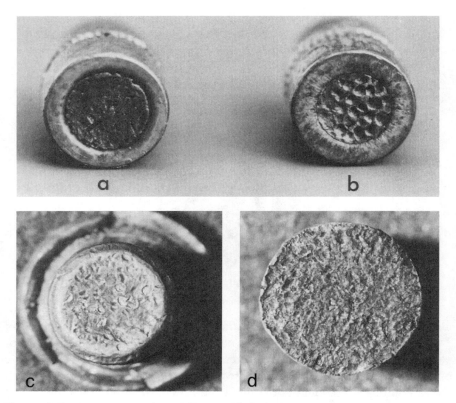

Figure 2.7 (a) Base of unfired full metal-jacketed bullet with exposed lead core. (b) Pitting of base of similar bullet due to ball powder. (c) Circular and linear marks on base of lead bullet due to disk powder. (d) Peppered appearing base of lead bullet due to black powder.

bullets whose lead core is exposed at the base. The shorter the barrel, the more numerous and the deeper the powder marks.[5] Different forms of powder produce different marks: spherical (true) ball powder produces numerous deep circular pits; disk powder produces shallow, circular imprints as well as linear markings (powder flakes striking on edge); black powder produces a characteristic peppered appearance (Figure 2.7).

Powder marks are more prominent on the exposed lead base of full metal-jacketed bullets than on the base of all lead bullets. Bullets with a jacketed base (partial metal-jacketed bullets) may show very faint powder markings on the base.

Powder grains may become adherent to the base of a bullet and be carried into and even through a body. This usually involves bullets with a lead base though on occasions this has been seen in a bullet with a jacketed base (Figure 2.8).

Figure 2.8 Powder adherent to base of full metal-jacketed .357 Magnum bullet.

Cytology on Bullets and Clothing

If a bullet passes through a body or intermediary target, or ricochets off a hard surface, fragments of tissue or target material may adhere to or be imbedded in the bullet. If the bullet is a hollow point, a relatively large wad of this material may be deposited in the cavity. Recovery and identification of foreign material from a bullet may identify the organs or intermediary object perforated or prove that the bullet was a ricochet. Nonorganic material, such as aluminum from a window screen perforated by a bullet or minerals from a stone off of which a bullet ricocheted, can be identified on a bullet by SEM–EDX.[6]

If a bullet is found at a scene, or if multiple bullets are found in a body cavity after perforating different organs, it might be possible to determine that the bullet at the scene perforated a body or to determine which bullet recovered from a body cavity perforated which organ. If the bullet perforated bone and particles of bone were deposited on/in the bullet, identification of this bone can be made by histological examination if the fragment is large enough, or if too small, by SEM–EDX.[6] That a bullet perforated tissue or even a specific organ may be determined by cytological means. Nichols and Sens have described a method of recovery and identification of tissue and foreign material too small to visualize.[7] This process involves rinsing unwashed recovered bullets in various solutions, filtering the solutions through a cytology filter, and then performing cytologic staining on the material. In the case of high-velocity bullets, they noted extensive fragmentation of the tissue with blood clots, bone fragments, muscle, and amorphous debris, the most common tissues recovered. Mesothelial cells and organ fragments were less common. Tissue recovered from low-velocity bullets was better preserved and more abundant. Adipose tissue, fragments of small vessels, clumps of spindle cells were most commonly found; skeletal and cardiac muscle, occasionally. Visceral organ fragments were not necessarily found even when the organs were perforated. Skin was the least commonly encountered. In regard to gunshot wounds of the head, bone chips, skeletal muscle, connective tissue, and strips of small vessels were commonly identified. Fragments of brain were present but were not readily recognizable as neural in origin.

In numerous cytologic preparations, black deposits, most likely representing soot and/or debris from the barrel, were present irrespective of the range, i.e., distant or close-range. If the bullet perforated clothing, fibers were commonly found.

While blood from the victim is often searched for on the clothing of the alleged perpetrator, it is not appreciated that in contact wounds of the head, brain tissue may be blown back on the perpetrator's clothing. The stains produced do not resemble blood but rather coffee or soft drink stains. If these areas are soaked in saline solution, cellular material may be extracted from the cloth. Brain tissue can then be identified by cytological methods.

DNA Typing of Tissue on Bullets

A bullet found at a scene may be linked to the specific individual through which the bullet had passed by examining tissue deposited on the bullet. This is possible even if no tissue is visible on macroscopic examination of the bullet and it is full metal-jacketed. As a bullet passes through a body, tissue is deposited on its surface even if the tissue is not visible. The tissue can be removed by swabbing the bullet; the DNA replicated and DNA "fingerprinting" performed by short tandem repeat (STR) analysis.[8] This DNA "fingerprint" can then be compared to the DNA "fingerprint" of the individual (living or dead) through which the bullet is thought to have passed.

Fingerprints

In contrast to what is seen on television and in the movies or read in mystery novels, it is rare for an identifiable fingerprint to be left on a firearm, especially a handgun. Only a small surface area is suitable for leaving prints, and the recoil of the weapon causes the fingers to slide and produce smudges. Partial prints may be seen.

Both the public and many police agencies do not realize, that identifiable fingerprints may be obtained from fired cartridge cases.[9] Thus, ejected cartridge cases at a crime scene should be collected in such a manner as to preserve prints that might be found on such casings. In one unusual case seen by the author, a .25 ACP bullet recovered from a body had a partial fingerprint etched in the jacket. This was obviously due to handling the bullet in the distant past with the "acids" from the fingertip etching the partial print on the bullet. There were too few points for positive identification.

Black Powder Firearms

Black powder weapons, on rare occasions, are involved in fatal shootings. Most of these cases involve percussion revolvers. As these weapons have rifled barrels, rifling marks will appear on the spherical or conical bullets fired from them. In addition, the loading rammer used to seat the bullet in the chamber may leave markings on the bullet of sufficient clarity and with individual characteristics to make ballistics comparison possible.

Figure 2.9 shows a .44-caliber ball removed from the arm of a woman accidentally shot with a percussion revolver. Examination of the bullet revealed absence of rifling, shearing of one surface, and markings from a loading rammer. The first two findings indicated that this bullet was not fired down the barrel but came out the side of a gun from a chamber that was not in line with the barrel. When a black powder revolver is fired, a large amount of flame and sparks are produced. This may ignite the powder in an adjacent chamber causing a ball or bullet to come out the cylinder. In such a case, no rifling will be imparted to the missile and lead will be sheared off the side of it. The markings on the ball from the rammer might possibly have been useful for a ballistics comparison.

Discharge of a Weapon

Now that we have attained a basic knowledge of firearms and ammunition, let us consider the sequence of events that occurs when one brings the two elements together. Pulling the trigger causes release of the firing pin. This strikes the primer, crushing it, igniting the primer composition, and producing an intense flame. The flame enters the main chamber of the cartridge case through one or more vents, igniting the powder and producing a large quantity of gas and heat. This gas, which may be heated to 5200°F, exerts pressure on the base of the bullet and sides of the cartridge case, which varies

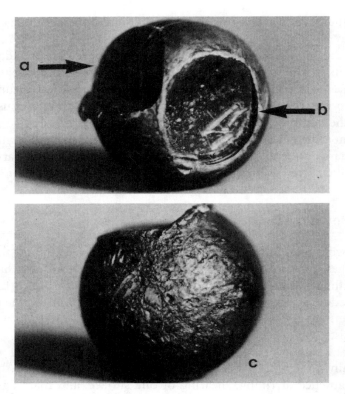

Figure 2.9   0.44-caliber ball showing (a) shearing of one surface, and (b) marking from loading rammer. Opposite surface has a peppered appearance due to black powder (c).

anywhere from several thousand to 50–60 thousand pounds per square inch.[10] The pressure of the gases on the base of the bullet propels it down the barrel. As the bullet travels down the barrel, some of the gas leaks past the bullet, emerging from the muzzle ahead of it. The bulk of the gas and any unburnt powder, however, emerge after the bullet (Figure 2.10).

When the bullet emerges from the barrel of the gun, it is accompanied by a jet of flame, gas, powder, soot, primer residue, metallic particles stripped from the bullet, and vaporized metal from the bullet and cartridge case. The powder results from incomplete combustion of the propellant, as burning of smokeless powder is never really complete. Thus, partially burnt, burning, and unburnt grains of powder invariably emerge with the bullet from the barrel. The amount of unburned or partially burned powder exiting depends largely on the burning properties of the powder and the length of the barrel. Smokeless powder does not explode; rather, it burns. The rate of burning can be controlled by the manufacturer by means of varying the size and shape of the powder grains, as well as by coating them with substances that retard

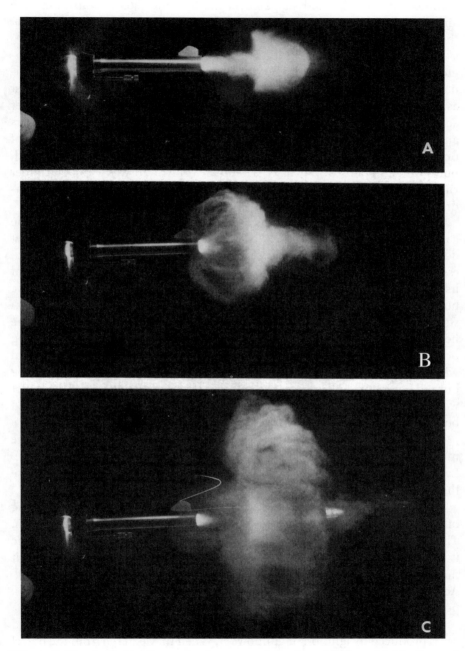

Figure 2.10 A–C. Small gas cloud emerges from barrel followed by bullet and larger cloud of gas (.38 Special Colt revolver).

combustion. The size and shape affect the burning rate by controlling the amount of surface area exposed to the flame. The greater the surface area, the faster the combustion.

The object of controlling the burning rate of powder is to achieve "progressive burning." Ideally, the propellant should start burning slowly, gradually increasing its rate of combustion until it is completely consumed just as the bullet leaves the muzzle. Such ideal burning powder is virtually never achieved because the same powder is used to propel bullets of various calibers and weights down barrels of different lengths. The author has knowledge of one case, where on test-firing a rifle, some amorphous black material exited, but no intact grains of powder.[11] The firearm involved was a .30–06 caliber rifle with a 22-in barrel firing a 220-gr. softpoint bullet propelled by cylindrical powder.

Bullet weight causes variations in burning by altering the pressure of the gases in the firing chamber. When powder is ignited and gas forms, the bullet does not begin to move immediately. There is a small interval of time necessary for the gas to overcome the inertia of the bullet and the resistance of its passing down the barrel. This interval increases with the weight of the bullet if everything else remains constant. As the interval increases, the pressure increases, causing the powder to burn faster and give off more heat. The heat in turn raises the gas pressure. If there is an ideally progressive burning powder for a specified bullet weight and that weight is increased, the interval will increase and the powder will burn faster. Therefore, the powder will be burned before the bullet leaves the barrel. Lightening the weight of the bullet would cause the opposite effect; in this case, not all the powder will be burned before the bullet emerges from the muzzle.

Varying the length of the barrel also affects how much powder exits the muzzle. Shortening the barrel causes more unburned powder to emerge. Lengthening the bullet results in the consumption of more powder before the bullet emerges.

When a bullet exits the barrel, it is accompanied by a "flame" consisting of incandescent superheated gases and a "ball of fire" — the muzzle flash. The flame is usually no more than 1 to 2 in. in length in handguns. The flame is of little significance except in contact and near-contact wounds, where it may sear the skin around the entrance wound. It cannot ignite clothing. Accounts of close-range firing igniting clothing date back to the use of black powder in cartridge cases.

The "ball of fire" emerging from the muzzle consists of oxygen-deprived gases produced by ignition of gunpowder. When they emerge from the barrel at extremely high temperatures, they react with the oxygen in the atmosphere, producing what is commonly known as the "muzzle flash." This should not be confused with the flame.

Figure 2.11 A cloud of gas can be seen emerging from the cylinder-barrel gap.

In revolvers, in addition to the gas, soot, vaporized metals, and powder particles emerging from the muzzle of the weapon, similar material emerges from the cylinder-barrel gap (Figure 2.11). If the cylinder of the weapon is not in perfect alignment with the barrel, fragments of lead will be avulsed from the bullet as it enters the barrel and will also emerge from this gap. In revolvers made to close tolerances, the amount of material escaping out the cylinder gap is relatively small and fragments of lead will be absent. In less well-made or worn guns, however, considerable debris may emerge. In either case, the soot and powder emerging from the gap may cause powder blackening and powder tattooing of the skin, if the weapon is held in close proximity to the body. The fragments of lead shaven from the bullet as a result of the misaligned cylinder may impact the skin causing stippling and even become embedded in the skin.

Hangfires

Haag defines a hangfire or delayed discharge "as one that is of abnormal duration and perceptible to the shooter by means of sight or sound".[12] The hammer falls; there is a click and after a delay, the gun discharges. The typical time interval from the firing pin striking a primer to the bullet exiting the barrel is 4 msec. The minimum time interval that a person can perceive a delay in firing is approximately 30 to 60 msec. Theoretically, hangfires can be caused by contamination and/or degradation of either primers or propellants. In a series of experiments attempting to induce hangfires, Haag was unable to do so by contamination or degradation of primers. The primers either discharged or misfired (failed to fire). No hangfires occurred. Contamination of propellant with oil or alcohol/water solutions resulted in both misfires (failure to fire) and hangfires. The duration of the hangfires was estimated at 200–250 msec. In addition to the delay, Haag noted other characteristics of hangfires: reduced velocity; reduced report; substantial quantities of unburnt powder in the cartridge case and/or bore of the gun; sooty deposits on the exterior wall of the cartridge case and little or no expansion of the case. Haag concluded that with modern ammunition hangfires are rare.

References

1. Mathews, J. H. *Firearms Identification* (3 vol). Springfield, IL: Charles C. Thomas 1972.

2. Ward, M. E., Conradi, S., Lawrence, C. H., and Nolte, K. B. Inappropriate use of .38 Special ammunition in .30–30 rifles, *J. Forensic Sci.* 39(5):1175–1181, 1994.

3. Smith, O. C., Jantz, L., Berryman, H. E., and Symes S. A. Effects of human decomposition on bullet striations. *J. Forensic Sci.* 38(3):593–598, 1993.

4. Krcma, V. Fluted and annular grooved barrel chambers in firearms. *J. Forensic Sci.* 41(3):407–17, 1996.

5. Experiments by author.

6. Di Maio, V. J. M., Dana, S. E., Taylor, W. E., and Ondrusek, J. Use of scanning electron microscopy and energy dispersive x-ray analysis (SEM–EDX) in identification of foreign material on bullets, *JFSCA* 32(1):38–47, 1987.

7. Nichols, C. A. and Sens, M. A. Recovery and evaluation by cytologic techniques of trace material on retained bullets, *Amer. J. Forensic Med. Path.* 11(1):17–34, 1990.

8. Karger, B., Meyer, E., and DuChesne, A. STR analysis on perforating FMJ bullets and a new VWA variant allele. *Inter. J. Legal Med.* (1997);110:101–103.

9. Given, B. W. Latent fingerprints on cartridges and expended cartridge casings. *J. Forensic Sci.* 21(3):587–594, 1976.

10. Lowry, E. D. *Interior Ballistics: How a Gun Converts Chemical Energy into Projectile Motion.* Garden City, NY: Doubleday and Co., 1968.

11. Personal communication with R. J. Shem.

12. Haag, L. C. To create a hangfire. *AFTE Journal* 23(2):660–667. April 1991.

General References

Dillon, J. H. Jr., Black powder background. *AFTE Journal* 23(2):689–693), April 1991.

Dillon, J. H. Jr. The manufacture of conventional smokeless powder. *AFTE Journal* 23(2):682–688, April 1991.

Wound Ballistics

3

Ballistics is the science of the motion of projectiles. It is divided into interior ballistics, external ballistics, and terminal ballistics. Interior ballistics is the study of the projectile in the gun; exterior ballistics, the study of the projectile through air; and terminal ballistics, the study of penetration of solids by the missile. Wound ballistics can be considered a subdivision of terminal ballistics concerned with the motions and effects of the projectile in tissue. In this chapter we shall review wound ballistics.

A moving projectile, by virtue of its movement, possesses kinetic energy. For a bullet, this energy is determined by its weight and velocity:

$$K.E. = WV^2/2\,g$$

where g is gravitational acceleration, W is the weight of the bullet, and V is the velocity.[1]

From this formula, it can be seen that velocity plays a greater role in determining the amount of kinetic energy possessed by a bullet than does weight. Doubling the weight doubles the kinetic energy, but doubling the velocity quadruples the kinetic energy.

The concept of a gunshot wound held by most individuals is that of a bullet going through a person like a drill bit through wood, "drilling" a neat hole through structures that it passes through. This picture is erroneous. As a bullet moves through the body, it crushes and shreds the tissue in its path, while at the same time flinging outward (radially) the surrounding tissue from the path of the bullet, producing a temporary cavity considerably larger than the diameter of the bullet.[1,2] This temporary cavity, which has a lifetime of 5 to 10 msec from initial rapid growth until collapse, undergoes a series of gradually smaller pulsations and contractions before it finally disappears, leaving the permanent wound track (Figure 3.1). It is the combination of the crushed and shredded tissue and the effects of the temporary cavity on tissue

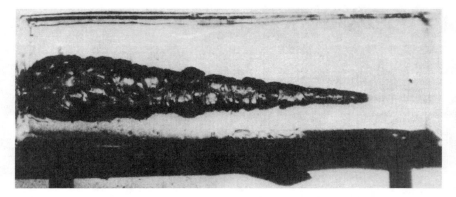

Figure 3.1 Temporary cavity produced in gelatin block by 110-gr. semi-jacketed hollow-point .38 Special bullet.

adjacent to the bullet path (shearing, compression, and stretching) that determines the final extent of a wound.

The location, size, and the shape of the temporary cavity in a body depend on the amount of kinetic energy lost by the bullet in its path through the tissue, how rapidly the energy is lost, and the elasticity and cohesiveness of the tissue. The maximum volume and diameter of this cavity are many times the volume and diameter of the bullet. Maximum expansion of the cavity does not occur until some time after the bullet has passed through the target. The temporary cavity phenomenon is significant because it has the potential of being one of the most important factors in determining the extent of wounding in an individual. For this potential to be realized, however, not only must a large temporary cavity be created but it must develop in strategically important tissue, e.g., a cavity in the liver is more significant than one located in the thigh.

In the case of handgun bullets, the bullet produces a direct path of destruction with very little lateral extension within the surrounding tissues, i.e., only a small temporary cavity is produced. As a general rule, the temporary cavity plays little or no role in the extent of wounding. To cause significant injuries to a structure, a handgun bullet must strike that structure directly. The amount of kinetic energy lost in the tissue by the bullet is insufficient to cause the remote injuries produced by a high-velocity rifle bullet.

The picture is radically different in the case of a high-velocity rifle bullet. As the bullet enters the body, there is a "tail splash," or backward hurling of injured tissue. This material may be ejected from the entrance. The bullet passes through the target, creating a large temporary cavity whose maximum diameter is up to 11 to 12.5 times the diameter of the projectile.[3] The maximum diameter of the cavity occurs at the point at which the maximum rate of loss of kinetic energy occurs. This occurs at the point where the bullet is at maximum yaw, i.e., turned sideways (at a 90° angle to the path) and/or when it fragments. If fragmentation does not occur and the path is long enough, the yawing continues until the bullet rotates 180° and ends up in a base-forward position. The bullet will continue traveling base first with little or no yaw as this position puts the center of mass forward.

The temporary cavity will undulate for 5 to 10 msec before coming to rest as a permanent track. Positive and negative pressures alternate in the wound track, with resultant sucking of foreign material and bacteria into the track from both entrance and exit. In high-velocity centerfire rifle wounds,, the expanding walls of the temporary cavity are capable of doing severe damage. There is compression, stretching and shearing of the displaced tissue. Injuries to blood vessels, nerves, or organs not struck by the bullet, and a distance from the path, can occur as can fractures of bones, though, in the case of fractures, this is relatively rare.[3] In the author's experience, fractures usually occur when the bullet perforates an intercostal space fracturing ribs above and below the bullet path.

The size of both the temporary and the permanent cavities is determined not only by the amount of kinetic energy deposited in the tissue but also by the density and elastic cohesiveness of the tissue. Because liver and muscle have similar densities (1.01 to 1.02 and 1.02 to 1.04), both tissues absorb the same amount of kinetic energy per centimeter of tissue traversed by a bullet.[4] Muscle, however, has an elastic, cohesive structure; the liver, a weak, less cohesive structure. Thus, both the temporary and the permanent cavities produced in the liver are larger than those in the muscle. In muscle, except for the bullet path, the tissue displaced by the temporary cavity returns to its original position. Only a small rim of cellular destruction surrounds the permanent track. In liver struck by high-velocity bullets, however, the undulation of the temporary cavity loosens the hepatocytes from the cellular supporting tissue and produces a permanent cavity approximately the size of the temporary cavity. Lung, with a very low density (specific gravity of 0.4 to 0.5) and high degree of elasticity, is relatively resistant to the effects of temporary cavity formation, and has only a very small temporary cavity formed with very little tissue destruction.[4]

It is not the high velocity of the rifle bullet per se that is responsible for the aforementioned picture, but rather the amount of kinetic energy possessed by the bullet by virtue of the high velocity and which is deposited in the tissue. With most modern rifles, the kinetic energy possessed by the bullet is acquired by virtue of high velocity. A high level of kinetic energy can also be acquired by increasing the mass of the bullet, though this is not as efficient. To illustrate this point, consider the .223 (5.56 × 45-mm) and the .45–70 cartridges. The 5.56 × 45-mm cartridge, fired in the M-16 rifle series, is the most famous of the new high-velocity military cartridges. It fires a 55-gr. bullet at 3250 ft/sec with a muzzle kinetic energy of 1320 ft-lbs (1790 J). The .45–70 U.S. government black powder cartridge, adopted by the U.S. Army in 1873, fired an all-lead bullet of 405 gr. at a velocity of 1285 ft/s and with a muzzle kinetic energy of 1490 ft-lbs (2020 J), 170 ft-lbs (230.5 J) more than that of the .223 bullet. These bullets, a light-weight, high-velocity one and a heavy, slow-moving one, possess relatively equivalent amounts of kinetic energy and, thus, are capable of producing identical-sized temporary cavities. What will determine their effectiveness is where in the body they will produce their respective cavities.

Energy loss along a wound track is not uniform. Variations may be due either to behavior of the bullet or changes in the density of the tissue as the bullet goes from one organ to another. An increase in kinetic energy loss is reflected by an increase in the diameter of the temporary cavity. A full metal-jacketed rifle bullet will produce a cylindrical cavity until it begins to yaw. At this time, the bullet's cross-sectional area will become larger, and the drag force will be increased. The result is an increase in kinetic energy loss and thus an increase in the diameter of the temporary cavity (Figure 3.2A). In addition to the increase in size of the temporary cavity, there will also be an increase in the amount of tissue crushed as the bullet is presenting a larger impacting surface area. For the 7.62-mm NATO M 80 bullet, gelatin studies reveal that yawing begins after 15 cm of penetration, with maximum tissue disruption at approximately 28 cm where the yaw is 90 degrees.[3]

Projectile fragmentation can amplify the effects of the temporary cavity increasing the severity of a wound (Figure 3.3). This is the reason for the effectiveness of the 5.56 × 45-mm cartridge and the M-16 rifle. For the M-193 55-gr. bullet, on the average, the yaw becomes significant at 12 cm with marked tissue disruption occurring most commonly at 15 to 25 cm due principally to bullet fragmentation.[3,5]

In contrast to full metal-jacketed military bullets, with hunting ammunition, the bullet begins to expand (mushroom) shortly after entering the body, with a resultant rapid loss of kinetic energy. Thus, a large temporary cavity is formed almost immediately on entering the body (Figure 3.2B). This is augmented by shredding of the lead core.

A lead shotgun pellet produces a cone-shaped temporary cavity with the base of the cone at the entrance (Figure 3.2C). The diameter of the cavity gradually lessens as the velocity of the pellet decreases. The loss of velocity is much more rapid for shotgun pellets because of their unfavorable ballistic properties (large cross-sectional area in relation to mass).

It has been found that above a certain critical velocity 800 to 900 m/sec (2625 to 2953 ft/sec), the character of a wound changes radically with tissue destruction becoming much more severe.[2] Trans- or supersonic flow within

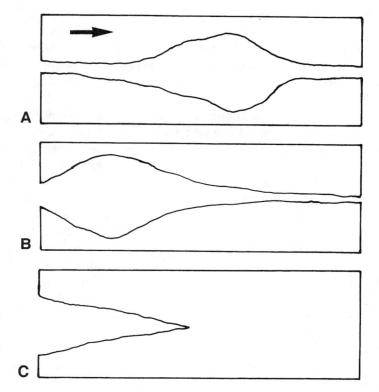

Figure 3.2 Appearance of temporary cavities in gelatin blocks due to (**A**) full metal-jacketed rifle bullet, (**B**) hunting rifle bullet, and (**C**) shotgun pellet.

the tissue causing strong shockwaves has been assumed to be responsible for this effect. In experiments by Rybeck and Janzon, 6-mm steel balls weighing 0.86 g were fired at the hind legs of dogs.[6] They found that at a velocity of 510 m/sec, the volume of macroscopically injured muscle was only slightly larger than the diameter of the bullet. At 978 and 1313 m/sec, the volume of devitalized muscle was seen to be 20 to 30 times the volume of the permanent cavity.

It is the author's belief that rather than there being a critical velocity above which the severity of wounds increases dramatically, there is instead a critical level (amount) of kinetic energy loss above which tissue destruction becomes radically more severe. This level is different for each organ or tissue. When a bullet or missile exceeds this kinetic energy threshold, it produces a temporary cavity that the organ or tissue can no longer contain, i.e., one that exceeds the elastic limit of the organ. When the elastic limit is exceeded, the organ "bursts." For full metal-jacketed rifle bullets and steel balls to reach this critical level of kinetic energy loss, these missiles must be traveling at very high velocities (greater than 800 to 900 m/sec; 2625 to 2950 ft/s). For soft-point and hollow-point rifle bullets, however, the same loss of kinetic energy will occur at lower velocities as a result of the deformation and breakup of the bullets. Thus, in the author's experience, for hunting bullets the critical velocity, appears to be between 1500 and 2000 ft/sec (457 to 610 m/sec).

In the case of hunting ammunition for centerfire rifles, no matter the caliber, once the critical level of kinetic energy lost in an organ is reached, the extent of destruction is relatively the same. Thus, these wounds generally do not appear any different in severity, regardless of the caliber of the rifle.

Centerfire rifle wounds of the head are especially destructive because of the formation of a temporary cavity within the cranial cavity. The brain is enclosed by the skull, a closed, rigid structure that can relieve pressure only by "bursting." Thus, high-velocity missile wounds of the head tend to produce bursting injuries. That these bursting injuries are the result of temporary cavity formation can be demonstrated by shooting through empty skulls. A high-velocity bullet fired through an empty skull produces small entrance and exit holes with no fractures. The same missile fired through a skull containing brain causes extensive fracturing and bursting injuries.[7] Wounds due to hunting bullets are more destructive to the structure of the head than wounds produced by military ammunition even if the same weapon is used. This is because, even though both bullets may possess the same amount of energy on impact, the hunting bullet will lose more energy in the head due to its construction.

With a centerfire rifle bullet, the permanent cavity in tissue is usually larger in diameter than the bullet. With a low-energy projectile such as a handgun bullet, the permanent track is often distinctly smaller in diameter. Tissue elasticity with contraction of the surrounding tissue accounts for this latter phenomenon. If, however, the elastic limit of the tissue has been exceeded by the handgun bullet, the tissue tears, and a large irregular wound track is produced. This latter phenomenon is seen most often in the liver.

Loss of Kinetic Energy

The severity of a wound, as determined by the size of the temporary cavity, is directly related to the amount of kinetic energy lost in the tissue, not the total energy possessed by the bullet. If a bullet penetrates a body but does not exit, all the kinetic energy will be utilized in wound formation. On the other hand, if the bullet perforates the body and goes through it, only part of the kinetic energy is used in wound formation. Thus, bullet A with twice the kinetic energy of B may produce a wound less severe than B, because A perforates the body whereas B does not. This, of course, assumes the bullets follow the identical paths through the body.

The amount of kinetic energy lost by a bullet depends on four main factors.[1] The **first** is the amount of kinetic energy possessed by the bullet at the time of impact. This, as has been discussed, is dependent on the velocity and mass of the bullet.

The **second factor** is the angle of yaw of a bullet at the time of impact.[1] The yaw of a bullet is defined as the deviation of the long axis of the bullet from its line of flight. When a bullet is fired down a rifled barrel, the rifling imparts a gyroscopic spin to the bullet. The purpose of the spin is to stabilize the bullet's flight through the air. Thus, as the bullet leaves the barrel, it is spinning on its long axis, which in turn corresponds to the line of flight. As soon as the bullet leaves the barrel, however, it begins to wobble or yaw. The amount or degree of yaw of a bullet depends on the physical characteristics of the bullet (its length, diameter, cross-sectional density), the rate of twist of the barrel, and the density of the air.

Angles of yaw have been determined with certainty only in military weapons. The maximum angle of yaw at the muzzle may vary from 1.5 degrees for a 150-gr. .30–06 Spitzer bullet, to 6 degrees for a 55-gr. .223 (5.56 mm × 45) bullet.[8] Extremes in temperature can increase yaw and thus the stability of the bullet. Altering the rate of twist in the barrel or the weight of the bullet can also alter the angle of yaw. The AR-15/M-16, as originally designed, had a barrel twist of 1/14 in. (1/356 mm). This twist was too slow, however, so that bullets fired from the weapon were so unstable as to cause significant problems in accuracy. In order to correct this flaw and to stabilize the bullet, the twist rate was changed to 1/12 in (1/305 mm). While this twist rate was sufficient to stabilize the 55-gr. bullet, when the U.S. military adopted the 62-gr. bullet, this rifling was found to be too slow to stabilize the heavier bullet and the rifling was changed to 1/7 in. (1/178 mm)

The greater the angle of yaw of a bullet when it strikes the body, the greater the loss of kinetic energy.[1] Because retardation of a bullet varies as the square of the angle of yaw, the more the bullet is retarded, the greater is the loss of kinetic energy.

As the bullet moves farther and farther from the muzzle, the maximum amplitude of the yaw (the degree of yaw) gradually decreases. At 70 yards, the degree of yaw for the 55-gr. .223 (5.56 × 45-mm) caliber bullet decreases to approximately 2 degrees.[8] This stabilization of the bullet as the range increases explains the observation that close-up wounds are often more destructive than distant wounds. It also explains the observation that a rifle bullet penetrates deeper at 100 yards than at 10 feet.

Although the gyroscopic spin of the bullet along its axis is sufficient to stabilize the bullet in air, this spin is insufficient to stabilize the bullet when it enters the denser medium of tissue. Thus, as soon as the bullet enters the body, it will begin to wobble, i.e., its yaw increases.[1] As the bullet begins to wobble, its cross-sectional area becomes larger, the drag force increases, and more kinetic energy is lost. If the path through the tissue is long enough, the wobbling will increase to such a degree that the bullet will become completely unstable, rotate 180 degrees and end up traveling base forward.

Tumbling of a bullet causes a much larger cross-sectional area of the bullet to be presented to the target. This in turn results in greater direct destruction of tissue as well as greater loss of kinetic energy and a larger temporary cavity. The sudden increase of the drag force or tumbling puts a great strain on the bullet which may eventually break up. A short projectile will usually tumble sooner than a longer one.[9]

The **third factor** that influences the amount of kinetic energy lost in the body is the bullet itself: its caliber, construction, and configuration. Blunt-nose bullets, being less streamlined than spitzer (pointed) bullets, are retarded more by the tissue and therefore lose greater amounts of kinetic energy. Expanding bullets, which "open up" or "mushroom" in the tissue, are retarded more than streamlined full metal-jacketed bullets, which resist expansion and lose only a minimum amount of kinetic energy as they pass through the body.

The caliber of a bullet and its shape, i.e., the bluntness of the nose, are important in that they determine the initial value of the area of interphase between the bullet and the tissue and thus the "drag" of the bullet. Shape and caliber decrease in importance when deformity of the bullet occurs. The amount of deformation in turn depends on both the construction of the bullet (the presence or absence of the jacketing; the length, thickness, and hardness of the jacket material; the hardness of the lead used in the bullet; the presence of a hollow-point) and the bullet velocity. Lead roundnose bullets will start to deform at a velocity above 340 m/sec (1116 ft/sec) in tissue. For hollow-points, it is above 215 m/sec (705 ft/sec).[10]

Soft-point and hollow-point centerfire rifle bullets not only tend to expand as they go through the body, but also shed lead fragments from the core (see Chapter 7, "Lead Snowstorm"). This shedding occurs whether or not they strike bone. The pieces of lead fly off the main bullet mass, acting as secondary missiles, contacting more and more tissue, increasing the size of the wound cavity and thus the severity of the wound. Such a phenomenon, the shedding of lead fragments, does not happen to any significant degree with handgun bullets, even if they are soft-point or hollow-point, unless they strike bone. Breaking up of missiles appears to be related to the velocity. The velocity of handgun bullets, even of the new high-velocity loadings, is insufficient to cause the shedding of lead fragments seen with rifle bullets.

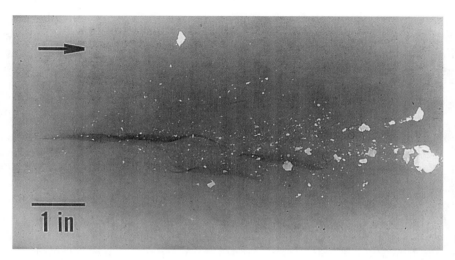

Figure 3.3 X-ray of gelatin block struck by 55 gr. FMJ M-16 bullet illustrating breakup of bullet.

A fact not often appreciated is that full metal-jacketed rifle bullets may break up in the body without hitting bone. This phenomenon was not seen in the .30–06 (7.62 × 63 mm) M-1 round but gained considerable medical attention with the M-193, 55-gr., 5.56 × 45 mm, M-16 round (Figure 3.3). Thus, there were press and medical reports stating that this bullet "blows-up" in the body. The M-193 M-16 bullet does tend to break up after penetrating the body, but it does not blow up. Although this round has a reputation for causing extremely severe wounds, the amount of kinetic energy lost by this round is less than that from the relatively low-velocity .30–30 (circa 1895) hunting cartridge.

The tendency of a full metal-jacketed bullet to break up in the body is governed by its velocity and tendency to radically yaw.[11] When the bullet yaws significantly, its projected cross- sectional area becomes much larger, with a resultant increase in the drag force acting on the bullet. The sudden increase in this drag force puts a great strain on the structure of the bullet, resulting in a tendency to break up. All this causes a greater loss of kinetic energy with an increase in the severity of the wound. Callendar and French, commenting on the tendency of high-velocity, full metal-jacketed bullets to break up, observed that blunt-nosed bullets break up from the tip, whereas pointed bullets break up from the base.[2] In both types of full metal-jacketed bullets, the lead core can be squeezed out the base if the bullet is exposed to severe stress, due to tumbling.

Breakup of the military M 193, 55-gr., 5.56 × 45-mm bullet initiates when it begins to yaw. The bullet tends to flatten on its longitudinal axis and bend at the cannula. The tip of the bullet remains relatively intact while the core and rest of the jacket shred and lead is expelled out the base. Certain minimum velocities are necessary for this to occur. The bullets flatten at velocities in the low 2,000 ft/s range, breaking up in the mid to high 2,000 ft/s range.[5] Breakup of the 62-gr. version of this bullet is similar. The 7.62 × 51 bullet also starts to break up at the cannula.[11]

The **fourth** characteristic that determines the amount of kinetic energy loss by a bullet is the density, strength, and elasticity of tissue struck by a bullet as well as the length of the wound track. The denser the tissue the bullet passes through, the greater the retardation and the greater the loss of kinetic energy. Increased density acts to increase the yaw as well as shorten the period of gyration. This increased angle of yaw and the shortened period of gyration lead to greater retardation and increased loss of kinetic energy.

One final point should be made about kinetic energy and temporary cavity formation. No matter how large a temporary cavity a bullet produces, it will have little or no effect unless it forms in an organ sensitive to injury from such a cavity. A 3-inch cavity in the liver is more effective as a wounding agent than the same cavity in the thigh muscle.

References

1. French, R. W. and Callendar, G. R. Ballistic characteristics of wounding agents. In Beyer, J.C. (ed), *Wound Ballistics,* Washington, D.C.: Superintendent of Documents, U.S. Government Printing Office, 1962.

2. Callender, G. R. and French, R. W. Wound ballistics: studies in the mechanism of wound production by rifle bullets. *Mil. Surg.* 77:177–201, 1935.

3. Fackler, M. L Wound Ballistics: A Review of Common Misconceptions. *JAMA* 259(18): 2730–2736, 1988.

4. Amato, J. J. Billy, L. J., Lawson, N. S., and Rich, N. M. High-velocity missile energy: an experimental study of the retentive forces of tissue. *Am. J. Surg.* 127:454–459, 1974.

5. Fackler, M. L. The wound profile and the human body: damage patterns correlation. *Wound Ballistics Review* 1(4):12–19.

6. Rybeck, B. and Janzon, B. Absorption of missile energy in soft tissue. *Acta Chir, Scand.* 142:201–207, 1976.

7. Harvey, E. N., McMillen, H., Butler, E. G., and Puckett, W. O. Mechanism of wounding. In Beyer, J. D. (ed.) *Wound Ballistics.* Washington D.C.: Superintendent of Documents, U.S. Government Printing Office, 1962.

8. Personal communication with Edgewood Arsenal.

9. Berlin, R., Gelin, L. E., Janzon, B., Lewis, D. H., Rybeck, B., Sandegrad, J., and Seeman, T. Local effects of assault rifle bullets in liver tissues. *Acta Chir. Scand.* [Suppl] 459: 1976.

10. Bruckey, W. J. and Frank, D. E. *Police Handgun Ammunition: Incapacitation Effects. Volume I. Evaluation.* Washington, D.C.: Superintendent of Documents, U.S. Government Printing Office, 1984.

11. Nordstrand, I., Janzon, B., and Rybeck, B. Break-up behavior of some small calibre projectiles when penetrating a dense medium. *Acta Chir. Scand* [Suppl.] 489:81–90, 1979.

General References

Evaluation of Wound Data and Munitions Effectiveness in Vietnam (Vol. 1). Joint Tech. Coord. Group for Munitions Effectiveness, December 1970.

La Garde, L. A. *Gunshot Injuries,* 2nd ed. New York: William Wood & Co, 1916.

Scott, R. Projectile Trauma. *An Enquiry Into Bullet Wounds.* Crown Copyright.

Scott, R. Pathology of injuries caused by high-velocity missiles. In DiMaio, V. J. M. (ed), *Forensic Pathology. Clinics in Laboratory Medicine.* 3(2): 273–274, 1983.

An Introduction to the Classification of Gunshot Wounds

4

> "There is nothing more exhilarating than to be shot at without result."
>
> **Winston Churchill**

Gunshot wounds are either penetrating or perforating. Penetrating wounds occur when a bullet enters an object and does not exit; in perforating wounds, the bullet passes completely through the object. A wound, however, can be both penetrating and perforating. A bullet striking the head may pass through the skull and brain before coming to rest under the scalp, thus producing a penetrating wound of the head, but a perforating wound of the skull and brain.

Gunshot wounds can be divided into four broad categories, depending on the range from the muzzle to target: contact, near contact, intermediate, and distant.

Contact Wounds

In contact wounds, the muzzle of the weapon is held against the surface of the body at the time of discharge. Contact wounds may be hard, loose, angled, or incomplete (a variation of angled).

Hard-Contact Wounds. In hard-contact wounds, the muzzle of the weapon is jammed "hard" against the skin, indenting it, so that the skin envelops the muzzle. In hard contact wounds, the immediate edges of the entrance are seared by the hot gases of combustion and blackened by the soot (Figure 4.1). This soot is embedded in the seared skin and cannot be completely removed either by washing or by vigorous scrubbing of the wound.

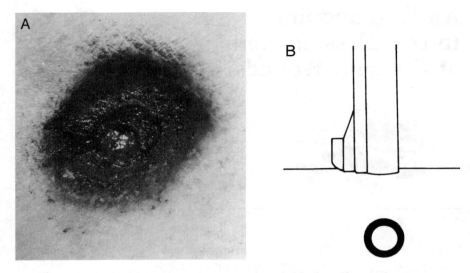

Figure 4.1 (A,B) Hard-contact wound with blackened seared margins.

Loose-Contact Wounds.   In loose-contact wounds, the muzzle, while in complete contact with the skin, is held lightly against it. Gas preceding the bullet, as well as the bullet itself, indents the skin, creating a temporary gap between the skin and the muzzle through which gas can escape. Soot carried by the gas is deposited in a zone around the entrance (Figure 4.2). This soot can be easily wiped away. A few unburnt grains of powder may also escape out this gap and be deposited on the skin in the zone of soot.

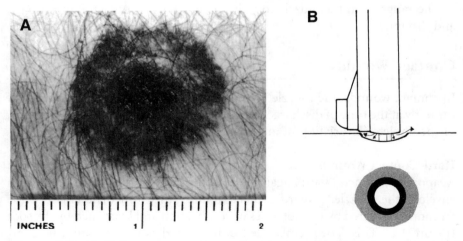

Figure 4.2 (A–B) Loose-contact wound with soot deposited in zone around entrance.

Angled-Contact Wounds. In angled-contact wounds, the barrel is held at an acute angle to the skin so that the complete circumference of the muzzle is not in contact with it. Gas and soot escaping from the gap, where contact is not complete, radiate outward from the muzzle, producing an eccentrically arranged pattern of soot. The soot is arranged in two different zones. The most noticeable zone, and often the only one seen, is a blackened seared area of skin or cloth having a pear, circular, or oval configuration (Figure 4.3A). Less conspicuous is a larger fan-shaped zone of light-gray soot that radiates outward from the gap. On the skin, this light zone is usually washed away, obscured by bleeding or removed in cleaning the wound for examination. A few unburnt grains of powder may be deposited in these zones.

The entrance wound is normally present at the base of the seared blackened zone. All or at least the majority of the seared blackened zone will be on the opposite site of the wound from the muzzle, and thus "points" the way the gun was directed. As the angle between the barrel and the skin **increases**, i.e., the barrel moves toward a perpendicular position to the skin, the entrance hole will be found more toward the center of the zone.

If the angle between the barrel and the skin **decreases**, the gap between the muzzle and skin becomes larger, and more material can escape through the gap. At some point, the gap becomes sufficiently large that unburnt grains of powder escaping through the gap will skim over the zone of seared skin, fanning out from the entrance, impacting distal to the entrance wound in a fan shaped pattern of powder tattooing (see Figure 4.3C).

Incomplete-Contact Wounds. Incomplete-contact wounds are a variation of angled-contact wounds. In these, the muzzle of the weapon is held against the skin, but, because the body surface is not completely flat, there is a gap between the muzzle and the skin. A jet of soot-laden gas escapes from this gap producing an area of seared, blackened skin. The location of this seared, blackened zone can be anywhere in relationship to the muzzle circumference, depending on where the gap is. Incomplete contact wounds are most often seen in self-inflicted contact wounds of the head due to long arms, i.e., rifles and shotguns. In these cases, a zone of blackened and seared skin extends downward from the entrance. The most probable cause for the appearance of this wound is a momentary break in contact between the muzzle and skin along the lower margin of the barrel as the victim reaches for the trigger with one hand while holding the muzzle against the skin with the other hand. A jet of hot sooty gases escapes from the gap producing the elongated blackened and seared zone of skin (Figure 4.4).[1] Scattered grains of powder may accompany the jet of gas and be deposited on the skin.

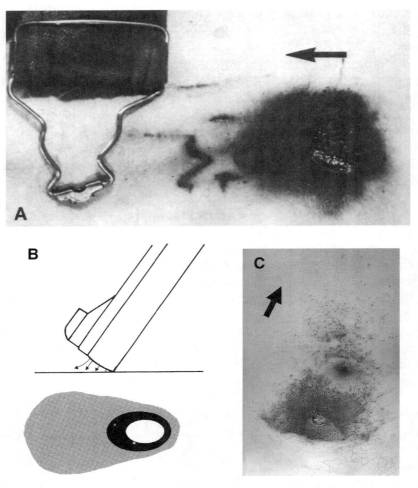

Figure 4.3 **(A–B)** Angled-contact wound with seared blackened zone of skin on opposite side of wound from muzzle pointing the way the gun was directed. **(C)** Angled-contact wound with powder tattooing on opposite side of wound from muzzle.

In all contact wounds, soot, powder, carbon monoxide, and vaporized metals from the bullet, primer, and cartridge case are deposited in and along the wound tract.

Near-Contact Wounds

Near-contact wounds lie in a gray zone between contact and intermediate-range wounds. There is an overlap between the appearance of near- and

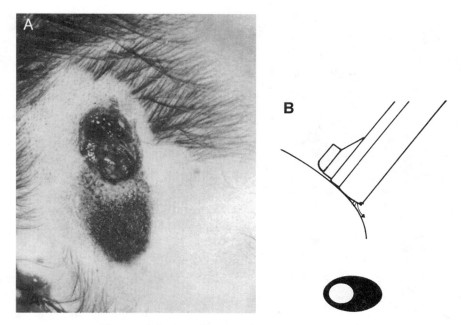

Figure 4.4 (A–B) Incomplete contact wound.

loose-contact wounds making it difficult to differentiate the two. In near-contact wounds, the muzzle of the weapon is not in contact with the skin, being held a short distance away. The distance, however, is so small that the powder grains emerging from the muzzle do not have a chance to disperse and mark the skin, producing the powder tattooing that is the *sine qua non* of intermediate-range wounds. In near-contact wounds, there is an entrance wound, surrounded by a wide zone of powder soot overlying seared, black-ened skin (Figure 4.5). The zone of searing is wider than that seen in a loose-contact wound. The soot in the seared zone is baked into the skin and cannot be completely wiped away. Small clumps of unburned powder may be present in the seared zones.

In near-contact angled wounds (Figure 4.6), just as in angled contact wounds, soot radiates outward from the muzzle creating two zones: the pear-shaped, circular, or oval blackened seared zone and the light-gray fan-shaped one. The location of the blackened seared zone to the entrance•hole is dif-ferent from that seen in angled contact wounds, however. In near-contact angled wounds, the bulk of the blackened, seared zone is on the same side as the muzzle, i.e., pointing toward the weapon. This is the opposite of what is found in angled contact wounds.

The importance of understanding the difference in the distribution of soot deposition for angled near-contact and contact wounds is that the range

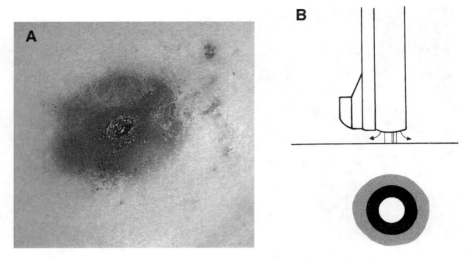

Figure 4.5 (A–B) Near-contact wound with wide zone of powder soot overlying seared blackened skin.

and direction in which the muzzle was pointing at the time of discharge cannot be deduced by looking at the soot pattern alone. In both contact and near-contact angled wounds, one gets an eccentric area of seared blackened skin. In contact wounds, however, this area lies on the side opposite to the muzzle, pointing the direction in which the bullet was fired. In near-contact wounds, the seared and blackened area lies on the same side as the muzzle of the weapon. By correlating the location of the blackened, seared zone with the path of the bullet through the body, one can differentiate an angled

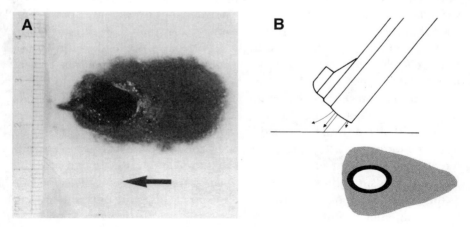

Figure 4.6 Angled near-contact wound with blackened seared zone on same side as muzzle, i.e., pointing toward the weapon.

contact wound from an angled near-contact wound. Thus, if both the bullet and the zone point in the same direction, an angled contact wound has occurred; if, however, the zone is on one side of the wound with the bullet going the other way, an angled near-contact wound has taken place.

This interpretation assumes the ideal presentation of contact and near-contact angled wounds. Things are never as simple as one might wish, however. Thus, in angled contact wounds, the entrance wound should be present at the base of the seared, blackened zone. By increasing the angle between the barrel and the skin, however, this entrance will move toward the center of the zone. This same picture can also be produced by a near-contact angled wound if the distance from muzzle to target is approximately 5 mm. In such an instance one cannot always differentiate between a contact and a near-contact angled wound. When the distance from muzzle to target increases to 10 mm in near-contact angled wounds, there is usually no difficulty differentiating it from an angled contact wound. The seared, blackened zone on the side of the muzzle is much wider than it is on the opposite side. Powder grains may be seen in the seared zone on the side opposite to the muzzle.

Intermediate-Range Wounds

An intermediate-range gunshot wound is one in which the muzzle of the weapon is held away from the body at the time of discharge yet is sufficiently close so that powder grains expelled from the muzzle along with the bullet produce "powder tattooing" of the skin (Figure 4.7). These markings are the *sine qua non* of intermediate-range gunshot wounds.

Just as there is a gradual transition from loose-contact to near-contact wounds, there is also a gradual transition from near-contact to intermediate wounds. The powder grains emerging from the muzzle may be deposited in the seared zone around near-contact wounds though individual tattoo marks are not seen. As soon as one sees individual tattoo marks, one is dealing with an intermediate-range wound. For handguns, powder tattooing begins at a muzzle-to-target distance of approximately 10 mm.

Tattooing consists of numerous reddish-brown to orange-red punctate lesions surrounding the wound of entrance. The distribution around the entrance site may be either symmetric or eccentric, depending on the angle of the gun to the target at the time of discharge, the nature of the target (flat or angled), and any covering of the skin, e.g., hair or clothing which may prevent powder grains from reaching the skin. When the muzzle of the weapon is at an angle to the skin, the skin under the muzzle, i.e., on the same side as the barrel, will show denser tattooing than the skin on the other side of the entrance hole (Figure 4.8).

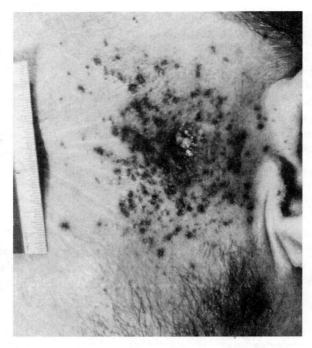

Figure 4.7 Powder tattooing of skin due to flake (disk) powder.

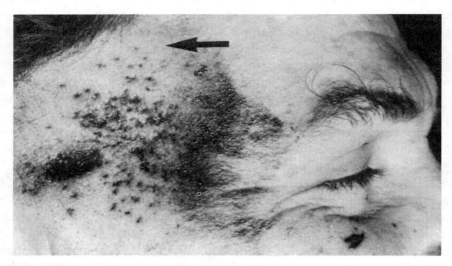

Figure 4.8 Intermediate-range gunshot wound with muzzle of weapon at angle to skin. Powder tattooing of skin on same side as barrel. Arrow indicates direction of bullet.

Powder tattooing is an **antemortem** phenomenon and indicates that the individual was alive at the time they were shot. If the individual was dead before being shot, although the powder may produce marks on the skin, these marks have a moist gray or yellow appearance rather than the reddish-brown to orange-red coloration of an antemortem wound. There should be no difficulty with differentiating the two.

Powder tattoo marks are produced by the impact of powder grains on the skin. They are not "powder burns", but rather are punctate abrasions. Similar markings can be produced by noncombustible particles such as poly-ethylene granules. The term "powder burns" should never be used because one does not know to what phenomenon the term is being applied. Some individuals use the term "powder burns" to signify powder tattooing, whereas others use it to signify searing and blackening of the skin due to the hot gases that occur from combustion of the propellant.

The term "powder burns" dates back to the black powder era, when burning grains of black powder emerging from the muzzle, were deposited on the skin and clothing, where they smoldered, apparently producing actual burns on the skin. Black powder grains could also penetrate into the dermis and produce literal tattooing. The burning grains of black powder were capable of setting clothing on fire, a characteristic not possessed by smokeless powder.

Some authorities use the term "stippling" synonymously with "powder tattooing." The author prefers to use the term "stippling" in a more generic manner to indicate punctate abrasions of the skin, which while they may be due to powder, may also be due to other materials, e.g., shotgun filler, frag-ments of intermediary targets. In other words "powder tattooing" is just one form of stippling with the term "powder tattooing" used to refer to stippling **unquestionably** and **exclusively** due to powder grains. If the marks are due to material other than powder or if one is not certain of their origin, then, one uses the term "stippling."

The punctate abrasions of powder tattooing cannot be wiped away. Powder tattoo marks usually heal completely if the individual survives. This is logical, as the injuries are generally confined to the superficial layers of the epidermis. Grains of ball powder, and less commonly flake powder, however, may pene-trate into the upper dermis thus producing actual tattooing of the skin.

The author has never seen true powder tattooing of the palms or soles of the feet caused by powder emerging from the muzzle of a handgun though he has seen cases in which powder grains were embedded in the palms without any vital reaction (Figure 4.9). It is probable that the thickness of the stratum corneum in this area protects the dermis from any trauma — direct or indirect — arising from the impact of powder grains; thus there is no dermal vital reaction and, therefore, no true tattooing.

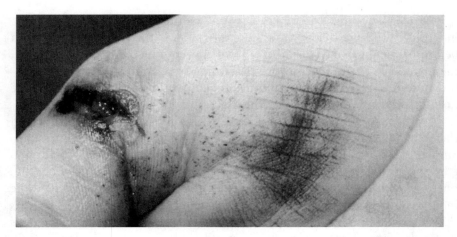

Figure 4.9 Intermediate-range gunshot wound of palm with entrance at base of thumb, soot on thenar eminence and powder grains embedded in skin of palm. No true powder tattooing present.

When a weapon is discharged, in addition to powder, soot produced by combustion of the gunpowder emerges from the muzzle of the weapon. The soot, which is carbon, contains vaporized metals from the primer, bullet, and cartridge case. If the muzzle is held close to the victim, this soot may be deposited on the body. The size, intensity, and appearance of the soot pattern and the maximum range out to which it occurs depend on a number of factors:

1. Range
2. Propellant
3. Angle of the muzzle to the target
4. Barrel length
5. Caliber of the weapon
6. Type of weapon
7. Target material and the state of the target (bloody or non-bloody)

As the range from the muzzle to the target increases, the size of the zone of powder soot blackening will increase, whereas the density will decrease. Beyond a certain point, however, the overall dimensions of the powder soot pattern will begin to decrease, and it will be impossible to delineate exactly the outer border of the soot, as it has become so faint.

The propellant is a determinant as to the amount of powder soot present in that some powders burn more cleanly than others. Thus, in a test using a .22-caliber revolver with a 6-in. barrel, two forms of .22 Long Rifle ammunition were fired at white cotton cloth. One form of ammunition was loaded with flake powder; the other with ball powder. The cartridge loaded with flake powder deposited powder soot out to a maximum of 30 cm, whereas soot from the ball powder disappeared between 20 cm and 25 cm. Powder loaded in Federal centerfire cartridges seems to be "dirtier" than that of other American manufacturers.

Differences in the barrel length of a weapon may affect the amount of soot reaching the target. Thus, Remington 158-gr. .38 Special cartridges loaded with flake powder were fired at white cotton cloth. A 6-in. barrel weapon produced soot out to a maximum of 30 cm; a 4-in. barrel weapon to 25 cm; and a 2-in. barrel weapon, out to 20 cm. The longer barreled weapons produced a soot pattern that was smaller and denser. On the basis of the author's experience, the maximum distance out to which powder soot deposition occurs for most handguns is 20 to 30 cm.

The orientation of the muzzle of the weapon to the target will determine whether the soot deposit around the wound of entrance in the skin or clothing is symmetric (concentric) or eccentric. If the muzzle is at a 90-degree angle to the target, the soot pattern should be circular in shape, with the entrance hole in the center. At ranges from loose contact up to 1 to 2 cm, there is usually a circular area of extremely dense dark-black powder blackening (soot) surrounded by a zone of light gray powder soot. Beyond this range (1 to 2 cm), one begins to get the blossom or petal pattern described by Barnes and Helson.[2] As the range increases farther, this pattern increases in diameter, reaches a maximum size, and then gradually begins to shrink and fade, disappearing by 15 to 25 cm of range. In some instances, the classical petal or blossom pattern will not be present; rather, there will be a dense black center surrounded by a lighter gray outer zone, with this zone possibly having a scalloped appearance.

Not uncommonly, a gunshot wound is covered with blood — wet, dried, or caked. In the process of cleaning the blood off the wound, soot may be wiped off. There are two methods of removing the blood without removing the soot. The first and simplest is to direct a spray of hot water at the wound. After a time, the water will wash away the blood but leave the soot. Blood can also be removed by pouring hydrogen peroxide on it. This will dissolve the blood, breaking up any clots. Any residual blood can then be washed away with a spray of water. Use of a hot water spray is sufficient in most cases. The hydrogen peroxide is useful when there are adherent clots of blood that will not wash away.

Cylinder Gap

When a revolver is fired, gas, soot, and powder emerge not only from the muzzle but also from the gap between the cylinder and the barrel (see Figure 2.11). This material emerges at an approximate right angle to the long axis of the weapon. In addition to the pattern produced by soot emerging from the muzzle, a soot pattern can be produced by soot escaping from the cylinder-barrel gap. If the weapon is held parallel to the body at the time of discharge, the jet of soot-laden gas escaping from the cylinder-barrel gap may produce a linear, a L-shaped or a V-shaped gray sooty deposit on the skin or clothing (Figure 4.10). The skin or cloth at this point may be seared. If the

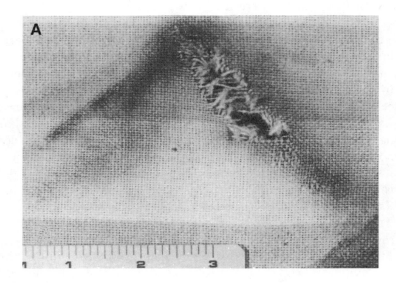

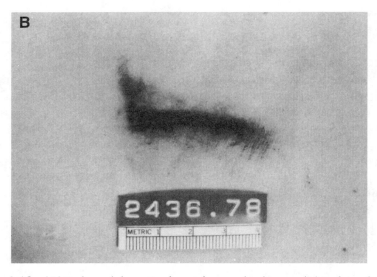

Figure 4.10 (A) V-shaped deposit of soot from cylinder gap; (B) L-shaped deposit of soot on skin from cylinder-barrel gap.

clothing is 100% synthetic, the hot gas may burn completely through the material with formation of the soot pattern on the underlying skin.

If a gun is held at an acute angle to the body, there will be a deposit of soot, possibly associated with a zone of searing, from the cylinder gap as well as searing and soot at the entrance from gas emerging from the muzzle. Measurements from the cylinder mark to the entrance will give an approximation of the barrel length (Figure 4.11).

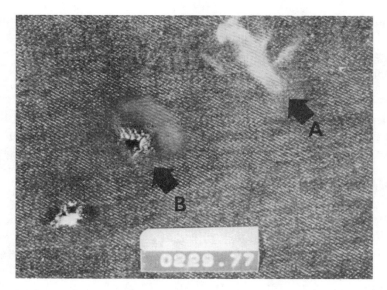

Figure 4.11 Angled near-contact gunshot wound through blue jeans. The arrows indicate (**A**) a strip of seared material due to the hot gases from the cylinder-barrel gap and (**B**) the point of entrance of the bullet seared by the hot muzzle gases. The distance between these two points indicates the weapon was a short barrel revolver.

In addition to the soot, powder escaping from the cylinder gap may produce tattooing of the skin. This tattooing will be relatively sparse. If the cylinder of the revolver is out of alignment with the barrel, as the bullet jumps from the cylinder to the barrel, fragments of metal may be sheared off the bullet. These fragments can produce marks (stippling) on the skin that resemble powder tattoo marks. Such marks, however, are larger, more irregular, and more hemorrhagic than traditional powder tattoo marks. In addition, fragments of lead are often seen embedded in the skin at these marks. These fragment wounds (stippling, pseudo-tattooing) often are intermingled with the true powder tattooing produced by powder escaping from the cylinder gap (see Figure 5.18).

Silencers

A silencer is a device for diminishing the sound of a discharging firearm. No silencer is completely effective and some individuals prefer the term "sound suppressor" for these devices. One can not practically silence a revolver because the noise of discharge exits the cylinder gap as well as the muzzle. Thus, silenced weapons are either semi-automatic pistols or rifles. The noise created on firing a weapon originates from the fall of the hammer or firing pin; detonation of the primer; the wave of gas and air exiting the barrel before the bullet; the bullet exiting; the propellant gas wave and the operation of the gun mechanism as the fired case is extracted and ejected and a new round chambered. This last noise may be deleted by locking closed the action of the weapon so that ejection and chambering of a new round is done manually. Firing a .22 Long Rifle cartridge produces approximately 150 decibels; a 9-mm Parabellum cartridge 165 decibels.

Silencers may be either an integral part of a weapon or attached to the muzzle. Most silencers are cylindrical devices attached to the muzzle of a gun. The cylinder is typically filled with metal or rubber baffles (disks) with a central hole through which the bullet can pass. In crude silencers, the cylinder may be stuffed with steel wool or fiberglass.

The noise produced on firing a weapon is only partly due to discharge. If the bullet travels faster than the speed of sound, e.g., the 9-mm Parabellum, it produces a sonic wave that may equal the sound of discharge. The way to prevent such a noise is to use: a weapon chambered for a subsonic cartridge, e.g., the .45 ACP; a subsonic loading of a high-velocity round, e.g., the 147 gr. 9-mm Parabellum cartridge or to alter the weapon so that on firing supersonic ammunition, the bullet is subsonic on exiting the muzzle.[3] This last solution is accomplished by drilling multiple holes down the barrel so as to bleed off some of the propellant gas causing the bullet to be traveling at subsonic velocity when it exits.

A silencer may filter out most if not all of the soot and powder that emerges from the barrel. Missliwetz et al. noted an absence not only of soot, powder, and tattooing in a series of close-range wounds inflicted with silenced weapons, but also absence of the abrasion ring in some entrances.[4] The weapons used were .32 ACP pistols and a 9-mm submachine gun. It is probable that the absence of the abrasion ring was due to the nature of the bullets rather than the fact that the weapons were silenced. The author has noticed an occasional absence of the abrasion ring in entrance wounds due to jacketed and semi-jacketed bullets.

Muzzle Brakes/Compensators

Silencers are rarely encountered. More common are muzzle-brakes and compensators. Just as in a silencer, they may be integral with the barrel or attached to the muzzle. A muzzle brake works by re-directing some of the gases at the muzzle so as to generate a forward thrust on the muzzle countering the force of recoil, i.e., reducing recoil. A compensator diverts gas upward to counteract the tendency for the muzzle to rise on firing. The terms muzzle brake and compensator are often used interchangeably.

Muzzle brakes often function as compensators as well. In their simplest form, they consist of gas ports cut in the muzzle end of the barrel. In some contact wounds, the jets of gas escaping out the ports may produce characteristic soot patterns on the skin or clothing. Figure 4.12A shows a contact wound under the jaw from a 7-mm Magnum rifle equipped with a muzzle brake (Figure 4.12B). Figure 4.12C shows a "rabbit-ear" pattern produced by a .22-caliber target pistol with a compensator having two slits.

Flash Suppressors

Modern military rifles and some civilian rifles have flash suppressors attached to the muzzle. These devices are intended to break up the "fireball" that emerges from the muzzle of the rifle when fired at night. Such a device is useful in combat to decrease the possibility of counterfire. Flash suppressors generally consist of a cylinder, having a number of longitudinal slits along its length, that is attached to the muzzle of the weapon (Figure 4.13A). On firing, the gas emerging from the muzzle is bled out the slits rather than emerging as one large cloud. Soot is present in this cloud of gas. If the muzzle of such a weapon is held in contact with the body, the flash suppressor will produce a distinctive pattern of seared, blackened zones around the entrance. If fully formed, this results in an unusual flower-like pattern of soot and seared skin (Figure 4.13B–C). The number of slits will determine the number of "petals" to the "flower" and may give one an idea of the type of weapon used. Thus, for the M-14 with five slits in the flash suppressor, there are five "petals" to the "flower" pattern. The flash suppressor on the M-16A1 and AR-15 rifles initially had three slits which was changed to six slits. The M-16A2 and AR-15A2 have a suppressor with five slits with absence of the slit at the 6 o'clock position. The skin underlying these linear deposits of soot is seared, with the soot often being baked into the skin. The "flower" pattern of the suppressor is more prominent when the wound is in an area of the body with loose skin that can enclose the suppressor (Figure 4.13B). In contact wounds on flat surfaces, the pattern may be more subtle (Figure 4.13D).

Gas Ports/Vents

Gas-operated self-loading shotguns and centerfire rifles have gas ports where the gas, after operating the gun's mechanism, is vented. In some semi-automatic centerfire rifles, e.g., the Remington M 7400 and shotguns, e.g., the

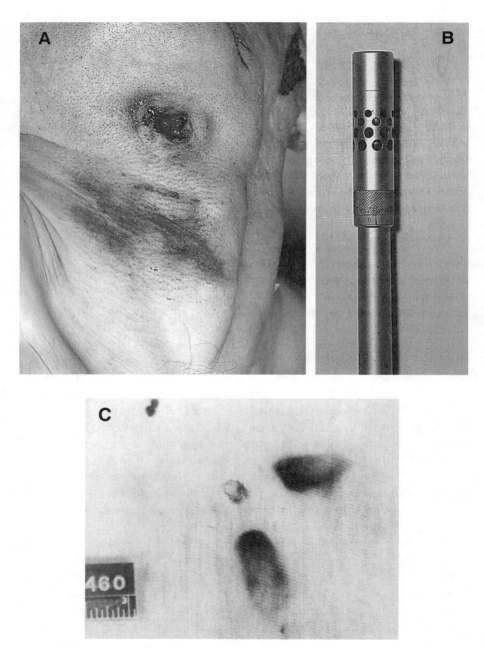

Figure 4.12 (A) Contact wound under jaw with muzzle imprint; seared zone of skin below entrance from (B) muzzle break. (C) "rabbit ear" pattern of soot on T-shirt produced by .22-caliber target pistol with muzzle break at end. Two slits on top of the muzzle break directed gas upward and forward, producing the soot pattern.

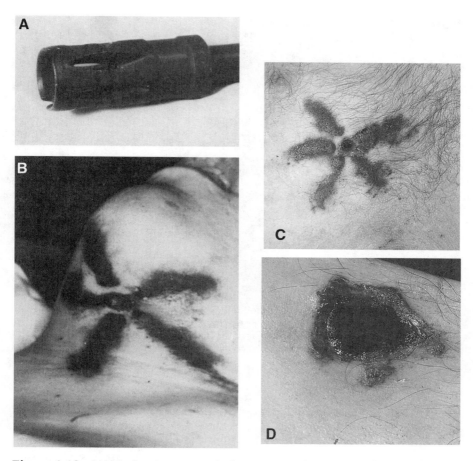

Figure 4.13 (A) Flash suppressor. Flash suppressor burns on undersurface of chin (B) and chest (C) from M-14 rifle; (D) burns on chest from AK-47 suppressor.

Winchester M 1400, there are two slots in the top of the forearm—one on each side of the barrel—through which soot-laden gas is vented. Knowledge of this arrangement was instrumental in the correct certification of the manner of death in a case seen by the author. The death was presented by the police agency as a case of suicide. The weapon was a Winchester M 1400 shotgun; the wound a near-contact wound of the forehead. There was a heavy deposit of soot and some fragments of tissue and blood on the left hand which had to have been holding the muzzle at the time of discharge (Figure 4.14A). On the palm of the right hand was a linear deposit of soot (Figure 4.14B). The only possible source for this soot was one of the vents. Thus, one hand was at the muzzle; the other partially overlying the vents on the top of the shotgun forearm. There was no way that the deceased could have pulled the trigger. The manner of death was certified as homicide.

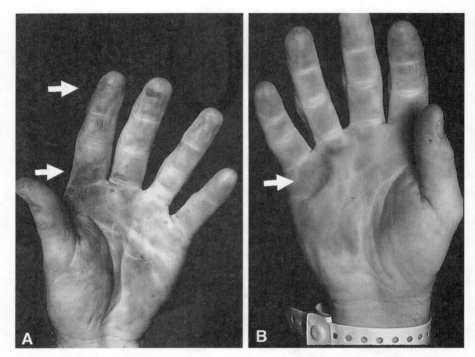

Figure 4.14 (A) Soot on left hand from muzzle and on right hand; (B) from gas port.

Miscellaneous Powder Patterns

An unusual powder pattern may be due to specific peculiarities of a gun. Thus, in the case illustrated, a 20-year-old Puerto Rican male shot himself twice in the chest (Figure 4.15A). The two contact wounds showed extensive blackening of the skin. Approximately 3.2 cm above each entrance wound there was a small, irregular area of powder soot deposit. The weapon used to inflict the wounds was a .22-caliber starter's pistol (Figure 4.15B) whose barrel had been reamed open. On the top of the barrel was a vent that was intended to channel off gases when blank cartridges were fired. When the two live rounds were fired; the vent in the weapon directed some of the gases in an upward and forward direction, causing the observed patterns. The two bullets recovered from the body were free of rifling.

Distant Gunshot Wounds

In distant wounds, the only marks on the target are those produced by the mechanical action of the bullet in perforating the skin.

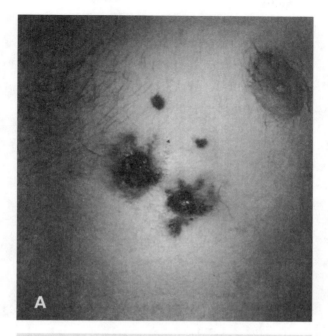

Figure 4.15 (A) Two contact wounds of chest with deposit of powder soot above the wound entrances; (B) top view of .22 caliber starter pistol barrel with vent visible (arrow).

Entrance Versus Exit Wounds

Entrance Wounds

Most entrance wounds, no matter the range, are surrounded by a reddish, reddish-brown zone of abraded skin — the abrasion ring (Figure 4.16). This is a rim of flattened, abraded epidermis, surrounding the entrance hole. Fresh entrance wounds have an abrasion ring with a moist, fleshy appearance. As the abrasion ring dries out, however, it assumes the more familiar appearance.

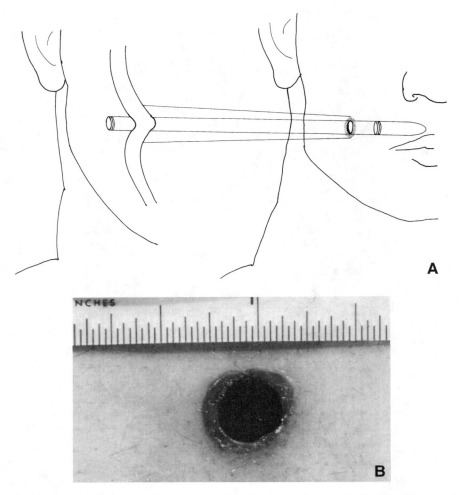

Figure 4.16 (A) The bullet indents the skin, punching a hole through it and abrading the margins of the entrance wound in the skin; (B) typical entrance wound with abrasion ring of margins.

The abrasion ring occurs when the bullet abrades, ("rubs raw") the edges of the hole as it indents and pierces the skin (Figure 4.16). This ring is not due to the bullet's rotational movement as it goes through the skin, as even a very rapidly rotating bullet, e.g., a 62 gr. 5.56 × 45 mm, fired in the M-16A2, makes only one complete rotation in 7 in. (178 mm) of horizontal travel.

The abrasion ring is also not due to the bullet burning the skin. While bullets may easily attain a surface temperature of over 100°C after leaving the muzzle, the contact time between the bullet and skin is extremely short, insufficient to cause a burn. Thus, while thermographic measurement of a copper jacketed 9-mm Parabellum bullet in flight showed a surface temperature of 147 to 152°C, contact time with the skin at a velocity of 1148 ft/s (350m/s) would be approximately 0.1 ms.[5] That bullets do not burn the skin has been known for some time. In the late nineteenth century, Von Beck conducted experiments to determine the amount of heat imparted to both lead bullets of large caliber and jacketed .30-caliber rifle bullets.[6] He found that the temperature of a recovered lead bullet of .45 caliber was 69°C; a steel-jacketed .30-caliber bullet 78°C and a copper-jacketed .30-caliber rifle bullet 110°C. The missiles were handled by the fingers and never possessed sufficient heat to burn skin.

The abrasion ring can vary in width, depending on the caliber of the weapon, the angle at which the bullet entered, and the anatomic site of entrance. Entrance wounds in the skin overlying the clavicle generally have a wider abrasion ring than those in other parts of the body, possibly due to reinforcement of a thin layer of skin by curved bone (Figure 4.17A).

The abrasion ring around the entrance hole can be concentric or eccentric, depending on the angle between the bullet and the skin. A bullet striking perpendicular to the skin should produce a concentric abrasion ring (see Figure 4.16). If the bullet penetrates at an oblique angle, the zone of abrasion in the skin will be eccentric, with the zone wider on the side from which the bullet comes (Figure 4.17B). This however, assumes that the skin is flat. People, however, are three-dimensional, with curves, depressions, and projections. Thus, the bullet may be fired perpendicular to the body but strike a projecting surface, e.g., the breast so that an eccentric abrasion ring wound is produced even though the bullet is going straight into the body. Thus, it is never possible to say with certainty in which direction a bullet has traveled through the body from examination of the entrance wound alone.

Abrasion rings may have very unusual configurations. In Figure 4.18A, the abrasion ring, besides being markedly eccentric, is divided into two sections. The medial end of each is "squared" off. The individual was shot in the center of her chest, between her breasts which were pushed together by her brassiere. The bullet abraded the inner surface of both breasts before penetrating the chest wall in the cleft between the breasts. The individual shown in Figure 4.18B was crouching when shot. Both bullets followed the same path through the body. Their abrasion rings, however, are markedly different because of the irregular dips and peaks in the skin caused by bending over.

Occasionally an entrance wound will not have an abrasion ring observable either by naked eye or by dissecting microscope. This can be due to the nature of the bullet or the location of the entrance wound. Entrance wounds from centerfire rifle bullets and jacketed/semi-jacketed handgun bullets (usually of high velocity, e.g., the .357 Magnum and 9-mm Parabellum) may not have

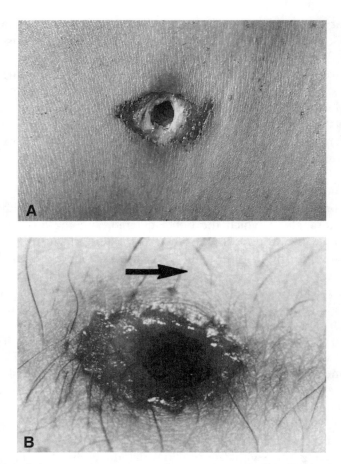

Figure 4.17   (A) Atypical entrance in skin overlying clavicle; (B) entrance wound with eccentric abrasion ring due to bullet striking skin at angle. Arrow indicates direction of bullet.

abrasion rings (Figure 4.19A). In one unusual instance, an entrance from a .38 Smith & Wesson lead bullet (a very low-velocity round) also did not have an abrasion ring (Figure 4.19B). Entrance wounds of the palms and the soles as well as re-entry wounds of the axilla usually do not have abrasion rings.

Distant or intermediate entrance wounds of the palms and soles differ from wounds of the skin in other areas of the body in that the entrance is stellate, with tears 1 to 3 mm in length radiating from the entrance perforation; or are "H" shaped or slit-like. These wounds typically have no abrasion ring (Figure 4.20 A–B). They resemble and are often mistaken for exit wounds or cuts. The same picture may be seen in entrance wounds of the elbow. The common factor tieing together these three locations is the increased thickness of the skin in these regions.

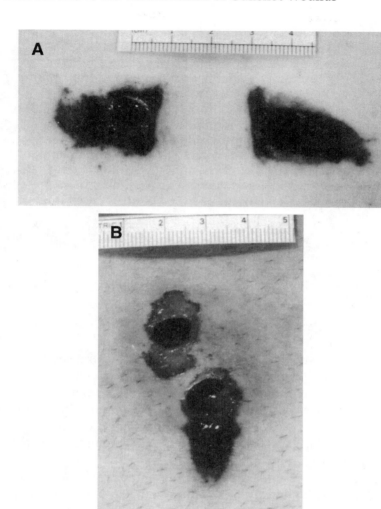

Figure 4.18 (A) Two areas of abrasion (compound abrasion ring) due to single bullet entering middle of chest, between breasts pushed together by brassiere. (B) Two entrance wounds with markedly different abrasion rings, though trajectory of bullets through body was identical.

In addition to the absence of an abrasion ring, wounds from high-velocity centerfire rifle bullets may show small splits or tears radiating outward from the edges of the perforation (Figure 7.12). These "micro-tears" usually involve the complete circumference of the entrance wound, though like abrasion rings they may involve only a partial circumference. Although micro-tears may be barely visible with the naked eye, they are readily apparent with the dissecting microscope. Micro-tears may also be seen, though rarely, in entrance wounds from partial metal-jacketed .357 Magnum bullets. In the

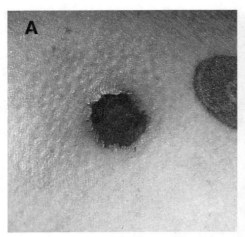 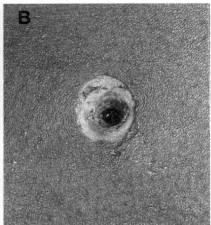

Figure 4.19 (A) Entrance of partial metal-jacketed .357 Magnum bullet showing absence of abrasion ring and presence of microtears; (B) entrance of .38 caliber S & W bullet showing absence of abrasion ring.

wound shown in Figure 4.19A due to a .357 Magnum bullet, there is both absence of an abrasion ring and micro-tears.

There is usually no difficulty determining that an entrance wound without an abrasion ring is truly an entrance. With the exception of the palm, sole, and elbow, these wounds are oval to circular with a punched-out clean appearance to the margins, totally unlike that of exit wounds. The exceptions to this are reentry wounds of the axilla and scrotum, which may be slit-shaped and resemble exits. Fortunately, these latter wounds are virtually all penetrating rather than perforating.

In rare instances, a circular punched-out entrance without an abrasion ring is associated with an exit that also has a circular punched-out appearance, leading to confusion as to which wound is the entrance and which the exit. In such an instance a determination as to entrance versus exit may not be possible. In a case seen by the author, the victim had a through-and-through gunshot wound of the left calf with wounds on the lateral and posterior-medial surfaces of the calf. Both wounds appeared identical, having a circular punched-out appearance and no abrasion ring. It was the author's opinion on examining these wounds that the lateral wound was the entrance and the posterior-medial wound the exit. An x-ray, however, showed a fracture of the fibula with bone fragments following a lateral path, thus indicating that the bullet entered the posterior-medial aspect of the calf and exited from the lateral aspect (Figure 4.21). Because of doubts concerning this interpretation, the fibula and the bulk of the bone fragments were removed from the leg. When the bone was reassembled from the fragments, it was obvious that

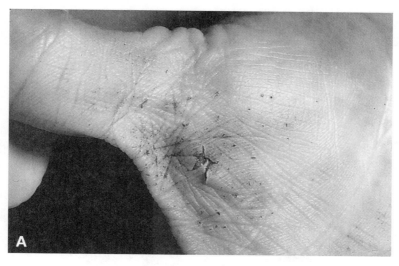

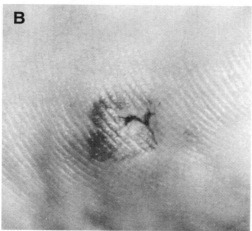

Figure 4.20 (A) Stellate entrance wound of palm without abrasion ring. Note embedded grains of powder but no true tattooing. (B) Entrance wound of sole of foot.

the x-ray interpretation was correct; the entrance in the leg was posterior-medial and the exit was lateral.

Distant gunshot wounds of the head may have a stellate or irregular appearance simulating a contact wound. This phenomena is seen with both handgun and rifle bullets. It is most common over bony prominence such as the orbital ridges. The author has seen this phenomena in other areas of the head as well, e.g., at the hairline; between the eyebrows; over the cheekbone; along the edge of the mandible; on the top and on the back of the head (Figure 4.22). These wounds may be incorrectly interpreted as contact wounds or exits.

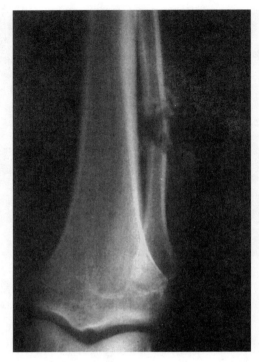

Figure 4.21 X-ray showing fracture of fibula, with bone fragments following lateral path.

Microscopic sections through a gunshot wound of entrance show a progressive increase in alteration of the epithelium and dermis as one proceeds from the periphery of the abrasion ring to the margin of the perforation. The most peripheral margin of the abrasion ring shows a zone of compressed, deformed cells many of which show nuclear "streaming." As one proceeds centrally, there is loss of superficial cellular layers so that only the rete pegs remain adjacent to the perforation.[7] Such epithelial changes occur in contact, near-contact, intermediate, and distant wounds.

In contact and near-contact wounds, large quantities of black amorphous material, predominantly soot, are found on the skin around the entrance and in the wound track. It is often not realized that soot, as well as occasional powder grains, may be seen in the wound tracks of distant wounds, carried in on the sides and base of the bullet. In virtually all such cases, the amount of such material is extremely small. Exceptions occur. Thus, an individual was seen by numerous witnesses to be shot in the head at a distance of 50 to 60 feet with a full metal-jacketed 9-mm bullet. The entrance was that of a distant wound. The underlying subcutaneous tissue showed a large black sooty deposit. Examination of bullets fired in the weapon revealed heavy

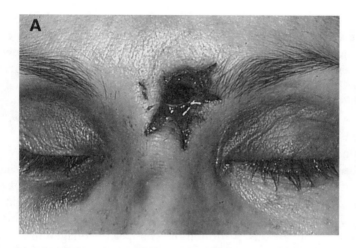

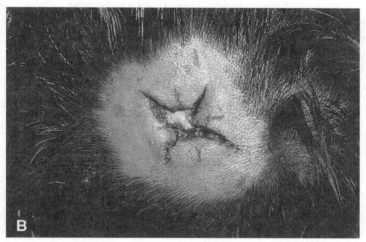

Figure 4.22 Distant range, stellate entrance wounds of: (**A**) forehead; (**B**) top of head.

deposits of soot covering one-third to one-half the surface area of the copper jacketing. This was the source of the deposit of soot.

In intermediate-range wounds, microscopic sections of the entrance should show grains of powder embedded in the skin adjacent to the entrance hole. Although true ball powder quite commonly embeds itself in the skin, flake powder generally bounces off. For the most part, the grains of powder are embedded in the epidermis. Ball powder, and on occasion flake powder, may however, perforate the epidermis, coming to rest in the upper dermis. Flake powder that does become embedded usually consists of small, thick disks and not the more common large thin disks (flakes).

Identification of a wound as contact or intermediate is best made with either the naked eye or a dissecting microscope rather than the microscope. Positive identification of material recovered from a wound as powder can usually be made by the shape of the powder grains if they are intact. If they are partially burned and there is no definite shape, the material can be analyzed by thin-layer chromatography to identify the material positively as powder.[8] A cruder test involves touching what appears to be a powder grain with a red-hot probe. This will cause the powder to burn.

In gunshot wounds, the dermis underneath the abrasion ring and adjacent to the wound track shows alterations in the appearance of the collagen. These alterations have been ascribed to the thermal effects of hot gases in close range wounds and the thermal effects of a "hot bullet" in distant wounds.[7] The collagen fibers stain from deep-red to gray-blue and appear swollen and homogeneous. Although the changes in collagen in contact and near-contact wounds may be due to heat, the changes in intermediate and distant range wounds are not. Rather, the changes are due to the mechanical action of the bullet stretching the epidermis and dermis as it pushes its way through the skin. Bullets are never "red-hot." In fact, a bullet never stays hot enough to sterilize itself. This fact has been demonstrated experimentally a number of times since the nineteenth century. Typically in such tests, bullets are dipped in a bacterial culture, fired, and recovered. The bacteria are then plated from the fired bullet.[6,9]

Exit Wounds

Exit wounds, whether they are the result of contact, intermediate, or distant firing, all have the same general characteristics. They are typically larger and more irregular than entrance wounds and, with rare exception, do not possess an abrasion ring. Exit wounds can be stellate, slit-like, crescent, circular, or completely irregular (Figure 4.23). Stellate exit wounds can be seen in the scalp and may be confused with contact wounds.

The larger but more irregular nature of exit wounds is due to two factors. First, the spin that stabilized the bullet in the air is not effective in tissue because of the greater density of the tissue. Thus, as the missile travels through the body, its natural yaw is accentuated; if it travels through enough tissue it will eventually tumble ending up traveling base first. Second, the bullet may be deformed in its passage through the body. Both factors result in the presentation of a larger area of bullet at the site of exit, with resultant larger and more irregular exit wounds. That deformation and tumbling of the bullet are the reasons why the exit wound is usually larger and more irregular than the entrance was proved by a number of experiments in which steel balls were fired through animals at high velocities.[10] These balls were not deformed by the tissue and, because of their configuration, could not tumble. The exit

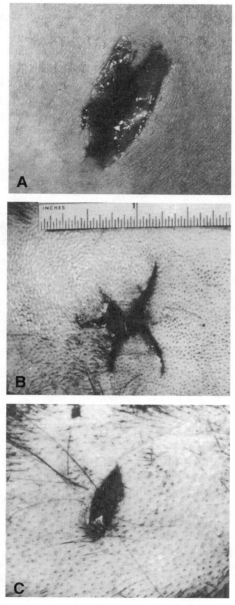

Figure 4.23   (a–c) Exit wounds.

wounds produced were smaller than the entrances because the missiles had less energy at the time of exit compared to when they entered the body.

In unusual circumstances, exit wounds will have abraded margins (Figure 4.24). These are called **shored** exit wounds. They are characterized by a broad, irregular band of abrasion of the skin around the exit. In such wounds the skin is reinforced, or "shored," by a firm surface at the instant the bullet exits. Thus, individuals shot while lying on the floor, leaning against a wall, or sitting back in a chair may have shored exit wounds. As it exits, the bullet everts the skin, with the everted margin impacting against the wall, floor, or back of a chair, thus being abraded or "rubbed raw." Shored exit wounds can also occur from tight supportive garments, such as girdles, brassieres, and

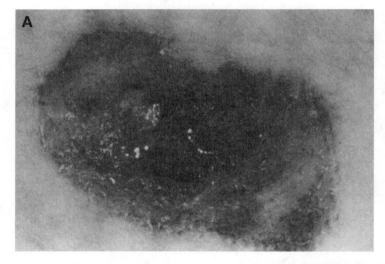

Figure 4.24   (A) Shored exit. (B) Shored exit — incising the skin lateral to the shored exit reveals the bullet.

belts, as well as from tight clothing. Fresh shored wounds have a moist succulent appearance. The pattern of the material overlying the shored exit may be imprinted on the edges of the wound. Shored wounds have very wide, irregular, abrasion collars and when dry may simulate contact wounds.

Occasionally, a bullet traveling through the body will lose so much velocity that, while it may have sufficient velocity to create an exit hole, the bullet will not exit. This may be due to the elastic nature of the skin or resistance to its exiting by either an overlying garment or an object such as a seat back or wall. In the latter case, the "exit" may show shoring of its edges. Occasionally, a bullet may be found protruding from its exit (Figure 4.25).

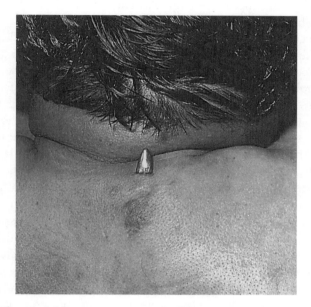

Figure 4.25   7.62 × 39 mm bullet projecting from exit.

The size and the shape of the exit wound are dependent to a certain degree on the location of the exit. In lax skin, the exit wounds tend to be small and slit-shaped. In contrast, where the skin is stretched tightly across a bony surface, e.g., the scalp, exit wounds tend to be larger and more irregular, often with a stellate configuration.

Although exit wounds are typically larger than entrance wounds, it is possible for an exit to be smaller than the entrance and in fact smaller in diameter than the bullet. The last phenomenon is due to the elastic nature of the skin. Another significant fact to be remembered concerning exit wounds is that the shape of an exit wound does not correlate with the type of bullet used, e.g., roundnose, hollow-point.

If one examines the whole spectrum of incomplete, partial, and complete exit wounds, one sees a progression in their development. First is the bullet lodged subcutaneously without disruption of the overlying skin. Next is the incomplete exit, consisting of one or two small superficial slit-like lacerations in the skin with the bullet still in the underlying subcutaneous tissue. These lacerations do not communicate directly with the bullet or wound tract. They are "tears" in the skin produced by eversion of the skin as the bullet attempts to exit. The elastic limit of the skin is exceeded, and the skin tears. The paired lacerations may represent the opposite ends of a bullet attempting to exit sideways. Next is the bullet that breaks the skin, but cannot exit and rebounds back into the wound because of the elasticity of the skin. The exit may or may not be shored. The missile had sufficient velocity to cause the exit but insufficient velocity to leave the body. Then comes the bullet that exits, hits a hard surface and is deflected back into the exit wound (see Figure 4.24B). Such exits are virtually always shored exits. Last is the complete exit.

A common and seemingly logical assumption that is not usually true is that a bullet on exiting the body will continue in a straight path that is a continuation (projection) of the path the bullet followed in the body. As a bullet passes through the body, however, it becomes unstable and its yaw increases. If the path is sufficiently long, the bullet will tumble, ending up traveling base forward. Thus, an exiting bullet may be wildly yawing and/or traveling base forward. Such a bullet is no longer aerodynamically stable and can go off in any direction. The farther such a bullet moves from the exit, the more the bullet will veer from its projected trajectory. If in passing through the body the bullet undergoes deformation, this will also contribute to the tendency of the bullet to veer off its projected course. Knowledge of this phenomenon is important in trying to reconstruct the shooting scene. Thus, with bullets embedded in a wall, one can accurately and confidently determine their point of origin, i.e., where they were fired from, by projecting backward along their trajectory, only if these bullets have not passed through a body.

Miscellaneous Entrance Wounds

A **graze wound** is one in which a bullet strikes the skin at a shallow angle, producing an elongated area of abrasion without actual perforation or tearing of the skin (Figure 4.26A). In a **tangential wound**, the injury extends down through to the subcutaneous tissue (Figure 4.26B). The skin is torn, or "lacerated," by the bullet.

In both graze and tangential wounds, it may be difficult to tell the direction in which the bullet was traveling when it produced the wound. Examination of the two ends of a tangential wound will often but not always reveal the entrance end to have a partially abraded margin, i.e., a cap of abraded tissue, while the exit end will be split. Tears along the margin of a tangential wound point in the direction the bullet moved (Figure 4.26B). In both types of wounds, piling up of tissue may occur at the exit end.

Superficial perforating wounds are shallow through-and-through wounds in which the entrance and exit are close together. They may be difficult to interpret. The entrance will usually have a complete but eccentric abrasion ring, whereas the exit will have abrasion of only a portion of the circumference. The abrasion at the exit points the way the bullet was moving; the eccentric abrasion of the entrance, the way the bullet was coming from. If the path of the bullet is immediately under the skin, the overlying skin may show traumatic stretch stria (Figure 4.26C).

Re-entry wounds occur when a bullet has passed through one part of the body and then reentered another part. The portion of the body initially perforated serves as an intermediary target. Most commonly, this occurs when a bullet perforates an arm and enters the thorax. The reentry wound is usually characterized by a large irregular entrance hole whose edges are ragged and a wide, irregular abrasion ring (Figure 4.27).

Reentry wounds of the axilla caused by missiles that have passed through the arm often have a very atypical appearance. Such wounds may be oval to slit-shaped with a very thin or even absent abrasion ring (Figure 4.28). They often so nearly resemble a wound of exit that they cannot be differentiated from an exit wound if considered alone.

Shoring of an entrance wound may be seen with a re-entry wound of the chest from a bullet that perforated the arm. This occurs when the arm is against the chest at the time the bullet perforated the arm and entered the chest. The chest "shores up" the exit in the arm and the arm "shores up" the entrance in the chest (Figure 4.29). These shored entrance wounds are due to skin around the reentry site slapping back against the arm that was against the chest.

Intermediary Targets

Passage of a bullet or pellets through an intermediary object before striking a victim usually results in alteration in the appearance of the wound or wounds incurred. In the case of shotgun pellets, the object may cause the pattern to "open up" sooner than it would have otherwise. The fact that the pellets passed through an intermediary target has to be taken into account when conducting range determinations based on the size of the pellet pattern on the body. Increased dispersion of pellets by an intermediary object can lead to the conclusion that the individual was shot at a greater range than they actually were.

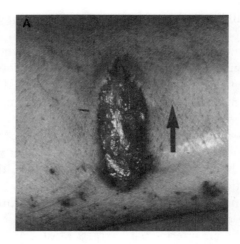

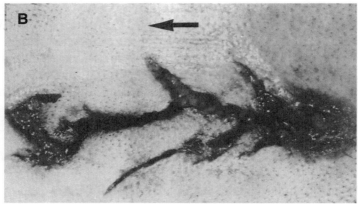

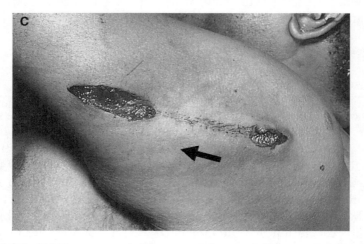

Figure 4.26 (A) Graze wound; (B) tangential wound; (C) superficial perforating wound. Arrow indicates direction of bullet in A–C.

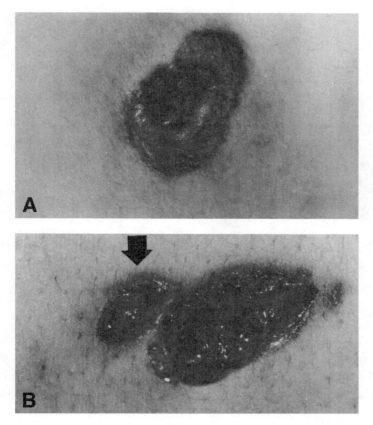

Figure 4.27 **(A)** Reentry wound with wide irregular abrasion ring and large irregular entrance hole. **(B)** Primary entrance wound (as indicated by arrow) adjacent to large irregular reentry wound.

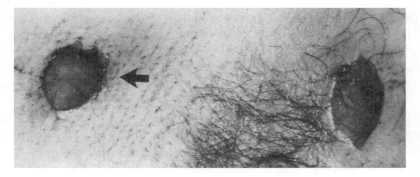

Figure 4.28   Exit and reentry wound (indicated by arrow) of axilla.

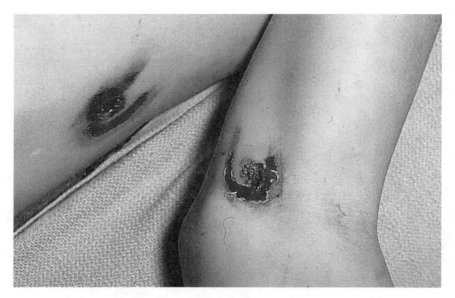

Figure 4.29 Shored entrance of chest and shored exit of arm.

In passing through an object, a bullet may propel fragments of the object forward with the bullet. If the victim is close to the intermediary object, these fragments may strike the individual, embedding themselves in the clothes or skin. In addition, these fragments may produce pseudo-powder tattoo marks (stippling) of the skin (Figure 4.30). With perforation of wire screens, the pattern of the wire may also be imprinted on the tip of the bullet. In lead or lead-tipped bullets that have passed through glass, glass fragments may be embedded in the tip of the bullet; these may be seen with a dissecting microscope.

The gyroscopic spin that stabilizes a bullet as it travels through the air is insufficient to stabilize the bullet as it passes through a solid object. Because of this, the bullet's yaw is accentuated and the bullet may wobble violently. In addition, the bullet may be deformed in its passage through the object. As a result of these factors, when the bullet does strike the victim, the entry wound is usually atypical (see Figure 4.27). The perforation will be larger and more irregular with ragged margins. The surrounding abrasion ring will be irregular and wider.

Passage of a semi-jacketed bullet, whether from a rifle or handgun, through an intermediary target can result in separation of the jacket and the core. Thornton found that this occurred in half the instances when a .38 Special jacketed hollow-point bullet passed through a tempered-glass automobile window.[11] In one of the author's cases, a .223 semi-jacketed soft-point

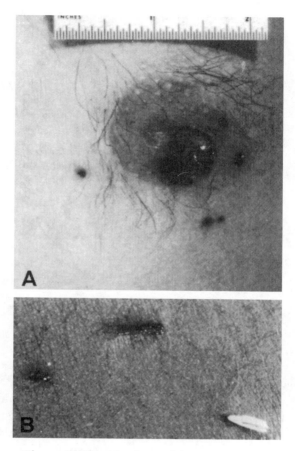

Figure 4.30 (A–B) Wood fragment marks.

bullet was fired through a wood door. On passing through the wood, the jacket and core separated with a 16-gr. fragment of jacket penetrating into the brain of a woman, killing her.

The most common intermediary targets seen in forensic medicine are the upper extremities, doors, and car windows. As previously stated, in about half the instances when a semi-jacketed handgun bullet passes through the tempered-glass window of a car, there will be jacket and core separation. The core, because of its greater mass, may continue the original trajectory for a short distance, retaining most of the impact velocity and, thus, can readily penetrate the victim. The jacket, because of its light weight, rapidly loses velocity and usually flies off at an angle from the path of the core. If the jacket does hit the victim, it can either bounce off or penetrate. Occasionally both jacket and core will penetrate, and the victim will have two entry wounds

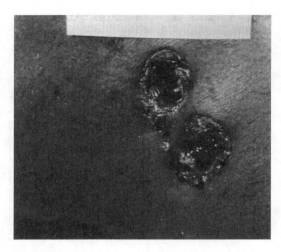

Figure 4.31 Separate entrance wounds from jacket and core of same bullet. Bullet perforated intermediary target.

from one bullet (Figure 4.31). The jacket often does not penetrate the body to any significant degree with handgun bullets.

Rarely, the bullet on hitting glass may completely disintegrate, showering the individual with fragments of lead, jacket, and glass. This is shown in Figure 4.32, where the individual was shot through the side of a window of a car by a police officer using 110-gr. semi-jacketed hollow-point ammunition.

The author has seen a number of individuals shot through car doors with centerfire rifles. The bullets were both full metal-jacketed and hunting. The hunting bullet tended to break up, inflicting multiple (scores even hundreds of) fragment wounds on the victims. The wounds of the torso were penetrating rather than perforating. Fragments of steel from the car doors were recovered from the bodies. In the case of full metal-jacketed bullets (5.56 × 45 and 7.62 × 39), the picture was more variable, depending to some degree, on whether the cores were steel or lead. Some bullets fragmented; others flattened along their long axis, while others appeared unaffected by their perforation of the door.

In his paper on the effects of tempered glass on bullet trajectory, Thornton has made some other observations.[11] Tempered-glass automobile windows are usually angled inward. On tests with such glass at 20 degrees to the vertical plane, hollow-point pistol ammunition showed an average deflection of 16 degrees from the original trajectory (range, 13.2 to 19.9 degrees), with separation of the jacket from the core in half the tests. Lead bullets showed an average 10.7 degree deflection.

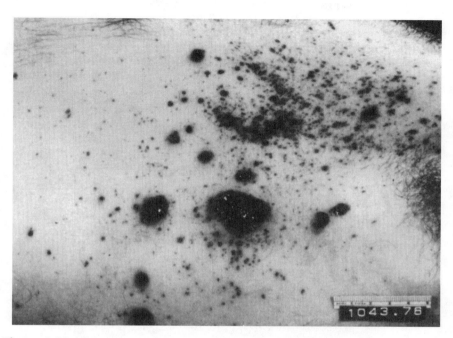

Figure 4.32 Fragment wounds of left side of chest due to disintegration of bullet and side window of car.

Stippling: Powder Tattooing and Pseudo-Powder Tattooing

Stippling consists of multiple punctate abrasions of the skin due to the impact of small fragments of foreign material. If this material is gunpowder, the author calls this form of stippling **powder tattooing**. If the material is not powder, but the punctate abrasions produced appear identical to those due to powder, the phenomena is referred to as **pseudo-powder tattooing**. Most stippling of a non-gunpowder origin does not resemble powder tattooing and can easily be differentiated from it. The exception is stippling from shotgun filler.

If a bullet passes through a sheet of glass, stippling may be produced by the fragments of the glass. This is seen most commonly in individuals shot through the tempered-glass side window of an automobile. Such glass stippling tends to be scant, as well as larger and more irregular, with greater variation in size compared to powder tattoo marks (Figure 4.33). Fragments of glass are usually found embedded in the skin at these sites or adherent to the clothing. Examination of the recovered bullet with a dissecting microscope

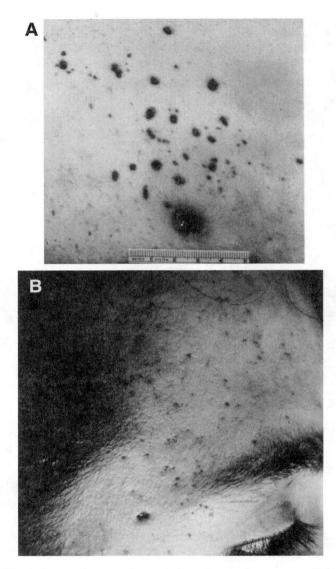

Figure 4.33 (A) Irregular stippling of skin due to fragments of glass; (B) fine stipple marks due to fragments of glass.

may reveal minute fragments of glass embedded in the tip. High-velocity bullets striking glass may break up, showering the individual not only with glass fragments but also with fragments of the core and metal jacketing. Thus, the stippling marks may be due not only to the glass but to the fragments of the bullet (see Figure 4.32).

A bullet ricocheting off a hard surface can generate secondary fragments that may produce stippling of the skin. These marks can be due to fragments of wood or stone from the surface from which the bullet ricocheted or to metal fragments from the bullet itself. Such markings are usually larger, more irregular, and considerably more sparse than powder tattoo marks. Fragments of wood or metal often will be found embedded in or adjacent to these markings.

Stippling can be produced by fragments of the plastic casing used to enclose the shot in handgun shot cartridges. The fragment marks are usually very large and irregular (see Figure 10.17).

Occasionally, individuals construct crude silencers, using steel wool as the packing material in the silencer. On firing the weapon, fragments of the steel wool may be propelled out the end of the silencer, embedding themselves in the skin around the entrance. These markings are relatively sparse and fragments of the steel wool often can be found embedded in the skin.

Postmortem insect activity may produce lesions on the skin that resemble powder stippling (Figure 4.34A). These lesions, however, are larger, more irregular, and usually have a dry, yellow color to them. They often are arranged in a linear pattern, indicating the feeding path of the insects across the body. Fresh wounds may ooze serosanguineous fluid that on drying forms a dark brown or black crust that may cause the insect bites to more closely resemble powder tattoo marks.

Gunshot wounds in hairy areas may result in hemorrhage in hair follicles (Figure 4.34B). If the hair is shaved from the area of the wound, a cursory examination of the skin surrounding the entrance may cause the examiner to interpret the hemorrhage in the follicles as powder tattoo marks. Closer examination, however, will reveal the true nature of the markings.

Occasionally surgical manipulation of a wound may produce markings that simulate powder tattoo marks. In the case illustrated, the wound was sutured closed by a surgeon (Figure 4.34C). When the sutures were removed, the needle puncture marks were interpreted by a number of individuals as powder tattoo marks.

One of the more unusual cases of lesions simulating powder tattooing involved a young boy who after shooting himself in the head survived a short time at a hospital. At autopsy, "powder tattoo marks" were seen on the flexor surface of the left forearm. Because the weapon was a bolt-action rifle, such tattooing could not have occurred. Subsequent investigation revealed the deceased had had a tourniquet placed on his arm when seen in the emergency room. This tourniquet was never removed. Close examination of the markings on the skin, originally interpreted as tattoo marks, revealed them to be petechiae.

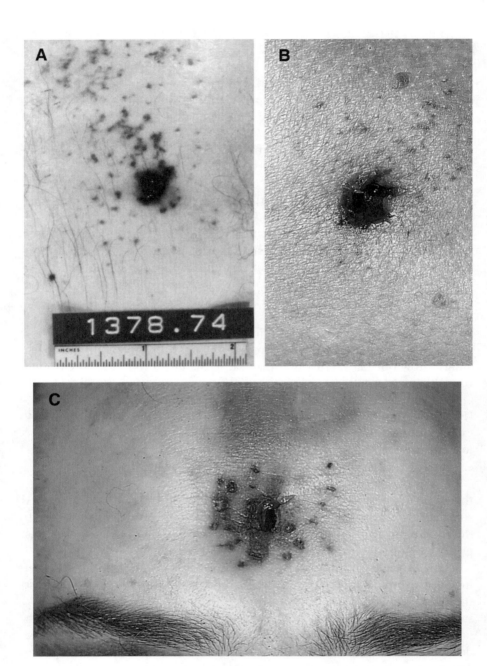

Figure 4.34 (A) Postmortem insect bites around gunshot wound of entrance; (B) hemorrhage into hair follicles simulating powder tattooing; (C) suture marks simulating powder tattoo marks.

Pseudo-Soot

Just as various materials can simulate powder tattooing, so can one have simulation of powder soot. While there is usually no problem differentiating an oily material such as grease from soot, problems arise with material such as fingerprint dusting powder, graphite, powdered asphalt and powdered lead.

One case that initially caused a problem involved an individual shot in the left chest just above the pocket of his shirt. On examination, there appeared to be a large quantity of soot around the bullet hole. Witnesses at the scene, however, said that the deceased had been shot from several feet away. Subsequently, it was discovered that the deceased habitually carried lead pencils in the pocket with the points directed upward. As he moved about, the graphite wiped off the tips of the pencils onto the shirt. When the bullet was fired through this area, the graphite was interpreted mistakenly as soot.

Another case involved an individual shot at multiple times with a high-velocity rifle while lying on an asphalt parking lot. The bullets striking the asphalt reduced some of it to a fine black powder that coated the clothing and body. Other bullets then entered the body in these areas. The powdered asphalt was initially mistaken as powder soot and partially burnt grains of powder associated with the gunshot wounds.

In two cases, involving victims shot with 7.62 × 39 caliber rifles, one individual was lying on gravel and the other on concrete. In the first case, the cartridges were loaded with hunting bullets; in the second, with full metal-jacketed bullets having lead cores. In both instances, the bullets impacted the ground immediately adjacent to the victim, breaking up, with bullet fragments penetrating the body. In the first case, powdered lead from the disintegrating core was deposited on the back of a jacket in a linear pattern that paralleled the ground. Associated with this deposit were multiple holes from bullet fragments. In the second case, the powdered lead was deposited in a U-shaped pattern, with a large irregular entrance wound at the base of the "U" where the bulk of the bullet entered. Multiple small fragment wounds streamed outward along the arms of the "U" (Figure 4.35A). In a study of this phenomena by Garavaglia et al., 7.62 × 39-mm hollowpoint and full metal-jacketed bullets were fired at an angled steel plate.* The cores of the full metal-jacketed bullets were of two styles: all-lead and mild-steel sheathed in lead, with a small conical lead core in front of the steel core. A target draped with white cloth was placed at different distances behind the steel plate. The impacting bullets fragmented, ricocheting off the plate at a shallow angle, in a fan-shaped pattern parallel to the ground. The fragments hit the cloth producing a linear pattern of defects lying in a horizontal plane.

* Personal communication with author.

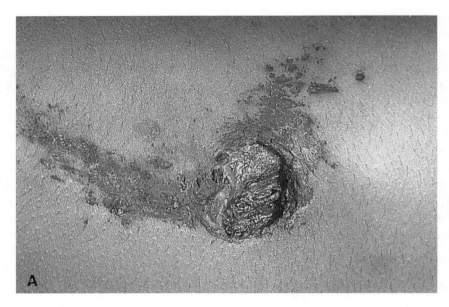

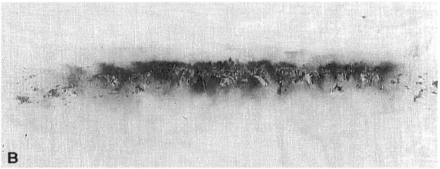

Figure 4.35 **(A)** "U"-shaped deposit of powdered lead with large entrance at base of "U." **(B)** Linear deposit of powdered lead and bullet fragments on cloth from 7.62 × 39 bullet that struck steel plate at shallow angle.

Overlying these defects was a linear deposit of powdered lead (Figure 4.35B). The closer the cloth was to the point of ricochet the denser (darker) the lead deposit. As the distance increased, the lead deposit grew lighter and disappeared at between 14 and 18 inches. These observations were true for both the hollow point and full metal-jacketed bullets.

Subcutaneous hemorrhage at an entrance may have a purple-black appearance and on cursory examination appear to be soot. Closer examination will readily reveal the subcutaneous nature of the deposits. More commonly, mistakes are made when the edges of a gunshot wound have dried out, giving the edges a black appearance. An inexperienced pathologist may interpret this as soot and searing. Use of a dissecting microscope readily differentiates soot from artifact. If there is any doubt as to the nature of the entrance, it should be excised and submitted for SEM-EDX analysis. Soot itself is of course carbon and nonspecific, but primer residues will accompany the soot and can be identified in the sooty deposit.

Ricochet Bullets

For both solid surfaces and water there is a critical angle of impact (incidence) below which a bullet striking the surface will ricochet rather than penetrate.* The critical angle is determined by the nature of the surface, the construction of the bullet and the velocity of the bullet.[12] Thus, round nose bullets are more likely to ricochet than flat-nosed; full metal-jacketed than lead and low velocity more than high velocity. If the angle of incidence is greater than the critical angle, the bullet either penetrates the surface or breaks up. In the latter case, if fragmentation is extensive, the fragments may come off the surface in a fan-shaped spray paralleling the plane of the ricochet surface.

Table 4.1 gives the approximate critical angle of impact in water for representative cartridges and bullet types.[13] The critical angles listed are those at which the particular bullet just began to ricochet. As one can see, the critical angles are small (3 to 8 degrees). At an impact angle of 15 degrees, all the listed projectiles penetrated water. Bullets ricocheting off water invariably ricochet off at angles greater than the impact angle, typically 2 to 3 times the impact angle.[13] Not surprisingly, these ricocheting bullets lose their gyroscopic stability.[14]

Bullets ricocheting off solid surfaces usually ricochet-off at angles smaller than the impact angle.[14] Such bullets are unstable and will tumble. Houlden fired full metal-jacketed 9-mm Luger (115 gr.) and .45 ACP bullets (230 gr.) at a 5-mm thick concrete slab and a 6-mm thick steel sheet, at angles from 10 to 60 degrees.[15] For both calibers, at angles of incidence of 30 degrees or more, the bullets fragmented. At angles below 30 degrees, they tended to remain in one piece though they flattened out.

The ricochet angles off the steel plate (incident angles 10 to 60 degrees) were less than 5 degrees for the 9-mm bullets; less than 4 degrees for the .45 ACP bullets. These figures were also true for the concrete slab with but one exception. A .45 ACP bullet, with an incident angle of 50 degrees, fragmented with a fragment of copper jacketing coming off the slab at a ricochet angle of 12.37 degrees.

---

* The angle of incidence is the angle formed by the trajectory of the bullet prior to ricochet and the surface from which the ricochet occurs.

Table 4.1   Approximate Critical Angles for Various Cartridges and Bullet Types: Water

Caliber	Bullet	Approximate Critical Angle (degrees)
.22 Short	29-gr. solid-point	8
	27-gr. hollow-point	5
.22 Long Rifle	40-gr. hollow-point	7
	37-gr. hollow-point	5
.38 Special	158-gr. lead roundnose	6
	125-gr. jacketed hollow-point	6
.380 Auto	80-gr. full metal-jacket	7
.222 Remington	50-gr. jacketed soft-point	3
.30 MI Carbine	110-gr. full metal-jacket	5
.30–06	150-gr. full metal-jacket	7

Modified from Haag, Reference 13.

Houlden also determined the remaining energy of the ricocheting bullets and fragments.[15] The determining factors were the angle of impact and the nature of the surface impacted. In the case of the steel plate, for both calibers, for angles of incidence of up to 30 degrees, the bullets tended to stay in one piece and retained approximately 75% of their impact energy. At angles greater than 30 degrees the retained energy declined in a linear relation with the angle of impact. Thus, at an impact angle of 50 degrees, the bullets retained only 20% of impact energy. In the case of the concrete surface, the retained energy of both calibers followed a linear relationship with the angle of impact. At an impact angle of 10 degrees, retained energy was approximately 75%; declining to approximately 20% at 50 degrees.

Ricocheting bullets commonly tumble in their path through the air, having an unpredictable trajectory. Their entrance wounds tend to be larger and more irregular; the edges ragged, with the surrounding zone of abraded skin large and irregular. These wounds tend to be penetrating rather than perforating because when the ricocheting bullet impacts the skin it is deformed, unstable, and has lost a significant amount of its energy by ricocheting off a hard surface.[15] Almost immediately after penetration, the bullet begins to tumble in the body, losing its remaining velocity and kinetic energy in a short distance. In the case of lead bullets, the ricochet bullet when recovered from the body typically has a flattened, mirror-like surface on one side (Figure 4.36). It is not uncommon to have the weave pattern of the clothing overlying the entrance imprinted on the side or base of the bullet, as the bullet may enter sideways or even backwards. In Figure 4.36 the bullet ricocheted off a steel rail, passed through a screen door, and then struck the deceased. The pattern of the screen is on one side of the bullet.

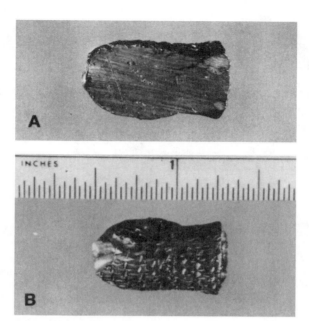

Figure 4.36 (A) Ricochet lead bullet with mirror-like surface on one side and imprint of screen on other side (B).

Full metal-jacketed bullets also ricochet. The bullet may flatten along one surface or even pancake with the core partly extruded from the base. Portions of the jacket may be avulsed off the bullet exposing the core. The weave imprint of cloth may be present on the lead base or exposed core of such bullets.

Partial metal-jacketed bullets have a greater propensity to breakup on striking a hard object in comparison to lead and full metal jacketed bullets. They may pepper the body with fragments of jacket and lead core (Figure 4.37). Fragments are often found embedded in or just beneath the skin. Ricocheting shotgun pellets spread out in a fan-like pattern, parallel to the surface.

Occasionally, a lead bullet recovered from a body is flattened on one surface like a ricocheted bullet, even though the bullet could not have ricocheted. This occurs when the bullet, on entering the body, strikes a heavy bone such as the femur, flattening on the bone. Such occurrences usually involves small-caliber low-velocity lead bullets, e.g., the .22 rimfire and a large, heavy bone such as the femur or humerus.

Rarely, a non-ricocheting full metal-jacketed bullet recovered from a body may have the appearance of a ricochet. The author has seen this in two circumstances. A bullet may strike a heavy bone such as the femur and either pancake or fragment. The jacket will be squeezed together and most of the

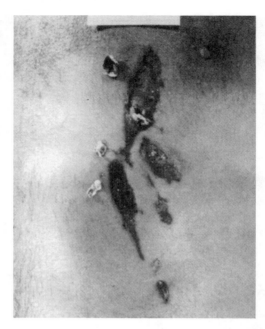

Figure 4.37 Fragment wounds of chest due to partial metal-jacketed bullet that disintegrated on striking ground.

lead core will extrude out the base. The bone may or may not be fractured. The author has seen this phenomenon in calibers from .25 to .45. In the other circumstance, the full metal-jacketed bullet perforates two adjacent sheets of metal, e.g., a car door before penetrating a body. The first sheet of metal destabilizes the bullet such that it is traveling sideways when it impacts and perforates the second sheet. This second sheet of metal flattens the bullet along its long axis so that when the bullet is recovered from the body it has the appearance of a ricochet bullet.

If an individual was close to the surface from which a bullet ricocheted, fragments of material from the surface as well as fragments of bullet torn off at the time of ricochet may impact around the wound of entrance, producing secondary missile wounds. These wounds are typically of minor significance in that the fragments are usually of insufficient mass and velocity to cause any serious harm. The marks produced may on occasion be confused with powder tattoo marks. The marks, however, are larger and more irregular in shape than powder tattoo marks.

Occasionally a bullet that exits a body will strike a hard surface, flatten out, and rebound back into the clothing. The author has seen this in a number of instances. In two cases the individuals were leaning against concrete walls, and in a third the individual was lying on a concrete floor. The bullets were pancaked, having a thickness of less than a nickel.

Bone

Bone is a specialized form of dense connective tissue composed of calcium salts embedded in a matrix of collagenous fibers. Whether a bullet perforates bone is dependent on a number of factors: the velocity of the bullet at impact, its construction (lead, full metal-jacketed, partial metal-jacketed), the weight of the bullet, the angle of interaction between the bone and the bullet, the type of bone (long, flat), its thickness, and its surface configuration.

A minimum velocity of 200 ft/sec is often cited as the minimum velocity required by a bullet to effect penetration of bone.[16] This figure is suspect. A review of the original paper reveals that this determination was made using the long bones (femur and humerus) of cattle, with the outer layer of compact bone sawed away, thus, exposing the softer spongy layer.[17] Steel spheres were used as missiles.

A limited number of tests by the author using fresh human bone and 9-mm Parabellum ammunition loaded with 125 gr. roundnose lead bullets has resulted in some additional data on this subject. With flat bone (cranial vault), 4- 6-mm thick, bullet penetration (depressed fractures) began at about 250 ft/s with perforation the rule at 290 to 300 ft/s. With bone 7–9 mm thick, perforation began at approximately 350 ft/ sec. At 10 mm of thickness, no perforation occurred even with velocities up to 460 ft/s (three tests at 400 ft/s plus). In eight tests using femurs, there was no perforation until 552 and 559 ft/s. Because of the limited nature of this study, these figures should be used with caution.

Once penetration of bone has been effected, the bullet's remaining velocity operates to effect deeper penetration in direct proportion to the square of the velocity and the sectional density of the bullet. As the bullet penetrates, it fragments the bone, creating a temporary cavity. The fragments are initially propelled laterally, toward the periphery of the cavity, as well as forward in the direction of the bullet. As undulation of the cavity occurs, some fragments return to the center. Bony fragments, moving outward and forward with the bullet, act as secondary missiles, causing additional injury.

The direction in which a bullet was traveling when it perforates a bone can be determined by the appearance of the wound in the bone. When a bullet perforates bone, it bevels out the bone in the direction in which it is traveling (Figure 4.38A). The entrance has a round to oval, sharp-edged, "punched-out" appearance (Figure 4.38B). The opposite surface of the bone, i.e., the exit side, is excavated in a cone-like manner (Figure 4.38C). This

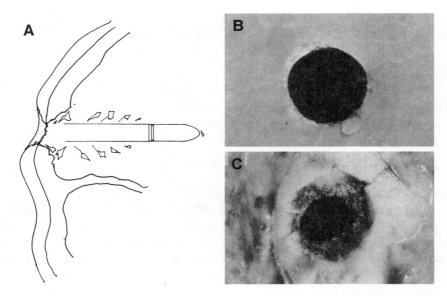

Figure 4.38 (a) Bullet perforating bone; (b) entrance in bone; (c) exit in bone.

difference in appearance of entrance and exit wounds is best seen in the flat bone of skull. As the bullet enters, it creates a round to oval sharp-edged hole in the outer table of the skull, with a large, bevelled-out hole on the inner table. When the bullet exits the cranial cavity, the inner table is the entrance surface and the outer table the exit surface.

Chips of bone can flake off the edge of an entrance hole. This flaking is usually very superficial and should not lead to confusion with an exit hole. Coe reported a number of cases (all but one involving contact wounds) that showed partial or complete beveling of the outer table of bone at the entrance sites.[18] The beveling is of such a degree that it easily could be ascribed to an exiting bullet (Figure 4.39). Such entrances should not be confused with exits, as examination will show beveling of both the inner and the outer tables. Since Coe's original paper, a number of confirmatory reports to his observations have appeared. While this phenomena can occur in both distant and contact wounds, it is more common with the latter.

Differentiation of entrance versus exit often is not possible in the case of paper-thin bones such as the orbital plates or the temporal bones of children. In both instances the bone is too thin for creation of the funnel-shaped wound tract that makes differentiation of entrance versus exit possible.

When a lead bullet perforates bone, it often leaves a thin deposit of lead on the edges of the entrance hole. This thin gray rim should not be confused with the wider zone of powder blackening seen in contact wounds overlying bone. Examination of the entrance with a dissecting microscope will readily differentiate lead from soot.

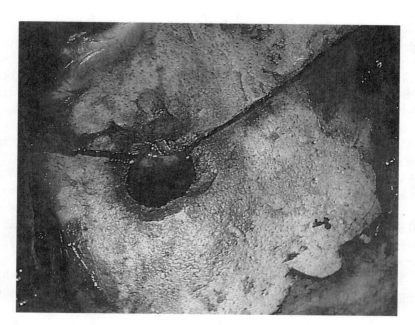

Figure 4.39   Contact entrance wound of bone with external bevelling.

As a general rule, after striking or perforating bone, bullets are not deflected from their original trajectory through the body. The only commonly encountered exception involves a bullet that has exhausted virtually all of its forward velocity at the time it hits the bone. In such instances, the bullet is usually found within an inch or two of the impact point on the bone. The author has seen two rare cases of bullets deflected by bone that do not fit this latter scenario. Both involved gunshot wounds of the legs. In both these cases, the victims were shot in the thigh with full metal-jacketed 9-mm Parabellum bullets. In both instances, the bullet struck and fractured the femur and was then deflected straight upward through the muscle, paralleling the femur, for a distance of approximately 6 inches. In one case, the bullet severed the femoral artery, causing death. The recovered bullets were flattened along one surface like a ricochet bullet.

Teeth, like bone, show a sharp-edged, punched-out appearance on the entrance surface and beveling of the exit surface when a bullet perforates them.

Bullet Wounds of the Skull

Tangential wounds of the skull have classically been called "gutter wounds."[19] In first-degree gutter wounds only the outer table of the skull is grooved by the bullet, with resultant carrying away of small bone fragments. In second-degree wounds pressure waves generated by the bullet fracture the inner table.

In third-degree wounds the bullet perforates the skull in the center of the tangential wound (Figure 4.40). The outer table is fragmented, and there are depressed fragments of the internal table if not comminution and pulverization of both tables in the center of the wound track. Fragments of bone can be driven into the brain causing death. After third-degree wounds come "**superficial perforating wounds**." Here there is production of separate entrance and exit wounds in the bone.

A low-velocity bullet may strike the skull at a shallow angle such that it does not penetrate but rather flattens out, forming a thin oval lead disk. The bullet may then slide along the surface of the skull beneath the scalp. When this occurs, this usually involves a .22 Short bullet.

A bullet striking the skull at a shallow angle may produce a punched out oval defect in the skull without the bullet actually entering the cranial cavity. The bullet may flatten out and either be recovered from beneath the scalp or exit. The fragments of bone may be driven into the brain and cause death.

A bullet striking the skull at a shallow angle may produce a **keyhole wound** of the bone. In the most common presentation, the bullet, impacting at a shallow angle, begins to punch out an entrance in the bone. Because of the stresses generated, part of the bullet shears off and travels a short distance beneath the scalp before either coming to rest or exiting. The bulk of the bullet enters the cranial cavity. This process results in a keyhole-shaped wound of bone (Figure 4.41). One end of this keyhole wound will have the sharp edges typical of a wound of entrance, whereas the other end will have

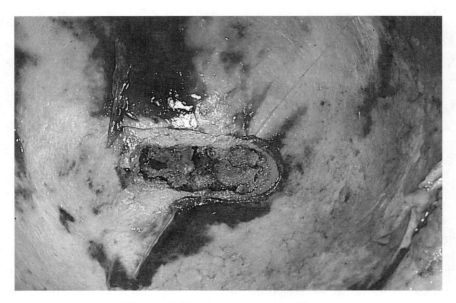

Figure 4.40 Gutter wound of bone.

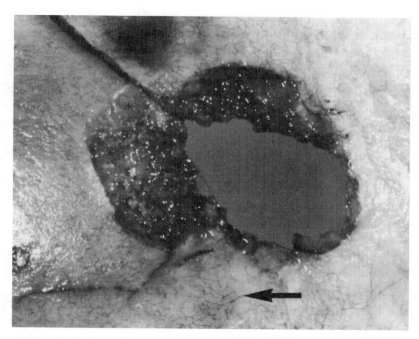

Figure 4.41 Keyhole wound of bone. Arrow indicates path of bullet.

the external beveling of a wound of exit.[20] In a less common variant of keyhole wounds, the bullet does not split but enters the cranial cavity intact. This type of keyhole wound is common with full metal-jacketed bullets. The exit aspect of the bony defect is do to pressure waves generated by the impacting bullet lifting and breaking off the bone at the exit end.

Bullet wounds of the head may produce cerebral injury and death without entrance into the cranial cavity. Thus, the author had a case of a 65-year-old white male who shot himself in the ear with a .32 revolver. The bullet traveled through the petrous bone before coming to rest adjacent to the sella turcica. Although the bullet caused extensive comminuted fractures of the petrous bone, it did not enter the cranial cavity. The dura overlying the petrous bone was intact. Examination of the brain revealed extensive contusions of the ventral surface of the temporal lobe overlying the bone. No lacerations of the brain were present.

The production of secondary fractures of the skull due to intracranial pressure waves is dependent on two factors: the range at the time of discharge and the kinetic energy possessed by the bullet. The most common sites for secondary skull fractures are the paper-thin orbital plates. These are extremely sensitive to a sudden increase in intracranial pressure such as that produced by a bullet entering the cranial cavity.

Secondary fractures are very common in contact wounds of the head. This is due to the gas produced by discharge entering the cranial cavity, expanding, and contributing to the stress placed on the bony chamber by the temporary cavity. The more gas produced, the more that enters the skull and the more likely that the fractures will be produced. An extreme example of this is provided by contact wounds from a centerfire rifle or shotgun. These weapons cause explosive wounds of the head, with large fragments of bone and brain typically being ejected from the head.

In distant wounds, gas plays no part in the production of fractures. These fractures are produced by the pressure built up in the skull as a result of temporary cavity formation. The size of this cavity is proportional to the amount of kinetic energy lost by the bullet in its passage through the head. The greater the amount of kinetic energy lost, the larger the cavity; the larger the cavity, the greater the pressure produced on the walls of the cranial chamber and the more likely a fracture is to occur. Thus, secondary skull fractures are rare with wounds inflicted by a low-energy .22 Short cartridge, but are the rule with wounds from a centerfire rifle. With the .22 Short cartridge, fractures are usually limited to the orbital plates. Although secondary skull fractures are uncommon with .22 Short ammunition (even in contact wounds), .22 Long Rifle cartridges usually produce secondary fractures in contact wounds and not uncommonly in distant wounds.

The fact that the fractures in a skull are due to temporary cavity formation was demonstrated by a series of experiments with skulls.[16] When the skulls were empty, the bullets "drilled" neat entrances and exits without any fractures. When the skulls were filled with gelatin to simulate the brain, massive secondary skull fractures were produced.

On occasion one will be presented with what initially appears to be a perforating gunshot wound of the head but in fact is a penetrating wound. There will be both an entrance and an "exit" wound in the scalp. The autopsy reveals the bullet still to be in the head. What happens is that the bullet, after perforating the brain, strikes the opposite side of the skull with sufficient force to fracture it and propel a piece of bone out through the scalp. The bullet itself had insufficient velocity to exit the head. In a variation of this involving semi-jacketed ammunition, the lead core exits while the copper jacket remains. Rarely, the jacket exits and the core remains. This again points out the need for x-rays in all gunshot wounds of the head.

Caliber Determination from Entrance Wounds

The caliber of the bullet that caused an entrance wound in the skin cannot be determined by the diameter of the entrance. A .38-caliber (9-mm) bullet can produce a hole having the diameter of a .32 caliber (7.65-mm) bullet and vice versa. The size of the hole is due not only to the diameter of the bullet but also to the elasticity of the skin and the location of the wound. An entrance wound in an area where the skin is tightly stretched will have a diameter different from that of a wound in an area where the skin is lax. Bullet wounds in areas where the skin lies in folds or creases may be slit-shaped.

The size of an entrance hole in bone cannot be used to determine the specific caliber of the bullet that perforated the bone though it can be used to eliminate bullet calibers. Thus, a bullet hole 7.65 mm in diameter would preclude it having been caused by a 9-mm (.38 caliber) weapon. Bone does have some elasticity, however, so that a 9-mm bullet may produce a 8.5-mm defect.

In the author's experience, the size of a bullet hole in bone is determined not only by the diameter of the bullet but also by its construction. Entrance holes of the temporo-parietal region from .25 ACP (6.35-mm) and .22 (5.45-mm) rimfire bullets were compared. The .25 ACP bullets were of full metal-jacket design while the .22 bullets were of lead. The holes in the bone from the .25 ACP bullets averaged 6 to 7 mm in diameter. In contrast, the entrance holes from the lead .22 caliber bullets ranged in diameter from 5 to 11 mm. The only major difference between the two calibers is the construction of the bullets: full metal-jacketed versus lead. The lead bullets expanded to some degree on impacting and perforating the skull, thus, producing the larger entrance holes.

Bullet Wipe

Bullet holes of entrance in the skin may have a gray coloration to the abrasion ring. This gray rim around the entrance is very common, and more prominent, in clothing, where it is called "bullet wipe" (see Chapter 12). Bullet wipe consists principally of soot, deposited on the surface of the bullet as it moves down the barrel, which is rubbed off the bullet by the skin or clothing as it penetrates the body. In the case of revolver bullets, some of this material may be lubricant as well. Bullet wipe should not be confused with the soot and searing found in contact wounds. While bullet wipe has been said to be characteristic of lead revolver bullets, this is incorrect as it is also seen in association with full metal-jacketed bullets as well.

Backspatter

Backspatter is the ejection of blood and tissue from a gunshot wound of entrance. While blood and tissue are often ejected from exit wounds, this is not the case for entrance wounds. The occurrence and degree of backspatter depends on the anatomical location of the wound, the range and the caliber of the weapon. A contact wound of the head from a large-caliber weapon is more likely to produce backspatter than a distant wound of the torso from a small-caliber weapon. Backspatter is important because the resultant stains may be found on the weapon, the shooter and objects in the vicinity.

There are three possible etiologies for backspatter in the case of head wounds: expansion of gas trapped subcutaneously; intra-cranial pressure generated by the temporary cavity and tail splashing. The last phenomena refers to backward streaming of blood and tissue along the lateral surfaces of the bullet. This may represent an early stage of the temporary cavity effect. The effects of expanding gas subcutaneously is only relevant in close range wounds while the other two etiologies of backspatter are independent of range.

Karger et al. studied backspatter using live calves shot with 9 × 19-mm pistol.[21-22] The calves were shot in the head at ranges of: tight contact; loose contact; 5 cm, and 10 cm. The resultant backspatter was divided into macro-backspatter (stain diameter of >0.5 mm) and microbackspatter (stain diameter 0.5 mm or less). There was **macrospatter** after every shot with the maximum distance traveled varying from 72 to 119 cm. The vast majority of stains were between 0 and 50 cm. The direction of the exiting droplets was at every possible angle resulting, overall, in a 180 degree semi-circle spray. For individual shots, the distribution of the droplets is usually uneven and asymmetrical.

In the case of **microbackspatter**, there was microspatter after each shot with the maximum distance traveled 69 cm. The vast majority of stains were between 0 and 40 cm. Microspatter stains tended to be more numerous than macrospatter. The stains produced were exclusively circular or slightly oval in contrast to macrostains that showed variations ranging from circular to exclamation mark forms. Just like macrospatter, the direction of the exiting droplets was at every possible angle resulting in a 180 degree semi-circle spray, though the distribution of the individual droplets was uneven and asymmetrical.

The authors felt that the number of droplets and the maximum distance these droplets would travel would be greater for humans because of the anatomical differences between calf heads and human heads. They also speculated that the maximum shooting distance that would result in backspatter in gunshot wounds of the head is likely more than 10 cm, the maximum range that they shot the calves.

References

1. Di Maio, V. J. M. and Kaplan, J. A. An unusual entrance wound associated with rimfire rifles. *Amer. J. Forensic Med. Path.* 12(3): 207–208, 1991.

2. Barnes, F. C. and Helson, R. A. An empirical study of gunpowder residue patterns. *J. Forensic Sci.* 19(3): 448–462, 1974.

3. Allen, W. G. B. *Pistols, Rifles and Machine Guns.* London: English University Press Limited, 1953.

4. Missliwetz, J., Denk, W., and Wieser, I. Shots fired with silencers — a report on four cases and experimental testing. *J. Forensic Sci.* 36(5):1387–1394, 1991.

5. Marty, W., Sigrist, T., and Wyler, D. Measurements of the skin temperature at the entry wound by means of infrared thermography. *Amer. J. Forensic Med. Path.* 15(1):1–4, 1994.

6. Von Beck, B. Cited by La Garde, L. A. Can a septic bullet infect a gunshot wound? *N.Y. Med. J.* 56: 458–464, 1892.

7. Adelson, L. A microscopic study of dermal gunshot wounds. *Am. J. Clin. Pathol.* 35: 393, 1691.

8. Peak, S. A. A thin-layer chromatographic procedure for confirming the presence and identity of smokeless powder flakes. *J. Forensic Sci.* 25(3): 679–681, 1980.

9. Thoresby, F. P. and Darlow, H. M. The mechanisms of primary infection of bullet wounds. *Br. J. Surg.* 54: 359–361, 1967.

10. Light, F. W. Gunshot wounds of entrance and exit in experimental animals. *J. Trauma* 3(2): 120–128, 1963.

11. Thorton, J. The effects of tempered glass on bullet trajectory. (Summary), *AFTE Journal* 15(3): 29, July 1983.

12. Burke, T. W. and Rowe W. F. Bullet ricochet: a comprehensive review. *J. Forensic Sci.* 37(5):1254–1260, 1992.

13. Haag, L. C. Bullet ricochet from water. *AFTE Journal* 11(3): 27–34, July 1974.

14. Haag, L. C. Bullet ricochet: an empirical study and a device for measuring ricochet angle. *AFTE Journal* 7(3): 44–51, December 1975.

15. Houlden, M. The distribution of energy among fragments of ricocheting pistol bullets. *J. Forensic Sci. Society* 34(1):29–35, 1994.

16. Beyer, J. D. (ed). *Wound Ballistics.* Washington, D.C.: Superintendent of Documents, U.S. Government Printing Office, 1962.

17. Grundfest, H. Penetration of steel spheres into bone. National Research Council, Division of Medical Sciences, Office of Research and Development. *Missile Casualty Report* No. 10, 20 July 1945.

18. Coe, J. I. External beveling of entrance wounds by handguns. *Am. J. Forensic Med. Pathol.* 3(3):215–220, September 1982.

19. La Garde, L. A. *Gunshot Injuries,* 2nd ed. New York: William Wood and Co., 1916.

20. Dixon, D. S. Keyhole lesions in gunshot wounds of the skull and direction of fire. *J. Forensic Sci.* 27(3):555–566, 1982.

21. Karger, B., Nusse, R., Schroeder, G., Wustenbecker, S., and Brinkmann, B. Backspatter from experimental close-range shots to the head. I. Macrobackspatter. *Int. J. Legal Med.* 1996 (109):66–74

22. Karger, B., Nusse, R., Troger, H. D., and Brinkmann, B. Backspatter from experimental close-range shots to the head. II. Microbackspatter and the morphology of bloodstains. *Int. J. Legal Med.* (1997) 110:27–30.

Wounds Due to Handguns

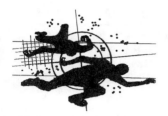

5

"God created men equal. Sam Colt made 'em equal."

Annonymous

Handguns are the most commonly used form of firearm in both homicides and suicides in the United States. Handguns are low-velocity, low-energy weapons having muzzle velocities generally below 1400 ft/sec. Advertised velocities of revolver cartridges traditionally have not been accurate because they are obtained in test devices that have no cylinder gap. Even in well-made revolvers, this gap will cause a velocity loss of approximately 100 to 200 ft/sec, depending on initial velocities and pressure as well as the construction tolerances of the weapon. Advertised velocities for semiautomatic pistols are more accurate as there is no cylinder gap from which gas can escape. The length of the barrel also influences muzzle velocity. The longer the barrel, the greater the velocity. Table 5.1 gives the advertised muzzle velocities of some .22-caliber and .38 Special ammunition compared to the actual velocities determined in revolvers with 2-, 4-, and 6-in. barrels. The velocity of .22-caliber ammunition in a rifle is also given.

The Remington Firearms Company developed a method of measuring the performance of revolver ammunition that reflects ballistic results more accurately. This method involves use of a vented test barrel. The technique takes into account the cylinder gap (controlled at 0.008 in.), barrel length (4 in.), powder position (horizontal), and production tolerances, as well as allowing for reasonable wear and tear.[1] Table 5.2 shows a comparison between the ballistic data that Remington previously published concerning its ammunition and the results obtained with a vented test barrel. Significant differences in the results can be seen.

Theoretically, the muzzle velocity in Saturday Night Special revolvers should be less than that in well-made revolvers because of greater tolerance

Table 5.1   Advertised Muzzle Velocities Versus Actual Velocities

Cartridge	Advertised Muzzle Velocity (ft/sec)	2-in. Barrel	4-in. Barrel	6-in. Barrel	Rifle
.22 Long rifle	1255	916	1034	1052	1237
.22 Short	1095	851	861	960	1005
.38 Special	855	687	722	765	

Table 5.2   Conventional Test Barrel Ballistics Versus Vented Test Barrel Ballistics

| | Bullet | | Muzzle Velocity | |
| | | | Conventional Test Barrel | Vented Barrel |
Cartridge	Wt (gr.)	Style[a]	(ft/sec)	(ft/sec)
.38 Special	125	SJHP	1028	945
	148	WC	770	710
	158	Lead RN	885	755
	200	Lead RN	730	635
.357 Magnum	125	SJHP	1675	1450
	158	SJHP	1550	1235
	158	Lead SWC	1410	1235

[a]   SJHP = semi-jacketed hollow-point; WC = wadcutter; RN = roundnose;
SWC = semiwadcutter.

differences in the Saturday night specials. Experiments, however, do not always substantiate this. The results of one such test can be seen in Table 5.3. There are no significant differences between the muzzle velocities of the Saturday night specials and those of well-made Smith & Wesson revolvers.

Handgun wounds can be divided into four categories, depending on the distance from muzzle to target. These are: contact, near contact, intermediate, and distant (see Chapter 4).

Table 5.3   Muzzle Velocities of .38 Special Cartridges Fired in Smith and Wesson and "Saturday Night Special" Revolvers of Various Barrel Lengths

| | Muzzle Velocity (ft/sec ± 1 S.D.) | |
Barrel Length	Smith & Wesson	R.G.
2 in.	687 ± 8	677 ± 11
4 in.	687 ± 15	722 ± 31
6 in.	765 ± 13	748 ± 18

Contact Wounds

A **contact wound** is one in which the muzzle of the weapon is held against the body at the time of discharge. Contact wounds can be hard, loose, angled, or incomplete. In contact wounds gas, soot, metallic particles avulsed from the bullet by the rifling, vaporized metal from the bullet and cartridge case, primer residue, and powder particles are all driven into the wound track along with the bullet.

In **hard contact** wounds, the muzzle of the weapon is held very tightly against the skin, indenting it so that the skin envelopes the muzzle at the time of discharge. All the materials emerging from the muzzle will be driven into the wound, often leaving very little external evidence that one is dealing with a contact wound. Inspection of the entrance, however, will usually disclose searing and powder blackening (soot) of the immediate edge of the wound (Figure 5.1). Subsequent autopsy will reveal soot and unburnt powder particles in the wound track.

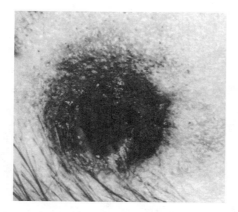

Figure 5.1   Close-up of hard-contact wound of head with a .38 revolver.

Hard contact wounds of the head from .22 Short or .32 Smith & Wesson Short cartridges are often difficult to interpret because of the small powder charge loaded into such cartridges. These wounds may appear to be distant because of an inability to detect the small amount of soot produced and to recover unburned powder grains in the wound track. Compounding this problem is the fact that in distant wounds from .22 Short and .32 S & W Short cartridges, drying of the edges can simulate the blackened and seared margins of hard contact wounds. In situations such as this, as well as in cases of decomposition of a body, examination of the wounds with the dissecting microscope for soot and powder grains is of value.

In the author's experience, with use of the dissecting microscope, soot is always present in contact handgun wounds, with powder particles identified in virtually all cases. Unfortunately, recognition of material as soot is to a certain degree subjective. Drying, hemolyzed blood, and decomposition can simulate or mask soot. Generally, blood can be removed by running or spraying hot water over the wound. Clots resistant to the hot water can be dissolved with hydrogen peroxide. Neither hot water nor hydrogen peroxide will remove the soot. In cases in which one is not sure whether a wound is contact and in which no powder particles can be identified by the dissecting microscope, the use of energy dispersive x-ray (EDX) or scanning electron microscope-energy dispersive x-ray (SEM–EDX) should be employed. Using these devices, one can analyze for the vaporized metals from the bullet, cartridge case, and primer.

In contact wounds, muscle surrounding the entrance may have a cherry-red hue, due to carboxyhemoglobin and carboxymyoglobin formed from the carbon monoxide in the muzzle gas. Even if this discoloration is not present, elevated levels of carbon monoxide may be detected on chemical analysis. Control samples of muscle should always be taken from another area of the body if such determinations are to be made. It should be realized that, whereas elevated carbon monoxide levels in the muscle are significant, the lack of carbon monoxide is not, as carboxyhemoglobin formation does not always occur. By using gas chromatography, carbon monoxide has been detected in wounds inflicted up to 30 cm from the muzzle.[2]

The presence of both powder particles and carbon monoxide in a gunshot wound would seem to leave no doubt that one is dealing with an entrance wound. In fact, on occasion both carbon monoxide and powder may be found at an exit. In the case illustrated in Figure 5.2, the deceased shot himself

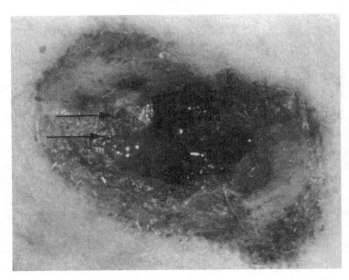

Figure 5.2   Shored exit wound of back with grains of ball powder in exit wound.

in the left chest with a .357 Magnum revolver. A perfect imprint of the muzzle was seen on the chest, thus indicating the contact nature of the wound. Examination of the exit in the back, however, revealed grains of ball powder in the exit wound and a cherry-red color in the adjacent muscle caused by carbon monoxide. The presence of carbon monoxide was confirmed analytically. To further confuse the interpretation of the wounds, the exit was shored. Thus, the exit in this case was characterized by an abraded margin, powder grains, and carbon monoxide.

The author has seen a number of cases in which ball powder traveled through the body and was found at the exit. All cases involved contact wounds, with the entrances in both head and trunk. The weapons involved were of .22 Magnum, .38 Special, 9-mm Luger, .357 Magnum and .44 Magnum caliber. In one case, an individual had his hand in front of his face and in hard contact with the muzzle of a .357 Magnum when it discharged. Ball powder traveled through the hand tattooing his face.

The author has never seen a case in which flake powder traveled completely through either the head or trunk and was in or adjacent to the exit. He has knowledge, however of one case involving cylindrical powder in which an individual shot himself in the head with a .44 Magnum handgun and cylindrical powder grains were present in the wound tract through the brain, and at the exit in the scalp.[3]

Though carbon monoxide and powder may travel through a body and be found at the exit, the author has never personally seen soot do so.

Contact Wounds Over Bone

Contact wounds in regions of the body where only a thin layer of skin and subcutaneous tissue overlies bone usually have a stellate or cruciform appearance that is totally unlike the round or oval perforating wounds seen in other areas (Figure 5.3A). The most common area in which stellate wounds occur is the head. The unusual appearance of contact wounds over bone is due to the effects of the gas of discharge. When a weapon is fired, the gases produced by the combustion of the propellant emerge from the barrel in a highly compressed state. In hard contact wounds, they follow the bullet through the skin into the subcutaneous tissue where they immediately begin to expand. Where a thin layer of skin overlies bone, as in the head, these gases expand between the skin and the outer table of the skull, lifting up and ballooning out the skin (Figure 5.4). If the stretching exceeds the elasticity of the skin, it will tear. These tears radiate from the entrance, producing a stellate or cruciform appearing wound of entrance. Re-approximation of the torn edges of the wound will reveal the seared, blackened margins of the original entrance site.

In some contact wounds over bone, instead of the classical stellate or cruciform wound, one finds a very large circular wound with ragged, blackened, and seared margins. This type of wound is more common with the less powerful calibers such as the .32 ACP or .380 ACP (see Figure 5.3B). On occasion, however, it is seen with even the larger more powerful cartridges such as the .38 Special and .45 ACP.

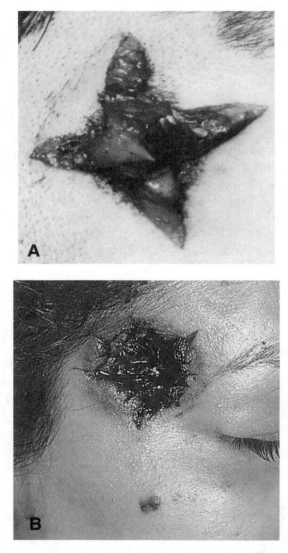

Figure 5.3 Contact wounds of head. **(A)** Stellate wound of temple from .38 Special revolver; **(B)** circular wound of entrance from .380 ACP.

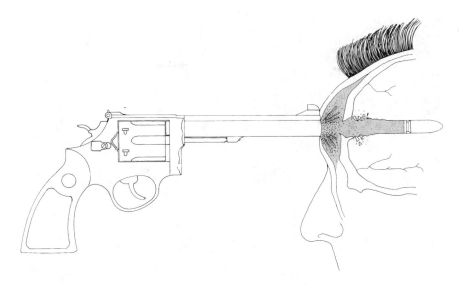

Figure 5.4 Contact wound of head showing dissection of gas between scalp and skull.

The presence of tearing of the skin as well as its extent depends on the caliber of the weapon, the amount of gas produced by the combustion of the propellant, the firmness with which the gun is held against the body, and the elasticity of the skin. Thus, contact wounds of the head with a .22 Short usually produce no tearing, whereas those due to a .357 Magnum usually do. It must be stressed, however, that exceptions occur.

Irregular, cruciform, or stellate entrance wounds can occur in individuals shot at intermediate or distant range, where gas plays no role in the production of a wound. These occur when the bullet perforates the skin over a bony prominence or curved area of bone covered by a thin layer of tightly stretched skin (Figure 5.5). The head is the most common site for such wounds. The forehead as it slopes back at the hairline; the top and back of the head; the supraorbital ridges and the cheek bone are common sites (Figures 4.22; 5.5A). An uncommon site is the elbow (Figure 5.5B). If the bullet is deformed or tumbles prior to striking the body, the tendency to produce cruciform or stellate wounds is further accentuated. A tangential gunshot wound of the face may simulate a stellate contact wound (Figure 5.6).

In contact wounds of the head, if the skin and soft tissue are retracted, soot will usually be found deposited on the outer table of the skull at the entrance hole (Figure 5.7). Soot may also be present on the inner table and even on the dura. Soot is usually not seen on bone when the wound is inflicted by either a .22 Short or a .32 Smith & Wesson Short cartridge.

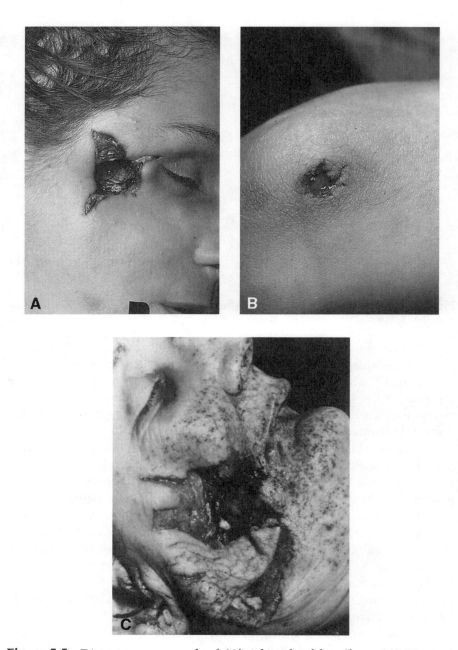

Figure 5.5   Distant range wounds of: **(A)** right side of face (from .357 Magnum revolver) and **(B)** elbow; **(C)** intermediate-range gunshot wound from .357 Magnum — range approximately 1 ft.

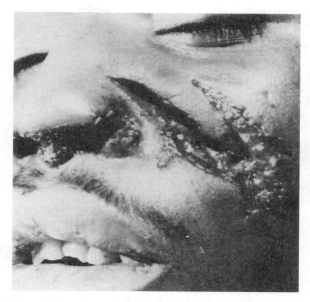

Figure 5.6 Tangential gunshot wound of left cheek from 9-mm bullet.

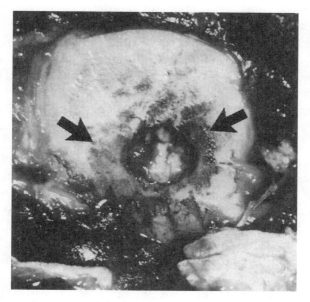

Figure 5.7 Powder soot deposited on outer table of skull around entrance site.

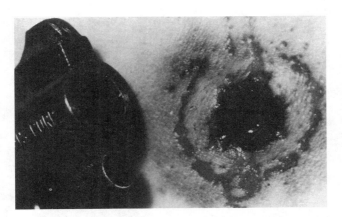

Figure 5.8 Contact wound with muzzle imprint.

Rarely, in contact wounds of the head from weapons of .38 Special caliber and greater that fire cartridges loaded with true (spherical) ball powder, the large irregular or stellate wounds produced may initially appear to show neither soot nor powder. Careful examination with a dissecting microscope will reveal small clusters of ball powder. It must be kept in mind, that the presence of only one or two grains of powder does not necessarily indicate a close range wound. The author has seen a number of distant entrance wounds in which one or two grains of powder have been carried to and deposited in the entrance wound by a bullet.

In contact wounds of the trunk, stellate or cruciform entrances in the skin usually do not occur, even when the weapon and ammunition used produce large volumes of gas, because the gas is able to expand into the abdominal cavity, chest cavity, or soft tissue. Rarely, contact wounds of the chest overlying the sternum, inflicted by handguns firing high-velocity pistol ammunition, may produce extremely large circular wounds of entrance with ragged margins.

In contact gunshot wounds in areas where only a thin layer of skin overlies bone (usually the head), the gas expanding in the subcutaneous tissue may produce effects other than tearing of the skin. The ballooned-out skin may slam against the muzzle of the weapon with enough force to imprint the outline of the muzzle on the skin (Figure 5.8). Such imprints may be extremely detailed. The more gas produced by the ammunition and weapon, the harder the skin will impact against the muzzle, and thus the greater the detail of the imprint.

Imprints of the muzzle of the weapon occur not only in regions where a thin layer of skin overlies bone but also in the chest and abdomen (Figure 5.9). Here, the gas expands in the visceral cavities and adjacent soft tissue. Thus, instead of just the skin flaring out against the muzzle, the whole chest or

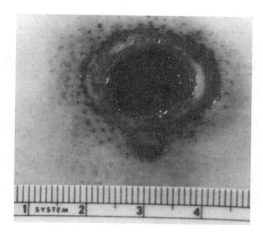

Figure 5.9 Muzzle imprint on chest from .38 Special Colt revolver. The diameter of the imprint is 24 mm, not quite double the actual diameter of the muzzle of the gun which was 13 mm.

abdominal wall will bulge out. These imprints are often larger, sometimes twice, the actual dimensions of the muzzle of the gun. Thus, in Figure 5.9, the muzzle imprint measures 24 mm in diameter while the muzzle diameter was actually 13 mm.

In contact wounds of the trunk in which there is a muzzle imprint, one may see a wide zone of abraded skin surrounding the bullet hole (Figure 5.10). This zone of abrasion is due to the skin rubbing against the muzzle of the weapon when, on firing, the skin flares back impacting and enveloping the muzzle. This zone is often interpreted incorrectly as a zone of searing from the hot gases of combustion. Differentiation is usually possible in that

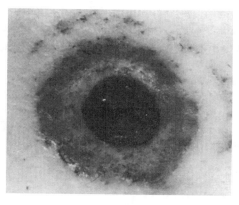

Figure 5.10 Hard-contact wound of chest from 9-mm automatic. Abraded skin around entrance.

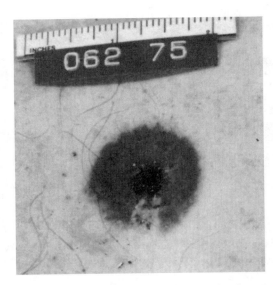

Figure 5.11 Loose-contact wound with circular zone of soot around entrance.

in seared zones, such as seen in near-contact wounds, the seared skin is heavily impregnated with soot, whereas in this impact zone it is not. This zone is often wider than the diameter of the barrel because the skin has been bent back around the end of the barrel, totally enclosing it.

A **loose-contact wound** is produced when the muzzle of the weapon is held in very light contact with the skin at the time of discharge. The skin is not indented by the muzzle. Gas preceding the bullet, as well as the bullet itself, indent the skin, creating a temporary gap between the skin and the muzzle through which gas can escape. Soot carried by the gas is deposited in a band around the entrance (Figure 5.11; see also Figure 4.2). This soot can be easily wiped away. A few unburnt grains of powder may also escape out this gap and be deposited on the skin in the band of soot. Particles of powder, vaporized metals, and soot will be deposited in the wound track along with carbon monoxide.

Angled and **incomplete-contact wounds** and their appearances have been discussed in detail in Chapter 4 (see Figures 4.3 and 4.4).

Near-Contact Wounds

These wounds and their characteristics have already been discussed in detail in Chapter 4. However, a number of additional points can be made. Small clumps of unburned powder may pile up on the edges of the entrance and in the seared zone of skin found in such wounds. These collections of powder are most prominent in wounds inflicted by .22 Magnum handguns whose cartridges contain ball powder. Near-contact wounds with handguns usually occur at ranges less than 10 mm. There is some variation depending on caliber, ammunition, and barrel length.

Hair

Many textbooks, in their descriptions of contact and near-contact wounds in hairy regions, put great stress on the presence of burned hair. In actual practice, charred or seared hair is rarely seen, most probably because the gas emerging from the barrel blows it away. Even in seared zones of skin, however, unburned hairs are numerous. Occasionally, seared hair is seen when a revolver is discharged close to the head while long hair overlays the cylinder gap.

Gas Injuries

The gas produced by combustion of the propellant can produce internal injuries as severe as or more severe than injuries produced by the bullet. Gas-produced injuries are most severe in the head because of the closed and unyielding nature of the skull. The skull, unlike the chest or abdominal cavity, cannot expand to relieve the pressure of the entering gases. In contact wounds of the head from high-velocity rifles or shotguns, large quantities of gas entering the skull produce massive blow-out fractures with extensive muti- lating injuries. The top of the head is often literally blown off with partial or complete evisceration of the brain. Contact wounds of the head with hand- guns, while often producing secondary skull fractures, do not ordinarily produce the massive injuries seen in high-velocity rifles and shotguns.

Massive injuries from contact handgun wounds of the head, when they do occur, are associated with Magnum calibers, e.g., the .357 Magnum, the .44 Magnum or high velocity, high-energy cartridge loadings of medium caliber weapons, e.g., .38 Special +P+ cartridges. These cartridges can inflict contact wounds that in their severity mimic wounds from rifles and shotguns. Such a wound is illustrated in Figure 5.12, where the deceased was an elderly white female who shot herself in the head with a .38 Special revolver. The ammunition used was Remington 125-gr., jacketed, hollow-point, loaded with ball powder. Because of the severe nature of the wound, on the initial viewing of this body it was suspected that the woman had been shot with a shotgun.

Contact wounds of the abdomen and chest from handguns ordinarily do not produce striking injuries of the internal viscera due to gas. Exceptions occur with the high-velocity +P+ loadings and the .44 Magnum, especially if the wound is inflicted over the heart or the liver.

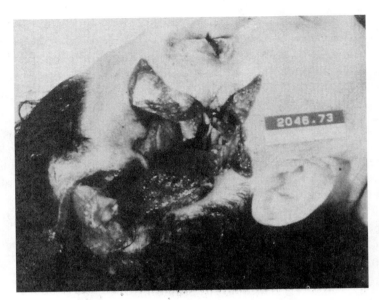

Figure 5.12 Contact wound of right temple from .38 Special revolver firing a high-pressure load.

Intermediate-Range Wounds

An intermediate-range gunshot wound is one in which the muzzle of the weapon is away from the body at the time of discharge yet is sufficiently close so that powder grains emerging from the muzzle strike the skin producing powder tattooing; this is the sine qua non of intermediate-range gunshot wounds.

In addition to the powder tattooing, there may be blackening of the skin or material around the entrance site from soot produced by combustion of the propellant. The size and density of the area of powder blackening vary with the caliber of the weapon, the barrel length, the type of propellant powder, and the distance from muzzle to target. As the range increases, the intensity of powder blackening decreases and the size of the soot pattern area increases. For virtually all handgun cartridges, soot is absent beyond 30 cm (12 in.). (For a more detailed discussion of powder soot, see Chapter 4.)

Although soot usually can be wiped away either by copious bleeding or intentional wiping, powder tattooing cannot. Tattooing consists of numerous reddish-brown to orange-red, punctate lesions surrounding the wound of entrance (Figure 5.13). Powder tattooing is due to the impact of unburned, partially burned, or burning powder grains onto and into the skin. Powder tattooing is an antemortem phenomenon and indicates that the individual was alive or at least that the heart was beating at the time the victim was

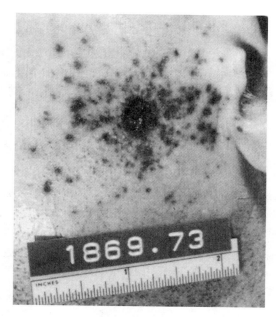

Figure 5.13 Powder tattooing from disk powder.

shot. If an individual is shot at intermediate range after the heart has stopped beating, mechanical markings will be produced on the skin. These markings, however, will not have the reddish color, i.e., the vital reaction of antemortem tattoo marks. Postmortem tattoo marks have a yellow, moist appearance. They are less numerous than markings produced in the living subject at the same range.

For handguns, forensic textbooks generally have stated that the powder tattooing extends out to a maximum distance of 18 to 24 in. (45 to 60 cm) from the muzzle. Such statements do not take into account the different physical forms of propellant powder. At present, in the United States, handgun cartridges are loaded with four forms of propellant: flake, spherical (true) ball powder, flattened ball powder, and cylindrical powder (Figure 5.14). Ball powder is favored in high-pressure loadings such as the .357 Magnum cartridge—because for consistent homogenous ignition of ball powder, high pressure, and thus high temperature conditions are necessary. In the past, however, ball powder was used for pistol loadings down to the .25 ACP. Some manufacturers use uncoated ball powder for better ignition. Grains of uncoated ball powder are a pale green color.

Flake powder usually is in the form of disks though some foreign manufacturers produce flake powder in the form of quadrangles. Circular disks of flake powder can vary greatly in diameter and thickness. If the graphite coating is lost the flakes have a pale green translucent appearance.

Figure 5.14   Ball, flattened ball, and flake (disk).

Handgun cartridges loaded with cylindrical powder are uncommon in the United States.

As a result of animal experiments, it appears that in a .38 Special revolver with a 4-in. barrel, cartridges with flake powder produce powder tattooing out to 18 to 24 in. (45 to 60 cm); cartridges loaded with flattened ball out to 30 to 36 in. (75 to 90 cm), and cartridges loaded with true or spherical powder out to 36 to 42 in. (90 to 105 cm) (Table 5.4).[4] In contrast, a .22 caliber rimfire revolver with a 2-in. barrel, firing .22 Long rifle cartridges produces powder tattooing out to 18 to 24 in. (45 to 60 cm) with flake powder and 12 to 18 in. (30 to 45 cm) with ball powder (Table 5.5).

In centerfire cartridges, powder tattooing extends out to greater ranges with ball powder (both spherical and flattened ball) than with flake powder, because of the shape of the powder grains. The sphere has a better

Table 5.4   Maximum Range of Powder Tattooing from .38 Special Revolver with 4-in. Barrel

Range (cm)	Flake[a]	Flattened Ball[a]	Ball[a]
30	+	+	+
45	+	+	+
60	+	+	+
75	0	+	+
90		+	+
105		0	+
120			0

[a] + = tattooing; 0 = no tattooing.

Table 5.5   Maximum Range of Powder Tattooing from .22 Revolver with 2-in. Barrel Firing Long Rifle Ammunition

Range (cm)	Type of Powder[a]	
	Flake	Ball
15	+	+
30	+	+
45	+	+
60	+	0
75	0	0

[a]   + = tattooing; 0 = no tattooing.

aerodynamic form than a flake; thus, ball powder can travel farther retaining more velocity, enabling it to mark the skin at a greater range. In .22 rimfire ammunition, however, flake powder produces tattooing out to a greater distance than ball powder. The explanation is that the individual grains of ball powder used in the .22 ammunition are so fine that any aerodynamic benefit obtained from the shape is lost as a result of its lighter mass.

The maximum ranges for powder tattooing that have been given should only be used as a rough guide as this data is based on animal tests.[4]

The maximum range at which tattooing occurs, as well as the size and density of the powder tattoo pattern, depends not only on the form of the powder but on a number of other variables, including the barrel length, the caliber, the individual weapon, and the presence of intermediary objects such as hair or clothing that will absorb some or all of the powder grains.

The greater the range, the larger and less dense the powder tattoo pattern. The increase in size of the pattern is due to gradual dispersion of the powder grains, with decreased density of the pattern resulting not only from dispersion but also from rapid loss of velocity of the individual grains; fewer grains reach the target and those that do may not have enough velocity to mark the skin. At close range, a gun with a short barrel will produce a wider and denser tattoo pattern than a longer barrel weapon as more unburned particles of powder will emerge from the short barrel (Figure 5.15). Tattooing will, of course, disappear at a closer range with a short-barreled gun compared with a long-barreled gun. Silencers will filter out a great proportion of the soot and powder particles, thus making the range from muzzle to target appear greater than it actually was.

To a degree, hair and clothing prevent powder from reaching the skin. In centerfire cartridges, ball powder readily perforates hair and clothing at close and medium range. In contrast, except at close range, flake powder usually does not produce powder tattooing through clothing or dense hair, as the grains of flake powder have difficulty in perforating these materials.

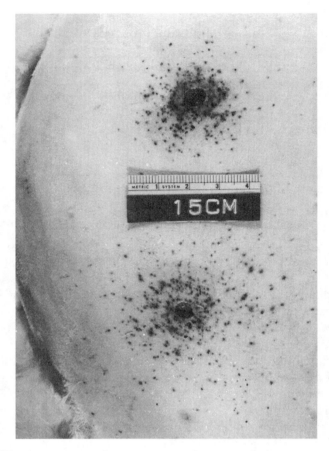

Figure 5.15 Two intermediate-range gunshot wounds (range, 15 cm). Upper tattoo pattern produced by weapon with 6-in. barrel; lower pattern from weapon with 2-in. barrel.

The influence of the type of powder on the extent and degree of powder tattooing and blackening was exhibited in a case in which an individual was shot with a .45 automatic loaded with Norma ammunition. Testing revealed that the maximum range of powder tattooing and blackening in this particular weapon with this particular ammunition was only 6 in.

Although powder tattooing may extend out to almost four feet with a .38-caliber revolver, individual powder grains can travel much farther. In an experiment using a .38 Special 4-in. barrel revolver firing standard velocity Remington ammunition in which the bullet weighed 158-gr. and the powder was flake, individual flakes of powder were deposited on material out to a maximum of 6 ft. from muzzle to target (Table 5.6).[5] A high-velocity Remington cartridge loaded with a 125-gr. semi-jacketed hollow-point bullet and ball powder, discharged from the same weapon, deposited powder grains on a target 20 ft. from the muzzle. An identical cartridge loaded with flake powder deposited powder on clothing out to a maximum of 9 ft. from the muzzle (Table 5.6). Additional tests were carried out with a .357 Magnum revolver having a 4-in. barrel. Cartridges loaded with flattened ball powder deposited grains of powder out to a maximum of 15 ft. Cartridges loaded with flake powder deposited flake powder out to a maximum of 10 ft. (Table 5.6).

Table 5.6 Maximum Distances Traveled from Muzzle to Target by Different Forms of Powder from Different Caliber Weapon (both with 4-in. barrels)

Caliber	Type of Powder in Cartridge Case	Maximum Distance Traveled by Powder Grains (ft)
.38 Special	Ball	20
	Flake[a]	9
	Flake[b]	6
.357 Magnum	Ball	12
	Ball	15
	Flake	10

[a]High-velocity loading; [b]standard velocity loading.

In view of the fact that powder grains can travel such great distances, the presence of a few unburned grains of powder around an entrance in the skin or clothing does not necessarily indicate an intermediate-range wound but, depending on the individual form of powder, can be produced by a weapon being discharged as much as 15 to 20 ft. from the victim. At these ranges, however, the powder has insufficient velocity to mark the skin.

In addition to soot and powder grains, other materials are deposited on the body when a weapon is discharged in close proximity to the body. These materials include: antimony, barium and lead from the primer; copper and zinc (sometimes nickel) vaporized from the cartridge case by the intense heat; fragments of metal stripped from or vaporized from previously fired bullets and deposited in the barrel; copper, aluminum or lead stripped or vaporized from the bullet that was fired; and the grease and oil that had coated the barrel or bullet before discharge. The metallic particles can be detected on the body or on clothing by soft x-ray if they are large enough. Trace metal deposits of these metals can be detected by EDX and SEM–EDX.

The appearance of powder tattoo marks on the skin depends on the physical form of the powder. Powder tattoo marks produced by flake and cylindrical powder are irregular in shape, reddish brown in color, and show great variability in size (see Figure 5.13). Such markings are usually relatively sparse compared to tattooing from ball powder. Slit-like tattoo marks due to grains of flake powder striking on their side may be seen. Occasionally, fragments, intact flakes or both will be found lying on the skin. The number of such flakes is relatively small. Flakes can on occasion penetrate into the dermis, in which case they may produce bleeding from these sites. Small blood clots at the points of penetration may give the appearance of a spray of dried blood. The author has seen a few cases involving flake powder where large numbers of flakes were embedded in the epidermis with some pene-trating into the dermis. The flakes of powder were found to be very small, very thick yellow-green disks. The tattooing produced by these thick disks very closely resembled the tattooing of ball powder. Differentiation was pos-sible only by observation of the thick disks in the wound.

In contrast to flake powder, powder tattooing due to spherical (true) ball powder is considerably more dense with numerous fine, circular, bright red tattoo marks, many containing a ball of unburned powder lodging in the center of the lesion (Figure 5.16A). On seeing the powder tattoo marks from spherical ball powder, one is struck immediately by the resemblance to the petechiae of an intravascular coagulation disorder. Attempts at wiping away the ball powder grains are only partly successful, as many if not most of the little balls of powder are deeply embedded in the skin.

In powder tattoo patterns due to flattened ball, the number of markings produced is greater than in the case of flake powder but fewer than from ball powder. The individual markings tend to be finer, more uniform and more hemorrhagic than flake, approaching those of ball powder in their appearance (Figure 5.16B). Powder grains are recovered embedded in the skin, but they are not nearly as numerous as in cases of true ball powder tattooing.

The previous descriptions of powder tattooing concerned centerfire handguns. Powder tattooing from .22 rimfire cartridges is different. Those cartridges are loaded with either small, thick disks or very fine ball powder (Winchester ammunition). Ball powder produces extremely fine but faint tattooing, whereas flake powder produces a larger, more prominent tattoo pattern. These latter markings more closely resemble those of centerfire flat-tened ball powder than those of traditional flake powder. In some instances flake or parts of flakes have penetrated into the dermis.

Powder tattooing may be present in **angled contact wounds**. In such wounds, as the angle between the barrel and skin decreases, the gap between the skin and barrel increases. At some point the gap becomes sufficiently large that unburnt grains of powder escaping through the gap will skim over the zone of seared skin, fanning out from the entrance, impacting distal to the entrance wound (see Figure 4.3C). In contrast, if a weapon is discharged at intermediate range with the barrel at an angle to the skin (an **angled inter-mediate wound**), dense tattooing is predominantly on the same side of the wound as the gun with scattered tattooing on the opposite side (Figure 5.17).

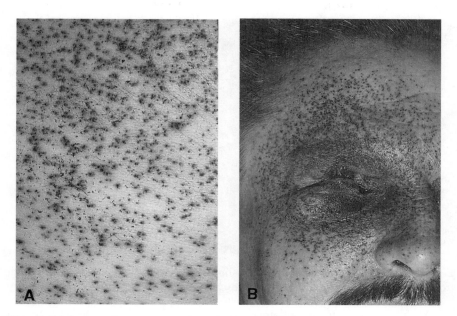

Figure 5.16   Powder tattooing from **(A)** true ball powder and **(B)** flattened ball powder.

The author has never seen *true* powder tattooing of the palms of the hands from powder exiting the muzzle of a gun. He has, however, seen numerous cases in which powder grains were embedded in the palm without the vital reaction that gives tattooing its appearance (Figure 4.9; 4.20A). Lack of tattooing in the palms is apparently due to the thicker stratum corneum protecting the dermis from any trauma. The author has seen rare cases where there were what appeared to be four to five powder tattoo marks on the palm. In these cases, the powder would have had to have come out the cylinder gap. Therefore, it is possible that the marks on the palm were not tattoo marks, but stippling due to fragments of lead accompanying the powder out the cylinder gap.

The size and density of the powder tattoo pattern on the body around the wound of entrance can be used to determine the range at which the weapon was discharged by replication of this pattern on test material. To do this however, the same weapon, and ammunition identical to that of the fired round, should be used in the testing. Selection of ammunition used for test firings is extremely important because different brands and lots of ammunition contain different powders and quantities of propellant. Therefore, ideally, unfired cartridges recovered from the gun or cartridges that came from the same box of ammunition that the fired ammunition came from should be used in the tests.

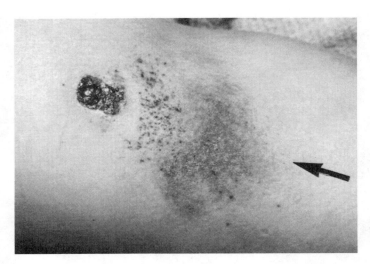

Figure 5.17 Angled intermediate gunshot wound with powder tattooing on side from which the bullet came. Arrow indicates direction of bullet.

Muzzle-to-victim range determinations from powder tattoo patterns on the skin are made by Firearms Examiners, using measurements of the tattoo pattern obtained by the pathologist or from photographs. The distance at which a test pattern identical in size and density to the powder tattoo pattern on the body is produced is assumed to be the range at which the gun was fired at the individual. Test patterns generally are produced on white blotting paper. Unfortunately, experiments have shown that powder tattoo patterns on paper are consistent with skin tattoo patterns only up to 18 in. of range.[4] At ranges greater than 18 in., there is no correlation between the size and density of the tattoo pattern produced on the body and the pattern produced on blotting paper.

Another potential problem with range determinations that are based on the size of powder tattoo patterns is a simple one of variation in measuring. Different individuals measuring the same powder tattoo pattern may produce different measurements.[4] This is due to the fact that some individuals measure the whole pattern, whereas others measure the main area of the pattern, excluding occasional "flier" tattoo marks.

Cylinder Gap

When a revolver is fired, gas, soot, and powder emerge not only from the end of the muzzle but also from the gap between the cylinder and the barrel (see Figure 2.11). This material emerges, fan-like, at an approximate right angle to the long axis of the weapon. If the revolver is in close proximity to the body at the time of discharge, there may be searing of the skin, deposition of soot or even powder tattooing from gas and powder escaping from the cylinder gap. The tattooing will be relatively scant. If there is intervening clothing, it may be seared, blackened or even torn by the gases. In rare cases, if a hand is around the cylinder gap at the time of discharge, the gases may lacerate the palm (Figure 14.5).

If the cylinder of the revolver is out of alignment with the barrel, as the bullet jumps from the cylinder to the barrel, fragments of lead may be sheared off the bullet. These fragments can produce marks on the skin that resemble powder tattoo marks. Such marks, however, are larger, more irregular, and more hemorrhagic than traditional powder tattoo marks. In addition, fragments of lead are often seen embedded in the skin. These fragment wounds are usually intermingled with powder tattooing produced by powder escaping from the cylinder gap (Figure 5.18).

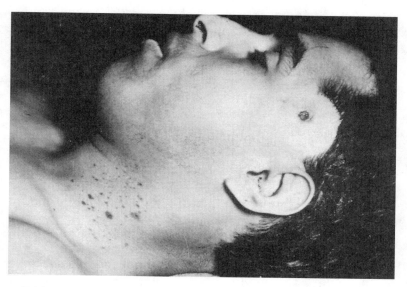

Figure 5.18 Suicide contact wound of left temple with powder tattooing and lead fragment stippling of left side of neck. The larger areas of hemorrhage are due to the lead fragments.

Distant Wounds

In distant gunshot wounds, the muzzle of the weapon is sufficiently far from the body so that there is neither deposition of soot nor powder tattooing. For centerfire handguns, distant gunshot wounds begin beyond 24 in. (60 cm) from muzzle to target for cartridges loaded with flake powder and beyond 42 in. (105 cm) for cartridges loaded with ball powder. The exact range depends on the particular weapon and ammunition and can be determined exactly only by experimentation with the specific weapon and ammunition.

All these figures presuppose the lack of clothing. Clothing will absorb soot and powder, in some cases making close-range wounds appear to be distant by examination of the body alone. This points out the need for examination of the clothing in conjunction with the autopsy. The presence of isolated powder particles on either the clothing or the body does not necessarily signify that one is dealing with an intermediate range wound, as individual powder particles may travel considerable distances before deposition on the body.[5]

Whether powder perforates clothing to mark the skin depends on the nature of the material, the number of layers of cloth, and the physical form of the powder. With handguns, ball powder can readily perforate one and even two layers of cloth to produce tattooing of the underlying skin (Figure 5.19). Rarely, ball powder will perforate three layers. The author has never seen it perforate four layers and produce tattooing. While flake powder usually does not perforate even one layer of cloth, at very close range, it may do so.

Range determinations cannot be made for distant gunshot wounds. Bullets fired from 5, 50, or 500 ft will produce identical entrances. Gunshot wounds of entrance, whatever the range, are identified by the presence of a reddish zone of abraded skin (the abrasion ring) around the entrance hole. This zone becomes brown and then black as it dries. The abrasion ring is due to the bullet rubbing raw the edges of the hole as it indents and pierces the skin. Occasionally, entrance wounds will not have an abrasion ring (Figure 5.20). In handguns, this is most commonly associated with high velocity cartridges such as the .357 Magnum and 9-mm Parabellum, loaded with jacketed or semi-jacketed bullets. Rarely, the wounds will have small tears radiating outward from the margins ("micro-tears") (Figure 4.19A).

In some areas of the body, e.g., the palms, it is the rule not to have an abrasion ring. This is discussed in more detail in Chapter 4.

Addendum: Centerfire Handgun Cartridges

There are scores of centerfire handgun cartridges. A few of the more common ones will be described.

.25 ACP (6.35 × 16)

The .25 ACP, the smallest of the currently manufactured centerfire handgun cartridges, was introduced in the first decade of the twentieth century. The

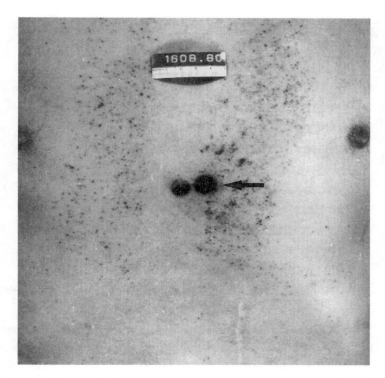

Figure 5.19 Unusual ball powder tattoo pattern resulting from shirt. The powder passed through the shirt, except for the center facing, where there were four layers of cloth rather than one. Arrow indicates entrance. Circular mark medial to entrance is imprint of button.

cartridge generally is loaded with a 50-gr. full metal-jacketed bullet. Muzzle velocity is around 760 ft/sec. A limited production of cartridges loaded with a hollow-point jacketed bullet was made by Winchester in the early 1970s. All these cartridges were loaded with ball powder. These bullets as a general rule do not expand in the body. In 1981, Winchester-Western introduced a cartridge loaded with a 45-gr. expanding-point projectile. The bullet is lead, unjacketed, but coated with a copper Lubaloy® finish. The bullet has a hollow point filled with one No. 4 steel birdshot pellet. The projectile without the shot weights approximately 42.6 gr. CCI cartridges are loaded with bullets having lead cores covered on all surfaces by a thick (0.004 inch) electroplated coating of copper.

.32 ACP (7.65 × 17SR)

The .32 ACP was introduced in 1899 by Fabriqué Nationale for the first successful semiautomatic pistol ever manufactured. It is used extensively in

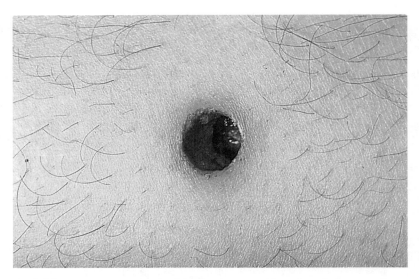

Figure 5.20 Entrance wound of back showing absence of abrasion ring. The bullet was a semi-jacketed .357 Magnum.

Europe. Czechoslovakia manufactured a submachine gun for it, the Scorpion. The cartridge is semirimmed and will chamber and fire in a .32 revolver. It is generally loaded with a 71 gr. full metal-jacketed bullet, with a muzzle velocity of 905 ft/s. Winchester markets a cartridge loaded with a 60-gr. aluminum-jacketed hollow-point bullet. Muzzle velocity is 970 ft/sec.

.32 Smith & Wesson and .32 Smith & Wesson Long

The .32 Smith & Wesson and .32 Smith & Wesson Long cartridges were introduced in 1878 and 1903, respectively. They are revolver cartridges. The .32 S & W is loaded with an 85-gr. lead roundnose bullet. Muzzle velocity is 680 ft/sec. The .32 S & W Long is loaded with a 98-gr. lead roundnose bullet. Muzzle velocity is 780 ft/sec. These cartridges were used extensively in cheap weapons of the Saturday Night Special design. They are essentially obsolete.

.38 Smith & Wesson (9 × 20R)

The .38 Smith & Wesson revolver cartridge was introduced in 1877 with a black powder loading. In Britain, it is called the .380/200. The cartridge is usually loaded with a 145-gr. lead bullet. Muzzle velocity is 685 ft/sec. A 200-gr. loading with a muzzle velocity of 630 ft/sec used to be available. The .38 S & W is essentially an obsolete cartridge. It is rarely seen in the United States.

.38 Special

Introduced in 1902, the .38 Special is the most popular centerfire handgun cartridge in the United States. The standard loading for more than 50 years was a 158 gr. round nose lead bullet having a muzzle velocity of 755 ft/sec. Since the mid-1960s, numerous high velocity semi-jacketed hollow-point and soft-point loadings have been introduced. Bullet weights are generally 95, 110, 125, and 158 gr. in these new loadings. Muzzle velocities range from 950 to 1200 ft/sec. Any weapon chambered for the .357 Magnum cartridge will chamber and fire the .38 Special cartridge.

.357 Magnum

Introduced in 1935 by Smith & Wesson, the .357 Magnum is the .38 Special cartridge case lengthened about 1/10 in. so that it will not chamber in the .38 Special revolver. Standard loading was a 158-gr. lead semiwadcutter bullet with a muzzle velocity of 1235 ft/sec. New semi-jacketed loadings are generally 110, 125, and 158 gr. with muzzle velocities ranging from 1235 to 1450 ft/sec.

.380 ACP (9 × 17 mm/9-mm Kurz/9-mm Corto/9-mm Browning Short)

The .380 cartridge was introduced in the United States in 1908 by Colt and in Europe in 1912 by Fabriqué Nationale. Standard loading is a full metal-jacketed, 95-gr. bullet with a velocity of 955 ft/sec. Semi-jacketed hollow-point loadings are commercially available. This cartridge is increasingly popular in the United States.

9 × 18-mm Makarov

This cartridge was developed by the former USSR as their standard pistol cartridge. In power, it is slightly superior to the .380 ACP. It was not seen in the United States until the early 1990s when large quantities of Makarov pistols began to be imported from China, Russia, and other former Warsaw Pact countries. The standard military loading is a full metal-jacketed 95-gr. bullet having a muzzle velocity of 1060 ft/s. This cartridge is not a true 9 mm as the bullet has a diameter of 0.364 inches compared to 0.355 for the 9 × 19mm.

.38 Colt Super Auto (9 × 23SR)

The .38 Colt Super Auto cartridge was introduced in 1929 as an improved version of the .38 Colt Auto cartridge introduced in 1900. It has never really gained much popularity in the United States. Standard loading is a 130-gr. full metal-jacketed bullet with a muzzle velocity of 1275 ft/sec.

9-mm Luger (9-mm Parabellum/9 × 19-mm)

Introduced in 1902, the 9-mm Luger is the most widely used military handgun cartridge in the world. All modern submachine guns are chambered for this cartridge. A typical military cartridge is loaded with a 115-gr. full metal-jacketed bullet and has a muzzle velocity of 1140 ft/sec. Standard loadings are with 115, 124 and 147 gr. bullets, full metal-jacketed or hollow-point bullets. The 147 gr. bullet as loaded is subsonic. The 9 mm was considered by many American shooters as inferior to the .45 ACP. Studies by the military, a number of civilian government agencies as well as by private individuals have shown that this is incorrect; there is no appreciable difference in the effectiveness of the 9 mm and the .45 ACP cartridges. This cartridge became the standard pistol caliber for the United States military in 1985 and is used by many if not most police agencies in the United States.

.40 Smith & Wesson

This cartridge was introduced in early 1990. It is ballistically similar to the .45 ACP but the cartridge is closer in size to the 9-mm Parabellum. Because of the smaller size than the .45 ACP cartridge, weapons designed originally for the .45 ACP can accommodate more rounds in the magazine. This cartridge is popular with many police organizations. Standard loadings are with 155 and 180 gr. bullets. Muzzle velocity is 1125 and 990 ft/s, respectively.

.45 ACP (11.43 × 23)

The .45 ACP cartridge was adopted as the official military caliber of the United States in 1911. It has never been popular outside the United States. Adoption was based on a series of wound ballistics tests by the U.S. Army prior to its adoption. It was considered a great "man stopper," but more recent testing has shown it no more effective than the 9-mm Luger cartridge which has replaced it in the U.S. military. Standard military loading is with a 230-gr. full metal-jacketed bullet that has a muzzle velocity of 855 ft/sec. Semijacketed hollow-point cartridges are available. This cartridge should not be confused with the .45 Colt cartridge introduced in 1873 by Colt for their Peacemaker single-action revolver.

.44 Smith & Wesson Magnum

The .44 Smith & Wesson Magnum is the most powerful commercially successful handgun cartridge produced. It was introduced in 1955. Not only are a number of revolvers chambered for this cartridge but also a pistol and a number of carbines. The cartridge is loaded with either a 240-gr. lead soft-point bullet or a semi-jacketed hollow-point bullet. Muzzle velocity is 1180 to 1350 ft/sec. This cartridge is unpleasant to shoot for most individuals.

References

1. Remington Ammunition Catalogue, 1982.

2. Menzies, R. C., Scroggie, R. J., and Labowitz, D. I. Characteristics of silenced firearms and their wounding effects *J. Forensic Sci.* 25(2): 239–262, 1981.

3. Personal communication with Patrick Besant-Matthews, M.D.

4. DiMaio, V. J. M., Petty, C. S., and Stone, I. C. An experimental study of powder tattooing of the skin. *J. Forensic Sci.* 21(2): 367–372, 1976.

5. Unpublished experiments by DiMaio, V. J. M. and Norton, L.

Wounds from .22 Caliber Rimfire Weapons

The most popular and most commonly fired cartridge in the United States is the .22 rimfire. It is estimated that over 2.2 billion rounds of this ammunition are produced each year in the United States. There are four types of .22 rimfire ammunition: the .22 Short, the .22 Long, the .22 Long Rifle and the .22 Winchester Magnum rimfire (Figure 6.1).

The Flobert BB cap was the ancestor of the .22 rimfire cartridge. It was developed in 1845 by necking down a percussion cap and inserting a lead ball. The primer was the sole propellant. Subsequent development by Smith & Wesson resulted in the .22 Short cartridge. Introduced in 1857, this is the oldest commercial metallic cartridge. It was loaded with a 29-gr., conical-shaped lead bullet with a diameter the same as that of the case and with outside lubrication. A heel was put on the back of the bullet, so that it could be inserted into the case. The case then was crimped into the bullet. The cartridge originally was loaded with 4 gr. of black powder.

The .22 Long cartridge appeared in 1871. This consisted of a lengthened case (the current .22 Long Rifle case), loaded with the 29-gr. Short bullet. Five grains of black powder were used as a propellant.

The .22 Long Rifle cartridge appeared in 1887. It consisted of the .22 Long case loaded with a 40-gr. bullet and 5 gr. of black powder. This is the most useful and most accurate of the rimfire cartridges.

In the years following the introduction of these three rimfire cartridges, there were a number of significant evolutionary changes. Smokeless powder and the hollow-point design appeared in the 1890s; noncorrosive priming was introduced by Remington in 1927. In 1930, the first high-velocity loadings appeared. In these loadings, bullets of the same weight are propelled at higher velocities than the standard loadings.

153

Figure 6.1 From left to right: .22 Short, .22 Long, .22 Long Rifle, and .22 Magnum.

.22 Magnum

The introduction of the .22 Magnum (Winchester Magnum Rimfire—WMR) occurred in 1959. It was developed as a rimfire cartridge that would possess a velocity close to that of a centerfire. It is loaded with either jacketed hollow-point or full metal-jacketed bullets. Both handguns and rifles are chambered for this cartridge. The .22 Magnum has a larger cartridge case diameter than the other rimfire cartridges and will not chamber in weapons chambered for the standard .22 rimfire cartridges. The .22 Short, Long, and Long Rifle cartridges will fit loosely in a weapon chambered for the Magnum cartridge. They ordinarily will not fire; if they do, the cases will split.

The .22 Magnum cartridge is loaded with an 0.224-in. bullet compared with the 0.223-in. bullet used in the other .22 rimfire cartridges. Some rimfire revolvers have interchangeable cylinders designed so that one cylinder is for the ordinary .22 rimfire cartridges and the other is for the .22 Magnum. The barrel has a groove diameter of 0.224-in., i.e., that of the Magnum bullet. When non-magnum rimfire ammunition is fired, the 0.223-in lead bullet expands, as a result of gas pressure, to fill the rifling.

.22 Magnum cartridges are loaded with either a 40 gr. full metal-jacketed bullet or a jacketed hollow-point (JHP) bullet whose weight varies depending on the manufacturer. Winchester loads a 40 gr. JHP; Federal, a 50 gr. and a 30 gr.; CCI, a 40 gr. and a 30 gr. The CCI 30 gr. JHP bullet has a pentagonal hole in its tip and is loaded in a nickel-plated case. Muzzle velocity from a rifle is 2200 ft/s; 1910 ft/s; and 1650 ft/s for the 30 gr., 40 gr. and 50 gr. bullets, respectively, with velocities of 500 to 600 ft/s less for handguns. Muzzle energy in the rifles is between 300 and 325 ft-lbs.

.22 Short, Long, and Long Rifle Cartridges

The .22 Short, Long, and Long Rifle cartridges can be fired in both handguns and rifles. The term "Long Rifle" as it is applied to the most powerful of these three cartridges does not indicate that the cartridge is intended exclusively for rifles.

Rifles and handguns chambered for the .22 Long Rifle cartridge will fire the Short and Long cartridges as well. In the case of semi-automatic weapons, however, the weak recoil generated by the Short and Long cartridges is generally insufficient to work the action. A few semi-automatic rifles can fire .22 Short, Long, and Long Rifles interchangeably.

Repeated firing of .22 Short cartridges in a weapon chambered for the Long Rifle cartridge may cause leading of the firing chamber, with subsequent difficulty in inserting Long Rifle cartridges. Some handguns and rifles are designed to use Shorts only and will not chamber the longer cartridges.

Weapons chambered for the .22 rimfire cartridge have an 0.223-bore diameter with a 1-in/16 in. (1/16) twist. Optimum velocity is said to be obtained from a 14- to 16-in. barrel. No notable reduction in velocity occurs until the barrel reaches 18 in. in length.[1] Table 2.1 (see Chapter 2) gives the rifling characteristics of the more commonly available .22 rimfire rifles. Marlin uses Micro-Groove® rifling in the rifles they manufacture. There are 16 lands and grooves in Marlin rifles chambered for the .22 Short, Long, and Long Rifle cartridges and 20 lands and grooves in their .22 Magnum rifles. Recovery of a bullet with Micro-Groove® rifling indicates that the individual was shot with a rifle since such rifling is not found in handguns (Figure 6.2). Jenning's Firearms and Phoenix Arms produce semi-automatic pistols chambered for the .22 LR cartridge that have barrels with 16 lands and grooves

Figure 6.2 .22 Long Rifle bullets with Micro-Groove® rifling.

with a right twist. Rifling imparted to a bullet fired down such a barrel can be confused with Microgroove® rifling. The difference is that Microgroove® rifling has extremely narrow lands with grooves twice the width of the lands. In contrast, in Jenning's weapons the lands and grooves have equal widths while the Phoenix pistols have lands that are only slightly narrower compared to the grooves.

The .22 Short, Long, and Long Rifle cartridges are available in either standard-velocity loadings designed for target shooting, short-range hunting, and plinking or high-velocity cartridges containing the same bullet that is loaded in standard velocity cartridges but loaded to a higher velocity. All three cartridges are loaded with unjacketed lead bullets. A small number of full metal-jacketed, .22 rimfire bullets were produced for the military during World War II. These are rare. Tracer Long Rifle rimfire cartridges have been manufactured by the French.

There are four major manufacturers of .22 rimfire ammunition in the United States and probably hundreds in the world. The major manufacturers in the United States are:

Remington-Peters
Winchester-Western
Federal
CCI (Blount Industries)

The head stamp imprinted on the flat base of every .22-caliber rimfire cartridge made in the U.S. will identify the manufacturer. Representative symbols used by the manufacturers are shown in Figure 6.3. All Remington ammunition now has the inscription "Rem" on the base. These four ammunition companies sell their ammunition not only under the company name but also under secondary brand names. Thus, ammunition manufactured by Remington-Peters has been sold under the Remington, Peters, Thunderbolt, Cyclone, and Mohawk brands; Federal under the Federal, American Eagle, and Lightning brands and Winchester-Western under the names Winchester, Western, and Wildcat. Some large chain stores have sold ammunition under a house brand. The head stamps on these cartridges may show who the manufacturer is. In addition to American manufactures, increasing quantities of .22 rimfire ammunition are being imported from throughout the world. The author has seen ammunition from the Philippines, Korea, China, Russia, Serbia, Mexico, etc.

.22 Rimfire ammunition, like all other ammunition, is made in batches called "lots." A lot is a large quantity of one type of ammunition that is manufactured under the same conditions and with materials as nearly identical as possible. Each lot is assigned a number, which is stamped on the box.

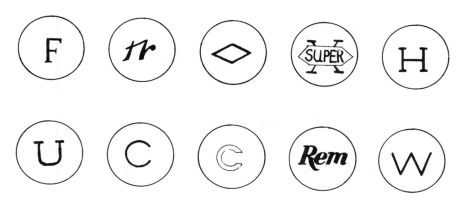

Figure 6.3 .22 Headstamps. Top row (from left to right): Federal, Winchester, Winchester, Winchester, and Winchester. Bottom row (from left to right): Remington, CCI, CCI, Remington, and Winchester.

.22 Short Cartridge

The .22 Short cartridge is available in both standard and high-velocity loadings. The cartridge is generally loaded with either a solid-lead, round-nose, 29-gr. bullet or a 27-gr. hollow-point bullet. The high-velocity bullets generally have a thin copper plating or in the case of Remington ammunition, a "gold" coat (copper and zinc). High-velocity ammunition sold under secondary brand names; standard velocity loadings and target ammunition do not, as a rule, have a copper coat. .22 caliber high-velocity and hollow-point bullets manufactured by CCI have a thick layer of electroplated copper on all surfaces. On initial appearance, they appear jacketed. Manufacturing of .22 Short ammunition appears to be decreasing.

.22 Long Ammunition

The .22 Long round serves no useful purpose and is obsolete.

.22 Long Rifle Ammunition

The .22 Long Rifle cartridge is available in either standard or high-velocity loadings. It is manufactured by all four major companies and is the most popular of the rimfire cartridges. The cartridge is usually loaded with either a 40 gr., lead round-nose bullet or a hollow-point bullet. The weight of the hollow-point bullet varies, depending on the manufacturer. CCI and Remington load 36 gr. hollow-point bullets; Winchester 37 gr. and Federal 38 gr. Remington also loads a 38 gr. subsonic hollowpoint. Winchester manufactured a special Long Rifle cartridge loaded with a 40-gr. hollow-point bullet called the "Dynapoint." This round had a very shallow cavity at the tip of the bullet. It is no longer manufactured.

The high-velocity loadings, whether hollow-point or solid, have a thin copper coating when manufactured by Federal and Winchester and a "gold" (copper zinc) coat when manufactured by Remington. High-velocity ammunition sold under secondary brand names, e.g., Mohawk and Wildcat, does not have the copper coat. Bullets manufactured by CCI, except target and standard velocity loadings, are electroplated with copper on all surfaces. On initial appearance, they appear jacketed and can be confused with .25 ACP bullets.

Winchester manufactures a silhouette round loaded with a 42 gr. lead truncated cone bullet. The bullet is not copper coated. Muzzle velocity is 1220 ft/s in a rifle. CCI makes a 38 gr. truncated cone small-game cartridge that is not electroplated and a 36 gr. high velocity round that is electroplated.

Shot Cartridges

In addition to the regular Long Rifle cartridges with which most people are familiar, .22 Long Rifle Shot cartridges are also available. As loaded by Federal, the cartridges have a crimped metallic mouth and contain approximately 25 gr. of #12 shot. Winchester manufactured a similar shot cartridge loaded with 37 gr. of #12 shot. The cartridge loaded by CCI contains 31 gr. (165 pellets) of #12 pellets in a blue plastic capsule. Muzzle velocity for this particular round is said to be 950 ft/sec. CCI also manufactures a .22 Magnum Shot cartridge which contains 52 gr. of #11 shot enclosed in a blue plastic capsule.

Deaths due to .22 shot cartridges are rare. Both suicides and homicides have been reported.[2,3] The Federal .22 Long Rifle shot cartridge will perforate the temporal bone out to five inches of range (Figure 6.4A).[2] In areas of the skull where the bone is thicker or at a range of greater than 5 in., close range wounds with this cartridge produce depressed skull fractures (Figure 6.4B). Di Maio and Spitz observed an unusual amount of powder blackening with the Remington "birdshot" cartridges, with soot out to 18 in. of range.[2]

Hyper-Velocity .22's

In late 1976, CCI introduced a special .22 rimfire cartridge called the Stinger®. This cartridge is loaded with a 32-gr. electroplated hollow-point bullet; it is intended principally for use in rifles. A velocity of 1687 ft/sec is claimed by the manufacturer, compared to 1370 ft/sec for the conventional high-velocity 37-gr. hollow-point bullet. The Stinger® originally had a pentagonal hole in the point to speed expansion. As presently manufactured the hole is round. A heavier charge of slower burning powder, developed especially for this

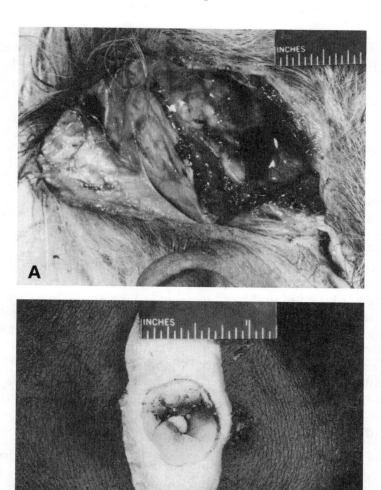

Figure 6.4 **(A)** Contact wound of right temple with Remington .22 shot cartridge. Incised wound revealing soot deposited on outer table of bone. **(B)** Distant gunshot wound of head from .22 shot cartridge. Wound incised revealing depressed fracture.

cartridge, is used. The cartridge case, which is nickel-plated, is approximately 1/10 in. longer than the standard .22 Long Rifle case. The overall length of the Stinger® and the regular .22 Long Rifle cartridge are the same, however.

The Winchester-Western Company countered the Stinger with the Xpediter®. This high-velocity .22 rimfire cartridge, which was introduced in

1978, was loaded with a 29-gr. hollow-point bullet. Muzzle velocity was 1680 ft/sec from a 24-in. barrel. The cartridge case was nickel-plated and was somewhat longer than the .22 Long Rifle case. This cartridge could be fired in any weapon chambered for the .22 Long Rifle cartridge, except those with match chambers. Pressure limits were within those intended for the .22 Long Rifle ammunition. This cartridge was discontinued in 1982.

In 1979, Remington introduced their Yellow Jacket® ammunition. This is a high-velocity .22 Long Rifle cartridge with a 33-gr truncated cone hollow-point bullet having a "gold coat" (copper zinc). The muzzle velocity in a .22 rifle with a 24-in. barrel is 1500 ft/sec compared with 1200 ft/sec for the Remington .22 Long Rifle, 40 gr., high-velocity round. Muzzle velocity in a Ruger automatic pistol with a 4 3/4-in. barrel is 1269 ft/sec compared to a muzzle velocity of 1048 ft/sec for an ordinary 40-gr. high-velocity, .22 LR cartridge. Unlike the CCI Stinger® and the Winchester Expediter®, the cartridge case length is the standard Long Rifle length. Imprinted on the base of the cartridge case is an outline of a yellow jacket. A solid bullet version of the Yellow Jacket called the Viper® appeared in 1982. The bullet weighs 36 gr. and has a muzzle velocity of 1410 ft/sec in a rifle.

Federal introduced their high-velocity .22 Long Rifle cartridge, the Spitfire®, in January 1983. This round is loaded with a 33-gr. lead hollow-point bullet or a 36 solid lead bullet. Muzzle velocity is 1506 ft/sec and 1410 in a rifle with a 24-in. barrel. With handguns, muzzle velocity is 1173 ft/sec in a 4-in. barrel for the "Spitfire." This cartridge is no longer manufactured.

BB and CB Caps

BB caps are imported from Europe and consist of a case shorter than the Short case loaded with a lightweight lead bullet. The propellant is just the primer. BB caps are not manufactured in this country. CCI, Remington, and Winchester produce CB cartridges. While Winchester produces only the .22 Short version, CCI and Remington produce both .22 Short and Long versions. The CCI and Winchester cartridges are loaded with 29-gr. Short bullets; the Remington with 30 gr. bullets. Reduced powder charges are used so that the muzzle velocity is approximately 706 ft/sec for both the Short and Long CB cartridges compared to 865 ft/sec for the standard velocity Short cartridge (in a 6-in. barreled weapon).

Frangible Rimfire Ammunition

.22 Frangible bullets were designed for use in shooting galleries and for stunning cattle for slaughter. The bullets consist of bonded fragments of iron or lead that disintegrate on striking a hard surface. Bullets composed of powdered iron show a slightly greater degree of fragmentation.

Although frangible bullets break up on striking a hard surface, such bullets readily penetrate the human body and have caused a number of deaths.[4] These bullets are of considerable forensic significance; when recovered from the body, they are unsuitable for ballistic comparison because of erosion of the bullet's surface. Both types of bullets show a fine particulate disintegration of the surface. At most, faint rifling marks unsuitable for ballistic comparison can be seen. The surface disintegration is due to the bonded fragment construction of the missile.

In a body, the iron bullets tend to break up into short cylinders or thick disks. An x-ray film of such a bullet in the body may be very characteristic. The iron gallery rounds can be identified easily by means of a magnet.

Iron and lead frangible rimfire cartridges are no longer manufactured.

CCI Rimfire Ammunition

Since the early 1970s, most .22 rimfire bullets manufactured by CCI are electroplated with copper. This plating, averaging 0.001 inches, covers all surfaces such that there is no exposed lead core. The plating is approximately 4/1000th (0.004) inches thick for the .22 Magnum bullets. The lead core is 0.85% antimony. Cartridge casings are copper with Stinger® and Maxi-Mag + V® casings nickel plated. The cartridges are loaded with flake powder for the most part though some ammunition has been loaded with flattened ball powder. The electroplated .22 LR and Magnum bullets when recovered from the body may be easily mistaken for jacketed .25 ACP bullets.

Wounds Due to Rimfire Ammunition

Contact Wounds

.22 Short.   Most contact wounds with .22 rimfire ammunition are self-inflicted wounds of the head. Hard contact wounds of the head inflicted with the .22 Short cartridge often present problems of interpretation. The small amount of powder in the cartridge and the resultant small amount of soot and gas produced result in an absence of tears at the entrance as well as very little or no deposition of soot or powder. These wounds often are mistaken for distant wounds; however, close inspection of the entrance, usually shows some blackening and searing of the edges. Distant wounds can simulate this appearance if the edges of the entrance have dried out. It is recommended, that in instances in which one cannot be sure whether the entrance wound is a hard contact or distant, that it be examined both externally and internally with a dissecting microscope for soot and powder.

If on examination of a wound both externally and internally, using both the naked eye and the dissecting microscope, there is still no evidence of soot or powder and the wound is suspected of being hard contact, the wound may be examined by energy dispersive x-ray (EDX) or SEM–EDX for metallic deposits from the primer, bullet, or cartridge case. Fortunately, such problems rarely arise. Often, with hard contact wounds from a .22 Short cartridge the problem is solved immediately by the observation of the imprint of the muzzle around the suspected contact wound of entrance.

Relative absence of soot and powder from a hard contact wound inflicted by a .22 Short cartridge will be more pronounced if the weapon used is a rifle. The longer barrel length permits almost complete combustion of the propellant.

In contact wounds of the head from the .22 Short cartridge, there are generally no skull fractures, except perhaps of the orbital plates. The bullet rarely exits the cerebral cavity. Internal ricocheting with such a round is extremely common. When recovered, the bullet usually is severely mutilated.

Hard contact wounds of the body from a .22 Short cartridge can be identified more easily than those of the head. Because most of these wounds are through clothing, there is often a band of soot on the skin around the entrance. In all cases, the edges of these wounds are seared and blackened to a greater degree than is seen in head wounds. Soot and powder often can be seen using a dissecting microscope. These differences in comparison to head wounds may result because there is less "blow-back" of gas due to absence of bone to deflect back the gas.

.22 Long Rifle and .22 Magnum Cartridges.   Hard-contact wounds of the head with the .22 Long Rifle cartridge range in appearance from a small circular perforation surrounded by a narrow band of blackened seared skin, to large, usually circular wounds, with ragged, blackened and seared edges. True stellate wounds are the exception, not the rule. Soot, powder, and searing are prominent. There should be no difficulty in distinguishing a distant from a contact wound with the .22 Long Rifle cartridge. The use of a dissecting microscope will reveal obvious deposits of soot and powder in the subcutaneous tissue. Muzzle imprints are much more common than in wounds from the Short cartridge because of the greater gas volume produced. Secondary fractures of the skull are frequent with fractures of the orbital plates virtually the rule. The bullet often exits the skull, though it may be found underneath the scalp, adjacent to the exit in the bone. X-ray of the head usually shows lead fragments at the entrance site and along the bullet track. However, the author has seen a number of instances of perforating .22 Long Rifle wounds of the head in which no lead was present on x-ray.

Contact wounds of the head with the .22 Magnum cartridge are more destructive than those from other .22 cartridges. In external appearance, they resemble .22 Long Rifle wounds excepting that cruciform tears (stellate wounds) are more frequent. In cartridges loaded with ball powder, powder grains can transverse the head and be found at the exit. .22 Magnum bullets usually exit the head. Secondary fractures of the skull are the rule and tend to be very extensive.

Contact wounds of the body from the .22 Long Rifle cartridge show searing and blackening of the edges of the wound, often with a cuff of soot (Figure 6.5). Muzzle imprints are common. The bullet may perforate the body in contrast to .22 Short bullets, which virtually never perforate.

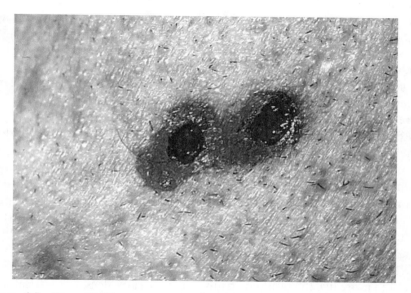

Figure 6.5 Two .22 LR contact wounds. There is searing and blackening of the edges of the wound.

Wounds of the body caused by .22 Magnum bullets resemble .22 Long Rifle wounds. Muzzle imprints are common. If the weapon is a handgun, there are often piles of unburnt ball powder at the entrance. Exit wounds of the trunk are common.

Intermediate-Range Wounds

The appearance of individual powder tattoo marks, the size of the pattern, and the maximum distance out to which tattooing occurs depend on the physical form of the powder (flake, ball, or cylindrical), the range from gun to target, and the barrel length. .22 Magnum cartridges may be found loaded with ball, flake or cylindrical powder. Winchester-Western .22 Short, Long, and Long Rifle cartridges are loaded with very fine ball powder. The other three American manufacturers use flake powder though some CCI cartridges loaded with flattened ball powder may be encountered.

In centerfire cartridges, powder tattooing from ball powder extends out to a greater range than that from flake powder, all other factors remaining the same. This is because a grain of ball powder has a better aerodynamic configuration than a flake. Consequently, as it travels from the muzzle of the gun, it retains its velocity better and can both travel further and impact the skin harder than a grain of flake powder of the same mass. Thus, the tattooing from the ball powder extends out to a greater range and is more prominent. In contrast, with .22 rimfire cartridges (excluding the Magnum), the exact opposite holds. This is because the balls of powder are very small and light and, consequently, have difficulty combating air resistance. In contrast, the flakes are large and dense, hence, better able to combat air resistance. They produce tattooing out to greater ranges than the ball powder.

Tattooing from .22 rimfire ammunition loaded with ball powder is extremely fine (Figure 6.6A). Animal tests, using a .22 handgun with a 2-in. barrel indicate that powder tattooing from Long Rifle cartridges loaded with ball powder extends out to a maximum of 18 in. (45 cm) from muzzle to target with tattooing absent at 24 in. (60 cm).

Cartridges loaded with flake powder produce fewer, larger, and more prominent powder tattoo marks (Figure 6.6B). Flakes may penetrate into the dermis. Animal testing with a 2-in. barrel .22-caliber revolver revealed powder tattoo marks from Long Rifle cartridges loaded with flake powder extend out to a range of 18 to 24 in. (45 to 60 cm). Tattoo marks were absent by 30 in. (75 cm).

.22 Magnum cartridges loaded with ball powder produce very dense tattooing more like the tattooing from centerfire cartridges. Cylindrical powder produces tattooing that resembles markings from flake powder.

Distant Wounds

Distant wounds of entrance from .22 rimfire bullets are generally circular in shape, measuring 5 mm in diameter, including the abrasion ring. In some areas of the body where the skin is very elastic and may be stretched when the bullet enters, e.g., the elbow, the entrance wound may be extremely small; in one case the complete diameter (including abrasion ring) was 3 mm. This wound initially was interpreted as a puncture wound and not a gunshot wound, as it was believed to be too small to be a gunshot wound. Distant wounds from .22 caliber bullets have been mistaken for ice-pick wounds and vice versa.

.22 Hollow-point bullets fired from handguns do not as a general rule mushroom. If they strike thick, dense bone, they can flatten out. More

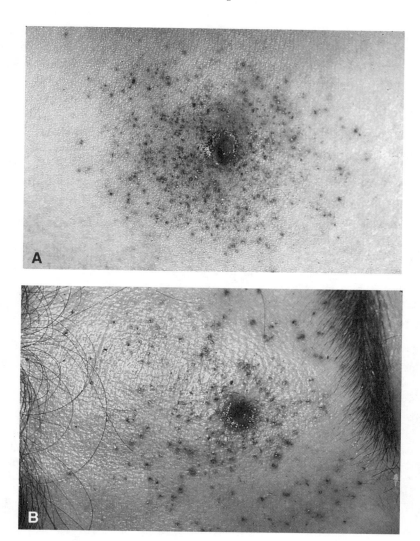

Figure 6.6 (A) Ball powder tattooing from .22 LR cartridge. (B) Flake powder tattooing from .22 LR cartridge.

commonly, both solid and hollow-point bullets, rather than flattening out on striking bone, penetrate it. On recovery, they may appear relatively intact and un-deformed. Close examination, however, will usually show fine, brush-like scrape marks on their surface. Long Rifle hollow-point bullets, fired from rifles, may mushroom without striking bone due to the increased velocity imparted to them by the longer barrel.

At distant range, .22 Long Rifle bullets penetrating the head can produce linear fractures of the skull whether the weapon used is a handgun or a rifle.

These fracture involve the cranial vault and orbital plates for the most part and are due to temporary cavity formation. In contrast, .22 Short wounds of the head usually do not produce fractures. If they do, the fractures are usually of the orbital plates.

References

1. Cochrane, D. W. Barrel lengths vs. velocity and energy. *A.F.T.E.* 11(1): 37–38, 1979.
2. DiMaio, V. J. M. and Spitz, W. U. Injury by birdshot. *J. Forensic Sci.* 15(3): 396–402, 1970.
3. DiMaio, V. J. M., Minette, L. J., and Johnson, S. Three deaths due to revolver shot shell cartridges. *Forensic Sci.* 4: 247–251, 1974.
4. Graham, J. W., Petty, C. S., Flohr, D. M., and Peterson, W. E. Forensic aspects of frangible bullets. *J. Forensic Sci.* 2(4): 507–515, 1966.

General References

Barnes, F. C. *Cartridges of the World*, 7th ed. Northfield IL: DBI Books Inc. 1993

Annual ammunition catalogs published by Winchester, Remington, Federal, and CCI.

Wounds from Centerfire Rifles

7

> "The U.S. exports Coca Cola; Japan exports Sony; Russia exports Kalashnikovs."
>
> **Anonymous**

Wounds caused by centerfire rifles are markedly different from those caused by handguns or .22 rimfire rifles. Handguns and .22 rimfire rifles are relatively low-velocity weapons with muzzle velocities of between 650 and 1400 ft/sec. With the exception of the .357 Magnum and the .44 Magnum, muzzle energies are well below 500 ft-lb. The widely proclaimed .45 automatic has a muzzle velocity of only 850 ft/sec, with a muzzle energy of 370 ft-lb. In contrast, the muzzle velocities of modern centerfire rifles range between 2400 and 4000 ft/sec (Table 7.1). The muzzle kinetic energy is never less than 1000 ft-lb; it is commonly in the 2000 ft-lb range and may be as high as 5000 ft-lb. Because of the low velocities and kinetic energies, injuries from both handgun and .22 rimfire rifle bullets are confined to tissue and organs directly in the wound path. In contrast, a centerfire rifle bullet can injure structures without actually contacting them.

Before the mid-nineteenth century, most shoulder arms were smoothbore with a caliber of .69 to .75. They fired of soft lead balls of 484 to 580 gr. The propellant was black powder. Muzzle velocity was from 590 to 754 ft/sec.[1] Because of the low velocities of these spherical balls, the injuries produced were confined to tissue and organs directly in the wound track.[2-4] The wound entrance was round and approximately the size of the ball; it was surrounded by an extensive area of ecchymosis. The wound track through the tissue was greater than the diameter of the ball. Musket balls usually lodged in the body. The exit wound, if present, was characteristically larger than the entrance. When these bullets struck bone, they often lodged in the bone or flattened against it. If the ball struck the bone at maximum velocity, it was capable of causing severe damage with extensive comminution of the bone and displacement of bone spicula along the wound track.

Table 7.1   Ballistics of Various Handgun and Rifle Centerfire Cartridges

Cartridge	Bullet Weight (gr.)	Muzzle Velocity (ft/sec)	Muzzle Energy (ft-lb)
Handguns			
.25 Auto	50	760	64
.32 ACP	71	905	129
7.62 × 25	87	1390	365
.380	95	955	190
9 × 18 Makarov	95	1060	237
9-mm Parabellum	124	1299	465
.40 S & W	155	1140	447
.45 Auto	230	855	405
.38 Special	158	755	200
.357 Magnum	158	1235	535
.44 Magnum	240	1350	971
Rifles			
5.56 × 45	55	3150	1218
	62	3020	1250
5.45 × 39	53	2985	1053
.243	100	2960	1945
.270	130	3060	2702
7.62 × 39	124	2300	1450
.30–30	150	2390	1902
7.62 × 51 (.308)	150	2750	2520
7.62 × 63 (.30–06)	150	2740	2500

The 1850s saw the introduction of conical bullets (Minie bullets). These bullets ranged in caliber from .67 to .69. They had a conical shape, were made of soft lead, and weighed from 555 to 686 gr.[1] These bullets could be loaded in either smooth-bore or rifled weapons. The most significant difference from the spherical bullets was the sharp increase in velocity. Initial velocity with such ammunition ranged from 931 to 1017 ft/sec. The wounds caused by these bullets showed enormous destruction of tissue and were much more severe than injuries from the old round balls. The use of these weapons in combat — for example, the American Civil War — brought about numerous accusations of the use of explosive bullets.[2-5] The increased wounding effectiveness of such ammunition was due to the fact that whereas the bullet weight was equal to or in many cases greater than that of the spherical bullet, the velocity was markedly increased. Thus, these conical bullets possessed significantly greater kinetic energy to inflict wounds.

Bone injuries from conical bullets were extremely severe.[2,3] The term used to described them at the time was "explosive."* Pulpefaction of soft tissue secondary to fragments of bone and disintegrating particles from the bullet were described. Large wounds of exit were present.

By the late nineteenth century, most rifles were generally of .40 to .50 caliber. The .45–70 cartridge adopted by the U.S. Army in 1873 is a typical example of the large-caliber black powder weapons in use. A typical loading for this cartridge was a 500-gr. bullet with a muzzle velocity of 1315 ft/sec and muzzle energy of 1875 ft-lb.

The introduction of smokeless powder at the end of the nineteenth century led to a general reduction of caliber so that most military weapons were of 6.5- to 8-mm caliber. Bullets used in these weapons were roundnosed and full metal-jacketed, weighed around 220 gr., and had a muzzle velocity of approximately 2000 ft/sec. Wounds produced by these bullets were believed by some authorities to be less severe than those due to the conical lead bullets.[2-4] Such observations were probably correct. These new bullets, being full metal-jacketed, tended to pass through the body without any deformation, thereby losing less kinetic energy than the conical lead bullets, which, being easily deformed in the body, lost large amounts of kinetic energy.

Almost immediately after the introduction of the roundnosed ammunition, full metal-jacketed Spitzer (pointed) bullets were introduced. These bullets, averaging 150 gr., had muzzle velocities of approximately 2700 ft/sec. Soon after the appearance of these new high-velocity loadings, the observation was made that the wounds produced by these cartridges appeared to be "explosive."[2-4] The external signs of injuries were slight, with small entrance and exit sites combined with extensive disruption and laceration of the internal viscera and soft tissue. These injuries not uncommonly involved structures distant from the actual bullet path. The extensive nature of these injuries is now known to be due to the temporary cavity formation described in Chapter 3. These wounds were still felt to be less severe than those due to lead conical bullets such as those used in the American Civil War.[3,4]

Discussion of rifle wounds in the medical literature is concerned almost exclusively with injuries from military ammunition. Wounds encountered by pathologists and medical examiners, however, often involve hunting ammunition. The design and construction of bullets used in hunting ammunition is radically different from that of military ammunition. Because of these differences, the wounds produced by hunting ammunition are much more devastating.

---

* In reviewing the literature concerning firearms wounds through the ages, one is struck by the recurrent use of the term "explosive" to describe wounds produced by newly introduced weapons or forms of ammunition. This term has been used to describe wounds produced by conical lead bullets, jacketed bullets, hunting bullets, and the M-16.

Before discussing rifle wounds from centerfire cartridges, one has to decide what a high-velocity centerfire rifle cartridge is. For the purpose of this discussion, it is defined as any cartridge with a centrally located primer intended to be fired in a rifle of caliber .17 or greater whose bullet is propelled at a velocity of more than 2000 ft/sec. The .30-caliber M-1 Carbine cartridge is neither a rifle nor a handgun cartridge. It has a bullet weight of 110 gr., a muzzle velocity just below 2000 ft/sec and muzzle energy of 955 ft-lbs. Wounds produced by the full metal-jacketed .30 Carbine bullet more closely resemble those from a Magnum handgun bullet than those from a centerfire rifle, whereas the wounds produced by soft-point or hollow-point ammunition are much too extensive to be ascribed to handgun cartridges and most closely resemble in severity those seen with a rifle cartridge. Thus, the .30 Carbine cartridge lies in a transition zone between rifle and handgun cartridges in terms of wounding. The construction of the bullet loaded in the .30 Carbine cartridge case determines whether the wound is handgun-like or rifle-like.

Beginning in the late 1930s, the Germans and the Russian military began the development of intermediate rifle cartridges. While these cartridges were considerably more powerful than pistol cartridges, they were significantly less powerful than traditional rifle cartridges. They were intended for a new class of weapons that we now know as Assault Rifles. Traditional rifle cartridges possess more than 1,900 ft-lbs (2,575 J) of muzzle energy. In contrast, intermediate cartridges have muzzle energies of between 1,000 and 1,500 ft-lb (1,360–2,030 J) (Table 7.2). The first of the intermediate cartridges to see use was the 7.92 × 33 mm. It was used in World War II by the Germans in the StG-44. Currently, only three intermediate rifle cartridges are in widespread use: the 5.45 × 39; the 5.56 × 45 and the 7.62 × 39 (Table 7.2). These are discussed in the section on assault rifles.

Table 7.2   Comparison of Intermediate Rifle Cartridges

Caliber	Bullet Weight (gr.)	Velocity (f/s)	Muzzle (ft-lb)	Energy (J)
7.92 × 33	123	2100	1214	1614
7.62 × 39	124	2300	1450	1960
5.56 × 45	55	3150	1210	1640
	62	3020	1250	1693
5.45 × 39	53	2985	1053	1428

Research by the military has revealed that the feature of a rifle bullet's interaction with soft tissue that contributes most to the severity and extent of the wound is the size of the temporary wound cavity (see Chapter 3). The size of this cavity is directly related to the amount of kinetic energy lost by a bullet in the tissue. Rifle bullets, by virtue of high velocities, possess considerably more kinetic energy than pistol bullets. Table 7.1 illustrates the muzzle velocities and kinetic energies of some typical handgun and rifle bullets. The marked contrast in the kinetic energy possessed by rifle bullets in comparison to handgun bullets is evident.

The severity and extent of a wound, however, are determined not by the amount of kinetic energy possessed by a bullet, but rather by the amount of this energy that is lost in the tissue. The major determinants of the amount of kinetic energy lost by a bullet in the body are:

1. The shape of the bullet
2. The angle of yaw at the time of impact
3. Any change in the presented area of the bullet in its passage through the body
4. The construction of the bullet
5. The biological characteristics of the tissues through which the bullet passes.

By virtue of high velocities and thus higher kinetic energies, rifle bullets have the potential to produce extremely severe wounds. For military ammunition, velocity, and stability of the bullet in the tissue are the most important determinants of the severity of the wound, as military bullets have a full metal jacket that usually prevents deformation of the bullet. In contrast, in hunting ammunition, bullet construction plays a role equal to or greater than that of velocity in determining the extent and severity of the wound. A hunting bullet is designed to deform in its passage through the body, producing an increase in its presenting area; this trait, plus a tendency to shed fragments of lead core, results in greater kinetic energy loss and thus greater tissue injury.

The two types of wound tracks produced when a bullet passes through tissue are the permanent wound track and the temporary cavity. As a bullet moves through the body, the tissue adjacent to the bullet's path is flung away in a radial manner, creating a temporary cavity. The size of this cavity is directly related to the amount of kinetic energy absorbed by the tissue. This cavity may be as much as 11 to 12.5 times the diameter of the bullet for centerfire rifle bullets.[6] The cavity undulates for 5 to 10 msec before it comes to rest as a permanent wound track. Organs struck by these bullets may undergo partial or complete disintegration. The pressures generated are sufficient to fracture bone and rupture vessels adjacent to the permanent wound track but not directly struck by the bullet. As the cavity collapses, tissue is often ejected from not only the exit but the entrance as well. Thus, when an individual is shot through a clothed area of the body with a rifle bullet, it is not uncommon to find ejected tissue, such as muscle or fat, on the inner surface of the clothing adjacent to both the entrance and exit holes. The amount of this tissue is usually greater at the exit site.

The severe nature of wounds from centerfire rifles is due to the large temporary cavities produced, exceeding the limits of elasticity of the tissue and organs. Body organs can absorb only a certain amount of kinetic energy and therefore a certain size of temporary cavity before the limits of their elasticity are exceeded and the organs shatter (pulpify). The severely destructive properties of rifle bullets are not possessed by handgun or .22 rimfire rifle bullets. The low velocity of the latter bullets, with resultant low kinetic energy imparted to the tissue, results in small temporary cavities that do not exceed the elastic limits of organs.

Centerfire Rifle Bullets

Centerfire rifle bullets differ in construction from handgun bullets in that rifle bullets have to have either full or partial metal jacketing. This is necessary because of the high velocities at which rifle bullets are propelled down a barrel. If the bullets were lead or lead alloy, these high velocities would result in the lead being stripped from the surface of the bullet by the rifling grooves. Some handloaders will load centerfire rifle cartridges with cast lead bullets. In such cases, however, they reduce the powder charge so that the muzzle velocities produced are generally below 2000 ft/sec. These bullets may or may not have a gas check. They are easily recognized by their long length and deep cannelures for lubricants (Figure 7.1).

Rifle bullets can be divided into four general categories on the basis of their configuration and construction. First is the full metal-jacketed bullet. This is the standard form of ammunition used by the military. The bullet

Figure 7.1 Cast rifle bullet with deep cannelures filled with grease.

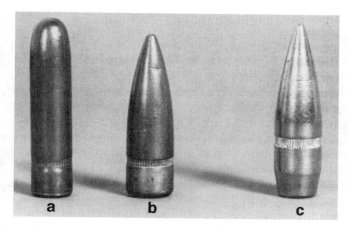

Figure 7.2 Full metal-jacketed military bullets. (a) 162-gr. roundnose; (b) 150-gr. Spitzer, (c) 150-gr. boat-tail.

has a lead or steel core, covered by a jacket of cupro-nickel, gilding metal or steel. The jacket encloses the tip of the bullet, preventing it from expanding when it reaches its target. The tip may be either pointed or rounded (Figure 7.2). The core is exposed at the base.

Some rifle cartridges are loaded with bullets whose core is made up of both mild steel and lead. The standard AK-47 military round produced in Russia and China has a mild-steel core, sheathed in lead, at the rear, with a small lead tip in front; the M-855 M-16A2 bullet, a small mild-steel core in front and a lead core in the rear.

Soft-point rifle bullets have a lead core with a partial metal jacketing that is generally closed at the base (Figure 7.3). The lead core is exposed at the tip so as to facilitate expansion when the bullet strikes. The tip of the soft-point bullet may either taper to a point or have a rounded, blunt end. Expansion of soft-point bullets can be facilitated further by scalloping the mouth of the jacket or cutting five or six notches around the jacket mouth. These modification allow uniform peel-back of the jacket when the bullet strikes the target. Soft-point bullets are the most widely used form of hunting ammunition. One variant of soft-point bullets is the Nosler Partition® bullet. Here the jacket is "H" shaped such that the lead core is in two segments, one above and the other below the horizontal bar of the "H". Thus, the bullet has an exposed lead tip and an exposed lead base. Federal makes a soft point bullet with the usual copper jacket and lead core but with a solid copper base. PMC makes a cartridge loaded with a solid copper bullet.

Hollow-point rifle bullets are a variant of soft-point bullets. They are partial metal-jacketed hunting bullets with a lead core and a cavity at the

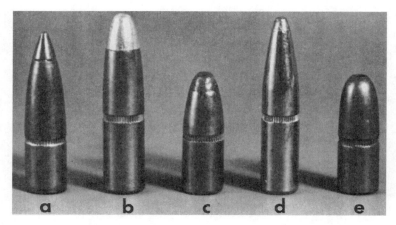

Figure 7.3 Hunting bullets. (a) Bronze-point, (b) Silvertip®, (c) soft-point, (d) soft-point, and (e) hollow-point.

tip of the bullet to facilitate expansion when the bullet strikes game (Figure 7.3). Hollow-point bullets are used for hunting and competitive shooting matches.

Winchester® makes a rifle bullet, the Fail Safe®, that has a solid copper-alloy front section, with a notched hollow-point cavity, and a solid rear lead core, partially sheathed in a steel insert. The base of the bullet is closed with a brass heel closure disk. The surface of the bullet is black due to a baked on molybdenum disulfide coating; the cartridge case is nickel plated.

The fourth category of rifle bullets is a miscellaneous one of controlled expansion projectiles. All are variants of soft-point bullets. This group includes Silver-Tip® ammunition by Winchester; the Bronze-Point® by Remington and the Nosler Ballistic Tip® bullets. The Silver-Tip® bullet is a soft-point bullet whose lead tip is protected by a thin jacket of aluminum alloy (Figure 7.3). This aluminum sheath extends back under the jacket almost to the cannelure. The purpose of the aluminum jacket is to protect the exposed lead core so as to delay expansion slightly. The Remington Bronze-Point® has a pointed, wedge-shaped nose inserted in the forward part of the lead core. This "bronze-point" projects out the tip of the bullet jacket. A small cavity underlies this wedge. When the bullet strikes the target, the wedge is driven back into the bullet, expanding it. Figure 7.4 is an x-ray of an individual shot in the head with this type of ammunition. Note the presence of the "bronze point."

In the case of Nosler Ballistic Tip® bullets, a solid polycarbonate tip is inserted into the tip of the lead core with the jacket crimped into the tip to hold it in place (Figure 7.5). As with the Bronze-Point®, there is an underlying

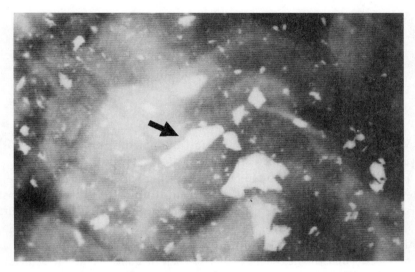

Figure 7.4 X-ray of individual shot in head with Bronze-Point® bullet; arrow-like "Bronze-Point" in center of bullet fragments.

Figure 7.5 Nosler Ballistic Tip®.

cavity into which the tip is driven on impact with the target. This tip is color coded for different calibers:

Orange	.22
Purple	6-mm
Blue	.25
Yellow	.270
Red	7-mm
Green	.30

Winchester, Remington, and Federal manufacture bullets with Nosler polycarbonate or similar tips.

From this discussion, we can see that hunting bullets differ from military bullets in that the former are designed to expand or mushroom so as to transfer energy more efficiently to the target and to kill game more effectively. Ammunition manufacturers control the rate and extent of expansion of hunting ammunition by controlling the bullet velocity and the physical characteristics of the bullet. Thus, the degree of expansion can be controlled by the thickness and hardness of the jacket, the location of the bullet cannelure, the amount of lead exposed, the shape of the bullet, the composition of the lead core (antimony is often added to the lead), and the design characteristic of the bullet.

Military bullets, by virtue of their full metal jackets, tend to pass through the body intact, thus producing less extensive injuries than hunting ammunition. Military bullets usually do not fragment in the body or shed fragments of lead in their paths. Because of the high velocity of such military rounds as well as their tough construction, it is possible for such bullets to pass through more than one individual before coming to rest. These bullets may be almost virginal in appearance after recovery from the body.

One notable exception to the aforementioned observations in regard to bullet breakup in full metal-jacketed bullets is the 5.56 × 45-mm (.223) cartridge. As originally loaded with a 55-gr. bullet and used in the original AR-15 and the M-16A1, this particular cartridge gained widespread notoriety in both the lay press and the medical literature in that the wounds inflicted often were described as "explosive" in nature. The 55-gr. bullet has been described as "exploding" in the body. Such statements are, of course, nonsense. The bullet does not explode in the body; it does, however, have a tendency to rapidly destabilize, bending at the cannelure, resulting in lead core being "squirted" out the base. Because of these characteristics, this cartridge tends to lose considerable amounts of kinetic energy, thus producing relatively severe wounds for the amount of kinetic energy that it possesses. The wounds produced by this round are, in fact, less severe than those produced by lower velocity hunting ammunition such as the .30–30.

When full metal-jacketed 55 gr. 5.56-mm bullets break up in the body, the tip of the bullet tends to break off at the cannelure with the tip remaining relatively intact, while the lead core and the rest of the jacket shred (Figure 7.6 A–B). The triangular shape of the tip of the bullet often can be seen on x-ray.

The M-193 (55 gr.) version of the 5.56 × 45 mm cartridge has been replaced in U.S. military service with the M-885 cartridge. This is loaded with a 62-gr. bullet. The bullet has a compound steel/lead core with a small mild steel core in front of a larger lead core. Just like the 55-gr. bullet, the 62-gr. bullet begins to yaw widely shortly after entering the body. The bullet tends to break at the cannelure resulting in loss of lead core (a "lead snowstorm"); a relatively intact triangular tip and the residual copper jacketing (Figure 7.6 C–D).

Centerfire Rifle Wounds

Wounds from centerfire rifles may be classified as contact, intermediate, or distant. Contact wounds of the head are the most devastating, producing a bursting rupture of the head (Figure 7.7). Large irregular tears in the scalp radiate from the entrance site. Powder soot and searing are typically present at the entrance. Rarely, virtually no soot will be present.

In some contact wounds of the head, the entrance may be difficult to locate because of the massive destruction. Large pieces of the skull and brain are typically blown away, with pulpification of the residual brain in the cranial cavity. Pieces of scalp may be sheared off. The skull shows extensive comminuted fractures. Such wounding effects are due partly to the large quantities of gas produced by combustion of the propellant, emerging from the muzzle under high pressure. This gas begins to expand as soon as it emerges from the muzzle of the weapon. If the gun is held in contact with the head, this gas follows the bullet into the cranial cavity, producing an effect that can only be described as explosive. That the massive wounds produced are due partly to the gas can be deduced from cases of suicides in which the weapon used was equipped with a flash suppressor. This device, attached to the muzzle of military rifles, breaks up the "ball of fire" produced on firing a rifle at night, making the soldiers firing these weapons less susceptible to enemy counterfire. The flash suppressor disperses the gas emerging from the barrel through a number of slits in the sides of the suppressor. If an individual shoots himself with a weapon equipped with a flash suppressor, such that the end of it is in contact with the head, the flash suppressor will divert much of the gas emerging from the barrel before it has an opportunity to enter the cranial cavity. Thus, the wound produced by a weapon with a flash suppressor will be less severe than a wound produced by the same weapon without a flash suppressor. In contact wounds, the gas diverted by the flash suppressor may produce a characteristic pattern of searing and soot deposition (see Figure 4.13).

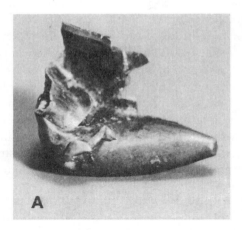

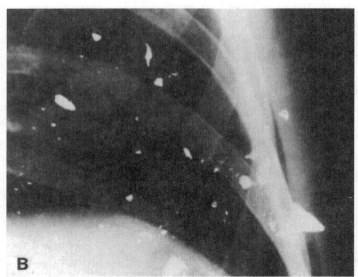

Figure 7.6 (**A**) Full metal-jacketed 55-gr. .223 bullet bent at cannelure. (**B**) "Lead snowstorm" resulting from 55-gr. full metal-jacketed .223 bullets; .223 bullet bent at cannelure can be seen on x-ray.

If a rifle is discharged in the mouth, massive wounds from the gas and the temporary cavity occur. Not uncommonly, lacerations of the corners of the mouth, the nasolabial folds, medial to the eyes, at the bridge of the nose and along the nasal ridge (Figure 7.8).

Contact wounds of the chest and abdomen do not have the dramatic external appearance of such wounds in the head. The wound of entrance is

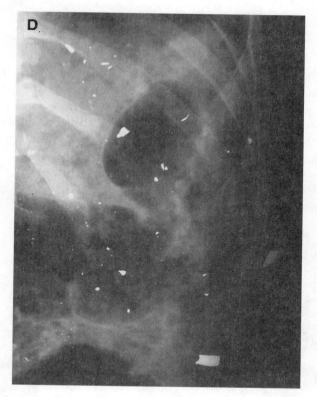

Figure 7.6 (continued) (C) Bullet tip and rectangular fragment of jacket; (D) "Lead snowstorm" 62-gr. bullet.

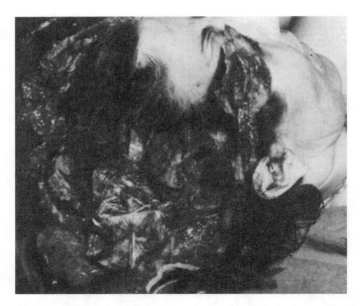

Figure 7.7   Homicidal contact wound of right temple from .30–30 rifle.

typically circular in shape and usually larger in diameter than those due to pistol bullets. There is almost never tearing of the skin due to gas. The edges of the wound are seared from the effect of the hot gases of combustion. Powder soot is deposited in and around the wound. The amount of soot, however, is less than that seen with most handguns. The imprint of the muzzle of the weapon is commonly present (Figure 7.9A). Such imprints are

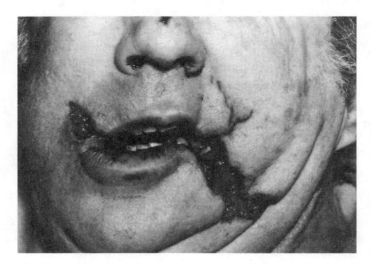

Figure 7.8   Tears at corners of mouth from intraoral gunshot wound.

due to the gas of combustion entering the chest and abdominal cavity, expanding in them, and slamming the chest or abdominal wall against the muzzle of the weapon. The fact that the whole wall is flung against the muzzle of the weapon by the gas, rather than just the skin as in head wounds, accounts for the fact that the skin is rarely torn. The outward moving chest or abdominal wall may envelop the muzzle to such a degree that the imprint of the front sight will be impressed on the skin even though the front sight is recessed a half inch from the muzzle of the weapon. In lever-action weapons with a magazine under the barrel, the imprint of the end of the magazine may be imparted to the skin (Figure 7.9A). While lacerations of the skin at the entrance in contact wounds of the chest and abdomen are rare, they do occur (Figure 7.9B).

In contrast to their benign external appearance, contact centerfire rifle wounds of the chest and abdomen produce massive internal injuries. The severe nature of these wounds, due to both the effects of the gas and the temporary cavity, literally pulpify organs, such as the heart and liver. In contact wounds of the thorax or abdomen, the musculature surrounding the entrance may show a cherry-red coloration due to the presence of large amounts of carbon monoxide in the propellant gases. This carbon monoxide may follow the missile through the body and may also be present in the muscle at the exit. In one case seen by the author, the concentration of carboxyhemoglobin in the muscle was greater at the exit than at the entrance.

In intermediate-range gunshot wounds, powder tattooing is present around the wound of entrance. Intermediate range and distant head wounds, show a wide range in the degree of severity, depending on the style of bullet and the entrance site in the head. Anything that tends to produce instability, deformation or breakup of the bullet as it enters the head results in more extensive injuries. Thus, bullets entering through the thick occipital bone cause greater injuries than those entering the temporal area. Intermediate and distant range wounds of the head can be just as devastating as contact wounds (Figure 7.10). This is especially true for hunting ammunition. As the hunting bullet rapidly expands, shedding fragments of core and sometimes jacket, large quantities of kinetic energy are lost in the cranial cavity. This produces a large temporary cavity with resultant high pressure, all within the rigid framework of the skull. The pressure produces extensive fragmentation of bone and brain tissue. Location of entrance and exit wounds may require extensive reconstruction of the skull, with careful realignment of the edges of the scalp and bone. Rarely, the entrance in the skin cannot be determined with absolute certainty. This is more common with exits, however.

Distant and intermediate-range entrance wounds in areas overlying bone—typically the head—may have a stellate appearance suggestive of a

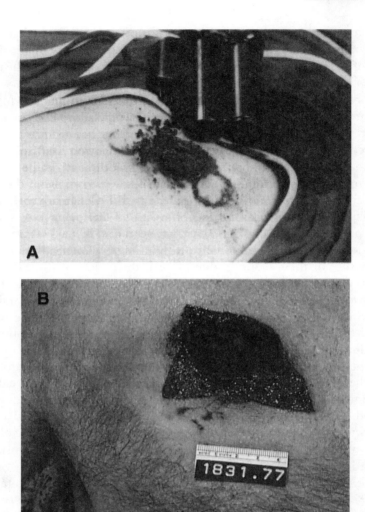

Figure 7.9 (A) Contact wound of chest from .30–30 rifle with muzzle imprint. (From DiMaio, V.J.M. *Clin. Lab. Med.* 3:257–271, 1983. With permission.) (B) Contact wound of chest with .30–06 with laceration of entrance.

contact wound (Figure 7.11). This is probably due to the temporary cavity ballooning out skin that is tightly stretched over bone, with resultant tearing of the skin.

Distant entrance wounds of the trunk inflicted by centerfire rifle bullets while often similar to those produced by handgun bullets, may differ by one or more of the following attributes: the abrasion ring around the entrance is narrower; the abrasion ring is absent; multiple small (less than 1 mm)

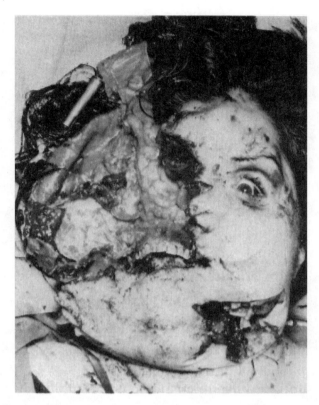

Figure 7.10 Centerfire rifle wound of right half of head from .30–30 rifle. Bullet entered in back of head; ejected cartridge case can be seen in hair. Second gunshot wound of left side of neck.

"micro-tears" radiate outward from the edges of the perforation. Micro-tears may or may not be found in association with an abrasion ring. Thus an entrance wound may appear as a round punched-out hole with micro-tears and no abrasion ring (Figure 7.12).

Distant entrance wounds of the lateral aspect of the thorax from approximately the mid-clavicular line to the posterior axillary line may be unusually large. Like most distant wounds they are circular in shape, but the diameter of the entrance perforation can be up to 1 in. (25 mm) in diameter from a .30 (7.62 mm) bullet. The cause of this is unknown.

Internal injuries of the trunk due to centerfire rifle bullets of hunting design, fired at intermediate and distant ranges are extremely devastating, with massive destruction and pulpification of the organs. This is due to temporary cavity formation, with its high-pressure effects. In distant wounds of the chest and abdomen, the thoracic or abdominal wall may be propelled

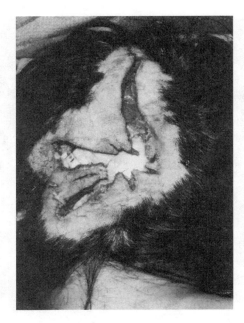

Figure 7.11   Large stellate distant wound of entrance in back of head from .30–30 rifle. (From DiMaio, V.J.M. *Clin. Lab. Med.* 3:257–271, 1983. With permission.)

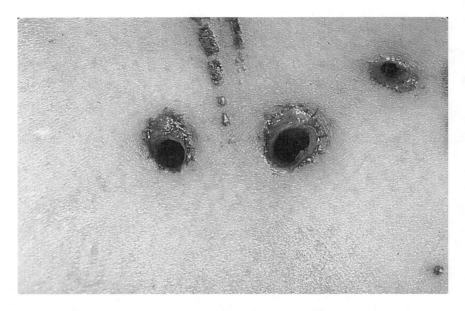

Figure 7.12   Entrance wounds of back from centerfire rifle. Note absence of abrasion ring and presence of microtears.

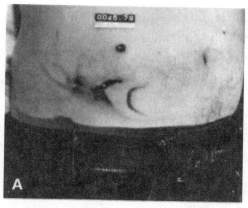

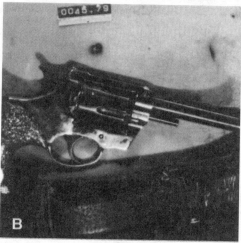

Figure 7.13 (A–B) Entrance wound from 7-mm Magnum rifle with patterned abrasions due to revolver tucked in waistband.

outward by the temporary cavity with such force that imprints of clothing or objects lying against the skin will be imparted to it (Figure 7.13).

Whatever the range, exit wounds of the chest and abdomen from centerfire rifle bullets all have the same appearance. They are larger and more irregular than the entrance wounds, with the majority of exit wounds 25 mm or less in diameter. The largest exit wound in the trunk that the author has seen measured 75 × 40 mm.

Powder Tattooing

The range out to which powder tattooing occurs from centerfire rifles depends on the physical form of powder in the cartridge cases. Two forms

Figure 7.14 Ball and cylindrical powder.

of powder are used in centerfire rifles cartridges manufactured in the U.S.: ball and cylindrical powder (Figure 7.14). A series of tests were carried out by the author on anesthetized rabbits. The chest and abdomen were shaved and the remaining hair was removed by depilatory cream. The rabbits were shot in the chest and abdomen at varying distances, using a Winchester Model 94 .30–30 rifle and a Remington 788, caliber .223, with a 24-inch barrel. Two brands of ammunition were used in each rifle. One was loaded with cylindrical powder, and the other had ball powder. The tests indicated that the maximum range at which powder tattooing occurs is different for the different forms of powder. For the .30–30 rifle, cartridges loaded with cylindrical powder produced heavy powder tattooing with deposition of soot at a range of 6 in. (15 cm). By 12 in. (30 cm) only a few scattered powder tattoo marks were present. No tattooing occurred at 18 or 24 in. (45 or 60 cm). Powder tattooing with ball powder extended out to 30 in. (75 cm), at which range it was present in moderate density. At a range of 36 in. (90 cm), ball powder no longer produced any tattooing (Table 7.3).

For the .223 rifle, cartridges loaded with cylindrical powder produced rare tattooing out to 12 in. (30 cm). By 18 in. (45 cm), no powder tattooing was present. Powder tattooing caused by ball powder was heavy at 18 in. (45 cm); scattered at 36 in. (90 cm) and absent at 42 in. (105 cm) (Table 7.3).

The skin of rabbits is thinner and more delicate than that of humans. Therefore, powder tattooing should theoretically occur out to greater maximum distances for rabbits than for humans. Thus, the data provided by these experiments should be considered only as a guide to the extreme maximum distances at which powder tattooing can occur.

Powder tattooing at greater ranges for ball powder compared with cylindrical powder is due to the shape of the powder grains. A sphere has a better

Table 7.3 Maximum Range Out to Which Tattooing Presents

Range (cm)	Cylindrical Powder	Ball Powder
Caliber: .30–30		
15	+++[a]	–
30	+	–
45	0	–
60	0	++
75	–	++
90	–	0
Caliber: .223		
15	+++	–
30	+	–
45	0	+++
60	–	–
75	–	++
90	–	+
105	–	0

[a] – = not tested. 0 = no tattooing. + = rare tattoo marks. ++ = moderate tattooing. +++ = dense tattooing.

aerodynamic form than a cylinder. Ball powder grains can travel farther with greater velocity, enabling them to mark the skin at a greater range.

Powder tattoo marks produced by these two different forms of powder have different appearances. The marks from ball powder are abundant and tend to be small, circular, and hemorrhagic (Figure 7.15A). Marks produced by cylindrical powder are larger, more irregular in shape and size, and relatively sparse in number compared with ball powder tattooing. Some markings have a linear configuration (Figure 7.15B). In tests, the number of tattoo marks from cylindrical powder at 6 in. was less than the number at 24 in. for ball powder.

Because rifles have long barrels, there is always the theoretical possibility that by pure chance a cartridge will be loaded with powder whose burning properties exactly match the length of the barrel. In such a case, essentially no unburnt powder will exit the muzzle. The author knows of only one case in which this situation occurred.* The weapon was a 30–06 Remington 760 pump-action rifle with a 22-inch barrel; the ammunition Remington 220 gr. Core-Lokt® loaded with cylindrical powder. On firing the weapon at a target six inches from the muzzle, no powder particles impacted the target material, though there was deposition of soot and some amorphous black residue. On firing a cartridge loaded with a 125-gr. bullet and cylindrical powder, grains of powder were deposited on the target as expected.

* Personal communication with Robert J. Shem.

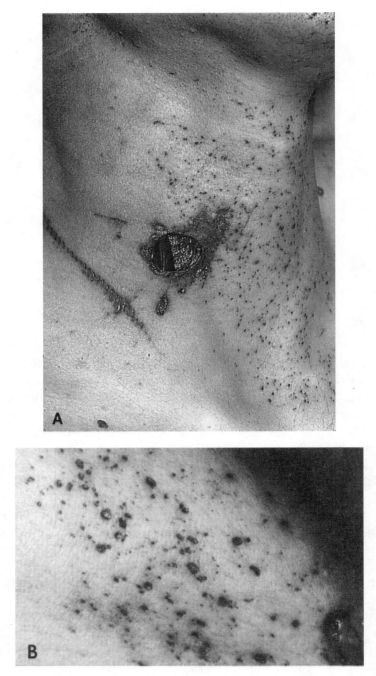

Figure 7.15 (A) Ball powder tattooing of neck with entrance wound and patterned abrasion from neck chain. (B) Tattooing of arm from cylindrical powder. (From DiMaio, V.J.M. *Clin. Lab. Med.* 3:257–271, 1983. With permission.)

X-rays

X-rays of individuals shot with hunting ammunition usually show a characteristic radiologic picture that is seen almost exclusively with this form of rifle ammunition—the so-called "lead snowstorm." As the expanding hunting bullet moves through the body, fragments of lead break off the lead core and are hurled out into the surrounding tissues. An x-ray shows scores, if not hundreds, of small radiopaque bullet fragments scattered along the wound track (the lead snowstorm) (Figure 7.16; see also Figure 11.4). These fragments vary from dust-like to large irregular pieces of metal. Occasional pieces of jacket may be seen. A rifle bullet does not have to hit bone for this phenomena to occur. This picture is not seen with handgun bullets, nor, with rare exception, with full metal-jacketed rifle bullets. Virtually, the sole exception with military bullets are the M-193 and M-885 5.56 × 45 mm cartridges with their 55- and 62-gr. bullets, whose propensity to fragment has been previously discussed (see Figure 7.6). Although the snowstorm appearance

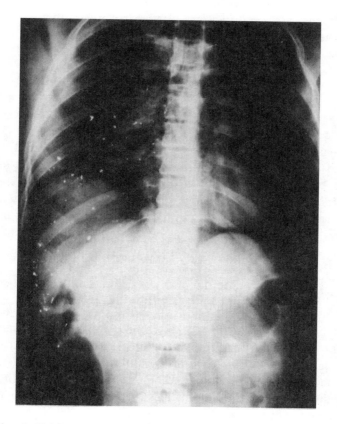

Figure 7.16 "Lead snowstorm" from .30–30 hunting bullet.

of an x-ray almost always indicates that the individual was shot with centerfire hunting ammunition, absence of such a picture does not absolutely rule out the possibility. The lead snowstorm from hunting ammunition is dependent on the velocity of the bullet. If a rifle bullet is traveling at a low velocity, either because of extreme range or having been slowed by passing through various other targets before striking an individual, x-rays will not show a lead snow-storm. It must be stressed that a rifle bullet does not have to hit bone for a lead snowstorm to occur.

A gunshot wound of the head from a high-velocity handgun bullet — typically the .357 Magnum — can produce an x-ray picture superficially resembling the lead snowstorm of hunting bullets. Breakup of the handgun bullet, however, requires perforation of bone which is not necessary with a rifle bullet. The fragments produced by the handgun bullet are fewer in number and larger. Lead dust is also not present (see Figure 11.5).

An x-ray of an individual shot with a full metal-jacketed rifle bullet, with the exception of the M-16 cartridge, usually fails to reveal any bullet fragments at all even if the bullet has perforated bone such as the skull or spine. If any fragments are seen, they are very sparse in number, very fine and located at the point the bullet perforated bone.

Perforating Tendency of Centerfire Rifle Bullets

Full metal-jacketed rifle bullets almost invariably exit if the deceased is the primary target and is within a few hundred yards of the muzzle of the weapon. The 5.56 × 45 mm round is the only full metal-jacketed round that has a tendency to stay in the body. Most hunting bullets of medium and large caliber also exit the body. Varmint cartridges such as the .222 or .22–250 tend to stay in the body. With a cartridge such as the .243, it depends on bullet weight, the area of the body struck and the length of the wound path.

Intermediary Targets

If a centerfire rifle bullet passes through an intermediary target, such as a wall or door, before striking an individual, the severity of the wound produced may be much greater than if the same bullet had not perforated the target. If the intermediary target is of sufficient thickness and resistance, the bullet will destabilize; be deformed or even break up. Such a bullet — when it strikes the victim — will more readily lose kinetic energy, thus, possibly increasing the severity of the wound. This is true even though the bullet has lost kinetic energy in piercing the intermediary target. This phenomenon is most pronounced in hunting bullets which because of their design and construction more readily deform and breakup. If multiple intermediary targets are perforated or if the intermediary target is very resistant, e.g., steel plates, the bullet may lose so much kinetic energy in passing through these targets that the wound has the characteristics of a handgun wound.

Almost invariably, the entrance produced by a bullet that has perforated an intermediary target is atypical in appearance with a large, irregular entrance hole surrounded by an irregular, non-symmetrical, often wide, abrasion ring. In passing through the intermediary target, the bullet, whether it be full metal-jacketed or hunting, may shed fragments of metal or even break up. If the individual is close to the intermediary target, they may be struck by fragments of the bullet and/or intermediary target. If the main mass of the bullet is intact and produces a single entrance, the skin around the entrance site may be "peppered" with small fragments of metal broken off the bullet and/or fragments of the target (Figure 7.17).

In some cases, in passing through the intermediary target the bullet breaks up. In the simplest scenario, the core and jacket separate producing

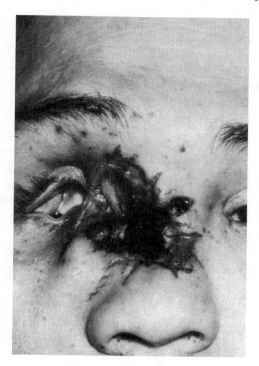

Figure 7.17   Large irregular entrance wound of the face from centerfire rifle bullet that passed through intermediate target. Stipple marks around entrance caused by fragments of bullet and intermediate target.

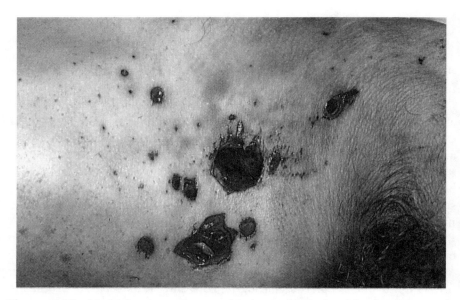

Figure 7.18 Multiple entrance wounds of top of left shoulder from .270 soft-point bullet that broke up after perforating wall boards. The two largest defects are the entrance sites of the core and jacket.

two entrances. More commonly, both the jacket and core are torn apart and multiple, sometimes scores, of fragments impact the skin. Figure 7.18 shows entrance wounds, on the top of the left shoulder, from a single .270 soft-point hunting bullet that passed through two layers of wallboard. The deceased was bending over at the time he was shot facing the wall perforated by the bullet. In passing through the wall, the core and jacket separated producing the two large entrances. Fragments of jacket and core produced the rest of the wounds. In Figure 7.19, the deceased was struck by two 7.62 × 39 mm full metal-jacketed bullets having steel jackets and lead cores. The bullets perforated the wall of a frame house and a sofa before striking the deceased. Both the jacket and core had fragmented prior to striking the deceased.

A bullet may carry large fragments of an intermediate target into the body. Figures 7.20 and 7.21 illustrate the case of an individual shot through an automobile car door with a .30–30 hunting rifle. The main mass of the bullet remained intact, penetrating into the chest and causing death. A small fragment of lead core also penetrated, with another fragment producing a superficial wound of the skin. In exiting the door, the bullet carried with it a large piece of steel, which in turn inflicted a fourth, penetrating wound. This piece of steel was recovered from the muscle of the side, not having penetrated into the chest cavity.

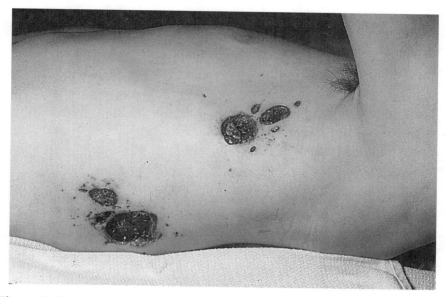

Figure 7.19 Two entrance wound complexes from two 7.62 × 39 bullets that broke up after perforating wall of house and sofa. Each entrance consists of a cluster of wounds from a fragmented bullet.

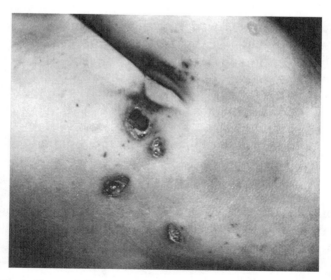

Figure 7.20 Bullet and shrapnel wounds of left side of chest from .30–30 rifle bullet that passed through car door.

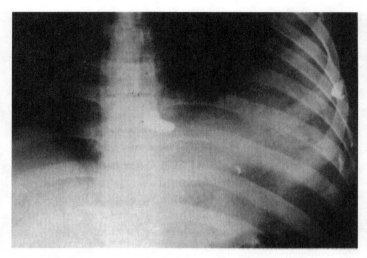

Figure 7.21 X-ray of chest showing bullet in midline with steel fragment in left side of chest.

Soot-Like Residues

If a bullet perforates an intermediary target of suitable resistance, the impact may be sufficient to vaporize lead from the core which is then propelled forward with the bullet. This lead can be deposited on a surface behind the entrance if the surface is in close enough proximity to the intermediary target. The lead deposit around the second entrance can simulate soot such that the wound is mistakenly interpreted as a contact or close range. This phenomena was described by Shem.[7] In his case, a .270 soft-point bullet perforated the sheet metal wall of the cab of a pickup truck before striking the driver. The bullet hole in the deceased's jacket was surrounded by vaporized lead simulating soot. Shem reproduced the same effect with a soft point .308 bullet. If the bullet had a full metal jacket, however, no deposit occurred.

In variance with this last observation in regard to full metal jacketed bullets, Dodson and Stengel reported a case of a full metal jacketed 7.62 × 39 bullet, that after perforating a window pane and a curtain behind the glass, deposited vaporized lead on the surface of the curtain facing the glass, i.e., the entrance side of the curtain.[8] They were able to reproduce the phenomena experimentally. The lead vapor around the entrance in the curtain apparently came from the exposed lead core at the base of the bullet.

A report by Messler and Armstrong described lead residue sprayed backward, rather than forward, when a bullet perforated a firm intermediary target.[9] The circumstance described was the reverse of that encountered by Dodson and Stengel. A rifle bullet perforated a window shade and then a pane of glass. A deposit of melted lead particles simulating soot was observed around the hole in the shade, but on its exit side, i.e., the side facing the glass. Thus, the bullet perforated the shade and then the glass, at which time melted lead particles were sprayed backward from the bullet onto the shade. This phenomena was reproduced experimentally for lead bullets and bullets with an exposed lead tip but not for Silvertip® or copper jacketed bullets.

Assault Rifles

The term "Assault Rifle" refers to an auto-loading rifle having a large capacity (20 rounds or more) detachable magazine, capable of full automatic fire and firing an intermediate rifle cartridge. This term has been corrupted by the media, politicians and the bureaucracy to include virtually all self-loading weapons that look "ugly" and/or "mean". Weapons that fire pistol ammunition, e.g., Intratec Tec-9's, Cobray M-11's, are not assault rifles by virtue of their firing pistol ammunition and that they were not designed for full-automatic fire. Nor are weapons that while firing an intermediate rifle cartridge have fixed magazines and were never intended for full automatic fire, e.g., the SKS-45. In the United States, civilian versions of true assault weapons, such as the AKS-47, MAK-90 and AR-15, that can only deliver semiautomatic fire, are widely available. Strictly speaking, these are also not assault rifles as they are designed for semi-automatic fire only. Conversion of these weapons to full-automatic fire capability is rare. Use of assault rifles in crimes is uncommon as they are not concealable.

The first true "Assault" ("Storm") rifle was the Sturmgewehr 44 (StG 44).[10,11] This rifle was developed as a result of the experience of the German Army in World War I. They wanted a short reliable rifle chambered for a mid-range (intermediate) cartridge. In 1938, the firm of Polte was given a contract to develop this cartridge while the firm of C.G. Haenel was awarded a contract for development of a weapon to fire it. The cartridge, the 7.9-mm Kurz Patrone (7.92 × 33 mm), completed development by late 1940–early 1941. The weapon, called a Maschinenkarabiner (machine carbine), completed initial development by 1940. The first prototype apparently appeared in late 1941. By July 1942, the first 50 test weapons were produced. In January 1941, Walther was also commissioned to develop a weapon. By July 1942, only two prototypes were developed. Mass production was to begin by Haenel in November 1942 and Walther in October. The Haenel weapon was designated the Maschinenkarabiner 42(H) and the Walther the Maschinenkarabiner 42(W). By February 1943, less than 2000 weapons of both types had been delivered. Also by this time, the Haenel design was selected over the Walther. Full-scale production of the Haenel weapon, now the MP 43, was begun in July 1943. The MP 43 was a simplified version of the MKb 42(H) with a modified gas system and the internal hammer firing system used on the Walther design. These weapons were first used by German troops on the Russian front in the winter of 1943. By January 1944, the Army had received more than 19,000 MP 43's. The name MP 43 was changed to Sturmgewehr 44 in late 1944. Total production of all weapons is estimated at approximately 425,000.

As can best be determined, in 1939, Russia began development of an intermediate-power rifle cartridge, probably independent of the work in Germany. The new cartridge the 7.62 × 39 mm was developed by 1943. The first weapon to utilize this cartridge was the SKS-45, a traditional semi-automatic rifle and not an assault rifle. The rifle synonymous with this cartridge, and which was to symbolize assault rifles throughout the last half of the 20th century, the Avtomat Kalashnikova Obrazets (AK-47) was adopted in 1949. It was not until 1957, that the first AR-15 chambered for the 5.56 × 45 mm cartridge was to appear and it was not until 1963 that the first "one-time" order was placed for this weapon by the United States Army. In the early 1970s, the AK-47 was replaced in the Russian Army with the AK 74 chambered for the 5.45 × 39-mm cartridge. Table 7.2 compares the assault rifle cartridges.

One of the common fallacies about assault rifles is that the wounds produced by them are more severe than those due to regular military rifles and hunting rifles. In fact, the wounds are less severe, even when compared to such venerable hunting rifles as the Winchester M-94 (introduced in 1894) and its cartridge the .30-30 (introduced in 1895).

In dealing with rifles, the severity of the wound is determined to a great degree by the amount of kinetic energy lost by a bullet in the body. The intermediate cartridges used in assault rifles possess significantly less kinetic energy than traditional military cartridges as well as rifle cartridges designed for hunting. Therefore, it is impossible for a intermediate-power rifle cartridge to produce severer injuries than a full-power rifle cartridge, all other factors being equal.

In the past few years, the author has had extensive experience with deaths due to the 7.62 × 39-mm cartridge loaded with full metal-jacketed bullets having either a mild steel core (standard Russian and Chinese military design) or a lead core. In a review of 50 cases involving this cartridge, the following observations were made:

1. All primary head wounds were perforating.
2. While entrance wounds of the head, and usually the exits, can easily be mistaken for wounds inflicted by handguns, internally, there are very severe injuries with multiple fractures of the skull and extensive lacerations of the brain. The severe nature of the internal injuries

clearly indicate that one is dealing with a centerfire rifle and not a handgun.

3. Tangential and shallow (superficial) perforating wounds of the head, are extremely mutilating. Evisceration of part or all of the brain is common. These wounds cannot be mistaken for handgun wounds.

4. In distant wounds of the trunk, the entrance wounds appear similar to small caliber handgun wounds. Exit wounds are variable in size, sometimes indistinguishable from those from handgun bullets, though at other times too large. The wounds to the internal organs (chest and abdomen) are often no more severe in appearance than those from 9 mm or .357 Magnum handgun bullets. In many cases, especially involving bullets with a mild steel core, after examining the wounds internally and externally, one can not say whether the individual was shot with a centerfire rifle or a handgun. The wounds are not anywhere as severe as those from hunting ammunition.

5. Most tangential wounds of the trunk, and some shallow (superficial) perforating wounds, are obviously too severe to be from handguns and thus have to be of rifle origin.

6. If the bullet has perforated an intermediary target, it may be retained in the body even if it does not appear deformed.

7. Wounds of the extremities are perforating. They usually cannot be differentiated from handgun wounds unless they are tangential.

That entry wounds of the skin from the 7.62 × 39-mm bullet are not different from wounds due to handgun bullets is not surprising. What is surprising is the relative innocuous appearance of the internal injuries to the trunk and extremities. The explanation for this has to due with the stability of the 7.62 × 39 bullet in the body. Most of the shootings seen by the author involved Chinese ammunition loaded with bullets having a full metal-jacket and a mild steel core. This construction is typical of military ammunition of this caliber. In ballistic gelatin testing, these bullets do not undergo significant yawing until 25 to 27 cm of penetration.[12] Thus, a 7.62 × 39-mm bullet with a mild steel core may pass through 25 to 27 cm of tissue, perforating vital organs, without production of a significant temporary cavity, with resultant injury no greater than that from a handgun bullet.

The M-16 rifle chambered for the 5.56 × 45 cartridge is considered by many to be more effective in its wounding ability than the AK-47. With either the 55 or 62-gr. full metal-jacketed military bullet, the average distance of penetration before significant yaw develops is 12 cm.[12] Thus, on an average, these bullets begin significant yawing in half the distance of penetration of the military AK-47 round (25 cm). The effectiveness of the 5.56 × 45 bullets is further enhanced by the fact that as the bullet reaches maximum yaw, it tends to deform and fragment while the 7.62 × 39 bullet with a mild steel core does not.

The 7.62 × 51 cartridge (.308) with a full metal-jacketed bullet begins to yaw after 15 cm of penetration. The yaw progresses until the bullet ends up traveling base forward.

Military Ammunition Converted to Sporting Ammunition

Ammunition loaded with full metal-jacketed bullets cannot be used for hunting in the United States. Some individuals have attempted to "sporterize" such ammunition by cutting or grinding off the tip of a full metal-jacketed bullet, exposing the core, in an attempt to facilitate expansion. This is potentially dangerous in that the base of such bullets is open. On firing, pressure of the gases of combustion on the exposed core may cause it to be propelled out the tip of the bullet with deposition of the jacket in the barrel. On firing the rifle a second time, the deposited jacket may cause the barrel to explode.

Plastic Wads in Rifle Bullets

Some Russian 7.62 × 39 hunting ammunition imported into the United States is loaded with bullets having a plastic base wad. The bullets have an overall spitzer configuration with an open tip (a hollow point) and an open base. The mild steel core of the military round has been replaced with a lead core. This core, however, does not extend the full length of the jacket so that the base is potentially empty. Into this base has been inserted a white plastic wad (Figure 7.22A). On entering the body, the bullets breakup producing a lead snowstorm (Figure 7.22B).

Addendum: Rifle Calibers

At present, at least 50 different caliber rifle cartridges are being manufactured in the United States. Some of these cartridges have been introduced recently, whereas others are almost obsolete with no weapons currently manufactured for them. Obsolete cartridges no longer manufactured are sometimes available from overseas sources as well as being manufactured by home reloaders or small specialized companies. Rifle cartridges that are not popular in the United States but are popular in other countries can be obtained from the overseas sources. A few of the more common centerfire rifle calibers will be described.

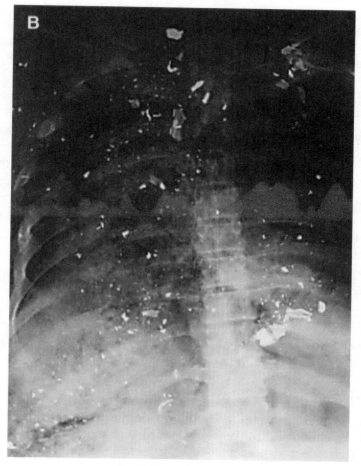

Figure 7.22 (A) Fired Russian 7.62 × 39 soft-point bullet with plastic wad extruding from base. (B) Chest x-ray of individual shot six times in chest with this ammunition and showing lead snowstorm.

.223 Remington (5.56 × 45 mm)

The .223 Remington cartridge was introduced in the Armalite AR-15 rifle (the precursor of the M-16) in 1957. It is the standard rifle caliber of the U.S. Army, having been adopted with the M-16A1 rifle in 1964. It is widely used overseas by other countries. The military cartridge was initially loaded with a 55-gr. full metal jacked boat-tail bullet (the M-193 Ball) with a muzzle velocity of approximately 3200 ft/sec. Muzzle energy is 1290 ft-lbs (1798 J). Civilian cartridges are loaded with either soft-point or hollow-point bullets weighing from 40 to 69 gr. These are used for varmint and small game hunting. In 1980, NATO adopted the SS109 cartridge loaded with a 62-gr. bullet. This has become the standard military loading in the United States where it is designated as the M855. The bullet has a mild steel core in front of a lead base core. Muzzle velocity is 3100 ft/s; muzzle energy 1325 ft-lbs (1680 J).

5.45 × 39

While firearms chambered for this cartridge are currently available in only small quantities in the United States, this cartridge deserves discussion because of its potential for worldwide use. It was introduced in the early 1970s for the AK-74 rifle which replaced the AK-47. The bullet weighs 53 gr. and has a steel jacket and a mild steel core with a short lead filler on top and an air space in the nose. Muzzle velocity is 2950 ft/s. Muzzle energy is 1045 ft-lbs (1383 J).

.243 Winchester (6.16 × 51 mm)

The .243 Winchester round was introduced in 1955. It is the .308 Winchester case, necked down to 6 mm. The round is intended for both varmints and deer hunting. It is loaded commercially with either an 85-gr. or a 100-gr. soft-point or hollow-point bullet. Muzzle velocity is 3320 and 2960 ft/sec; muzzle energy 2,080 and 1945 ft-lbs, respectively.

.270 Winchester

Introduced in 1925, this is the .30-06 cartridge necked down to 0.270 inches. It is a hunting caliber. It is generally loaded with 100, 130 or 150 gr. bullets with muzzle velocities from 3490 to 2850 ft/s and muzzle energies from 2612 to 2705 ft-lbs.

7-mm Magnum

Introduced in 1962, this cartridge has a belted case. It is a popular hunting round in the United States. Typical bullet weights are 139, 150, 165, and

175 gr. Corresponding velocities are 3150, 3110, 2950, and 2860 ft/sec. Muzzle energies range from 3063 to 3180 ft-lbs.

7.62 × 39

Introduced in 1943 by the then Soviet Union, it is the most widely used military cartridge in the world. The military round is loaded with a 122 gr. (7.91 g) full metal-jacketed bullet with a muzzle velocity of 2329 ft/s (710 m/s). Muzzle energy is 1470 ft-lbs (1993 J). Military rounds generally have a mild steel core encased in lead with a small lead core in front of the steel core.

.30 M-1 Carbine (7.62 × 33 mm)

The .30 M-1 Carbine cartridge is neither a rifle cartridge nor a pistol cartridge. The round was originally developed for the U.S. military M-1 Carbine. Commercially, this round is loaded with a 110-gr. soft- or hollow-point bullet. The military round is loaded with a 110-gr. (7 g) full metal-jacketed bullet. Muzzle velocity is around 1975 ft/s (579 m/s); muzzle energy 955 ft-lb (1173 J). The M-1 Carbine should not be confused with the M-1 Rifle (the Garand), which was chambered for the .30–06 cartridge.

.30–30 Winchester

The .30–30 Winchester was the first small-bore smokeless powder sporting cartridge in the United States. It was introduced in 1895 for the Winchester Model 94. This round is essentially a deer cartridge. It is loaded with either 150- or 170-gr. hunting bullets. Muzzle velocity is 2390 and 2200 ft/s, respectively, and muzzle kinetic energy 1902 and 1827 ft-lbs, respectively. This is probably the more popular hunting round in the United States.

.30-06 Springfield (7.62 × 63 mm)

The .30-06 Springfield cartridge was adopted in 1906 as the official military cartridge of the U.S. Armed Forces. It was replaced by the .308 Winchester (7.62 × 51 mm) in the early 1950s. Hunting bullets loaded in it weigh 110, 125, 150, 180, and 220 gr. Full metal-jacketed military cartridges are available. Muzzle velocities range from 3370 to 2400 ft/sec, depending on the weight of the bullet. The M2 military ball round weighed 150 gr. (9.72 g). Muzzle velocity was 2740 ft/s; muzzle energy 2500 ft-lbs.

.308 Winchester (7.62 × 51 mm)

The .308 Winchester round was introduced in 1952. It is used in medium and heavy machine guns. Military bullets are full metal-jacketed and usually weigh 150 gr. Civilian rounds are loaded with 110-, 125-, 150-, 180-, and 200-gr. hunting bullets. In ballistic performance it is approximately equal to the .30–06 cartridge. Muzzle velocities range from 3180 to 2450 ft/sec. The standard military round is the M-80. It has a 150 gr. (9.72 g) bullet with a muzzle velocity of 2750 ft/s (838 m/s) and muzzle energy of 2520 ft-lbs (3276 J).

7.62 × 54R (7.62-mm Mosin-Nagent)

This rimmed cartridge was introduced in the Russian M1891 Mosin-Nagent rifle. Rifles chambered for this cartridge are almost all of Russian or former Soviet-bloc manufacture. This cartridge is comparable in performance to the .30–06. A typical loading would be a 150 gr. bullet with a muzzle velocity of 2850 ft/s.

References

1. Butler, D. F. *United States Firearms, The First Century 1776–1875.* New York: Winchester Press, 1971.

2. La Garde, L. A. *Gunshot Injuries.* New York: William Wood & Co., 1916.

3. Longmore, T. *Gunshot Injuries.* London: Longmans Green and Co., 1895.

4. Scott, R. *Projectile Trauma. An Inquiry into Bullet Wounds.* New York: Crown, (date).

5. Edwards, W. B. *Civil War Guns.* The Stackpole Co., Harrisburg, PA, 1962.

6. Fackler, M .L. Wound ballistics: a review of common misconceptions. *JAMA* 259 (18): 2730–2736, 1988.

7. Shem, R. J. The vaporization of bullet lead by impact. *AFTE Journal* 25(2):75–78, 1993.

8. Dodson, R. V. and Stengel, R. F. Recognizing vaporized lead from gunshot residue. *AFTE Journal* 27(1):43, 1995.

9. Messler, H. R. and Armstrong, W. R. Bullet residue as distinguished from powder pattern. *J. Forensic Sci.* 23(4):687–692, 1978.

10. Senich, P. R. *The German Assault Rifle 1935–1945.* Paladin Press. Boulder, CO. 1987.

11. *Submachine Guns,* Vol. 1, pp 1–12, Aberdeen Proving Grounds, July 1958.

12. Bowen, T. E. and Bellamy, R. F. (Editors) *Emergency War Surgery.* U.S. Government Printing Office. Washington, D.C., 1988.

Wounds from Shotguns

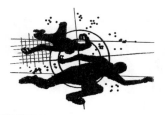

8

Shotguns differ from rifles and handguns in construction, ammunition, ballistics, and use. Rifles and handguns fire a single projectile down a rifled barrel. Shotguns have a smooth bore. Although they can fire a single projectile, they are usually employed to fire multiple pellets. Rifled shotgun barrels, intended for use with slugs, are available. Shotguns may be autoloaders, pump (slide action), over/unders, side-by-side, bolt action or single shot. Some shotguns intended for military and/or police use convert from semi-automatic to pump action and back as the user desires.

Barrel lengths of shotguns range from 18 to 36 inches with 26 and 28 in. the most common. Barrels 18 and 20 in. in length traditionally have been used only for police riot guns. With modern powders, barrel lengths greater than 18 and 20 in. produce only insignificant increases in velocity.[1] Longer barrels are really just a matter of tradition, styling, balance, or a desire for a longer sighting radius.

The usual shotgun barrel does not have a rear sight. It possesses only a small rudimentary front sight consisting of a small brass bead. With the increased use of shotguns in deer hunting, manufacturers are now producing shotgun barrels, 20 and 22 in. long, that are equipped with rifle sights as well as optional rifling.

A shotgun barrel is divided into three sections: the chamber, the forcing cone, and the bore.[1,2] The chamber is the portion of the barrel that encloses the shotgun shell. It is slightly larger in diameter than the bore. The chambers are cut to the exact full length of the unfold (fired) cartridge case. Between the chamber and the bore, there is a short, tapering section called the forcing cone. This section constricts the charge as it emerges from the shotgun shell, enabling the pellets to be pushed smoothly into the bore.

The archaic term "gauge" is used to describe the caliber of the shotgun.[1,2] This term refers to the number of lead balls of the given bore diameter that make up a pound. In 12-gauge for example, it would take 12 of the lead balls

to make 1 lb. The only exception to this nomenclature is the .410, which has
a bore 0.410 in. in diameter. The actual diameters of the most common
gauges are as follows:

| Gauge | Bore Diameter | |
	in.	mm
10	0.775	19.3
12	0.729	18.2
16	0.662	16.8
20	0.615	15.7
28	0.550	13.8
.410	0.410	10.2

These are, of course, the nominal bore diameters, as there can be a
variation of a few thousands of an inch due to mechanical operations. As the
bore size of the shotgun increases, so does the number of pellets that can be
loaded in the shot shell. This increase is important to a hunter, as the effectiveness of the shotgun depends on the accumulative effects of several pellets
hitting an animal rather than on a single wound by a single pellet. The most
popular gauge in the United States is the 12-gauge.

Most shotgun barrels have some degree of "choke," that is, a partial
constriction of the bore of a shotgun barrel at its muzzle so as to control
shot patterns. The choke may be permanent and built into the barrel or the
barrel may accept choke tubes that when screwed in the muzzle determine
the choke of the barrel. Choke constricts the diameter of the shot column,
increasing its overall length. The outer layers of shot are given inward acceleration as they pass through the area of constriction (the choke). This holds
the shot column together for a greater distance as it moves away from the
muzzle.

Different degrees of choke will give different spreads for a particular
shotgun charge and range. The tighter the choke, the smaller the pattern of
pellets. The usual degrees of choke in descending order are full, modified,
improved cylinder, and cylinder. The degree of choke is based on the percentage of pellets that will stay inside a 30-in. circle at 40 yd. The only
exception to this is the .410 shotgun, in which the pattern of shot is determined at 25 yd in a 20-in circle. In determining the spread of the shot
patterns, whether on paper or on the body, one must exclude "fliers," i.e.,
pellets deformed in the bore that stray from the main pattern.

The following table gives the percentage of shot that can be expected in
the various choke borings:

Choke	Percentage at 40 yards in 30-in. circle
Full choke	65–75
Modified choke	45–55
Improved cylinder	35–45
Cylinder	25–35

If one examines the table, one sees that a full-choke weapon is supposed to deliver a 65 to 75% pattern.[1] In fact, with modern ammunition, it may actually deliver a higher percentage of shot in a 30-in. circle because of improvements in shot shell design. Plastic wads, redesign of composite wads, and plastic envelopes for shot have resulted in an increase in percentage of shot delivered to the 30-in. circle, i.e., "a tighter" grouping of pellets. In a full-choke weapon, large shot sizes such as BB's or #2 shot may give 75 to 85% shot patterns.[2] This improvement in pattern performance is true for all chokes. It decreases with small shot sizes, however, so that for a No. 9 shot there is no improvement in patterning. The size of a shot pattern can also be influenced by the brand of ammunition.

In barrels with permanent choke, the chokes may start anywhere from 1 to 6 in. from the end of the barrel. They may end flush with the barrel or 1/2 to 1 in. before it. The amount of constriction, i.e., choke, is relative to the actual bore diameter of the gun, which, as mentioned, may vary a few thousands of an inch. In a 12-gauge shotgun with a 0.725-in. diameter, a full choke barrel has a diameter at the muzzle of approximately 0.694.[2]

In theory, the cylinder bore has no choke. In practice, however, gun companies put some degree of choke in these barrels because a true cylinder bore throws patterns that are irregular in density and shape and have "holes" in them. Addition of 0.003 to 0.005 in. of constriction will make the pattern round with a more even density of shot.

Unlike rifles or pistols, many shotguns have barrels that are easily removable, so that an individual may have one shotgun but a number of barrels of different choke. Over-and-under and double-barrel shotguns often have a different choke for each barrel. Most shotguns now manufactured accept choke tubes that when screwed into the muzzle of the shotgun barrel change the choke of the barrel. Some older shotguns were equipped with polychokes. These devices were installed at the end of the barrel and permit an individual to go from one choke to another simply by turning a sleeve.

There is one common area of confusion concerning gauge and choke. No matter what the gauge, weapons of identical choke produce approximately the same size patterns at the same range. The pattern will differ only in density. A full-choke barrel, whether 12-gauge or 20-gauge, should put 65 to 75% of the pellets in a 30-in. circle at 40 yd. The only difference is that the 12-gauge shotgun, with its greater number of pellets, will put more of these in the same area. Thus, assuming the same barrel length, choke, pellet size, and range, there should be no difference in the size of the patterns thrown by weapons of different gauges (with the exception of the .410).

Shotgun Ammunition

From the late nineteenth century until fairly recently, shotgun shells were constructed basically the same way. They consisted of a paper body (the tube); a thin brass or brass-coated steel head; a primer; powder; paper, cardboard or composition wads, and lead shot (Figure 8.1A).

The wads were of four types (Figure 8.1B). First was the base wad which was compressed paper or other material and was located inside the shotgun shell at its base. Its purpose was to fill up the space in the shell not occupied by the propellant powder. This wad was not expelled on firing. The overpowder wad was between the propellant and the filler wads. The overpowder wad was a disk of cardboard that acted as a gas seal and prevented contamination of the powder by grease from the filler wads. The filler wads lay in between the overpowder wad and the shot. The filler wads acted to seal the bore when the shotgun was fired, keeping the gas behind the pellets. In addition, they cushioned the shot against the blast of hot gases, preventing deformation, fusion, and melting of the pellets. Filler wads were greased so that they would lubricate and clean the bore as they moved down it. The mouth of the shotgun shell was closed by a thin cardboard disk—the overshot wad—with the edge of the mouth turned down over this wad in what was called a "rolled crimp."

The brass head of the shell has a rim on it. This rim aids in extraction and head spacing of the shell. In the latter function it prevents the case from moving too far forward into the shotgun chamber.

Until 1960 shotgun tubes were made of paper. In 1960, Remington introduced their SP shell (Figure 8.2a).[3] This shell had a polyethylene tube, a brass-plated steel head, and a non-integral base wad, made from an asbestos-like material molded to shape under pressure. In 1972, Remington introduced their plastic RXP shell, which has a solid head section, i.e., an integral base wad that is continuous with the tube wall.[3] Originally used only in the Remington skeet and trap loadings (Figure 8.2b), it is now the standard shell for all Remington shotgun ammunition replacing the SP shell.

Winchester introduced two types of plastic shot shells in 1964.[3] One was a shell with a corrugated or ribbed tube surface and a non-integral base wad.

Figure 8.1 (A) Traditional shotgun shell with paper tube, brass head, powder, cardboard over-the-powder wad, filler wads, shot, and an over-the-shot wad. (B) Disassembled traditional shotgun shell showing wadding.

This shell was subsequently phased out. The other plastic hull was produced by a combination of injection molding and die forming. There is no separate base wad, with the head section being of solid plastic and continuous with the walls (Figure 8.2c). The Federal Ammunition Company introduced plastic tubes in 1965.[3]

Although most shotgun shells are now made with plastic tubes, some manufacturers still produce shells with paper tubes. In fact, some competitive skeet and trap shooters prefer such paper tube shells.

Standard shot shells in 12, 16, 20, and 28 gauges are 2 3/4 in. (70 mm) long. This measurement is taken when the case has been fired, i.e., with the crimp unfolded. Unfired, the shells are approximately 1/4 in. (6.2 mm) shorter.

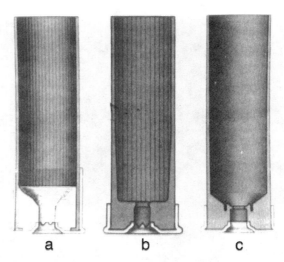

a   b   c

Figure 8.2   (a) Remington SP shell; (b) Remington RXP shell; and (c) Winchester shot shell.

Magnum shotgun shells in 12, 16, and 20 gauges come in the standard 2 3/4-in. (70 mm) length as well as a 3-in. (76 mm) version in the case of 12 and 20 gauge. The standard-length Magnums can be fired in strong modern guns, whereas the 3-in. shell is usable only in guns especially chambered for these rounds. The standard length shell presently manufactured for the 10 gauge is 3 1/2-in. (89 mm). There is no Magnum shell for the 28 gauge. The .410-gauge shells come in 2 1/2 (63.5 mm) and 3 in. (76 mm) length. The longer shell contains a little more extra shot. It is not called a Magnum, however.

The term "Magnum" in regard to rifle and handgun cartridges implies a larger cartridge, more propellant and a higher muzzle velocity. When speaking of Magnum shotgun shells, this is only partly true. Magnum shotgun shells contain more propellant; a heavier charge of shot; may or may not be longer, but they do not produce higher velocities. Rather, the heavier powder charge is used to propel the increased load of pellets at standard velocities. Magnum shells typically have a high brass head.

In 1961, Federal began the introduction of color coding of its shotgun shells.[3] At present, Federal shotgun shells are red in 12 gauge, yellow in 20 gauge, and purple in 16 gauge. Remington and Winchester-Western color code their 20-gauge shells yellow; this color coding is done to prevent using the wrong gauge ammunition in a weapon. Use of a 20-gauge shell in a 12 gauge is particularly dangerous. If a 20 gauge shell is inserted in a 12 gauge shotgun chamber, it will slide down into and lodge in the barrel. If a 12-gauge round is then inserted into the weapon and the gun is fired, the 20-gauge round will blow up in the barrel.

Figure 8.3 Low-brass and high-brass shotgun shells.

Shotgun shells often are spoken of as being either low-brass or high-brass, depending on how high the brass head extends up the length of the tube (Figure 8.3). Whether a shotgun shell is high or low brass is not an indication of the volume or strength of a shell. A high head is associated with heavy or Magnum loads; a low head with light field or target loads.

Currently manufactured shotgun shells have brass or brass-plated steel heads. It is possible to produce all-plastic shotgun shells without a metal head. In fact, such shells have been marketed, though unsuccessfully. Other apparently all-plastic cases, e.g., ACTIV, have an internal steel disc in the head to reinforce the rim of the shell and the primer pocket. Winchester states that its compression plastic hull is strong enough to be fired without the metal head, though they do not recommend this.[3]

By virtue of its design, the traditional shotgun shell had a number of defects. On firing, some of the hot gases from burning powder were able to bypass the over powder and filler wads and reach the shot charge. Here the hot gases partially melted and fused together a number of pellets. In addition to this problem, the rapid acceleration of the shot charge caused pellets at the bottom of the charge to be "welded" together by the pressure into small clumps. Furthermore as the charge moved down the barrel, pellets on the outer edge of the charge that were in direct contact with the barrel were flattened, as a result of both pressure and friction. Thus, by the time the pellets emerged from the barrel, only the central core of pellets, excluding those at the base, were round and undamaged. These undamaged pellets flew "true" toward the target, whereas the damaged pellets and clumps of pellets veered off at varying angles. These are the "fliers" seen in all shotgun patterns.

Another impairment to a good pattern was the overshot wad. This was supposed to slide off to one side of the shot column as it emerged from the barrel. This did not always happen, and the overshot wad sometimes fell into the shot column, disrupting it.

In an attempt to overcome these defects, ammunition manufacturers introduced a number of innovations. The first major change in shotgun shell design was the elimination of the rolled crimp and the overshot wad.[3] This was accomplished by introducing the "pie" crimp. In this procedure, closure of the paper shot shell was accomplished by having the tube folded in a number of equal segments and compressed inwardly to cover the shot column. Thus, the overshot wad was no longer necessary. Federal uses an eight-segment crimp in its plastic shells and a six-segment crimp in its paper shells.

The second innovation was the introduction by Winchester of the "cup" wad. This is a cup-shaped paper overpowder wad whose cupped surface faced the powder. On ignition of the powder, the gas produced drives the lips of the cup outward, producing a gas-tight seal against the inner wall of the tube. The cup wad was so effective that it became possible to reduce the charge of powder in the shotgun shells yet obtain the same ballistic performance. Cup wads are used in most of the shotgun ammunition loaded by Winchester-Western.

In 1962, Winchester introduced the shot protective sleeve, or plastic shot collar.[3] This consists of a rectangular strip of plastic surrounding the shot charge. The collar acts to eliminate the abrasive-type damage that occurs as the pellets move down the barrel. The use of such a shot collar eliminates lead fouling of the bore and increases the density of shotgun patterns. Plastic shot collars are used in most Winchester shotgun shell loadings. Figure 8.4 illustrates a typical present-day Winchester field load incorporating the cup wad, filler wads and a plastic shot collar.

In 1963, Remington introduced the Power Piston®.[3] The Power Piston® is a one-piece plastic assemblage that provides a cup wad for sealing, a resilient spring center to cushion the acceleration of the shot and a polyethylene cup to prevent the shot from rubbing against the inner wall of the barrel (Figure 8.5). The Powder Piston® eliminates the overpowder wad, the filler wads, and the need for a shot collar. On firing, the gas of propulsion expands the lips of the cup-shaped base outward, providing a gastight seal against the inner wall of the shot shell case. The gas moves the cup wad forward, compressing the plastic spring center between the cup wad and the shot. The Powder Piston® and the shot begin to move forward, breaking the seal at the mouth of the shotgun shell. The shot charge is accelerated down

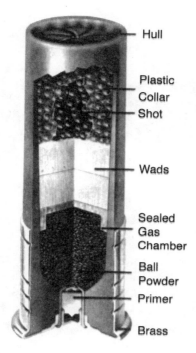

Hull

Plastic
Collar
Shot

Wads

Sealed
Gas
Chamber

Ball
Powder

Primer

Brass

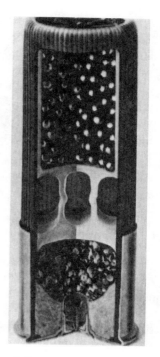

Figure 8.4 Cross-section of present-day Winchester birdshot shell. (Courtesy of Winchester-Western.)

Figure 8.5 Cross-section of present-day Remington birdshot shell.

the barrel, protected from contact with the barrel wall by the polyethylene cup and cushioned against the acceleration by the central spring section. The Power Piston® has four longitudinal slits the length of the shot container, dividing the walls of the container into four sections or "petals." As the wad assemblage containing the shot emerges from the barrel, the air pressure acts on the petals, bending them backward and releasing the shot (Figure 8.6). The wad then quickly falls away. Remington Power-Piston® wads are found in different colors apparently due to subcontracting of manufactures. There is apparently no significance to the different colors. Remington uses a variant of the Power-Piston® in some shells where the central portion has a "figure 8"-shaped configuration.

One slightly different approach to the plastic wad construction is the wad assemblage of the Federal Ammunition Company. In 1968, they introduced the two piece Triple-plus® wad column (Figure 8.7).[3] This consists of an all-plastic assemblage, made up of a gas-sealing overpowder wad with an integral plastic pillar that acts as a shock absorber (the pillar crushes on firing) and a plastic shot cup that is separate from the plastic wad.

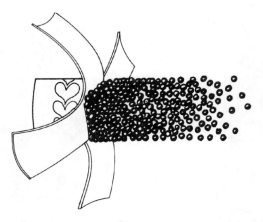

Figure 8.6   Power-Piston® opening up on leaving barrel.

Plastic wads similar to the Power Piston® are now produced by all the major U.S. shotgun shell manufacturers and used in some of their various loadings. Winchester and Federal use a single all-plastic wad with a collapsible central portion in their trap and skeet loads. .410 shells produced by Winchester, Remington, and Federal use plastic shot cups.

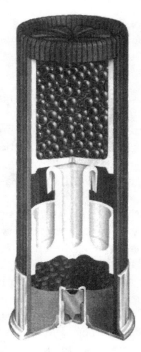

Figure 8.7   Cross-section of Federal birdshot shell.

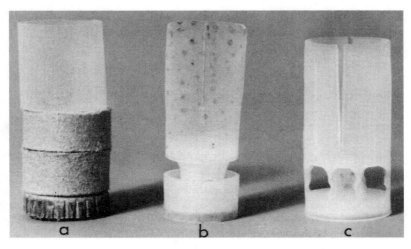

Figure 8.8 Wadding used in (a) Winchester, (b) Federal, and (c) Remington birdshot loads.

Figure 8.8 shows the wadding used in most shot shells manufactured by Winchester, Federal, and Remington. This wadding is not used in shells loaded with buckshot, slugs, or some trap and skeet loadings. It should be understood that manufacturers periodically change the wadding used in their shells, so that many variants exist on the "usual" loading.

In spite of all the new designs in shotgun shells, traditionally constructed shells containing felt or composition filler wads and shells with overshot wads still are manufactured and marketed. In addition, shells manufactured years, even decades ago are still around and may be encountered. Ammunition 40, 50 or more years old is still reliable as long as it was not exposed to extremes of temperature and humidity. This is true for rifle and handgun ammunition as well.

While recovery of a 20-gauge shotgun wad from a body should indicate that the deceased was shot with a 20-gauge shotgun there is an exception. Federal has used a 20-gauge filler wad, inserted in the bottom of a 12 ga plastic shot cup, to prevent low center crimps. Thus, an individual shot with such ammunition may present with both a 12-gauge plastic wad and a 20-gauge filler wad.[4]

In 1963, Winchester-Western began loading their buckshot shells with buckshot packed in granular white polyethylene filler (Figure 8.9).[3] This filler cushions the shot pellets on firing, reducing shot distortion and improving the shot pattern. Remington soon followed Winchester's lead. By the late 1970s, Winchester, Remington, and Federal were loading Magnum birdshot shells with granulated white filler. Filler is now available to handloaders. At

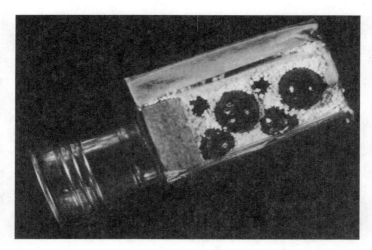

Figure 8.9 Winchester buckshot load showing buckshot packed in granulated white polyethylene filler.

close range, this filler can cause stippling (pseudo-tattoo marks) on the skin that can be mistaken for powder tattooing. This phenomenon will be discussed subsequently.

The white filler used in Winchester ammunition is polyethylene, whereas that in Remington is polypropylene. Federal uses both polyethylene and polypropylene, with the latter the most widely used at present.

Examination of a box of shotgun ammunition and sometimes individual shot shells will reveal a series of three numbers such as 3 3/4 – 1 1/4 – 7 1/2. The last number, e.g., 7 1/2, refers to the size of the individual shot pellets; the middle number, e.g., 1 1/4, indicates the weight of the shot charge in ounces. The first number indicates the "dram equivalent" of the particular shell. This is an obsolete term that indicates the comparative power of a shotgun shell loaded in relationship to black powder loads. When black powder was used in shotgun shells, the relative power of the shell was indicated by listing the number of drams of black powder loaded in each shell. The more drams loaded, the more powerful the loading. Modern smokeless powder is rated in dram equivalents. Thus, a certain loading of a shotgun shell will be said to have a dram equivalent value of 3. This indicates that the charge of powder in this shell will drive the charge of shot to approximately the same velocity as 3 drams of black powder. The dram equivalent rating bears no relation to the amount of smokeless powder in the shotgun shells; thus, two shotgun shell cartridges loaded with the same weight and size shot can have the same dram equivalent rating with different quantities of smokeless powder.

Shot

Three general types of lead shot have been made: drop or soft shot, which is essentially pure lead; chilled or hard shot, which is lead hardened by the addition of antimony, and plated shot. The last is lead shot coated with a thin coat of copper or nickel to minimize distortion on firing, thereby maintaining a good aerodynamic shape and increasing the range. Winchester-Western sells their copper plated shot under the trade name of Lubaloy® shot.

A fourth category of shot is now widely available. This includes steel, bismuth, and tungsten shot. These were produced because of government regulations prohibiting use of lead shot for migratory bird hunting. In the case of steel shot, the pellets are made of softened steel; weigh less than comparably sized lead pellets, lose velocity quicker and thus have less range. Steel shot may be copper plated or in the case of Remington zinc galvanized. Winchester manufactures shells loaded with bismuth pellets; Federal tungsten-iron and tungsten-polymer pellets.

Shotgun pellets fall into two general categories: birdshot and buckshot. Birdshot is used for birds and small game; buckshot is used for large game such as deer. Shot size generally ranges from #12 to 000 Buck. The smaller the shot number, the greater the pellet diameter. Table 8.1A gives the diameter, weight, and number of pellets per ounce for various lead birdshot pellet sizes; Table 8.1B, the diameter and pellets per ounce for steel shot.

Table 8.1A   Standard Lead Birdshot: Sizes and Weights

No.	Diameter (in.)	Average Weight of Pellets (grains)	(milligrams)	Approximate Number per ounce
12	.05	.18	11	2385
11	.06	.25	19	1750
9	.08	.75	49	585
8 1/2	.085	.88	57	485
8	.09	1.07	69	410
7 1/2	.095	1.25	81	350
6	.11	1.95	126	225
5	.12	2.58	167	170
4	.13	3.24	210	135
2	.15	4.86	315	90
BB	.18	8.75	567	50

Birdshot

The smallest lead birdshot is #12, which has a diameter of 0.05 in. (1.27 mm); the largest, commonly encountered, is BB shot — 0.18 in or 4.57 mm

Table 8.1B   Standard Steel Birdshot

No.	Diameter (in.)	Approximate Number per ounce
7	.10	422
6	.11	315
5	.12	243
4	.13	192
3	.14	158
2	.15	125
1	.16	103
BB	.18	72
BBB	.19	62
T	.20	52
F	.22	37

(Table 8.1A). BB shot should not be confused with the copper-coated steel BB's used in airguns. Airgun BB's have a diameter of 0.175 in. (4.44 mm).

The size of the shot in a shotgun shell usually is printed on the side of the tube. In shells where there is an overshot wad, the size of the shot may be printed upon this wad. Some shells are also marked with the weight of the shot charge and the dram equivalent. The number of pellets in such a shell can be determined by consulting tables such as Table 8.1A and B. Thus, a shell loaded with 1 oz of #7 1/2 lead shot contains approximately 350 pellets.

Theoretically, a shot shell loaded with #7 1/2 shot should contain only pellets of this size. However, if one cuts open enough of these shells, one will find an occasional shell inadvertently containing a few pellets of a different size, either one shot size larger or one size smaller. The vast majority of the pellets, however, will be #7 1/2. Remington produces what are called Duplex® shotshell cartridges. These are loaded with birdshot of two sizes e.g., BB and #2; #2 and #6; #7 1/2 and #8, etc.

Buckshot Ammunition

There are three major manufacturers of buckshot ammunition in the United States: Remington-Peters, Winchester-Western, and Federal. Smith & Wesson produced shotgun buckshot shells for a short time in the early 1970s.

Buckshot is usually manufactured in seven sizes, ranging from No. 4 (0.24 in.) to 000 (0.360 in.). With buckshot ammunition, the number of pellets loaded into the shell is stated rather than the weight of the charge. Table 8.2 gives the diameter and weight of various sizes of buckshot pellets.

In 1963, Winchester-Western began loading their shotgun shells with buckshot packed in a white, granulated, polyethylene filler material

Table 8.2 Buckshot: Sizes and Weights

No.	Diameter		Average Weight of Pellets	
	(in.)	(mm)	(grains)	(grams)
4	.24	6.10	20.6	1.32
3	.25	6.35	23.4	1.50
2	.27	6.86	29.4	1.87
1	.30	7.62	40.0	2.57
0	.32	8.13	48.3	3.12
00	.33	8.38	53.8	3.42
000	.36	9.14	68.0	4.44

(Figure 8.9). This filler cushions the shot on firing, reducing shot distortion and improving patterns. The shot and filler material are enclosed in a plastic shot collar. The end of the tube is closed with a "pie" crimp. Most Winchester buckshot loads seen by the author contain the filler, the plastic shot collar, filler wads, and a cardboard cup wad.

In 1967, Remington began loading their shells with buckshot packed in a black, granulated polyethylene material. In October 1978, however, Remington changed to a white polyethylene filler similar to that of Winchester. Current buckshot loads by Remington-Peters contain a white polypropylene filler material and either a plastic "H" wad used in the overpowder position or a plastic shot-cup.

Federal buckshot loads contain a white packing material, usually polypropylene and are closed with a pie crimp. In the past, no filler was used and the shells were closed with a thin plastic disk over-the-shot wad.

Absence of filler material is preferred by some police agencies, because if a shotgun is carried in a car, the constant stop-and-go action of the vehicle can cause the buckshot to force open a "pie" crimp. This results in the granulated filler material coming out, entering, and possibly jamming the shotgun action.

The granulated filler is of interest to the forensic pathologist in that on firing ammunition loaded with it large quantities of filler are propelled toward the target (Figure 8.10). This filler becomes adherent to clothing and skin. At close ranges, it can produce stipple marks (pseudo-tattooing) on the skin identical in appearance to powder tattoo marks. Marks from the filler can vary from large and irregular, to small and regular, depending on the size and shape of the individual granules. The white filler in Winchester shells has changed in form over the years. Older shells contain large coarse granules that produce large irregular marks on the skin (Figure 8.11A). These marks should not be mistaken for powder tattooing under usual circumstances. Newer ammunition contains fine white granules that produce marks virtually identical to powder tattooing(Figure 8.11B). The black filler formerly used

Figure 8.10 Buckshot pellets traveling through air, accompanied by white polyethylene filler.

in Remington 12-gauge buckshot shells was very fine and produced marks similar to powder. Because the filler was black, it was mistaken for powder by the unwary. Remington always loaded their 20-gauge buckshot with white filler, possibly because of the translucent hull used for 20 gauge. All Remington buckshot is now loaded with finely granular white material. Federal uses a fine white filler as well.

For a time Smith & Wesson produced 12-gauge buckshot loads. These shells were loaded with what appears to be chopped up blue plastic casing material. The marks produced by it are relatively large and irregular.

Winchester, Remington, and Federal now load Magnum birdshot loads with polyethylene or polypropylene filler. In all shells seen by the author the filler has consisted of fine white granules. Filler is also available to reloaders.

Animal experiments have shown that with a 12-gauge shotgun, stippling caused by filler extends out to a greater distance than powder tattooing. Although tattooing can extend out to a maximum of one (1) meter, stippling from filler material can extend out to 2 to 3 m of range. The white filler can be deposited on a body out to a maximum of 6 to 8 yd.[5]

The most popular buckshot load in this country is a 12-gauge 2 3/4 shell loaded with 9-00 Buck pellets. Some police agencies, however, have begun using either #1 or #4 Buck, as they feel that these loadings give a denser and more even pattern with a greater probability of a hit (Table 8.3).

Shotgun Slugs

Shotgun slugs are used for deer and bear hunting in heavily populated areas where the slug's rapid loss of velocity allegedly affords greater protection from shooting mishaps. Three types of shotgun slugs are on the market: the European Brenneke; the American Foster and the Sabot (Figure 8.12).

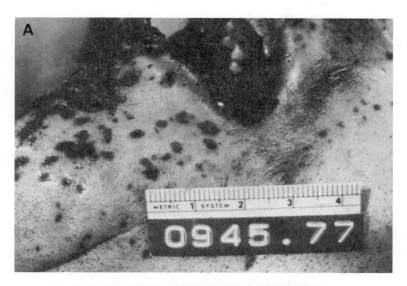

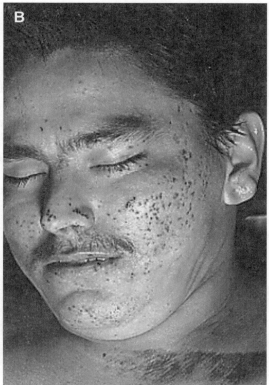

Figure 8.11 **(A)** Large, irregular stipple marks of face caused by coarse, white polyethylene filler loaded in early Winchester buckshot loads. **(B)** Fine stippling due to fine plastic filler.

Table 8.3 Buckshot Loads

Gauge	Length of Shell inches	(mm)	Shot Size	No. of Pellets
10	3 1/2	(89)	00	18
12	3 1/2	(89)	00	18
	3	(76)	000	10
			00	15
			1	24
			4	41
	2 3/4	(70)	000	8
			00	12
			00	9
			0	12
			1	20
			1	16
			4	34
			4	27
16	2 3/4	(70)	1	12
20	3	(76)	2	18
			3	24
	2 3/4	(70)	3	20

The Brenneke slug was developed in Germany in 1898. It is a solid lead projectile having a pointed nose with felt and cardboard wads attached to the base by a screw. Approximately 12 angled ribs are present on the surface of the slug. The longer profile provided by the wad allegedly decreases tumbling and improves accuracy. Brenneke slugs, originally rare in the United States, are now being imported in quantity. Nominal slug weights, including felt and cardboard wads, are 491 gr. in 12 gauge, 427 gr. in 16 gauge, and 364 gr. in 20 gauge. The weight of the slug will vary somewhat depending on

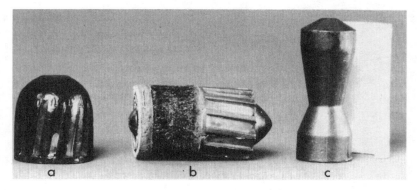

Figure 8.12 Shotgun slugs: (a) Foster, (b) Brenneke, and (c) Smith & Wesson sabot.

the country of manufacture. The advertised muzzle velocity ranges from 1593 ft/sec in 12 gauge to 1513 ft/sec in 20 gauge. The diameter of a 12-gauge slug, measuring from the top of one rib to the other, is 18.47 mm (0.727 in.) and 16.13 mm (0.635 in.), from groove to groove.

The Foster slug, introduced by Winchester in 1936, is considered the traditional American shotgun slug. It is a roundnose soft lead projectile, with a deep, concave base, and has anywhere from 12 to 15 angled, helical grooves cut into its surface. This slug is produced in a hollow-point version. The hollow-point cavity serves no purpose in the author's opinion in increasing the effectiveness of the slug. The Remington slug may have a plastic insert in its tip. Slugs manufactured by Federal have a one-piece plastic wad; Winchester's having a cup wad and cardboard (paper) filler wads — the one next to the slug being thinner and harder. Remington uses a combination of plastic and cardboard wads. Variations on these construction designs will be encountered as the type of wadding always seems to be in flux.

Both the Brenneke and Foster slugs employ the same principle to stabilize their flight. In both, most of the weight of the slug is forward of the center, thus causing them to fly point forward. The lead grooves or ribs cause the slug to slowly rotate on its long axis as it flies through the air increasing stability. This slow rotation, combined with the balance created by a heavy nose, results in greater accuracy.

Foster slugs are made in 10, 12, 16, 20, and .410 gauges. In diameter, the slugs are equal to or smaller than the tightest choke. On firing, the slugs expand and fill the bore. The weight and nominal velocity of the slugs is given in Table 8.4.

The Sabot slug was introduced to the United States by Smith & Wesson. They no longer manufacture ammunition. This slug was made only in 12 gauge. It had an hourglass configuration with a hollow base in which there was a white plastic insert. This slug lay in a sabot consisting of two halves of high-density polyethylene plastic. The slug, encased in the sabot made a projectile of 12-gauge diameter. On firing, the sabot with the enclosed slug, moved down the barrel as one unit. The sabot contacted the bore, not the slug. On exiting the muzzle, the sabot fell away.

Sabot slugs were made by Smith & Wesson in police and civilian versions. Both slugs had a nominal weight of 440 gr. The advertised muzzle velocity of the police round was 1450 ft/sec. The diameter at the front and rear was 0.50 in. The police slug was loaded into a blue, ribbed plastic case on whose side "Police" was lettered in white. The tip of the slug and the end of the sabot were visible at the mouth of the shotgun shell. The sabot was of white plastic. The civilian slug was in a similar shotgun tube, except that there was no white lettering. Again, the tip of the slug and the sabot were visible. The sabot in the civilian slug was made of black plastic. Both police and civilian

Table 8.4 Foster Slugs

Manufacturer	Gauge	Length (mm)	(inches)	Weight (grams)	(oz)	Advertised Muzzle Velocity	Muzzle Energy	Misc.
Federal	10	89	(3 1/2)	766	(1 3/4)	1280	2785	Hollow point
	12	76	(3)	547	(1 1/4)	1600	3110	Hollow point
		70	(2 3/4)	547	(1 1/4)	1520	2805	Hollow point
		70	(2 3/4)	438	(1)	1610	2520	Hollow point
	16	70	(2 3/4)	350	(4/5)	1600	1990	Hollow point
	20	70	(2 3/4)	328	(3/4)	1600	1865	Hollow point
	.410	63.5	(2 1/2)	88	(1/5)	1830	650	Hollow point
Remington	12	76	(3)	438	(1)	1760	3009	
		70	(2 3/4)	438	(1)	1560	2364	
		70	(2 3/4)	438	(1)	1680	2741	
	16	70	(2 3/4)	350	(4/5)	1600	1989	
	20	70	(2 3/4)	275	(5/8)	1580	1515	
	.410	63.5	(2 1/2)	88	(1/5)	1830	651	
Winchester	12	76	(3)	438	(1)	1760	3010	
		70	(2 3/4)	438	(1)	1600	2488	
	16	70	(2 3/4)	350	(4/5)	1600	1962	
	20	70	(2 3/4)	328	(3/4)	1600	1865	
	.410	63.5	(2 1/2)	88	(1/5)	1830	651	

shells were closed with a rolled crimp. In both shells, the sabot rested on a cardboard wad, which in turn rested on a white plastic wad. The police version of the sabot slug was intended to be fired in weapons having only a cylinder or modified choke. Firing in weapons of greater choke could cause the slug to snap at the hourglass waist. The civilian slug, of softer lead, could be fired in weapons of any choke.

Sabot shotgun shells are now manufactured by Federal, Remington and Winchester in 12 and 20 gauge (Table 8.5). The weight of the slug is usually 1 oz (438 gr.) in 12 gauge and 5/8 oz (275 gr.) in 20 gauge. Remington manufactures a 1 3/16 oz (520 gr.) sabot slug for its 3 in. (76 mm) 12 gauge loading. Its 20-gauge sabot slug weighs 3/4 oz (328 gr.). The Federal slugs have a "hollow point" and may be copper plated. Nominal velocity for the Sabot slugs ranges from 1200 to 1550 f/s. The Winchester Sabot has a pentagonal hole in the tip of the slug and a hole in the base closed with a plastic plug. The shell has a cup wad and a cardboard filler wad.

In 1993, Remington introduced Sabot slugs of solid copper rather than lead. There are four machined slots in its nose to produce expansion. The slug is encased in an eight-fingered plastic sabot. As the slug penetrates tissue, the nose sections open, increasing the diameter of the projectile and the loss of energy. Upon complete deployment, the nose sections, which each weigh 20 gr. each, separate from the main mass of the slug producing four additional wound tracks. Subsequently, Federal introduced a solid copper hollow point slug in a plastic sabot. These rounds are intended for use in rifled shotgun barrels.

Wounds Due to Slugs

The wound of entrance from a shotgun slug, whether it be a Foster, Brenneke or Sabot, is circular in shape, with a diameter approximately that of the slug. The edge of the wound is abraded. Determination of the gauge from the diameter of the entrance wound is not possible. At close range, the wads from a Foster shell either enter through the entrance hole or strike adjacent skin producing circular to oval imprints. In the case of the Sabot round, at close range the two halves of the sabot may either enter the body or impact the skin. If they impact sideways, the rectangular pattern produced is fairly characteristic (Figure 8.13). In the case of a Brenneke shotgun shell, no matter the range, the wadding enters with the slug because it is literally screwed into the base.

Shotgun slugs produce massive internal injuries comparable in severity to those produced by a centerfire rifle hunting bullet. As a Foster slug moves through the body, it tends to "pancake", usually remaining in the body. The slug may come to rest as a flattened lead disk or may break into a few large pieces. X-rays often show a central disk of lead with 2 to 4 comma-like pieces

Table 8.5 Sabot Slugs

Manufacturer	Gauge	Length (mm)	Length (inches)	Weight of Slug (grams)	Weight of Slug (oz)	Advertised Muzzle Velocity	Advertised Muzzle Energy	Misc.
Federal	12	76	(3)	438	(1)	1500	2400	Hollow point
		70	(2 3/4)	438	(1)	1450	2100	Hollow point
	20	76	(3)	275	(5/8)	1450	1285	Hollow point
Remington	12	76	(3)	520	(1 3/16)	1500	2498	Solid copper
		70	(2 3/4)	438	(1)	1450	1984	Solid copper
	20	70	(2 3/4)	328	(3/4)	1450	1480	Solid copper
Winchester	12	76	(3)	438	(1)	1550	2401	
		76	(3)	438	(1)	1300	1689	
		70	(2 3/4)	438	(1)	1450	2101	
		70	(2 3/4)	438	(1)	1200	1439	
	20	70	(2 3/4)	275	(5/8)	1400	1249	

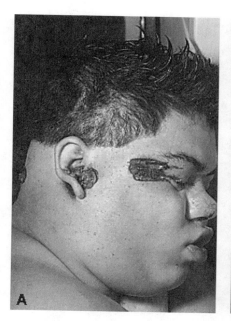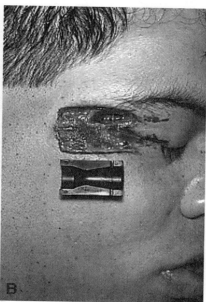

Figure 8.13 (A) Deceased shot immediately in front of ear with 12-gauge Winchester Sabot slug. Injury from sabot behind eye, range less than three feet. (B) Close-up of wound from plastic sabot and sabot.

of lead adjacent to or surrounding the disk. These comma-like pieces of lead break off from the edge of the pancaked slug (Figure 8.14). Foster slugs do not produce the x-ray picture of the "lead snowstorm" seen with high-velocity hunting rifle bullets. In the deaths seen by the author due to the Sabot round, the slug has always exited. Internal injury was very severe. Scattered fragments of lead were deposited if bone was struck but there was no true lead snowstorm.

Rarely, one will encounter jury-rigged slugs constructed from birdshot shells. In these instances, a deep groove is cut around the circumference of a birdshot shell just in front of the metal head. On firing, the tube is supposed to separate at this cut. The tube, containing its load of shot and wadding, then travels down the barrel, exits, and continues as one missile to the target, producing a single wound of entrance. At autopsy, one recovers from the body, the tube, the wadding and the pellets — sometimes still in one piece. Figure 8.15 illustrates such a case. The deceased was shot twice in the head with a 12-gauge shotgun firing birdshot shells. Recovered from the body was the plastic hull with the plastic wad inside.

In a second case involving a birdshot shell, separation did occur, but the pie crimp at the end of the shell was forced open by the pellets and wadding as the separated hull moved down the barrel. Because of this, the shot and wads exited the barrel but the severed portion of the hull remained in the

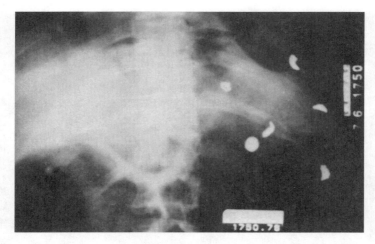

Figure 8.14 X-ray of body showing breakup of Foster slug.

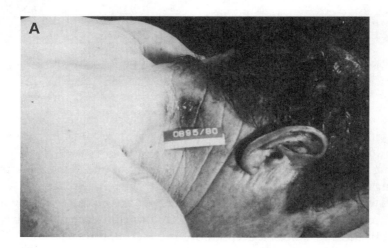

Figure 8.15 **(A)** Entrance wound of right side of back of neck; **(B)** Recovered portion of hull from wound.

barrel. On firing the weapon a second time, an unaltered buckshot shell was used. The buckshot and wads swept the deposited hull out the barrel into the body. Thus at autopsy, buckshot and wads from the second shell and the distal two-thirds of the tube from the birdshot shell were recovered from the body.

While separation at the point the hull is cut may have occurred consistently in the age of paper shotgun shells, with plastic tubes separation usually does not occur. In repeated attempts by the author to cause separation by cutting the hull just in front of the steel head, he found that he almost had to cut the shell in two to cause consistent separation. Separation at the point of notching was the exception not the rule.

Wound Ballistics of the Shotgun

At close range, the shotgun is the most formidable and destructive of all small arms. For birdshot and buckshot loads, the severity and lethality of a shotgun wound depends on the number of pellets that enter the body, the organs struck by the pellets and the amount of tissue destruction. Like handgun bullets, the extent of tissue destruction from each individual pellet is limited to that tissue they physically shred. Temporary cavities play no significant role in injury. This is, of course, not the case with rifle slugs which, like rifle bullets, produce injury both directly and from temporary cavity formation.

In rifled weapons, the weight of the bullet does not change no matter how great the distance. In contrast, in shotguns, as the range increases there is dispersion of shot with resultant decrease in the number of pellets that strike the target. Although velocity decreases with range in rifled weapons, this decrease is very little at the short ranges at which most killings occur. In contrast, the unfavorable ballistic shape of the shotgun pellet, combined with the lack of stabilizing spin, causes a rapid fall-off in velocity such that beyond a relatively close range, pellets have insufficient velocity to perforate skin. Thus, unlike rifled weapons, in shotguns, the range from muzzle to target is extremely important in determining the number of pellets that strike a body and enter it.

Larger sized shot is more effective at longer range because it retains its velocity better than smaller shot. Even then the term "longer range" is very short. Maximum effective range for hunting birds and small game with birdshot is 45 to 65 yards. The maximum range that lead birdshot can travel, as calculated by Journee's formula (maximum range in yards = shot diameter in inches times 2200), ranges from 110 yds for #12 shot to 396 yds for BB shot. For buckshot, the maximum range is 528 yds for #4 Buck and 726 yds for #00 buck. The actual effective range to produce wounding in humans is considerably less because of the minimum velocity necessary to perforate skin.

Shotgun Wounds

Figure 8.16A–D show the sequence of events that occur at the muzzle on firing a shotgun. Note the large gas cloud that is partly responsible for the severe nature of the wounds at contact range.

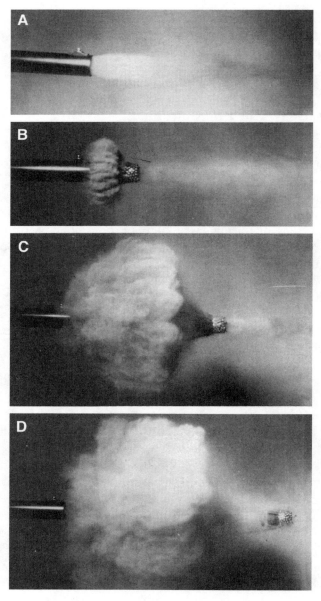

Figure 8.16 (**A–D**) Discharge of shotgun.

Contact Wounds of the Head

Contact shotgun wounds of the head are among the most mutilating firearms wounds there are. Extensive destruction of bone and soft tissue structures with bursting ruptures of the head are the rule rather than the exception. These are the wounds of which an individual is said to have "blown his head off." In some cases, this is almost literally true. The skull may be largely fragmented and the brain pulpified. Large fragments of the cranial vault and cerebral hemispheres are often ejected from the head. The scalp is extensively lacerated.

The severity of the injuries in contact wounds of the head is due to two factors: the charge of shot entering the skull and the gas from combustion of the propellant (Figure 8.16D). The shot directly fractures the skull and shreds the brain while at the same time producing pressure waves that increase the severity of these injuries as well as ejecting the brain tissue. The gas, entering the closed chamber of the head, expands rapidly, adding to the pressure waves acting on the bony framework of the skull. The only way for the skull to relieve the pressure produced is to shatter.

Most contact shotgun wounds of the head are suicidal in origin. In a study of 89 contact shotgun wounds of the head, Harruff found the most common site of entrance was the mouth (62%), followed by the temple (15%) and the submental region (13%).[6] In the case of wounds of the temple, most right-handed individuals shoot themselves in the right temple using the left hand to steady the gun against the head.

With similar sites of entrance, the internal injuries produced by shotguns of different gauge are very similar. This is not the case for external injuries. Harruff noted a marked difference in the external injuries depending on the gauge of the weapon used.[6] In the case of intraoral wounds, in 74% of the cases in which a 12 gauge shotgun was used there were bursting injuries extending from the mouth to the scalp. For 20-gauge shotguns, only 9% of the wounds produced were this severe. Rather, 55% of the cases with intra-oral wounds from 20 gauge shotguns had either no lacerations or the lacerations were limited to the perioral area. Only 8% of the cases involving 12-gauge shotguns showed this less severe pattern.

In suicidal contact wounds of the head, individuals tend to use their dominant hand to depress the trigger, steadying the muzzle against the head with the non-dominant hand. Because of this, powder soot may be visible on the non-dominant hand (Figure 8.17A). This is the exception, not the rule. In rare instances, there may be blowback of powder from the entrance with resultant tattooing of the web of skin between the thumb and index finger of the hand steadying the barrel (see Figure 14.9A). In other instances, this area of the hand may slightly overlap the lumen of the barrel and a graze wound from the exiting pellets and wadding may occur (Figure 8.17B). If a compensator was present at the end of the muzzle, a grid-like pattern of soot deposition may be present on the palm of the hand holding the muzzle (Figure 8.17C).

Even if there is no visible gunshot residue, residue may still be present on the back and/or palm of the hand steadying the muzzle. Because of this, testing for residue by FAAS or SEM–EDX should be performed.

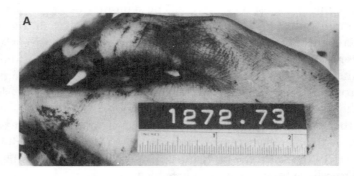

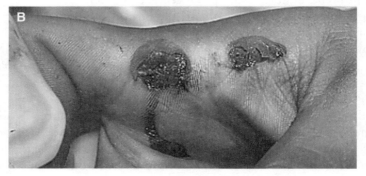

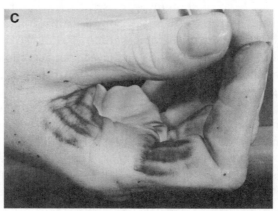

Figure 8.17 (**A**) Soot deposit on hand used to cradle muzzle end of shotgun. (**B**) Graze wound. (**C**) Patterned soot deposit due to compensator.

Although massive injuries of the head with evisceration of the brain are very common, they are not inevitable. The author has seen numerous cases in which an individual shot themself in the head with a shotgun and no pellets exited. Almost invariably, such wounds are inflicted in the mouth or under the jaw and not the temporal region. Even though no pellets exited, there are massive fractures of the skull and pulpification of the brain. The weapons in these cases ranged from .410 gauge to 12 gauge. In wounds where the brain is eviscerated, the great bulk of the pellets and the wad will exit. An x-ray of the head may show only 3 or 4 pellets remaining from a shell that held hundreds.

Occasionally, people shooting themselves in the mouth tilt the head too far backward before firing. This results in their "shooting off" the face and sometimes the frontal lobes (Figure 8.18). In such instances, death may not be immediate. The author has seen individuals survive weeks with such wounds. One individual who shot off his face survived a number of months in a vegetative state only to die from meningitis due to an intracranial abscess that formed about a tooth driven into the occipital lobe of the brain.

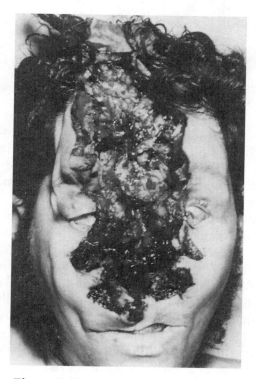

Figure 8.18   Intraoral shotgun wound.

In the typical contact wound of the head, the entrance site is easy to locate, as large quantities of soot will be found at it. The edges of the wound will be seared and blackened (Figure 8.19). The entrance is often bisected by large lacerations extending across the top of the head. Fragmentation of the skull usually occurs. The exit site of the pellets may not be found because of missing fragments of bone and scalp; the massive comminuted fractures of the skull and extensive lacerations of the scalp.

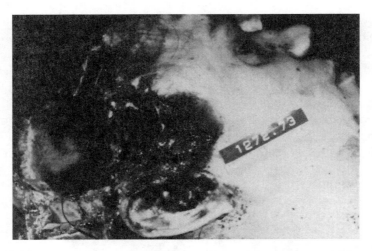

Figure 8.19 Contact wound of right temple with evisceration of brain. Note large amount of soot at entrance site.

In intraoral shotgun wounds, soot is present on the palate, the tongue, and sometimes the lips. Stretch-like striae or superficial lacerations of the perioral skin and nasolabial folds often occur because of the sudden transient "bulging out" of the face, caused by the temporary cavity and the gas (Figure 8.20). Lacerations of the tongue can also occur.

Although soot is seen around the entrance in most contact wounds of the head, this is not absolute. The author has encountered a number of cases in which no soot was seen either externally or internally (Figure 8.21). All but one case involved Winchester ammunition loaded with ball powder. In all but one of the Winchester cases, ball powder grains were readily identified in the wound. The most disturbing case involved an individual who shot himself in the temporo-parietal region with a 12-gauge shotgun firing Winchester birdshot. The suicide took place in front of scores of witnesses. The head injury was massive, with evisceration of the brain. Neither powder nor soot could be found on or in the head. Since not all the cranial contents were recovered from the scene, it is possible that a more diligent search would have revealed at least powder grains.

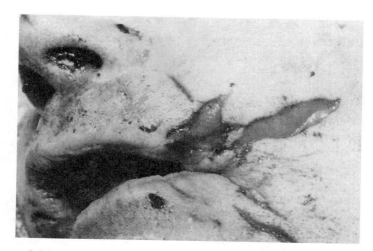

Figure 8.20 Tears at corner of mouth due to intraoral shotgun wound.

Intermediate and Close-Range Wounds of the Head

Intermediate-range and close-range shotgun wounds of the head are almost as mutilating as contact wounds because the pellets are still traveling in a single mass. Severe wounds are especially common if the mass of pellets strike the skull at a relatively shallow angle and exit. Large gaping tears of the scalp are present. Careful re-approximation of the scalp and examination of the edges will reveal the entrance site, which will be indicated by the abrasion

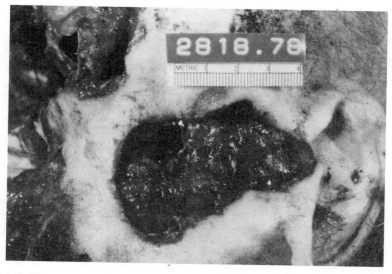

Figure 8.21 Contact wound of right temple with 12-gauge shotgun. Note absence of soot. Ball powder was recovered from entrance.

ring. Stretch-like striae may radiate from the entrance as well. The exact site of the exit of the pellets, however, is often not apparent. Reconstruction of the shattered skull may be helpful.

Contact Wounds of the Trunk

Contact wounds of the trunk appear relatively innocuous when compared with the massive destruction produced by such wounds in the head. The wound of entrance will be circular in shape and will have a diameter approximately equal to that of the bore of the weapon (Figure 8.22). In hard-contact wounds, no soot surrounds the entrance site, but the edges of the wound will be seared and blackened by the hot gases. The skin will not split, as in head wounds, because the gases disperse in the underlying soft tissue and visceral cavities. These gases, however, will cause the chest or abdominal wall to flare out abruptly, impacting the muzzle of the weapon with great force. This often will result in a detailed imprint of the muzzle of the shotgun. In double-barrel weapons, the imprint of the unfired barrel often will be present. The chest and abdomen may flare out to such a degree and with such force as to have impressed on them the outline of the hand holding the barrel or even a chain or medal that was present around the neck (Figure 8.23A). The flared-out chest or abdomen may envelope the end of the barrel so that an imprint of the front sight may be present, even though the sight is one inch from the muzzle.

In one case examined by the author involving a contact wound of the chest, there was neither soot nor powder around or in the contact wound of

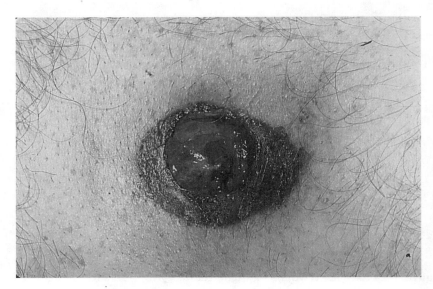

Figure 8.22 Contact wound of chest with seared edges.

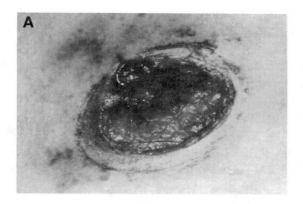

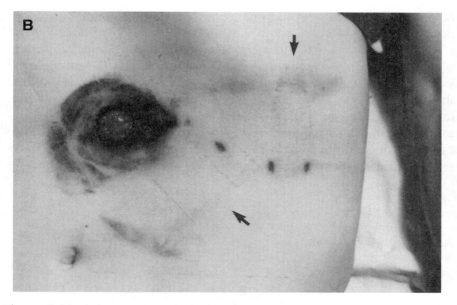

Figure 8.23 (**A**) Contact wound of chest without soot or powder but muzzle imprint. (**B**) Contact wound of abdomen with imprint of wrist and hand; note the watchband around wrist.

entrance. That the wound was a hard contact was easy to determine because of a muzzle imprint around the entrance (Figure 8.23B).

The wound of entrance may be surrounded by a wide zone of raw, abraded skin caused by flaring out of the skin of the chest or abdomen around the muzzle at the time of discharge. The mechanical action of the skin rubbing against the end of the barrel causes abrasion of the superficial layers.

If the muzzle of a shotgun is held in loose contact or near contact with the body, there will be a circular area of soot deposited on the skin surrounding the entrance hole. As the range increases, the diameter of the soot deposit increases, but the density decreases. Deposition of soot continues out to a range of approximately 30 cm.

If the skin is reflected from around a contact wound of entrance, the underlying muscle will usually have a cherry-red hue from carboxyhemoglobin and carboxymyoglobin formation, with the source of the carbon monoxide (CO) being the gases of combustion of the gunpowder. CO is not necessarily confined to the immediate adjacent muscle but can spread 15 cm or more from the entrance. CO also may accompany the shot in its path through the body; if a large mass of shot lodges subcutaneously in the back, CO may produce a cherry-red hue to the adjacent muscle.

Intermediate Range Wounds of the Body

As the range increases beyond one to two cm from the muzzle to target, powder tattooing will occur (Figure 8.24). Powder tattooing from a shotgun is less dense than the tattooing a handgun produces at the same range. This is due to more complete consumption of powder caused by the greater barrel length. The maximum range out to which powder tattooing occurs from a shotgun depends to a great degree on the type of powder, i.e., ball or flake. In shotgun shells loaded with flake powder and fired in a 28-in. barrel 12-gauge shotgun with a modified choke, powder tattooing was present out to 24 in. (60 cm) but disappeared by 30 in. (75 cm).[5] Using the same weapon and firing cartridges loaded with ball powder, definite tattooing was present

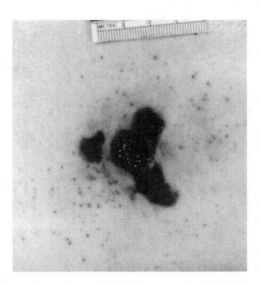

Figure 8.24 Intermediate-range .410 shotgun wound of chest with ball powder tattooing. The deceased was shot through flannel pajamas.

at 30 in. (75 cm), with a very few marks present at 36 in. (90 cm), but absent by 40 in. (125 cm). Just as in handguns, ball powder produces fine powder tattoo marks and can readily perforate clothing (Figure 8.24). All Winchester shotgun ammunition is loaded with ball powder while all Remington and Federal ammunition uses flake powder.

The above data on range of tattooing is based on tests done in rabbits, whose skin is thinner than that of humans; therefore, these figures should be considered only as maximum ranges out to which powder tattooing will occur in humans. In addition, other factors such as barrel length, also have an effect on the maximum range and density of powder tattooing.

Distant Wounds

As the muzzle of the shotgun is moved farther from the body, tattooing disappears and the diameter of the circular wound of entrance increases in size until a point is reached where individual pellets begin to separate from the main mass (Figure 8.25). From contact to 2 ft, birdshot fired from a shotgun, independent of its gauge (excluding the .410), generally produces a single round entrance wound approximately 3/4 in. to 1 in. in diameter. By 3 ft, the wound widens out to approximately 7/8 in. for a barrel with modified choke to 1 1/4 in. for a cylinder bore weapon. The edges of the wounds will have scalloped margins (Figure 8.26). By 4 ft, the modified choke barrel produces an entrance hole approximately 1 in. in diameter with the cylindrical bore barrel producing an entrance 1 3/4 in. in diameter. Scattered satellite pellet holes are present around the main entrances (Figure 8.27). By 6 to 7 ft, there is a definite cuff of satellite pellet holes around a slightly irregular wound of entrance for a shotgun with a modified barrel (Figure 8.28). For a cylindrical bore weapon, the wound is ragged with a prominent cuff of pellet holes around the entrance. Beyond 10 ft, there is great variation in the size of the pellet pattern depending on the ammunition used, the choke of the gun and most important, the range. At the same range, the pattern for different guns and brands of ammunition may vary from a central irregular perforation with numerous satellite wounds to a pattern of multiple individual pellet wounds.

In all deaths from shotgun wounds, the size of the shot pattern on the body should be measured so that the range can be determined accurately. There have been many formulas published to determine the range at which a shotgun has been discharged, but none of these formulas is reliable. The wound measurements given in the previous paragraphs should be used only as a rough guide in estimating range. The only reliable method of determining range is to obtain the actual weapon and the same brand of ammunition used and then conduct a series of test shots so as to reproduce on paper the

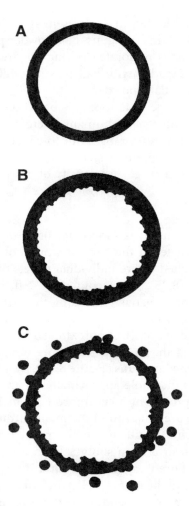

Figure 8.25 Shotgun pellet patterns: (A) contact to 2 ft, (B) 3 ft, and (C) 4 ft.

pattern of the fatal wound on the body. It must be stressed that identical weapons of the same choke may produce different patterns; thus, the actual weapon employed in a killing must be used. A fact not often appreciated is that ammunition plays a great part in the size of the pattern. Different brands of ammunition, even when loaded with the same shot size, produce different patterns at the same range.

Another factor often not considered, and that can cause errors in range determination, involves the measurement of the shot pattern on the body. Different individuals measure the same pattern differently. The occasional flier should be ignored, and only the main mass of the pellet pattern should be measured.

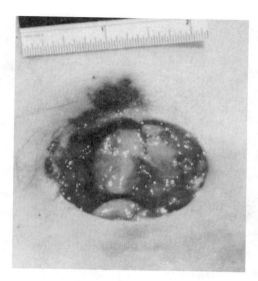

Figure 8.26 Shotgun wound of chest with scalloping of margins (range, approximately 3 ft).

At close range, when there is only a single large wound of entrance, the wad from a shotgun shell will be found inside the body. If the shell contained a plastic Power-Piston® wad or plastic shot cup, as the wad enters the body, the individual arms or "petals" that have peeled back in flight may produce a patterned abrasion around the wound of entrance (Figure 8.29). These petal marks can occur even if the entrance site is covered with clothing.

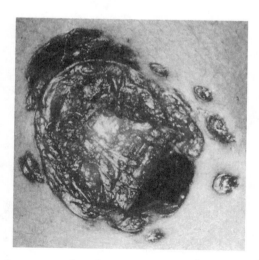

Figure 8.27 Entrance wound with scattered satellite pellet holes (range, approximately 4 ft).

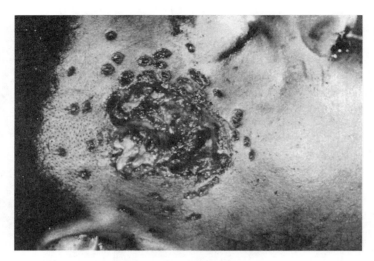

Figure 8.28 Slightly irregular wound of entrance surrounded by pellet holes (range estimated at 5 to 7 ft).

In 12, 16, and 20 gauges, one will have a circular wound of entrance in the center of a Maltese Cross abrasion. In .410 gauge shot cups have only three petals; thus, three equally spaced rectangular abrasions radiate from the entrance rather than four (Figure 8.30).

In the author's experience, petals marks from plastic shot cups have always been accompanied by powder tattooing of the adjacent skin if the skin

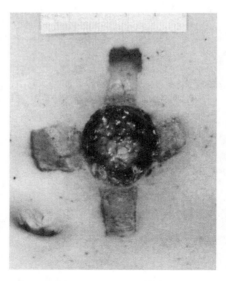

Figure 8.29 Intermediate range 12-gauge shotgun wound of abdomen with "petal" marks from Remington Power Piston® wad.

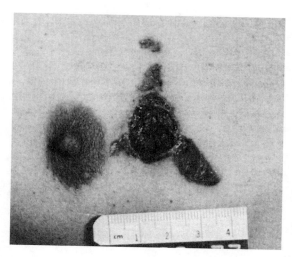

Figure 8.30   .410 shotgun wound of chest. Note the three equally spaced "petal" marks characteristic of the .410.

is bare. Petal marks are seen at ranges between 1 and 3 ft for 12, 16 and 20-gauge shotguns. Before 1 ft of range, the petals usually have not opened up sufficiently to mark the skin. By one foot, they will have. The increasing air resistance bends the petals back so that after 3 ft they are generally flush with the sides of the wad base, and no petal marks are produced. Sometimes not all the petals bend back uniformly, and one finds a circular wound of entrance with only one petal mark (Figure 8.31). In .410 shotguns, the petal marks appear at 3 to 5 inches (7.5 to 12.5 cm), reach a maximum spread at 12 to 21 inches (30 to 52.5 cm) and disappear at approximately 2 ft. (60 cm).[7] Dowling et al. attribute the earlier spread of the .410 petals to their long, narrow configuration.

As the range increases, the wads gradually fall behind and separate from the main shot mass. At relatively close range, the wad may impact the edge of the entrance before sliding into the body. Thus, one will have a circular entrance surrounded by a symmetric abrasion ring with a large, irregular area of abraded margin on one side where the wad impacted. As the range increases (5 to 8 ft), however, the wads will drift laterally until they impact on the skin adjacent to the entrance site and do not enter (Figure 8.32). At this time the wad will leave a circular or oval imprint on the skin. In shotgun shells loaded with both an over-the-shot wad and a plastic shot cup, one may get two sets of wad markings. As the range from muzzle to target increases still farther, the wads will miss the body or strike with so little energy that they will not leave a mark on the skin. The maximum range out to which wads will produce patterned abrasions on the body is unknown. Filler wads have produced marks at least out to 15 ft, and plastic wads out to 20 ft.

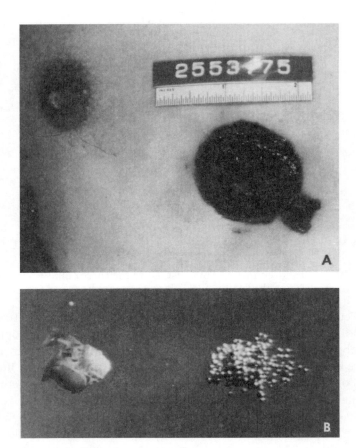

Figure 8.31 (A) 12-gauge entrance wound of chest with single "petal" mark. (B) Plastic wad falling behind shot. Note that three of the four petals have folded back, with one still protruding.

In some instances, for unknown reasons, the shot cup or Power Piston® does not open to release the shot. Thus, the mass of shot travels to and through the body in one compact mass. In the case illustrated, this happened to a limited degree (Figure 8.33). Most of the pellets stayed in the Power Piston® and exited with it. Some pellets, however, did emerge from the wad as it moved through the body.

Shot charges may strike an intermediary target, e.g., glass with a resultant increase in the dispersion of the shot. This occurs secondary to the "billiard ball" effect described by Breitenecker.[8-9] Here, the first pellets striking the intermediary target are delayed, allowing the following pellets to catch up and impact the first pellets, causing dispersion of the pellets. This phenomena has been thought to occur with intermediary targets as thin as a pane of

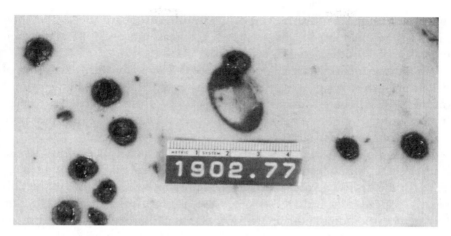

Figure 8.32   Circular abrasion of skin from composite wad.

window glass or a window screen. Coe and Austin demonstrated, however, that for the dispersion to occur the intermediary target has to have sufficient thickness and tensile strength to slow down the initial wave of pellets striking the target.[10] Their experiments revealed no dispersion when the intermediary

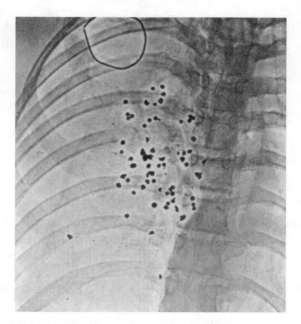

Figure 8.33   Perforating shotgun wound of chest. Note the small number of pellets present. The circular mark in the upper left-hand corner of the picture indicates where the pellets entered.

target was aluminum screen, window glass, thin cardboard (3 mm) or cow-hide (3 mm). Tempered and safety glass, 1/8" masonite and 3/8" fir plywood increased pattern diameters 2–3 times.

If an intermediary target is of sufficient thickness to cause dispersion of pellets prior to striking an individual, estimates of the range from the pattern on the body will be erroneous unless the effects of the dispersion are taken into account. The only way to determine the range correctly is to interpose a similar intermediary target when test firing.

While the effects of an intermediary target on pellets is obvious, less so is its effect on the appearance of a wound when the missile is a shotgun slug. Thus, in the case of a young boy accidentally shot with a 12-gauge slug, his hand — specifically, a finger — acted as an intermediary target. The slug fragmented the bone and soft tissue of the finger, propelling it against the deceased's chest, where these fragments produced irregular areas of abrasion (Figure 8.34).

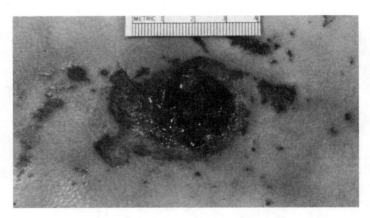

Figure 8.34 Entrance wound of chest from 12-gauge slug. The irregular abrasions around the entrance are due to fragments of the victim's finger.

In another unusual case involving an intermediary object, an individual was shot with birdshot, at a range of a few feet, through a pillow, with a 12-gauge shotgun. There was a single large entrance wound of the side of the chest, without satellite pellet holes, but with a wide irregular band of abrasion. A large clump of filler material from the pillow was recovered from the entrance in the chest.

On occasion, when bodies have been burned or are markedly decomposed, authorities have attempted to use the size of the shotgun pattern within the body as determined by x-ray for estimation of range. Experiments have revealed that this method is completely unreliable. Both close-range wounds and wounds of several yard's distance can give similar patterns on x-ray because of the billiard-ball effect of the pellets on entering the body in close range shotgun wounds.[8-9]

Internal injuries, due to shotgun pellets are extremely variable, depending on the range at which an individual is shot. In contact wounds, where one is dealing with the effects of both the pellets and the gas, there may be near disintegration of organs. Close-range wounds, in which the pellets enter in a relatively compact mass, can also result in pulpification of organs. As the range increases, and the pellets enter the body separately, the wounds produced will resemble those from a low-velocity handgun bullet.

Perforating wounds of the trunk from shotgun pellets are uncommon. When they do occur, they usually result from a superficial perforating wound; contact wounds in an extremely thin person, and contact or close-up wounds from shells loaded with buckshot. The wound of exit may vary from a large, irregular, gaping wound caused by a mass of pellets exiting to a single slitlike exit wound produced by one pellet. Only very rarely will one see exit wounds of the trunk from a direct hit with birdshot. Such cases may be due to the welding together of a number of pellets at the time of firing so that these pellets move through the body as a single mass.

In all shotgun deaths, the size of the pattern on the body should be measured and recorded. Photographs of the wound pattern are recommended. These can be used for subsequent range determinations. Shot and wads should be recovered and retained. Examination of the wad will give the gauge of the shotgun and make of the ammunition. Measurements of the pellets will give the pellet size. On rare occasions, irregularities at the end of the muzzle will impart scratch marks on plastic wads that are sufficiently distinctive so as to make positive ballistics comparison between the wad recovered from the body and a test wad fired from the suspect weapon. Such cases usually occur when the barrel of the shotgun has been sawed off, leaving jagged metal projections into the barrel. Such comparisons are also possible with the plastic sabot of shotgun slugs.

Wounds from Buckshot

The appearance of a wound resulting from buckshot depends principally on the range between the victim and the muzzle of the weapon. A contact wound will consist of a circular wound of entrance whose diameter is approximately the same as that of the bore of the shotgun. The edges of the wound will be seared and abraded. The wound of entrance often is surrounded by a wide zone of raw, abraded skin caused by flaring out of the skin around the muzzle at the time of discharge when the gas produced by the burning propellant enters the body. The mechanical action of the skin rubbing against the muzzle causes the abrasion of the skin. If the weapon is held in loose contact with the skin, there will be deposition of soot surrounding the entrance. Deposition of soot continues out to a range of approximately 30 cm.

As the range from target to muzzle increases beyond a few centimeters, powder tattooing of the skin appears. Depending on the form of powder present, i.e., ball or disk, powder tattooing in a 12-gauge shotgun will extend out to a maximum range of approximately 90 to 125 cm for ball powder and 60 to 75 for flake powder. The ability of granulated filler in buckshot loads to simulate powder tattooing has been discussed previously.

As the range increases, the diameter of the entrance will increase gradually. At approximately 3 ft, the edges of the wound will have a scalloped shape. At 4 ft, there will be separation of buckshot pellets from the main mass so that there will be a large gaping wound with a few satellite holes. By 9 ft, there will generally be individual pellet holes (Figure 8.35).

At close range, when there is still one large perforation, the wad usually follows the buckshot into the body. As the range increases, the wad will move outward from the main pellet mass path and will impact the skin either among or adjacent to the individual pellet holes, producing an oval or circular abrasion (Figure 8.35).

Federal buckshot cartridges were formerly closed with a thin plastic disk-like, over-the-shot wad. This wad does not fragment on firing and is recoverable intact at the scene or from the body (Figure 8.36). The author had a case of an individual shot in the chest with a Federal buckshot shell containing

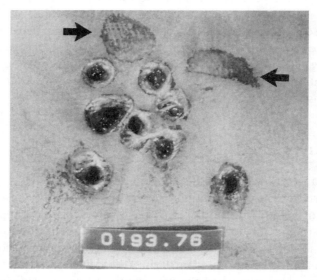

Figure 8.35 Wounds from 00 buckshot. Note the abrasions from wadding (arrows).

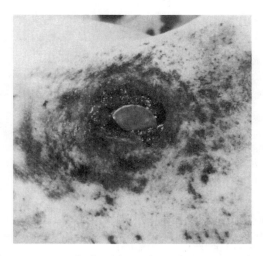

Figure 8.36 Shotgun wound of neck with a plastic over-the-shot wad from a Federal buckshot shell embedded in the entrance.

both composite and cork filler wads (Figure 8.37). The cork wad overlay the powder. The victim was shot at close range (approximately 1 1/2 to 2 ft). The single large entrance was surrounded by a number of irregular abrasions in addition to some powder tattooing (Figure 8.38). No intermediary targets were present. Test firings revealed, however, that the cork wad fragmented on firing and that the fragments of cork were responsible for the skin markings. This shows the importance of integrating findings at autopsy with the individual weapon and ammunition.

In most cases in which an individual is shot in the trunk with buckshot, the pellets will remain in the body. On some occasions, usually in contact or close-up buckshot wounds, the pellets may exit.

Pellet Holes in Window Screens

At ranges from contact to 4 ft, discharge of a shotgun through a window screen will result in production of a square hole in the screen. This is

Figure 8.37 Disassembled Federal buckshot shell showing the thin plastic over-the-shot wad, 00 buckshot pellets, a composite cushion wad, and a cork wad.

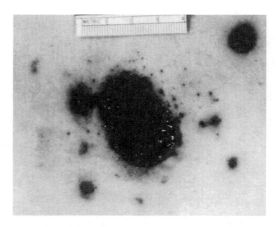

Figure 8.38 Intermediate-range shotgun wound of chest showing powder tattooing and large irregular areas of abrasion.

independent of the gauge, choke, barrel length, type of wad, and shot size.
The major factor in the production of a square hole is the distance from
muzzle to screen. A perfect square is not produced all the time, as one side
can have a rounded appearance. Examination of the square hole shows that
the individual wires of the screen are broken and bent outward by the pellets.
The wires tend to be longer in the corners and shorter on the sides. When
the strands are bent back into place, a circular hole is formed.

As the range increases beyond 4 ft, the pellets start to spread and the hole
takes on a circular appearance. At farther distances, individual pellet holes
appear around the circular defect. Slugs produce square holes at all ranges.

Sawed-Off Shotguns

Test firings, by the author, of sawed-off shotguns at ranges of 21 ft or less
revealed that decreasing the barrel length of a cylinder-bore shotgun has no
significant effect on the size of the pattern until the barrel has been sawed
off to less than 9 in. At this point, the patterns begin to open up significantly.

Moreau et al. found that with birdshot, as the barrel length decreased,
any change in the size of the pattern produced depended on the brand of
ammunition. Patterns either did not change or increased.[11] For 00 Buckshot,
the size of the pattern increased as the barrel length decreased. The greatest
increase occurred at 12 inches and less.

In a sawed-off shotgun in which the end of the barrel has not been reamed
out, slivers of steel may project into the bore. If plastic wads are fired in such
a weapon, the spicules of steel may mark the wad with individual markings,
making ballistic comparison possible.

Shotgun Diverters

A shotgun diverter is a device attached to the end of the shotgun barrel that changes the normal circular pattern of shot to a controlled, predictable, rectangular pattern. This rectangular pattern is formed by the diverting ribs integral with the bore of the device coupled with compounded angles. The mass of shot is reformed after it leaves the barrel and enters the forward diverter section. The action of the gases on the walls of the diverter reorient the shot, so that a rectangular pattern is formed after exiting the muzzle. Shotgun slugs may be fired through the diverter. These slugs, however, will be deformed, having a rectangular shape.

Automatic Ejection of Fired Hulls

The author has seen a number of irrefutable cases of suicide, utilizing pump shotguns, in which death was instantaneous, yet the pump shotgun used to commit suicide was found to have an empty chamber and an ejected hull was present adjacent to the gun. These circumstances, understandably, aroused the suspicion of homicide. Examination of the shotgun in these cases, as well as other pump shotguns, revealed that they would eject the fired case after discharge if the slide was not restrained in a forward position. Other pump shotguns will unlock and only partially extract the fired case. If this latter weapon falls to the ground, landing on its butt, enough momentum may be given the shotgun bolt to cause it to go backward, ejecting the fired case. Though ejection may occur in the aforementioned situations, there is never sufficient energy for the bolt to come forward and chamber a new round.

Miscellaneous Notes on Shotgun Shells

There are three major manufacturers of shotgun shells in the United States: Remington-Peters, Winchester-Western, and Federal.

Remington-Peters.   All shotgun ammunition produced by Remington has plastic tubes and is loaded with flake powder. Birdshot and buckshot shells are closed with a "pie" crimp. Power-Piston® wads are used in virtually all birdshot shells. A one-piece Figure 8™ plastic wad is used in some trap and skeet loadings. Filler is used in Magnum birdshot and buckshot shells.

Winchester-Western.   All shotgun ammunition marketed by Winchester-Western has plastic tubes and is loaded with ball powder. Birdshot and buckshot shells are closed with a pie crimp. Virtually all birdshot shells have a cardboard over-the-powder cup wad, composite filler wads, and a plastic collar. Trap and skeet loads use a one piece plastic wad with an integral shot cup. Shells loaded with steel shot use a two piece plastic wad — a cup and disk. Some shells are loaded with copper-coated (Lubaloy®) shot. Filler is used in Magnum birdshot and buckshot shells.

Federal Ammunition.   Virtually all shotgun ammunition manufactured by Federal uses plastic hulls. Federal shotgun shells use a wide variety of wad systems. The most common is the Triple-Plus wad. Some paper hull shells are manufactured for skeet and trap. These use a one-piece plastic wad. Federal hulls are color coded: red for 12 gauge, purple for 16 gauge, and yellow for 20 gauge. Plastic hulls loaded with birdshot are closed with an 8-piece pie-crimp. Paper shells are closed with a 6-piece pie crimp. Flake powder is used in all shells.

Miscellaneous Shotgun Ammunition

Shotgun Shells Loaded with Rubber or Plastic Pellets.   Fiocchi, a major European ammunition manufacturer, produces shotgun ammunition loaded with hard-rubber pellets. The ammunition, now available in the United States, is sold as a self-defense loading that is non-lethal except at close ranges. The 12-gauge shell has a transparent hull closed by a plastic disk and contains 15 rubber pellets, a felt wad, and a plastic over-the-powder wad. The pellets measure 8.4 to 8.5 mm in diameter and weigh an average of 1.016 g. On X-ray, they have a metallic density. Muzzle velocity is 302 m/s. Experiments by Missliwetz and Lindermann on corpses revealed that the pellets can cause fatal wounds at distances of 4 to 5 meters if the individual shot is wearing only light clothing.[12] These authors concluded that these pellets required a velocity of 130 to 140 m/s to perforate skin.

Brass Shotgun Shells.   Brass shotgun shells are now relatively uncommon in the United States. Remington, the last manufacturer of them, stopped production in 1957. Brass shotgun shells have been imported into the United States.

Winchester Tracer Rounds.   Winchester tracer rounds were introduced in 1965 in 12 gauge only. The 12-gauge tracer load was intended for use by skeet and trap shooters so that they could see where the shot had gone. This round contains a spherical aluminum capsule with a short hollow tail. The capsule containing the tracer compound lies above the filler wads among the shot (Figure 8.39). The tracer is ignited by powder gases through an opening in the center of the wad column that communicates with the lumen of the tail. When fired, the tracer appears as a glowing dart of yellow-white flame.

Figure 8.39 Disassembled Winchester tracer round.

Remington Modi-Pac. The Remington Modi-Pac refers to the Modified Impact Shotgun Shell. This round, which apparently was produced in the late 1960s, used an SP tube with a rolled crimp. It was intended by law enforcement agencies for riot control. Only 12-gauge shells were manufactured; these shells contain 1/4 oz of 0.120-in.-diameter plastic pellets. Approximately 320 pellets per load were used. The muzzle velocity was 1600 ft/sec. Loss of velocity was extremely rapid because of light weight of the pellets. Thus, at 15 yd, muzzle velocity was only 200 ft/sec. Maximum range was 25 yds. Given the low pressure generated in these shells, they would not function in auto-loading shotguns.

References

1. *The American Shotgun.* New York: Winchester Press, 1973.

2. Keith, E. *Shotguns by Keith.* New York: Bonanza Book, 1967.

3. Labisky, W. The ever-changing shotshell story. *Gun Digest.* Northfield, IL: Digest Books Inc., 1973.

4. Franovich, J. 20-gauge filler wads used in 12-gauge shotgun shells. *AFTE Journal* 28(2):92–94, 1996.

5. Experiments by the author.

6. Harruff, R. C. Comparison of contact shotgun wounds of the head produced by different gauge shotguns. *J. Forensic Sci.* 40(5):801–804, 1995.

7. Dowling, G. P., Dickinson A. H., and Cooke, C. T. Shotgun petal abrasions in close range .410-caliber shotgun injuries. *J. Forensic Sci.* 33(1):260–266, 1988.

8. Breitenecker, R. and Senior, W. Shotgun patterns. An experimental study on the influence of intermediate targets. *J. Forensic Sci.* 12(2): 193–204, 1967.

9. Breitenecker, R. Shotgun wound patterns. *Am. J. Clin. Pathol.* 52:258–269, 1969.

10. Coe, J. I. and Austin, N. The effects of various intermediate targets on dispersion of shotgun patterns. *Am. J. Forensic Med. Path.* 13(4):281–3, 1992.

11. Moreau, T. S., Nickels, M. L., Wray, J. L., Bottemiller, K. W. and Rowe, W. F. Pellet patterns fired by sawed-off shotguns. *J. Forensic Sci.* 30(1):137–149, 1985.

12. Missliwetz, J. and Lindermann, A. Gunshot wounds caused by Fiocchi Anticrime Cartridges (plastic bullets). *Am. J. Forensic Med. Path.* 12(3):209–212, 1991.

Bloody Bodies and Bloody Scenes

9

"Is there life after death? Trespass and find out."
"This property is protected by Smith & Wesson"

Bumper stickers

Violence as portrayed in the movies and television has traditionally been relatively bloodless. In real life, most gunshot scenes are quite bloody. As in many aspects of forensic pathology, this observation is not immutable. Some scenes show evidence of considerable bleeding; some essentially none. In the latter case, hemorrhaging is internal (into the chest or abdominal cavities) or is prevented by clothing. The only observable blood may be a dime-shaped area of bleeding on the clothing overlying the entrance site.

Minimal bleeding around an entrance site usually involves small-caliber weapons and locations on the body that are clothed and/or elevated, i.e., not in dependent areas where bleeding or leakage of blood would occur secondary to gravity. Clothing may act as a pressure bandage. When the deceased is wearing multiple layers of clothing, blood from the wound may be absorbed by the internal layers of clothing so that there is no evidence of bleeding on the outer clothing.

Gunshot wounds of the head usually bleed freely. This is not invariable, however. The author had a case in which there was a contact gunshot wound of the back of the head from a .22-caliber rimfire weapon whose entrance was sealed by the hot gases. There was no blood at the scene or visible on the body. The entrance was concealed by a bushy haircut and was found only when the head was opened as part of a routine autopsy on an apparent natural death.

In scenes where the deceased has walked or run from the scene of the shooting, there is usually a trail of blood. The quantity of bleeding, however, is very variable. In some cases there may be no blood because the bleeding was internal or the victim pressed their hand or a cloth against the wound, thus acting as a pressure bandage to prevent external hemorrhaging onto the floor or ground.

Physical Activity Following Gunshot Wounds

An individual may sustain a fatal gunshot wound and yet engage in physical activity.[1-2] Experienced forensic pathologists, not uncommonly, encounter cases in which an individual, after incurring a fatal gunshot wound of the heart, is able to walk or run hundreds of yards and engage in strenuous physical activity prior to collapse and death. In one case seen by the author, a young man was shot in the left chest at a range of 3 to 4 ft with a 12-gauge shotgun firing #7 1/2 shot. The pellets literally shredded the heart, yet, this individual was able to run 65 feet prior to collapsing. Such activity is not surprising if one realizes that an individual can function without a heart for a short time. The limiting factor for consciousness is the oxygen supply to the brain. When the oxygen in the brain is consumed, unconsciousness occurs. Experiments have shown that an individual can remain conscious for at least 10 to 15 sec. after complete occlusion of the carotid arteries. Thus, if no blood is pumped to the brain because of a massive gunshot wound of the heart, an individual can remain conscious and function, e.g., run, for at least 10 sec before collapsing.

In another case, a 17-year-old boy was shot once in the left back with a .25 ACP (6.35-mm) pistol. The bullet perforated the aorta, left main pulmonary artery, and left lung, embedding itself in the anterior chest wall. When the Emergency Medical Service technicians arrived at the scene, the victim initially refused to go to the hospital with them; he had to be forced into the ambulance. This scene was videotaped and shown on a local television station. He arrived at the hospital approximately 30 min. after having been shot. At the time, he was awake and alert with normal vital signs. Fifteen minutes after arrival at the hospital, (45 min. after being shot), he was noted to be agitated and combative. Over the next half hour he gradually exhibited shock, and 1 hr. and 15 min. after being shot, he was brought into the operating room. At this time, he developed irreversible shock and was pronounced dead 2 hr. and 20 min. after being shot.

Sudden blood loss causes interference with activity when it exceeds 20 to 25% of the total blood supply. Loss over 40% is life threatening. The rate of bleeding, the amount of blood loss, the nature of the injury, and the body's physiological response determines the time from injury to incapacitation and death. This can vary from seconds to hours.

As blood is lost, there is impaired perfusion of the tissue by blood with resultant cellular dysfunction (shock). The individual becomes anxious, weak, disoriented and restless. The pulse becomes weak, blood pressure falls, and breathing becomes rapid. The body initiates defensive mechanisms to counteract this loss of blood. Blood pressure (and thus tissue perfusion) is directly related to cardiac output and systemic vascular resistance (primarily the vasomotor tone of the blood vessels in the peripheral vascular system). As blood pressure falls, there is activation of the systemic nervous system. Epinephrine (adrenalin) and norepinephrine are released from the adrenals and sympathetic nerve endings. B_1 receptors in the heart respond by increasing the heart rate and force of contraction. This results in an increase in cardiac output. Stimulation of A_1 receptors in the peripheral vasculature causes selective vasoconstriction reducing the blood flow to the skin, gastrointestinal tract and kidneys, thus maintaining adequate perfusion of the heart and brain. The decease in arterial pressure also causes a decrease in the capillary hydrostatic pressure. As this falls, fluid from the interstitial space is drawn into the vasculature replacing the volume of the lost blood. Once the blood loss exceeds the ability of the body to compensate, there is confusion, disorientation and loss of consciousness.

Just as in the case of gunshot wounds of the heart or major blood vessels, individuals can perform tasks or even survive gunshot wounds of the brain, especially if the injury involves only the frontal lobes. Numerous individuals have survived perforating gunshot wounds of the frontal lobes though there may be associated personality changes and/or blindness. In documented cases of suicide, individuals have fired a bullet through the frontal lobes, to be followed by a second, fatal gunshot wound, of the basal ganglia.

If a bullet passes through the basal ganglia, one can ordinarily be certain of immediate unconsciousness and inability to move. The only exceptions to this rule that the author has encountered involved two cases of gunshot wounds of the anterior tips of the caudate nuclei. In one case, an elderly individual shot himself in the temple with a .32-caliber revolver. The bullet perforated both cerebral hemispheres injuring the tips of the caudate lobes. Following this, he was conscious for at least two hours during which time he spoke to his wife, a visiting nurse, and EMS personnel.

Gunshot wounds of the brainstem produce instant incapacitation, though death may not occur immediately. One individual who had a gunshot wound of the pons survived approximately one week, although in a totally vegetative state.

The fact that one can survive at least for a limited time with a wound of the head that would ordinarily be thought to cause instant death is shown in Figure 9.1. This elderly male shot himself in the right temple with a .357

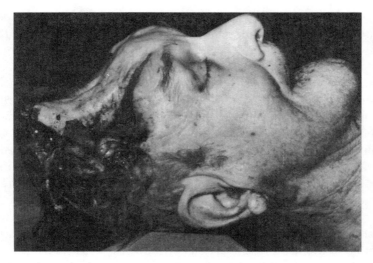

Figure 9.1 Contact wound of right temple with .357 Magnum. The deceased lived 1 hr and 34 min without any life-support systems.

Magnum. In spite of the obvious devastating nature of the wound, he lived 1 hr. and 34 min. without any life-support systems.

In addition to a wound not immediately causing incapacitation, in some instances individuals who have been shot do not initially realize it. This is not uncommon in combat situations, where the noise, violence, and activity so distract an individual that he may not realize that he has been wounded.

Wounds Seen in The Emergency Room

It is quite common for a pathologist at autopsy to discover gunshot wounds missed by the police at the scene or physicians in an emergency room. Emergency room physicians often miss head wounds because of long hair and back wounds because they fail to look at the patient's back. They also confuse entrances with exits. In a study of 46 cases of fatal multiple or exiting gunshot wounds by Collins and Lantz, 24 (52.2%) were misinterpreted by trauma specialists (emergency medicine, trauma surgery and neurosurgery physicians).[3] The failures involved errors in interpreting the number of projectiles as well as differentiating exits and entrances. In 27 fatal cases involving a single gunshot wound, 10 cases were misinterpreted. In five (5) cases, there were errors involving misinterpretation of entrance versus exit, in one (1) the number of projectiles, and in four (4) both these errors occurred. Therefore, one must approach medical records with a degree of caution in trying to determine how many times a person has been shot as well as whether a wound is an entrance or exit. It is also quite common for a physician to fail to note in the medical records the exact location of a wound and the presence or absence of soot or powder tattooing around it. A gunshot wound may be described only as "in the right back" without any other localizing information. Occasionally, such information may be found in the nurse's notes. One must also realize that soot may have been present initially, but that the nurse who saw the patient before the physician may have wiped it off. These factors again point out the importance of retention of clothing, as the wounds in question may have been due to bullets that went through the clothing. The ambulance crews, emergency rooms, and hospitals should be instructed never to discard clothing in cases of gunshot wounds.

Surgical intervention may make interpretation of gunshot wounds difficult if not impossible as a result of the obliteration or the alteration of wounds. In gunshot wounds of the chest, the surgeon may insert a chest tube into the wound or make his thoracotomy incision through it. In gunshot wounds of the head, it is usual for the surgeon to obliterate the entrance wound in the scalp and bone when performing a craniectomy.

Some surgeons, especially those who have had military training, perform wide debridement of entrance wounds in the skin from handguns and rimfire rifles even though this is unnecessary due to the small amount of kinetic energy possessed by these bullets. As the removed tissue is supposed to be sent to Surgical Pathology for examination, this tissue can often be retrieved and examined.

Surgeons often recover a bullet that caused an injury. One should instruct them in the correct marking of such missiles. Unfortunately, it is not uncommon for a surgeon to inscribe their initials on the side of a recovered bullet rather than the nose or base, thus obliterating its rifling characteristics. In shotgun wound cases, one should also inform the surgeons that the wadding and representative pellets should be retained for evidentiary purposes.

Concealment of a wound may occur not only through the actions of a physician but also as a consequence of an unusual entrance site. At some time in every forensic pathologist's career, a case will be encountered in which the bullet enters either the nostril or open mouth, thus, presenting the pathologist with a body with no observable entrance wound. Advanced decomposition may also conceal a gunshot wound. The use of x-rays on select decomposed bodies will prevent missing such cases.

In skeletal remains, x-ray of the bones for missiles should be done routinely. It is also wise to collect the dirt underneath the skeleton and x-ray it. The author had a case in which a .22-caliber bullet was found embedded in a vertebra. Up to that time no cause of death had been determined. The entrance defect had been missed on gross examination of this bone. Subsequent x-ray of the dirt underneath the body revealed two other bullets.

Minimal Velocities Necessary to Perforate Skin

Before a bullet can cause a significant injury, it must be able to perforate skin. Skin differs from other tissue in that a relatively high initial velocity is necessary for a bullet to effect perforation. Knowledge of this velocity is important to the forensic pathologist in cases of assault, attempted homicide, or homicide with airguns as well as in determining the maximum range out to which a bullet is capable of penetrating the body.

The first person to attempt to determine the minimum velocity needed to perforate skin was Journee in 1907.[4] He observed that missiles of relatively low velocity (80 to 200 m/sec) that rebounded from the skin of a horse could go through 20 cm of muscle after the skin had been removed. Thus, skin appeared to be more resistant to missiles than muscle. Experiments on human cadavers revealed that a lead sphere 11.25 mm in diameter and weighing 8.5 g needed a minimum velocity of 70 m/sec (230 ft/sec), with an energy/area of presentation (E/a) of 2.13 m-kg/cm^2, to perforate the skin and enter the underlying subcutaneous tissue and muscle.

Matoo et al. in 1974 obtained virtually the same results using human thigh muscle with intact skin.[5] A lead sphere 8.5 mm in diameter and weighing 4.5 gm required a velocity of 71.3 m/sec (234 ft/sec) to perforate skin and penetrate into subcutaneous tissue and muscle to a depth of 2.9 cm. The E/a was 2.06 m-kg/cm^2.

Both these studies involved relatively heavy large-caliber lead balls and not the lighter weight, bullet-shaped projectiles fired in modern firearms or the very lightweight projectiles used in airguns.

DiMaio et al. conducted a series of tests to determine the velocities necessary for .38-caliber lead bullets and lead airgun pellets (calibers .177 and .22) to perforate skin.[6] Human lower extremities were used in the tests. A 113-gr. lead roundnose .38- caliber bullet required a minimal velocity of 58 m/sec (191 ft/sec) to perforate skin (Table 9.1). The E/a was 1.95 m-kg/cm.^{2}

Caliber .22 wasp-waist Diabolo-style airgun pellets weighing an average of 16.5 gr. initially perforated skin at 75 m/sec (245 ft/sec), with perforation becoming consistent at 87 m/sec (285 ft/sec) and above (Table 9.1). The E/a at 75 m/sec was 1.30 m-kg/cm^2. At a velocity of 68 m/sec (223 ft/sec), a pellet embedded itself in, but did not perforate, the skin.

0.177 airgun pellets of wasp-waist Diabolo style weighing an average of 8.25 gr. required a minimum velocity of 101 m/sec (331 ft/sec) to initially perforate skin (Table 9.1). At velocities of 111 m/sec (365 ft/sec) and higher, perforation always occurred. At a velocity of 88 m/sec (290 ft/sec), a pellet embedded itself in the skin. The E/a at 101 m/sec (331 ft/sec) was 1.84 m-kg/cm^2.

Table 9.1 Minimum Velocities Necessary to Perforate Skin

Missile	Weight (gr)	Minimum Velocity (m/sec)
.177 airgun pellets	8.25	101 (331 ft/sec)
.22 airgun pellets	16.5	75 (245 ft/sec)
.38-caliber round-nose bullet	113	58 (191 ft/sec)

McKenzie et al. conducted a series of experiments involving the firing of 7.9 gr., .177 caliber, airguns pellets, pointed and blunt tipped, at a newly killed (within 10 minutes of experimentation) pig. The pointed tip pellets had a velocity of perforation of 384 +/– 4 ft/s; the blunt tip pellets 403 +/– 3 ft/s.[7]

These studies indicate that lightweight projectiles need a higher velocity to perforate skin than large caliber heavier bullets.

Now that we have an idea of the minimum velocity necessary for bullets and airgun pellets of different weights and calibers to perforate skin, we must ask whether the missiles lose this velocity in perforating the skin. The answer is no. In an unpublished extension of the previously mentioned study, DiMaio and Copeland conducted a number of test firings using a human lower extremity to determine how much velocity was lost by a missile passing through the thigh.[8] The bullets had to pass through two layers of skin and approximately 6 in. of muscle. Two different calibers of ammunition were used — .38 Special and .22 Long Rifle. In the tests with the .38 Special ammunition, two different types of ammunition were used. The first type was loaded with a 158-gr. lead round-nose bullet. Average impact velocity was 766 ft/sec. On an average, these bullets lost 280 ft/sec (36.8% of impact initial velocity) in passing through the thigh (Table 9.2). The velocity lost ranged from a minimum of 214 ft/sec to a maximum of 337 ft/sec.

Table 9.2 Velocity Lost by Bullets Perforating Human Skin and Muscle[a]

Caliber	Bullet Weight (gr)	Bullet Style	Average Velocity Lost (ft/sec)	Range of Velocity Lost (ft/sec)	Velocity Lost (%)
.38 Special	158	Lead roundnose	280	214–337	36.8
	158	Semi-jacketed hollow-point[b]	305	264–355	34.4
.22 Long Rifle	40	Lead roundnose	195	187–202	18
	36	Lead hollow-point	491	431–599	45.5

[a] Two layers of skin, 6 in. of muscle.
[b] This bullet did not mushroom.

The second type of ammunition was loaded with 158 gr., semi-jacketed hollow-point bullets. The average impact velocity was 884 ft/sec. With this velocity and weight of bullet, there is no mushrooming of the projectile in the body. Therefore, mushrooming was not a factor in loss of velocity. The average velocity lost was 355 ft/sec for an average loss of 34.4% of impact velocity (Table 9.2). The velocity lost ranged from a low of 264 ft/sec to a maximum of 335 ft/sec. The increased loss of velocity by the semi-jacketed hollow-point bullet compared with the roundnose bullet, if significant, could be due to either one or the other of two factors if not a combination. The first factor is the greater velocity at which the semi-jacketed bullet was pro-pelled and the second is the blunt shape of the tip necessitated by having a hollow point. Mushrooming of the bullet did not occur and therefore could not play a part in an increased loss of velocity. In all probability, the greater impact velocity caused the greater loss of velocity. This theory tends to be confirmed by the fact that the percentage loss of impact velocity for both styles of bullets was approximately the same.

The tests with the .22 ammunition were somewhat more extensive in that the loss of velocity was determined not only for the thigh when it was enclosed by skin but also for the muscle alone. This was accomplished by the removal of the skin after test-firing with it in place. The first ammunition tested was high-velocity .22 Long Rifle cartridges loaded with 40-gr. lead roundnose bul-lets. The average impact velocity was 1083 ft/sec. Average loss of velocity in passing through the thigh was 195 ft/sec, with velocity lost ranging from 187 to 202 ft/sec (Table 9.2). When the skin was removed from the thigh, this same ammunition lost an average of 151 ft/sec range (85 to 229 ft/sec). Thus, in passing through two layers of skin, the bullets lost only an average of 44 ft/sec.

The second type of ammunition was high-velocity .22 Long Rifle ammu-nition loaded with a 36-gr. lead hollow-point bullet. The average striking velocity was 1079 ft/sec. Average velocity loss was 491 ft/sec with a range of 431 to 599 ft/sec, approximately 2 1/2 times the velocity lost by the solid roundnose bullets (Table 9.2). When the hollow-point ammunition was tested against the thigh with the skin removed, there was an average loss of velocity of 383 ft/sec, with a range of 320 to 520 ft/sec. Thus, in passing through two layers of skin, the hollow-point bullets lost an average of only 108 ft/sec. The increased loss of velocity in passing through the skin compared with the solid lead bullets is consistent with the increased loss sustained while passing through muscle.

Bullet Emboli

Vascular embolization of a bullet is an uncommon occurrence. When it does occur, it usually involves the arterial system. Embolization should be suspected whenever there is a penetrating bullet wound with failure to discover the bullet in the expected region or to visualize the bullet on routine x-ray.[9] In the author's first encounter with a case of bullet embolization, he spent seven hours looking for a bullet in the chest and abdomen, when it was in the femoral artery (there was no x-ray equipment).

The most common sites of entrance for a bullet into the arterial system are the aorta and the heart. In a review of 153 cases of bullet emboli in the English-language literature, there were 100 cases of embolism to the arterial circulation and 53 to the venous.[10] The source of the embolism to the arterial circulation was the thoracic aorta in 37.9% of cases, the heart in 34.4% cases, and the abdominal aorta in 15.5% cases. The sources of the emboli to the venous circulation were the vena cava in 23.5% (the inferior vena cava was 20.6%), the iliac veins 29.4%, and the heart 17.6%. The bullets generally followed the direction of the blood flow though 14.7% of venous bullets followed a retrograde path. Although embolization usually occurs immediately following entrance of the bullet into the circulation, delays as long as 26 days have been reported.[11] The site of lodgment of the bullet is predominantly the right side of the heart and the pulmonary arteries for bullets entering the venous system and the lower extremities for bullets entering the systemic circulation. Whether there is predominant embolization to the right or left legs is debatable.[9] Embolization to the brain is rare. Virtually all such cases involve shotgun pellets.[12]

Bullet emboli are usually associated with small caliber, low-velocity missiles. Thus, in the review by DiMaio and DiMaio, in the 24 instances in which the caliber or type of weapon was known, a .22-caliber bullet accounted for 14 cases, an airgun pellet for 2 cases, and a shotgun pellet for 2 cases.[9] These missiles are all small-caliber, lightweight, low-velocity projectiles possessing low kinetic energy and usually causing penetrating rather than perforating wounds. If these missiles lose their forward velocity on penetration of a major blood vessel or the heart, they will be swept along by the blood to their final point of lodgement.

If an x-ray is not taken before autopsy, a bullet embolus secondary to a gunshot wound of the aorta may not be suspected because of the presence of both an entrance and an exit in this vessel. In such a case, the almost spent bullet, after exiting the aorta, strikes the vertebral column and rebounds back through the exit into the lumen of the aorta, where it is swept away to a lower extremity.

Bullet emboli may occur from wounds other than those in the chest and abdomen. In one of the author's cases, an individual was shot in the left eye with a .22-caliber bullet. The bullet entered the cranial cavity, traveled through the left cerebral hemisphere, and ricocheted off the inner table of the skull, penetrating into the left straight sinus. It was carried through the venous system, down the jugular vein, through the right atrium and ventricle, and into the pulmonary artery. The bullet came to rest lodged in a major branch of the left pulmonary artery.

A variant of the bullet embolus not involving vascular embolization is occasionally encountered. One such case involved an individual shot in the right back. The bullet traveled upward into the oral cavity, where it subsequently was coughed or vomited up by the victim. The bullet was found on the ground a number of feet away from the deceased in a pool of vomitus and blood. In another case, an individual incurred a gunshot wound of the chest. On admission to the hospital, the bullet was seen on x-ray apparently lodged in the parenchyma of the right lung. The individual survived a number of days in the hospital. At autopsy, the bullet was found in the bronchus of the left lung. Apparently the bullet entered the bronchial tree on the right side and subsequently was coughed up and aspirated into the left bronchial tree.

Gunshot Wounds of the Brain

Gunshot wounds of the brain constitute approximately one-third of all fatal gunshot wounds. Wounds of the brain from centerfire rifles and shotguns are extremely devastating. Such injuries are described in Chapters 7 and 8. This section will deal with gunshot wounds of the brain caused by low-velocity weapons — handguns and .22 rimfire rifles.

Bone Chips

When a bullet strikes the head, it "punches out" a circular to oval wound of entrance in the skull, driving fragments of bone into the brain. The bone chips generally follow along the main bullet track, contributing to its irregular configuration. Sometimes the bone chips create secondary tracks that deviate from the main path. These chips are detectable on digital palpation in approximately one-third of gunshot wound cases of the brain.[13] Use of high-resolution x-ray increases the percentage detected.

The presence of bone chips at one end of the bullet track through the brain provides conclusive evidence of the direction of the shot; in the author's experience, no bone chips are found in the brain parenchyma adjacent to the exit wound. This fact is of help in cases of perforating gunshot wounds where there has been surgical debridement of wounds in the skin and bone and where it is important to differentiate the entrance from the exit.

Secondary Fractures of the Skull

As the bullet perforates the brain, it produces a temporary cavity that undergoes a series of pulsations before disappearing. The pressure waves in the

brain in the case of high-velocity missiles may produce massive fragmentation of the skull. In the case of handgun bullets, the pressure waves are
considerably less but still may cause fractures. Linear fractures of the orbital
plate are the most common because of the paper-thin nature of the bone.
Fracture lines may radiate from the entrance or exit hole or even be randomly
distributed in the vault or base of the skull. These secondary fractures of the
skull are seen most commonly with medium- and large-caliber handguns,
though they occur even in distant .22-caliber Long Rifle wounds. No matter
what the caliber, secondary fractures are more common with contact wounds,
where the pressure waves from the temporary cavity are augmented by pressure from the expanding gas.

Shape of the Bullet Tracks

The shape of the permanent missile track in the brain is irregular, sometimes
larger near the entry, other times larger near the exit or the middle.[13] The
irregular shape of the cavity defies any attempt to determine the direction of
travel from its configuration. The size of the permanent cavity bears no
relationship to the caliber or muzzle energy of the missile. Wound tracks
produced by .22 rimfire ammunition may be as large and devastating as those
caused by .45 ACP bullets. The influence of gas from combustion of the
propellant on the volume of the permanent cavity appears to be small or nil.
In the study by Kirkpatrick and DiMaio, contact wounds accounted for both
the minimum and the maximum volume of missile tracks.[13]

Point of Lodgement of the Bullet

In many handgun wounds of the head, the bullet is retained either in the
cranial cavity or beneath the scalp. Whether a handgun bullet is retained or
exits is dependent on: the caliber of the weapon; the construction of the bullet
(lead, semi-jacketed, full metal-jacketed); the range and the site of entrance.
As the caliber of a bullet increases, the likelihood of its perforating also
increases. Full metal-jacketed bullets have a greater tendency to perforate the
head than lead or semi-jacketed bullets of the same or approximately the same
caliber. Distant wounds are more likely to produce penetrating wounds rather
than perforating wounds; contact wounds, perforating rather than penetrating. A bullet entering the skull through the thick occipital bone is less likely
to exit than a bullet entering through the thin temporal bone. Thus, a contact
wound of the temple, from a .357 Magnum handgun, firing a full metal-
jacketed bullet, should result in the bullet exiting while a distant wound of the
occipital area, from a .22 lead bullet, should result in the bullet being retained.
    Table 9.3 shows the percentage of bullets exiting the head in relationship
to caliber, range, bullet construction, and site of entrance. Virtually all the

suicidal wounds were contact, with the vast majority entering the temple region, while most of the homicides were distant wounds with the location of the entrances randomly distributed. All the .22 caliber bullets were lead; the .25 ACP's full metal-jacketed and the .357 Magnum's semi-jacketed hollow-point or, very rarely, soft-point. The 9 mm's were predominantly full metal-jacketed; the .38 Specials mostly semi-jacketed hollow-point, occasionally lead roundnose. The exact distribution of bullet styles for the 9 mm's and .38 Specials could not be determined because not all the exiting bullets were recovered and in some cases different bullet styles were used in the same gun.

Table 9.3 Percentage of Bullets Exiting Head in Relationship to Caliber

Caliber	Suicides		Homicides	
	Cases	Exiting	Cases	Exiting
.22	185	20.0%	60	6.6%
.25 ACP	90	50.0%	59	1.6%
.38 Special	258	63.1%	101	24.7%
9 mm	26	69.2%	26	57.6%
.357 Magnum	101	73.2%	25	36.0%
Total	660	51.0%	271	19.9%

Table 9.3 confirms the previously noted assertions in regard to caliber, bullet construction, range and site of entrance. In suicides (in which wounds are virtually always contact and predominantly in the temple), the bullet exited 51% of the times compared to homicides (predominantly distant wounds, randomly distributed over the surface of the head), where the bullet exited in only 19.9% of the cases. These observations are true even if one compares the percentage of exit for suicide versus homicide for each caliber individually. With the exception of homicides with the .357 Magnum, as the caliber increased so did the tendency for a bullet to exit the head.

Of the bullets that do not exit the head, the vast majority are retained in the cranial cavity. Thus, internal ricochet is fairly common, occurring in anywhere from 10 to 25% of the cases, depending on the caliber of the weapons and the diligence with which the evidence of internal ricochet is sought. As a general rule, internal ricochet is more commonly associated with lead bullets and bullets of small caliber. Thus, ricochet within the cranial cavity occurs most commonly with .22 lead bullets. The type of ricochet most commonly encountered results from a bullet that passes through the brain, strikes the internal table of the skull on the other side, and is deflected in a cortical or subcortical path parallel to the internal table. This results in a shallow gutter wound track in the cortex of the brain. Less commonly, bullets ricochet back into the brain at an acute angle or along the original bullet track (Figure 9.2).

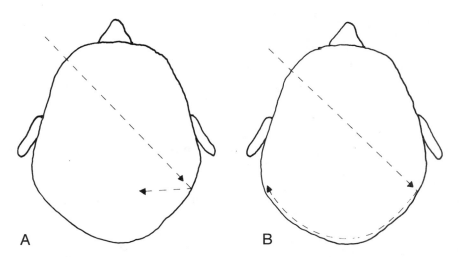

Figure 9.2 Patterns of bullet ricochet inside cranial cavity. Type B is the most common.

The length of the internal ricochet track may be quite long. In one case, a .38 Special lead bullet entered the right frontal lobe, perforated the brain, exiting the left frontal lobe. The bullet then ricocheted off the bone traveling along the lateral aspect of the left frontal, parietal, and occipital lobes; crossed the midline; and continued along the lateral aspect of the right cerebral hemisphere, coming to rest in the lateral cortex of the right frontal pole adjacent to where it had entered.

Examination of the brain in gunshot wounds reveals contusions around the entrance site in about half the cases.[13] These are probably due to in-bending of the bone against the brain at the moment of perforation. Contusions are equally frequent at the exit, although they do not necessarily occur in the same cases as entry contusions. Contusions can also be seen on the inferior surface of the frontal lobe.

In virtually all gunshot wound cases involving the brain, the brain will show signs of increased intracranial pressure. These signs consist of grooves of the uncal gyri from the tentorium as well as cone-shaped molding of the cerebellar tonsils at the foramen magnum. These findings may help explain death in some cases. Examination of gunshot-wounded brains reveals many cases in which the vital centers were not directly in the path of the bullet and in which the volume of the permanent cavity was relatively small (less than many spontaneous hematomas), i.e., the volume of grossly involved brain is trivial when compared with the brain itself. In such cases, deformation of the brain toward the foramen magnum still occurs. Pressure on the brainstem secondary to this deformation may be the fatal mechanism in these cases.[13]

Intrauterine Gunshot Wounds

Gunshot wounds of the pregnant uterus are relatively uncommon.[14] Maternal death in such cases is rare. The gunshot injury to the fetus or placenta usually results in intrauterine death or premature delivery with or without evidence of injury to the child.

The most significant question arising from fetal deaths due to gunshot wounds of the pregnant uterus concerns the ruling of the manner of death.[15] If the child dies in utero, no matter how advanced the state of development, there is no criminal culpability for the child's death attached to the person who did the shooting. Legally the child is not considered an individual until it is born alive. If, however, the child is born alive and then dies, even if the time of survival is a matter of only a few minutes, the death is considered a homicide, even if the bullet did not strike the child but just induced premature labor. In the latter case, one could rule the cause of death as "Prematurity secondary to gunshot wound of uterus — Homicide."

Lead Poisoning from Retained Bullets

Lead poisoning from a retained bullet or lead shotgun pellets is extremely rare in view of the large number of individuals with such retained missiles. Even rarer is death from lead poisoning resulting from the retained bullet, with only three such cases in the English literature.[16-18]

As of 1994, there were 35 laboratory-documented cases of lead toxicity from a retained lead missile in the English literature.[19-20] Fifteen of these have been reported since 1980. Onset of symptoms has occurred from months to up to 27 years after being shot.[16] In most of the cases, the missile was within a joint, a bone, or an intervertebral disk. It has long been recognized that synovial fluid is capable of dissolving lead. A rich vascular supply to the tissue surrounding the bullet and prolonged bathing of the bullet with either bursal or synovial fluid makes the development of acute lead intoxication more likely.

In a fatal case of lead poisoning reported by the author, the individual was a 54-year-old woman shot in the thigh by her son with a .32-caliber revolver.[17] X-rays taken at the time the deceased was shot showed a flattened, deformed lead missile lodged in the soft tissue near the distal femur, just proximal to the condyles and antero-lateral to the bone. Small fragments of lead were present adjacent to the main mass. The location of the bullet was consistent with its being in or in communication with the suprapatellar bursa. Five months after being shot, the victim was admitted to a hospital with severe anemia. Hemoglobin was 6.9 gm/dl, hematocrit 21%, MCV 84, and platelets 388,000 mm³, with a white blood cell count of 5600 mm². The reticulocyte count was 5%. A smear showed basophilic stippling. The patient had been seen 9 months previous to this admission, at which time her hematocrit was 39% and hemoglobin 13 gm/dl. One month before this last admission, she came to the hospital complaining of constipation and gnawing dull periumbilical and epigastric abdominal pain. She had had a 20-lb weight loss over the previous 4 months.

During her hospitalization, a diagnosis of lead poisoning was never considered. She suffered multiple episodes of grand mal convulsions and died 14 days after admission. At autopsy, the brain was swollen with uncal herniation and necrosis. Secondary brainstem hemorrhage was present. Analysis of the blood obtained postmortem revealed a lead level of 5.3 mg/L. Fortuitously, antemortem blood obtained 5 days before death had been retained and revealed a lead level of 5.1 mg/L. Any lead level above 0.6 mg/L was considered toxic in the hospital laboratory.

Microscopic examination of autopsy tissue in this case revealed eosinophilic intranuclear inclusions in hepatocytes and cells of the proximal tubules of the kidneys (Figure 9.3). Many of the perivascular spaces in the brain

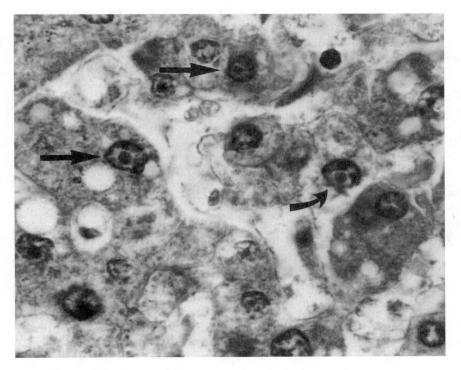

Figure 9.3 Eosinophilic intranuclear inclusions in hepatocytes.

contained aggregates of pink-staining homogeneous material that was PAS positive. These histological lesions are described as being associated with lead intoxication. It is interesting that a neurological examination conducted at the time of admission to the hospital was negative. This result most probably represents a cursory neurologic examination in a patient not expected to have neurological abnormalities. By coincidence, the other two fatal cases in the literature also involve women shot in the leg.[16-18]

Location of Fatal Gunshot Wounds

There have been no extensive civilian studies to show the location of fatal gunshot wounds in the body in non-suicide cases. The U.S. Army has conducted a number of studies involving combat casualties.[21-23] The most recent one, and probably the most applicable in view of changes in medical therapy, was the WDMET study from the Vietnam war.[21] This study found that, although the head and neck constituted only 6.5% of the body surface, wounds of this region accounted for 37.2% of fatal gunshot wounds. The thorax, with 13% of the body surface, was the source of fatal wounds in 36.4% of fatalities; the abdomen, 10.6% of the body surface, accounted for 9.2% of the fatal wounds.

It has been the author's experience that in civilian homicide cases 40% of fatal wounds involve the brain, approximately 25% involve the heart, 25% involve the aorta or other main blood vessels, and 10% involve solid viscera, e.g., lungs, liver, kidney, etc.

Behavior of Ammunition and Gunpowder in Fires

Occasionally a story appears in a newspaper describing how fire fighters fought a blaze in a sporting goods store as bullets from exploding ammunition "whizzed by" and cans of gunpowder "exploded" around them. Although this type of story makes fine newspaper copy, it bears no relation to what actually happens in a fire involving ammunition and gunpowder.

Smokeless powder is used in all modern cartridges. When it is ignited in a gun, heat, and gas are produced, both of which are confined initially to the chamber. As the pressure of the gas builds up, the chemical processes of combustion are speeded up so that the rate of burning becomes relatively instantaneous, and an "explosion" is produced. This explosion, however, occurs only when smokeless powder is ignited in a confined space such as the chamber of a gun. Outside of a gun, the powder will only burn with a quick hot flame.

In order to demonstrate the burning properties of smokeless powder, Hatcher conducted a series of experiments in which he burned cans of smokeless powder.[24] The amount of powder in each can varied from 1 lb to 8 oz. Each can was placed on a quantity of kindling wood, which was then ignited. After a period of from 40 sec to 1 1/2 min, the cans burst with a mild noise, followed by a yellow-white flame 3 to 4 ft in diameter. The underlying kindling wood was practically undisturbed. There were no violent explosions.

Black powder is a different matter. It burns faster than smokeless powder and may actually produce an explosion. Black powder is not loaded in modern ammunition. Hatcher burnt a 1-lb can of black powder. After a minute of heating, the can exploded with a heavy dull thud, producing a dense cloud of smoke but no flames. The can was hurled approximately 35 ft. It had been opened up and flattened by the explosion.

Experiments have been conducted to determine at what temperature a small-arms cartridge will detonate.[25] Cartridges were placed in an oven and the furnace was heated until the round exploded. It was found that .22 Long Rifle cartridges exploded at an average of 275°F, .38 Special rounds at 290°F, .30–06 at 317°F, and 12-gauge shotgun shells at 387°F. Whereas the cartridges detonated in every case, the primers did not. In some of the detonated rounds, the primers were removed, loaded into other cartridges cases, and fired.

Occasionally one hears that an individual has been "wounded" when a cartridge was accidentally dropped into a fire and detonated. Investigation of such incidents usually reveals that the victim was really injured when they or another individual was playing with a gun. When small-arms ammunition is placed in a fire, the cartridge case may burst into a number of fragments and the bullet may then be propelled forward out of the case. In centerfire cartridges, the primer may blowout. None of these missiles, however, is dangerous to life under ordinary circumstances. The bullet in fact is probably the most harmless of all these missiles because with its relatively great mass it will have very little velocity. Fragments of brass and the primer are the only components of an exploding round that have sufficient velocity to cause injury. These fragments can penetrate the skin or eye if the individual is very close to the exploding cartridge. With the exception of eye injury, however, no serious injury should occur, and certainly no mortal wound. As the distance between the exploding round and the individual increases, the primer and brass particles become harmless because of their relatively small mass and irregular shape, which produce rapid loss in velocity.

The aforementioned observations were verified in a series of experiments in which flame from a propane torch was applied to a total of 202 cartridges: 10 shotgun shells (.410 and 12 gauge); 30 .22 Long Rifle cartridges; 68 handgun cartridges from .38 Special to .44 Magnum and 94 rifle cartridges from .22 Hornet to .338 Magnum.[26] Heat applied to the base of the shotgun shells caused the primer to detonate, igniting the powder and rupturing the plastic hull. Any pellets expelled had a velocity too slow to record on a chronograph. When the primers were expelled, they had an average velocity of 860 ft/s for the .410 shells and 60 ft/s for the 12 gauge. Heat applied to the plastic hull would burn through, igniting the powder but not detonating the primers. The shot was not expelled.

In regard to the rifle and handgun cartridges, when heat was applied to the base of the cartridge case, while the primers always detonated, the powder burnt only half the time. In the instances when the powder ignited, the cases did not rupture but rather the gases were vented out the primer hole. Heat applied to the forward part of the case would cause the powder to burn with the cases usually rupturing. With few exceptions, the primers did not detonate. The velocity of the expelled bullets ranged from 58 to 123 ft/s with the exception of the .270 rifle cartridge where it was 230 ft/s. Primer velocity ranged from 180 to 830 ft/s.

Although unconfined cartridges are relatively innocuous in fires, ammunition in a weapon is dangerous if it is present in the chamber. Here we have the same conditions as if the cartridge had been fired in the weapon in a conventional manner. The heat of the fire may be sufficient to "cook off" the cartridge in the chamber. If the weapon is a long arm or an auto-loading pistol, only one round will be fired. If the weapon is a revolver, not only can the cartridge in line with the barrel discharge, other cartridges in the other chambers of the cylinder can discharge. In this situation, one bullet would have rifling marks whereas the other bullets would be free of such markings. The bullets not in alignment with the barrel would show shearing of one surface secondary to their striking the frame of the weapon as they exited the cylinder.

If one is in a situation in which a fired weapon is recovered from a burned-out residence or vehicle, it is usually very easy to determine whether the cartridge in the weapon was discharged by heat rather than by firing in the conventional manner. Examination of the primer will reveal it to be free of the normal firing-pin impression. In weapons in which the firing pin rests on the primer, a faint mark may be present on the primer as a result of slight rearward movement of the cartridge case at the time of discharge from the heat.

Blunt-Force Injuries from Firearms

Occasionally a firearm will be used not only to shoot a person but to beat that individual. Thus, individuals will be seen with evidence of "pistol whipping." This usually takes the form of semicircular or triangular lacerations of the scalp or forehead produced by the butt of the gun. Underlying depressed

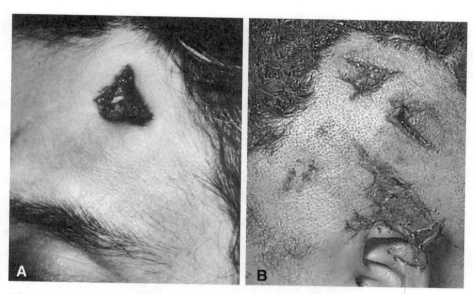

Figure 9.4 (A) Triangular laceration with underlying depressed skull fracture caused by pistol butt. (B) Rectangular lacerations of scalp from magazine well and base of magazine of 9-mm pistol.

fractures may be present (Figure 9.4). The butt of a rifle may also be used to beat a victim. Figure 9.5 shows an individual, who after being shot, had his jaw broken with the butt of a .22 rimfire rifle.

Multiple Gunshot Wounds Through One Entrance

Multiple gunshot wounds fired through a single entrance are rarely encountered. Jentzen et al. described a case where three separate bullets were fired through a single entrance.[27] The author has encountered a somewhat similar case in which two bullets were fired through a single entrance. This phenomena must be differentiated from Tandem bullets.

Falling Bullets

In some parts of the country, individuals celebrate New Years' Eve and July 4th by shooting guns in the air. Rarely, deaths are reported due to this practice. In most of these instances, the gun was probably not pointed straight up but at an angle to the horizon. In such a case, it is not unexpected for serious injuries to occur even if the bullet has traveled a great distance as a .30 caliber military rifle round has a maximum effective range of 4000 yards.

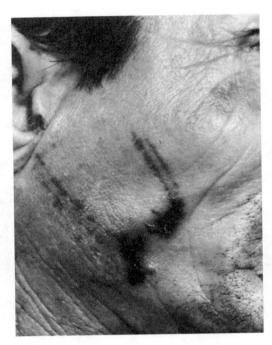

Figure 9.5 Patterned abrasion from rifle butt. Underlying fracture of mandible.

Haag, using a ballistic computer program, calculated the terminal velocity of bullets of various calibers if a weapon was fired straight up into the air.[28] When a gun is so fired, the bullet should return base forward. For some calibers, he also calculated the terminal velocity if the bullet was tumbling (Table 9.3). The terminal velocities of the bullets in Table 9.3, with the exception of the .22 Short and the buckshot pellets, are in the area of the minimum velocity necessary to perforate skin.

The author has had two cases in which individuals were struck by bullets fired into the air. In the first case, a 17-year-old male was struck in the upper left chest, by a full metal-jacketed .303 rifle bullet. The bullet perforated the chest wall through the second intercostal space, penetrating the upper lobe of the left lung and the pulmonary vein at the hilum. The bullet was then swept by the blood through the left atrium and ventricle into the thoracic aorta coming to rest just above the level of the diaphragm (Figure 9.6).

The second case involved a 5-year-old male child struck on the top of his head, in the left fronto-parietal region, by a full meatal-jacketed pistol bullet of probable 9-mm caliber. The bullet penetrated into the left cerebral hemisphere. The child survived and the bullet was not recovered. In both cases, the shooters were never apprehended. Whether the weapons were fired straight up or at an angle could not be determined.

Table 9.4 Terminal Velocity of Falling Bullets[a]

Caliber	Terminal Velocity	
	Base Forward (ft/s)	Tumbling (ft/s)
.22 Short	168	134
.22 LR	198	142
.25 ACP	191	146
.32 ACP	187	158
.380 ACP	187	
9 mm	219	
.38 Special	237	
.44 Magnum	249	
.45 ACP	228	
.223	244	141
7.62 × 39	264	158
.30–30	282	
.30–06	294	171
#4 Buck	134	
00 Buck	157	

[a] Based on data from Haag[28]

Reaction–Response Times in Handgun Shootings

Sooner or later a medical examiner will become involved in a shooting where an individual claims to have shot at another individual facing them but, at autopsy, the gunshot wound is found to be in the side or back. The question then arises as to whether the victim, on seeing the gun pointed towards them, or reacting to another outside stimulus, would have had sufficient time to turn 90 to 180 degrees in the time from when the shooter initiated the shooting process and the bullet hit. Cases such as this often involve police shootings.

Tobin and Fackler measured the minimum time needed for police Officers to fire, on signal, a drawn handgun, pointed at a target.[29] The tests were performed with both the trigger finger on the trigger as well as outside the trigger guard (the recommended way by many police agencies to hold a gun). The mean time from signal to firing the handgun was 0.365 seconds with the finger on the trigger and 0.677 seconds with the trigger finger outside the trigger guard. Volunteers were then videotaped as they turned their torsos 180 degrees as rapidly as possible. The mean time to turn the torso 90 degrees was 0.310 seconds while to turn 180 degrees it was 0.676 seconds. Thus, Tobin and Fackler concluded that if an individual was facing a shooter, it was possible for the individual to turn their torso and end up facing away from the shooter in the time from when the shooter decides to fire and the gun discharges.

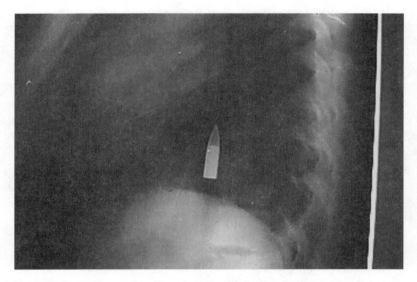

Figure 9.6   Full metal-jacketed .303 rifle bullet in lower thoracic aorta.

References

1. Karger, B. Penetrating gunshot wounds to the head and lack of immediate incapacitation. I. Wound ballistics and mechanisms of incapacitation. *Int. J. Legal Med.* (1995) 108: 53–61.

2. Karger, B. Penetrating gunshot wounds to the head and lack of immediate incapacitation. II. Review of case reports. *Int. J. Legal Med.* (1995) 108: 117–126.

3. Collins, K. A. and Lantz, P. A. Interpretation of fatal, multiple, and existing gunshot wounds by trauma specialists. *J. Forensic Sci.* 139(1): 94–99. January 1994.

4. Journeé, C. Rapport entre force vive des balles at la gravite des blessures qu'elles peuvent causer. *Rev. d'Artilleries.* 70(1): 81–120, 1907.

5. Matoo, B. N., Wani, A K., and Asgekar, M. D. Casualty criteria for wounds from firearms with special reference to shot penetration. Part II. *J. Forensic Sci.* 19(3): 585–589; 1974.

6. DiMaio, V. J. M., Copeland, A .R., Besant-Matthews, P. E., Fletcher, L A., and Jones, A. Minimal velocities necessary for perforation of skin by airgun pellets and bullets. J. Forensic Sci. 27(4): 894–898, 1982.

7. McKenzie, H. J., Coil, J. A., and Ankney, R. N. Experimental thoracoabdominal airgun wounds in a porcine model. *J. Trauma.* 39(6): 1164–1167, 1995

8. Unpublished study by DiMaio, V. J. M. and Copeland, A. R.

9. DiMaio, V. J. M. and DiMaio, D. J. Bullet embolism: Six cases and a review of the literature. *J. Forensic Sci.* 17(3): 394–398, 1972.

10. Michelassi, F., Pietrabissa, A., Ferrari, M., Mosca, F., Vargish, T., and Moosa, H. H. Bullet emboli to the systemic and venous circulation. *Surgery* 107(3): 239–245, 1990.

11. Keeley, J. H. A bullet embolus to the left femoral artery following a thoracic gunshot wound. *J. Thoracic Surg.* 21: 608–620, 1951.

12. Dada, M. A., Loftus, I. A., and Rutherford, G. S. Shotgun pellet embolism to the brain. *AJFMP* 14(1): 58–60, 1993.

13. Kirkpatrick, J. B. and DiMaio, V. J. M. Civilian gunshot wounds of the brain. *J. Neurosurg.* 49: 185–198, 1978.

14. Jafari, N., Jafari, K., and Sheridan, J. T. Gunshot wounds of the pregnant uterus. *Int. J. Gynecol. Obstet.* 13: 95–96, 1975.

15. Adelson, L., Hirsch, C. S., and Schroeder, O. Fetal homicide victims of maternally sustained violence. An occasional paper published by the Law and Medicine Center. Cleveland, OH: Case Western Reserve University, 1977.

16. McNally, W. D. Lead poisoning caused by a bullet embedded for twenty-seven years. *Industrial Med.* 18: 77–78, 1949.

17. DiMaio, V. J. M., DiMaio, S. M., Garriott, J. C., and Simpson, P. A fatal case of lead poisoning due to a retained bullet. *Am. J. Forensic Med. Pathol.* 4(2): 165–169, 1983.

18. Linden, M .A., Manton, W. I., Stewart, M., Thal, E. R., and Feit, H. Lead poisoning from retained bullets: pathogenesis, diagnosis and management. *Ann. Surg.* 195: 305–13, 1982.

19. Dillman, R. O., Crumb, C. K., and Lidsky, M. J. Lead poisoning from a gunshot wound: report of a case and review of the literature. *Am. J. Med.* 66: 509–514, 1979.

20. Dasani, B. M. and Kawanishi, H. The gastrointestinal manifestations of gunshot-induced lead poisoning. *J. Clin. Gastroenterol.* 19(4): 296–9, 1994.

21. *Evaluation of Wound Data and Munitions. Effectiveness in Vietnam,* Vol. 1. Prepared by Joint Technical Coordination Group for Munitions Effectiveness. December 1970.

22. Maughon, D. S. An inquiry into the nature of the wounds resulting in killed in action in Vietnam. Military Med. 135: 8–13, 1970.

23. Silliphant, W. M. and Beyer, J. C. Wound ballistics. *Military Med.* 113: 238–246, 1954.

24. Hatcher, J. S. *Powder Fires. NRA Illustrated Reloading Handbook.* Washington, D.C.: National Rifle Association of America.

25. *Cooking-Off Cartridges. NRA Illustrated Reloading Handbook.* Washington, D.C.: The National Rifle Association of America.

26. Sciuchetti G. D. Ammunition and fire. American Rifleman 144(3): 36–38, 59–60, March 1996.

27. Jentzen, J. M., Lutz, M. and Templin, R. Tandem bullet versus multiple gunshot wounds. *J. Forensic Sci.* 40(5): 893–895, 1995.

28. Haag L. C. Falling bullets: terminal velocities and penetration studies. *Wound Ballistics Review* 2(1): 21–26, 1995.

29. Tobin, E. J. and Fackler, M. L. Officer reaction-respose time in firing a handgun. *Wound Ballistics Review* (1997); 3(1): 6–9.

Weapons and Ammunition: Miscellaneous 10

Air Weapons

Air-powered guns are used throughout the world for target shooting, sport, and firearms training. These devices range from toys exemplified by the Daisy BB gun to expensive, highly sophisticated custom air rifles.

The device that most people think of when discussing an air-powered gun is the Daisy BB gun. The Daisy is in fact a toy that fires an 0.175-in. steel BB down a smooth bore at a muzzle velocity of 275 to 350 ft/sec. A BB gun can cause serious injury only if the BB strikes the eye. In such cases, perforation of the globe may occur. Based on animal studies, the V-50 velocity for corneal penetration and serious disruption of the globe from a steel BB is approximately 246–249 ft/sec.[1] At these velocities, 50% of steel BB's fired at an eye will penetrate.

There are, however, other air- and gas-powered guns with considerably greater velocity and striking energy than that of the Daisy BB gun. These devices are more properly classified as weapons as they can cause significant physical injury and occasionally death. Austrian armies used air rifles against the French during the Napoleonic wars from 1799 to 1809.[2] These weapons were rifles of 12.8-mm caliber with an effective range between 100 and 150 yd. Air rifles, air shotguns, and air pistols were used for hunting and target shooting during the late eighteenth and early nineteenth centuries. Air rifles are still used extensively for target shooting as well as gun training.

An air rifle is a weapon that uses the expanding force of compressed air or gas to propel a projectile down a rifled barrel.[2] The term "air rifle" is commonly but incorrectly applied to toys such as the Daisy airgun. An airgun is distinguished from an air rifle in that the airgun has a smooth-bored barrel and may be either a weapon or a toy. Air pistols may be either weapons or toys and may have either a rifled or a smooth bore. The same projectile used in airguns and air rifles are used in air pistols.

The standard calibers for air- and gas-powered guns in the United States are the 0.177 in., the Sheridan 0.20 in., and the .22 in. The basic form of airgun ammunition is the BB. These are steel balls having an average diameter of .175 in. and an average weight of 5.5 gr. The most common form of air rifle ammunition is the waisted Diabolo pellet, a soft-lead missile shaped somewhat like an hourglass (Figure 10.1A). The front edge of the pellet acts as a guide riding on the rifling lands of the bore. The bullet is waisted at the center and has a hollow base. The rear edge is flared to engage the rifling and to seal the bore. Diabolo pellets weigh an average of 8.2 gr. for caliber .177 and 15 gr. for caliber .22. The exact weight depends on the brand of the pellet. Because of their extremely light weight, these pellets lose velocity rapidly, becoming harmless in less than 100 yd. Air-rifle pellets can be fired in smooth-bore air guns without any difficulty. The firing of BB shot in a rifled bore, however, eventually results in damage to the rifling.

Pointed conical bullets are also made for use in air rifles. The Sheridan air rifle in .20 (5-mm) caliber fires pointed conical pellets averaging 15.3 gr. weight, with a hollow base and a narrow exterior flange to engage the rifling in the bore (Figure 10.1B). The forward portion of the pellet is bore diameter and rides on top of the lands.

Figure 10.1 (A) Diabolo air rifle pellets; (B) Sheridan air rifle pellets.

There are three basic power systems for air-powered guns.[2] In the pneumatic type, air is pumped into a storage chamber. When the trigger is pulled, the air is released, driving the pellet down the barrel. Varying the amount of air pumped into the reservoir by varying the number of pump strokes allows control of the velocity of the projectile. Increasing the number of pumps to a maximum can produce velocities as high as 770 ft/sec in a well-made airgun or air rifle.

The spring-air compression system uses a powerful spring that is compressed by manual action. On pulling the trigger, the spring is released, driving a piston forward in the cylinder and compressing the air ahead of it. The air is driven from the cylinder through a small port behind the projectile. Air drives the missile down the barrel. Velocities of 1000 ft/sec may be reached by .177 air rifles. Weapons of .22 caliber generally have slightly lower muzzle velocities. In contradistinction to pneumatic guns, spring-air compression rifles have only one power setting. Thus, the muzzle velocity is constant.

Both air rifles and toy airguns operate on the spring-air compression principle. In toy guns, however, cheap construction and low-power springs prevent the high performance achieved in quality rifles.

The third gas-compression system uses carbon dioxide from a disposable cartridge as the propellant. Carbon dioxide guns may be toys or weapons, rifles or pistols, smooth-bore or rifled. The rifles have approximately the same muzzle velocity as spring rifles of the same caliber.

Death from air-powered guns are rare. The author has seen only four cases. Three are described:

Case 1. During a heated argument between two boys, ages 14 and 17 years, respectively, the 14-year-old grabbed an air rifle from a friend and at a range of a few feet shot the other boy in the right eye. The victim was transported to a hospital, where he was pronounced dead.

The autopsy revealed a pellet wound of entrance in the medial half of the right eyelid. The wound measured 6 mm in diameter, with a 4-mm central perforation. The pellet traveled through the soft tissue of the orbit superior to the globe, not injuring it. The missile entered the cranial cavity through the right orbital plate adjacent to the cribriform plate. The pellet traveled across the ventral aspect of the right straight gyrus, crossed the midline, penetrating the left straight gyrus. It traveled upward, posteriorly and laterally, along the anterior limb of the left internal capsule, coming to rest subcortically in the left posterior gyrus, 5 cm to the left of the midline. A deformed, 5-mm lead air rifle pellet with rifling marks on its surface was recovered.

The weapon was a 5-mm Sheridan air rifle with a rifled barrel. Ballistic examination of the pellet removed from the brain confirmed it to have been fired from this weapon.

Case 2.   Two boys, age 7 and 8, respectively, were playing in the yard with an "empty" airgun of .177 caliber. A cousin who was baby sitting had taken the BB's for the gun away from the boys. The 8-year-old boy pointed the gun at the 7-year-old and pulled the trigger. The weapon discharged and the 7-year-old collapsed to the ground. The boy was dead at the scene.

At autopsy, there was a single 5 × 4 mm oval pellet wound of entrance in the left forehead, just above the middle of the eyebrow. The pellet perforated the underlying frontal bone, which was 2 mm thick at this point. The pellet entered the left frontal pole and traveled medially, posteriorly, and slightly upward in the left frontal lobe, exiting the medial surface. It then entered the right cerebral hemisphere, continued left to right, posteriorly, and in a slightly upward path through the right cerebral hemisphere. A standard .175-inch, copper-coated steel BB was recovered from the right Sylvian fissure.

Examination of the gun revealed it to be a smooth bore, pneumatic-type airgun of caliber .177. The weapon had a magazine that could hold 100 BB's. When testing the weapon, the author discovered that if a single BB is in the magazine, this BB is not delivered consistently to the firing chamber on working the action. Thus, with one BB in the magazine, it was possible to "fire" the weapon several times before the BB was actually chambered and propelled down the barrel. An individual unfamiliar with this eccentricity of the weapon might assume that the weapon was empty after discharging it a number of times and not firing a missile down the barrel. In fact, a missile might still be in the magazine and might be capable of being discharged on another firing.

Case 3.   This was a 12-year-old white male shot in the left chest by a friend with a .22 Benjamin Pump air rifle. The wasp-waist diabolo pellet perforated the second intercostal space and the pulmonary artery, penetrating the descending aorta just below the origin of the subclavian artery. The pellet was carried by the blood to the right femoral artery where it lodged. There was a 100 ml hemopericardium and a 220 ml left hemothorax.

The weapon used in the first case was a 5-mm Sheridan pneumatic air rifle. Average muzzle velocities for this particular rifle, as determined by tests conducted by the author for different numbers of pump stokes, is given in Table 10.1. The muzzle energy of these pellets is also listed. Fifty-eight foot-pounds of energy is considered the minimum energy necessary to cause a casualty by the military.[3] The amount of energy possessed by these pellets is less than 20% of this value. Death occurred because of the site of entrance: the orbit. Test firings of the same weapon at point blank range on skull caps from cadavers resulted in the air rifle pellets being deflected off the bone

Table 10.1   Performance Data of the 5-mm Sheridan Air Rifle in Case 1 (average weight of pellet, 15.3 gr.)

Number of Pump Strokes	Average Muzzle Velocity (ft/sec)	Muzzle Energy (ft-lbs)
1	0[a]	0[a]
2	303	3.1
3	388	5.1
4	435	6.4
5	470	7.5
6	502	8.6
7	531	9.6
8	553	10.4
9	554	10.4
10	566	10.9

[a] Pellet did not leave barrel.

without causing any damage. The only evidence that the pellets had struck the bone were 6 × 7 mm smears of lead at the point of impact.

The second death was caused by a smooth-bore pneumatic .177 air gun. By virtue of its high muzzle velocity, this gun is a weapon rather than a toy. Table 10.2 lists the average muzzle velocities for this particular air weapon as determined by the author for different numbers of pump strokes. Also listed is the muzzle kinetic energy at these velocities. All tests were conducted using BB's, as this was the form of missile that caused death.

The weapon used in Case 2 is relatively ineffective if one considers its muzzle energy. Death occurred in this case because the thin (2-mm) frontal bone of the child permitted the missile to enter the cranial cavity.

Table 10.2 Performance Data of the .177 Air Gun in Case 2 (average weight of BB, 5.5 gr.)

Number of Pump Strokes	Average Muzzle Velocity (ft/sec)	Muzzle Energy (ft-lbs)
1	294	1.1
2	416	2.1
3	492	3.0
4	540	3.6
5	581	4.1
6	606	4.5
7	620	4.7
8	646	5.1
9	657	5.3
10	669	5.5

A recent review of the English language literature described 11 reported deaths from air-weapons.[4] Most involved children. The portal of entry for the pellet was usually the head (10 of 11). The author's Cases #1 and #2 make up two of the 11 cases. Bond et al. state that in a 5-year period ending July 1994, 33 air gun deaths were reported to the United States Consumer Product Safety Commission.[5]

Zip Guns

The term "zip gun" as used in this book indicates either a crude homemade firearm or a conversion of a blank pistol, tear gas gun, or cap pistol to a firearm.[6] In the United States, zip guns had their peak of popularity in inner city areas during the juvenile gang wars of the 1950s. The quality of these weapons was extremely variable, with some so crude as to be a greater danger to the firer than to the intended victim. The simplest zip gun seen by the author was a metal tube in which a .22 Magnum cartridge was inserted. It was fired by striking the protruding base of the cartridge with a hammer. This weapon was used to commit suicide.

The zip guns of the 1950s in the New York area generally were constructed of a block of wood, a car antenna (the barrel), a nail (the firing pin), and rubber bands (to propel the pin). Most of these weapons were chambered for the .22 rimfire cartridge. The "chamber" was generally oversized, resulting in bulging and splitting, i.e., bursting, of the fired case. As the round was usually a low pressure .22 rimfire cartridge, injury to the firer was uncommon. The firing pin was often too long and too sharp, leading to piercing of the primer when the weapon was fired. The barrel was an un-rifled tube, often of greater diameter than the bullet. Thus, when the zip gun was fired, gas leaked out the ruptured case, the perforated primer, and around the bullet as it began to move down the barrel. This resulted in a very low muzzle velocity to the projectile. Because of the lack of rifling, the bullet was not stabilized and on leaving the barrel would almost immediately begin to tumble and lose velocity. The initial low velocity combined with the inherent instability of the projectile made the zip gun an extremely short-range weapon.

Cap firing conversions were more sophisticated zip guns. Cap pistols are made of light metal castings held together by rivets. Conversion to a firearm was made by inserting a piece of car radio antenna or similar metal tubing in the barrel and providing a firing pin. The firing pin usually was made by inserting a nail or screw into the hammer or by filing the hammer to a point. If the hammer fall was too light, it was strengthened by wrapping rubber bands around the frame in back of the hammer.

Blank firing pistols were also converted to lethal weapons by reaming out the barrel and altering the cylinder's chambers to accommodate live ammunition. Such a weapon at contact range may produce a characteristic soot pattern. Figure 4.12B shows such a case.

Zip guns were most commonly encountered in poverty-stricken areas where there were restrictive firearms legislation, as these weapons could be easily manufactured with inexpensive materials, few tools, and limited skills. In the 1950s in New York City, they were often manufactured in high school shop classes. The increased mobility and affluence of the population, combined with the ready availability of inexpensive handguns, has resulted in the disappearance of the zip gun from the crime scene in the U.S. The only exception appears to be conversion of tear gas pens to firearms. This still retains some minimal popularity, perhaps because these devices do not immediately appear to be firearms and can be carried openly without eliciting suspicion.

This picture is not the same in all countries. Thus, Book and Botha report widespread use of zip guns in Zululand, South Africa.[7] The design and materials used vary widely. Three-quarters employ no trigger utilizing only a sprung hammer that is drawn back and released. The great majority of these weapons fire 12-gauge shotgun shells due to their relatively low chamber pressure and widespread availability.

Stud Guns

Stud guns are industrial tools that use special blank cartridges to fire metal nails or studs into wood, concrete, or steel (Figure 10.2A). The blank cartridges range in caliber from .22 to .38. They are loaded with fast-burning propellants that develop pressures too high for a firearm to contain. Thus, they should never be used in firearms. The mouth of these blank cartridges is sealed with a cardboard disk that is color-coded to indicate the strength of the propellant.

Stud guns have a built-in safety mechanism that requires a guard at the end of the tool to be pressed firmly against a flat surface before the tool can be fired. Workers have been known to use stud guns for "plinking" at tin cans. They depress the safety guard with one hand and fire with the other.

Stud guns have caused a number of accidental deaths at industrial sites after the nails or studs have either perforated walls or ricocheted off a hard surface, striking and killing workers. In the cases in which a nail has ricocheted prior to penetrating the body, the nail usually appears bent (Figure 10.2B). On occasion, stud guns have been used in suicides.[8] The author has seen a number of accidents and one suicide with a stud gun. In the latter case, the deceased, a 50-year-old white male, shot himself in the forehead

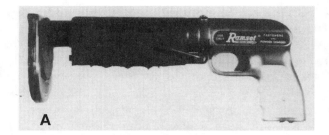

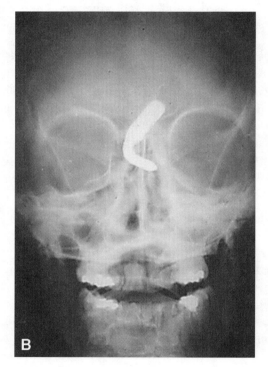

Figure 10.2 **(A)** Stud gun; **(B)** ricochet bolt.

with a nail propelled by a .22 industrial blank propellant cartridge.[9] A stellate-shaped entrance wound was present (Figure 10.3). The nail perforated the head, lodging in a wall behind the deceased. Interestingly, there was no visible soot blackening in the skin, soft tissue, or skull of the deceased.

Captive Bolt Devices (Pistols)

Captive bolt pistols are used in cattle slaughtering. In these devices, discharge of a blank cartridge drives a captive bolt, 7 to 12 cm long, out the muzzle of the device.[10] Free flight of the bolt out the muzzle is prevented by the design

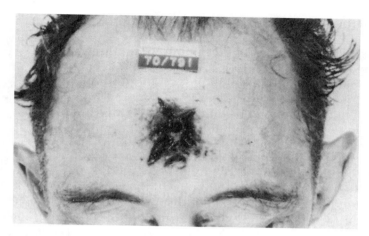

Figure 10.3   Contact wound of forehead from stud gun.

of the bolt, though it is possible to overcome this. Injuries occur when the device is discharged at a range less than the length of the bolt.

The end of the bolt is usually circular, 7 to 12 mm in diameter, with sharp edges. It produces a sharp-edged, circular hole in the skin and bone, whose diameter is slightly less than that of the bolt. In contact or near-contact wounds, the wound in the skin may be surrounded by either two or four symmetrically arranged deposits of soot produced by gas escaping from openings (2 or 4) at the end of the muzzle. These act as vents for the gas produced by the blank. The deposits of soot decrease in intensity, finally disappearing, as the range increases. Not all guns have vents at the muzzle, however.

Most deaths from this device are accidental. Death is usually not immediate and prolonged survival may occur. The report by Betz et al. is apparently the first report of a homicide with this device in the English literature.[10] The author of this book has seen only one death from a captive bolt device. This involved a 28-yr-old white male working in a slaughter house who was accidently shot in the head with a captive-bolt gun of German manufacture. At the time of the shooting, he was wearing a plastic safety helmet. Examination of the helmet revealed an 11 × 10 mm, roughly circular, punched out defect of the front 1/4 of an inch to the left of midline, with a black sooty deposit around the hole. The bolt punched out an 11.5 mm entrance in the cranial vault, just to the left of the midline, adjacent to the coronal suture. There was a hemorrhagic wound track along the medial aspects of the cerebral hemispheres with disruption of the caudate nuclei bilaterally. At the end of the track was an 11.5 mm plug of bone and an 11.8 mm white plastic plug. The bolt gun had a three inch (7.5 cm) long bolt with a circular, sharp-edged, concave end, 11 mm in diameter.

Bang Sticks

A Bang Stick is a device used by skin divers and fisherman to kill sharks, large fish, or alligators. It is also called a "fish popper", "shark stick" or "power head". A Bang Stick consists of a metal cylinder or barrel that contains a cartridge chamber. The front end of the cylinder is open to allow exit of the bullet. The other end is closed by a screw-on, cap-like breech through which a firing pin can project. The pin is ordinarily held out of the breech by a spring. A metal shaft, at least 26 inches in length, is permanently attached to the base of the firing pin. Sticks of varying length can, in turn, be attached to the back of the shaft. When the open end of the cylinder is jammed hard against a target, such as a shark, the chamber and breech are forced back, overcoming the tension of the spring. The firing pin is forced through a hole in the breech face into the chamber firing the cartridge. The bullet then exits the open end of the cylinder. Bang Sticks may be acquired in various calibers including centerfire handgun (.38 Special, .44 Magnum), rifle, and 12-gauge shotgun. Blanks can also be used and are just as effective. A number of suicides have been reported using Bang Sticks.[11-12] The wounds produced in humans are contact and may or may not show a muzzle imprint.

Sympathetic Discharge of Rimfire Firearms

In cheap .22 rimfire revolvers, "sympathetic" discharges may occur on firing. "Sympathetic" discharge occurs when, on firing a revolver, there is not only discharge of the cartridge stuck by the firing pin but also of a cartridge in an adjacent chamber. Such multiple discharges were quite common in percussion revolvers when a spark from a discharging round would ignite the black powder in other cylinders.

In sympathetic discharge of .22 rimfire revolvers, discharge of a cartridge by the firing pin causes recoil of the cylinder against the frame with resultant compression of the rim of a cartridge case in an adjacent chamber between the frame and cylinder, producing a second discharge (Figure 10.4). As this chamber is not aligned with the barrel, no rifling will be imparted to the bullet. In addition, the inner surface of the bullet will be partially shaved away by the frame of the revolver as the bullet travels forward. Sympathetic discharge can occur only in rimfire cartridges, not in centerfire cartridges, because of the centrally located primer in the latter type of cartridge.

In a case seen by the author, a young male was shot during an argument on a bus. There was a penetrating gunshot wound of the right cheek with an apparent graze wound of the right shoulder. The bullet recovered from the head was a .22-caliber rimfire bullet with rifling marks on its sides. The

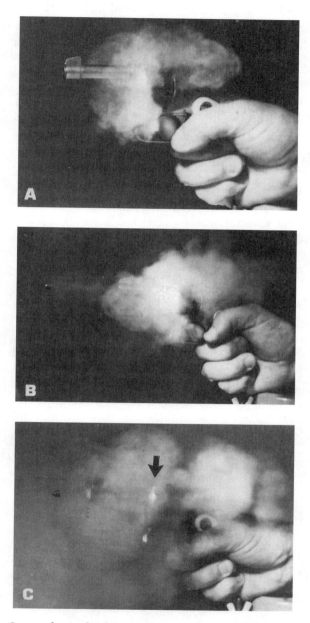

Figure 10.4 Sympathetic discharge of .22 rimfire revolver. (**A**) The weapon has just been fired; (**B**) a bullet has emerged from the barrel; (**C**) a second bullet has come out the left side of the cylinder and is approximately 1 in. ahead of the barrel. The arrow indicates where the bullet emerged from.

bullet that caused the graze wound was found loose in the clothing. Examination of this bullet showed shortening of its length (from base to tip), absence of rifling, one side sheared off, and an expanded (flared-out) base having a granular pock-marked surface resulting from impaction of powder grains (Figure 10.5). This appearance of the bullet is classical for sympathetic discharge of a weapon. Examination of the weapon confirmed the tendency of the gun to sympathetic discharge.

Bullets without Rifling Marks

Occasionally a bullet recovered at autopsy will show no rifling on its surface. Lack of rifling indicates that the weapon is a zip-gun, a smooth-bore handgun, or rifle, or a revolver whose barrel has been removed. Zip guns have been previously discussed.

Weapons intentionally manufactured with smooth-bores are almost all .22-caliber rifles made for the exclusive use of .22 shot cartridges. Rarely, weapons that are supposed to have rifled barrels, inadvertently, get out of a factory with smooth bores. Absence of rifling in a smooth-bore weapon does not indicate that a ballistic comparison cannot be made. The author had a case in which an individual was shot with a smooth-bore .22 rifle in which there was enough pitting of the bore to produce striations on the bullet, thus making possible a positive comparison with test bullets fired down the barrel.

An individual may remove the barrel of a revolver to prevent rifling marks being imparted to bullets fired from it. Such a weapon is effective only at short range, because the lack of gyroscopic spin on the bullet causes it to become unstable after leaving the cylinder and to tumble end over end. Bullets fired from such barrel-less revolvers often have a "flared" base. Flaring of the base of the bullet is most pronounced in ammunition that has a concave base

Figure 10.5   The bullet on the left is shortened, shows the absence of rifling, and has one side sheared off compared to the bullet on the right which emerged from the barrel.

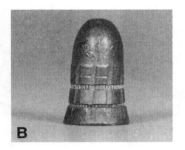

Figure 10.6 **(A)** .38-caliber lead hollow-base bullets fired from revolver without barrel; **(B)** .38-caliber bullet fired from derringer. The base is flared.

(Figure 10.6A). Flaring out of the base can also be seen, though to a lesser degree, in bullets fired from short barrel revolvers and derringers (Figure 10.6B). In such cases, however, the bullets still have rifling marks on them.

Elongated bullets

Rarely, one may recover an abnormally long thin lead bullet up to 2 to 3 times normal length. They are produced by a constriction at the end of the barrel which swages or compresses the bullets as they pass through the area of constriction. The author has seen this phenomenon only in association with .22 rimfire ammunition. In all instances the end of the barrel had been compressed in a vise while part of the barrel had been sawed off.

Cast Bullets

On occasion, individuals are shot with pistol ammunition reloaded with cast bullets. These bullets can usually be recognized on x-ray by the deep lubricating grooves. Upon recovery of the bullets, they usually have a dull silver-gray color. The lead is obviously harder than that used in commercial bullets; deep lubricating grooves are present, and the base of the bullet shows a circular marking caused by the sprue in the bullet casting mold (the sprue is the opening in the bullet mold through which the molten lead is poured) (Figure 10.7).

Sabot Ammunition

Sabot ammunition was introduced during World War II in an armor-piercing anti-tank role and is still used for this purpose. This ammunition consisted of a dense core of tungsten carbide covered with a steel sheath and a bore-and-sleeve assembly (the sabot). The sabot converts the core of the projectile

Figure 10.7 9-mm cast bullet showing circular mark on base resulting from sprue.

to the same diameter as the gun barrel. The sabot is discarded as the projectile leaves the bore of the weapon.

The U.S. Army experimented with sabot-flechette rifle ammunition as well as a 5.56-mm cartridge loaded with a 4.32-mm bullet in a 5.56-mm sabot. Sabot shotgun slug ammunition that uses a plastic sheath to bring the diameter of the projectile up to the desired gauge is currently manufactured. It is discussed in detail in Chapter 8.

In late 1976, Remington introduced rifle ammunition loaded with a sabot round. This cartridge is sold under the trade name of Accelerator®. The round was originally introduced only in .30–06. Other calibers have appeared (.30–30 and .308). In these three calibers, a standard .30 caliber cartridge case of the designated caliber is loaded with a subcaliber .224 (5.56-mm), 55-gr., partial metal-jacketed soft-point bullet, loaded in a plastic sabot weighing 5.7 gr. and having six equally spaced slits down its side (Figure 10.8). The manufacturer

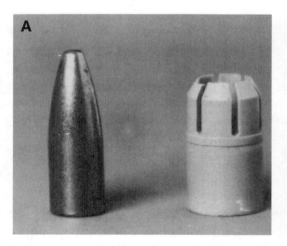

Figure 10.8 (A) .223 bullet and plastic sabot disassembled. (B) Bullet in sabot inserted in .30-caliber cartridge case. (From DiMaio, V.J.M. Wounds caused by centerfire rifles. *Clin. Lab. Med.* 3:257–271, 1983. With permission.)

claims a muzzle velocity of 4080 ft/sec for the .30–06; 3800 ft/s in .308 and 3400 ft/s in .30–30. This ammunition will not function in most semiautomatic rifles. A special fast-burning powder is used in this ammunition.

On firing, the rifling of the barrel engages the sabot. As it exits, the centrifugal force and increased air resistance spread the "petals" of the sabot, causing it to drop away from the bullet (Figure 10.9). The manufacturer claims complete separation of the plastic sabot from the bullet within 14 in. of the muzzle.

Figure 10.9   Sabot with open "petals" and rifling marks.

Tests in which the .30–06 cartridge was fired in a Model 1903 Springfield rifle revealed muzzle velocities of 3861 to 3950 ft/sec. Test firings were carried out at 3, 5, and 10 ft on paper targets. At 3 ft, the sabot entered the bullet hole. At 5 ft, the sabot impacted 2 cm to the right of the bullet hole of entrance; at 10 ft, 8.9 cm to the right in one test and 16.5 cm to the right in a second. In all tests, the sabot impacted to the right of the bullet hole. This trait possibly has to do with the right-handed twist of the rifle. The sabot traveled approximately 50 ft.

Tests on anesthetized pigs, using .30–06 Accelerator® ammunition, were conducted at the Armed Forces Institute of Pathology. At 3 and 6 ft. of range the bullet and sabot entered together with creation of a star-shaped (petal-shaped) entrance wound.[13] At 6 ft, there was an entrance with the deployed sabot embedded in the adjacent skin. At 12 feet, there was an entrance wound and a star-shaped abrasion from the sabot.

The most significant facet of sabot ammunition to the forensic pathologist is that, if a bullet is recovered from an individual shot with this cartridge, the bullet will not show any rifling; rather, the rifling will be on the plastic sabot. A ballistic comparison can be made between the markings on the sabot and a test round fired through a weapon, though this is difficult.

Tandem Bullets

On rare occasions, when a gun is fired, the bullet lodges in the barrel. This occurs because there is an insufficient quantity of propellant in the cartridge case or incomplete combustion of the propellant. The latter condition can occur if oil has leaked into the cartridge case, preventing some of the powder from being ignited or if there is a chemical breakdown of the powder because of age or prolonged exposure to high environmental temperatures or humidity.

If a bullet has lodged in the barrel and the weapon is fired a second time, one of two things may happen. The increased pressure in the barrel can cause it to rupture, or both bullets can be propelled out of the barrel.[14] At close range, both these bullets can enter a body through the same entrance hole. Thus, although a single wound of entrance will be found, two bullets will be present in the body. Careful examination of the bullets, however, will generally reveal that a "piggy-back" arrangement was present when they entered the body.

A very unusual variation to this was reported by Mollan and Beavis.[15] They reported the case of an individual shot in the knee in which on surgical exploration there were found to be two bullets and a cartridge case in the knee joint. All three missiles entered through one entrance wound. The bullets were of .32 ACP and .380 ACP caliber and the case was .32 ACP. It was hypothesized that a .32 ACP cartridge was inadvertently put in a .380 automatic. The cartridge slipped forward, lodging in the barrel. A .380 ACP cartridge then was chambered. On firing, the .380 bullet struck the .32 ACP primer, discharging the cartridge. The whole complex of two bullets and one case was swept down the barrel, emerged from the muzzle, and entered the victim.

New Forms of Handgun Ammunition

Up to the mid 1960s, commercial handgun bullet design had not changed since the early 1900s. Handgun bullets were either full metal-jacketed or all lead. Lead bullets were roundnose or, less commonly, wadcutter or semi-wadcutter. Recovery of a full metal-jacketed bullet meant that the individual had been shot with an automatic pistol; an all-lead bullet of medium or large caliber indicated a revolver; a small lead bullet a .22.

The 1960s saw the introduction of semi-jacketed soft-point and hollow-point bullets for both automatic pistols and revolvers and lead hollow-point bullets for revolvers. These bullets were usually lighter and driven at higher velocities than the traditional bullets. Of the new designs, the semi-jacketed hollow point has been the most successful. This bullet and the all lead hollow-point are designed to mushroom in the body, causing penetrating rather than perforating wounds, with loss of all their kinetic energy. The all lead hollow-point and the semi-jacketed soft point designs are uncommonly encountered nowadays. The semi-jacketed hollow-point configuration is gradually replacing both all-lead and full metal-jacketed bullets.

Soon after their introduction, hollow-point handgun bullets became the center of controversy. Many civil libertarian groups protested that they were "Dum-Dum bullets," violated the "Geneva Convention," and caused severe and more lethal wounds. All these statements are incorrect. The Dum-Dum "bullet" was in fact a .303 centerfire rifle cartridge loaded with a soft-point style bullet manufactured at the British Arsenal at Dum-Dum, India, in the late nineteenth century.

The "Geneva Convention" that outlawed Dum-Dum bullets was in fact the Hague Conferences of 1899 and 1907. The declarations issued at the conventions were applicable only to the use of expanding bullets in war. If one takes the declaration literally, even the all-lead bullets traditionally used by the police are outlawed.

In regard to charges that hollow-point ammunition is "more lethal", in an unpublished study of over 75 fatalities from hollow-point ammunition by the author, he was unable to demonstrate any death that would not have occurred if the bullet had been an all-lead bullet. As to increased severity of wounding, this is purely theoretical. To this day, the author cannot distinguish a wound by a hollow-point bullet from that by a solid-lead bullet of the same caliber until recovery of the actual bullet.

As the years have passed, semi-jacketed bullets of hollow-point design have, for the most part, replaced the traditional bullet designs. Except for wadcutters, all-lead revolver bullets are becoming uncommon. In the case of automatic pistols, full metal-jacketed bullets are still the rule only for calibers .25 ACP and .32 ACP. Medium- and large-caliber pistol cartridges are increasingly being loaded with semi-jacketed hollow-point bullets. Most police agencies now use this design.

Hollow-Point Design

As a result of research by manufacturers and redesign of the jacket and cavity, semi-jacketed hollowpoint pistol bullets now mushroom more consistently. Some of the designs of interest are:

Silvertip® Handgun Ammunition.   Produced by Winchester, this ammunition is loaded with hollow-point bullets having aluminum colored jacketing (Figure 10.10). The jacketing is open at the base with the lead core visible. The jacketing may be either aluminum or nickel plated copper-zinc. It is made in both revolver and pistol calibers, from .32 ACP to .44 Magnum. The

Figure 10.10   9-mm Silvertip® bullet.

9 mm, .38 ACP, and .357 Magnum are examples of cartridges that have the nickel-plated copper-zinc jackets. The first 1 1/2 year production of 9 mm used aluminum jacketing.

Black Talon®.   Produced by Winchester, this was a commercial success and a public relations nightmare. It was a line of pistol cartridges loaded with a hollow-point bullet having a distinctive black-colored copper jacket. The jacket was thicker at the tip than at the base with multiple notches such that when the bullet expanded in tissue it formed six, sharp triangular barbs (talons). If the bullet expands in the body, the x-ray picture is very characteristic (Figure 10.11). The pointed talons readily perforate surgical gloves if one is not aware of the nature of the projectile being recovered or if one is not careful. The news media went into a frenzy about this ammunition stating that the sharp "talons" were shredding organs producing devastating wounds. Because of the bad publicity, Winchester stopped production. In actual fact, the wounds produced are indistinguishable from wounds produced by solid and hollow-point bullets of the same caliber.

Supreme® SXT®.   Manufactured by Winchester, this appears to be the Black Talon® without the black color and pointed barbs.

Hydra-Shok®.   Manufactured by Federal, the cartridges are loaded with a semi-jacketed hollow-point bullet with a lead post in the center of the hollowpoint (Figure 10.12). The jacket is notched to further expansion. It is made in both revolver and pistol cartridges in calibers from .380 ACP and up. It is a favorite of many law enforcement agencies — both local and Federal. The recovered bullets often show remnants of the lead post in the mushroomed cavity.

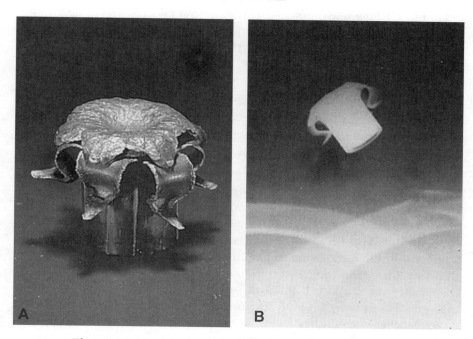

Figure 10.11 (A) Black Talon®; (B) x-ray of Black Talon.

Figure 10.12 Mushroomed Hydra-Shok® bullet.

Golden Saber®.   This is a semi-jacketed hollow-point bullet with a thick jacket of cartridge brass, notched at the tip in a folded spiral configuration that allegedly promotes expansion and produces larger petals. It is manufactured by Remington.

Miscellaneous Bullet Designs

In addition to hollow-point bullets more radical bullet designs have appeared in attempts to increase the effectiveness of handgun ammunition. Most have faded rapidly into oblivion. Some designs worth mentioning are:

Glazer Ammunition

Introduced in 1974, Glazer rounds are loaded with a bullet consisting of a copper jacket, open at the tip, containing multiple small lead pellets rather than a solid lead core (Figure 10.13). The tip of this jacket is closed with a colored plug. The design and materials used to construct the plug have changed over the years. In current ammunition, the plug is spherical in shape. On firing, the Glazer "bullet" travels to the target just like a traditional bullet. On penetrating the target, the lead pellets force the plug out and emerge from the jacket, radiating outward in a fan-like manner and producing a shotgun pellet wound effect. This ammunition is readily identifiable on x-ray by the presence of both copper jacketing and pellets (see Figure 11.3).

Exploding Ammunition

The 1970s saw the introduction of exploding ammunition for handguns.[16] Exploding ammunition dates back to the early nineteenth century and was used in rifles in the American Civil War. Present-day exploding ammunition intended for handguns has been manufactured in at least three forms for

Figure 10.13   Cross-section of Glazer round.

centerfire cartridges and one form for rimfire cartridges. Ammunition initially manufactured for centerfire weapons used ordinary commercial semi-jacketed hollow-point ammunition in which the nose of the bullet had been drilled out. Into this cavity was placed black powder and a lead shot. The tip of the cavity was then sealed with a percussion cap. Because of federal regulations regarding black powder, a second form of exploding ammunition was introduced to replace the first. The black powder was replaced by Pyrodex®, a smokeless powder substitute for black powder and a pistol primer replaced the percussion cap. The third form of exploding ammunition is essentially the same, but no lead shot is used.

Evaluation of a series of individuals shot with this ammunition reveals that both the entrance wound and the wound tracks are indistinguishable from wounds produced by similar non-exploding ammunition of the same caliber.[16] The fact that one is dealing with exploding ammunition may be determinable only on x-ray, as often the primer cap and primer anvil may be seen.

President Reagan was shot with .22 Long Rifle exploding ammunition. This ammunition was constructed from ordinary commercially available .22 Long Rifle hollow-point ammunition. A hole was drilled in the tip of the bullet, with insertion of an aluminum cylinder. The cylinder was filled with an explosive mixture and sealed at its open end. The cylinder was inserted with the sealed end toward the base of the bullet (Figure 10.14). Originally, RDX explosive was used in the cylinder, but this was replaced with lead azide.

Exploding ammunition is no longer commercially manufactured.

Figure 10.14 Longitudinal section through .22-caliber exploding round.

Blitz-Action Trauma (BAT) Bullet

This cartridge is a product of Geco, a division of Dynamit Nobel. Also known as the Action Safety Bullet, the cartridges are loaded with 86-gr. copper alloy hollow-point 9-mm Luger bullets.[17] The primers contain neither lead nor barium. The nose cavity of the bullet is closed with a plastic nose cap, that has a plastic post at its base. This post inserts into a cylindrical channel that has been drilled from the base of the hollow-point cavity to the base of the bullet.

The plastic nose cap gives a roundnosed shape to the tip of the bullet for reliable feeding from the magazine to the chamber. On firing, gas enters the channel in the base of the bullet propelling the plastic nose cone out of the hollowpoint cavity, down the barrel, ahead of the bullet. Because of an asymmetrical shape, the cap flies off at an angle to the trajectory of the bullet. The plastic post at the base of the bullet snaps off and flies separately from the body of the nose cap. Because of this, at close range, one may get three wounds: the entrance from the bullet; a circular abrasion or superficial penetrating wound from the cap and a punctate abrasion from the post. This constellation of injuries may extend out to two (2) meters.

Multiple Bullet Loadings

Pistol and rifle ammunition in which more than one bullet is loaded into a cartridge case has been produced by both civilians and the military. Figure 10.15 illustrates a .38 Special cartridge that has been loaded with four 50-gr. lead bullets. This ammunition was produced commercially. If an individual was shot at close range with this ammunition, there would be a single wound of entrance and four bullets in the body. At various times, handgun ammunition loaded with buckshot pellets has been produced.

The U.S. Army has used a 7.62 × 51 mm Duplex round designated M-198.[18] This cartridge was loaded with two 80-gr. bullets of conventional flat-based design. The base of the rear bullet, however, was canted at an angle of approximately 9 degrees (Figure 10.16). At 25 m, the velocity of the lead

Figure 10.15   .38 Special round loaded with four 50-gr. bullets.

Figure 10.16   Military duplex round. Note the canted base of bullet on right.

bullet was 2800 ft/sec (850 m/sec), with the second bullet having a velocity of 2600 ft/sec (790 m/sec). The canting of the second bullet's base was for the purpose of controlled dispersion. The M-198 cartridge had a green bullet tip for identification purposes.

Ammunition Intended for Use In Indoor Ranges

In order to reduce lead pollution in indoor ranges, all the major U.S. ammunition manufacturers have introduced handgun ammunition loaded with lead free primers and bullets that either have the lead core completely enclosed (sealed) or are made of solid copper or zinc. Sealing the lead core is important in that lead vaporized from the exposed core at the base of the bullet may contribute more to atmospheric contamination than primer lead.

Blount (CCI) produces Clean-Fire® ammunition. The primers are without lead, barium, or antimony using strontium instead. The bullets have lead cores completely enclosed by copper jackets formed by electroplating. The case may be either aluminum or brass.

Remington manufactures Leadless® ammunition. The primer is lead-free with the lead core of the bullet enclosed in a thick copper jacket sealed at the base with a copper disc. Winchester makes Super Clean NT™. The primer is lead free. The bullet has a copper jacket with a tin core. Federal makes BallistiClean® which uses a primer free of lead and a copper jacketed bullet with a zinc core.

NYCLAD® Revolver Cartridges

This ammunition was originally manufactured by Smith & Wesson. When they stopped manufacturing ammunition, Federal purchased the exclusive manufacturing rights. These cartridges are loaded with nylon-coated lead bullets of roundnose, hollow-point and semi-wadcutter hollow-point. This black coating significantly reduces the amount of lead particles in the air of firing ranges. Rifling is impressed on the coating and not on the lead. If these bullets go through thick bone, the nylon jacketing may be shredded or stripped from the core, making bullet comparison difficult if not impossible.

Frangible Bullets

Centerfire handgun ammunition, and to a lesser degree rifle ammunition, loaded with frangible bullets are now produced by all major ammunition manufacturers. The bullets are constructed of various materials depending on the manufacturer: copper powder compressed under high pressure; copper with a polymer binding agent; powdered tungsten, copper and a nylon matrix; twisted strands of zinc and powdered iron encased in an electroplated jacket. Kaplan et al. tested frangible ammunition composed of copper particulate material in calibers .38 Special, 9-mm Parabellum and .223 by firing them into the heads of pigs.[19] The wounds caused by the handgun bullets were comparable in severity to those caused by regular bullets. The frangible handgun bullets, when recovered, while demonstrating class characteristics, did not possess individual markings necessary for bullet-to-gun comparison. The .223 frangible bullets fragmented in the heads. The x-ray picture produced was similar to the "lead snowstorm" seen with hunting bullets but differed in that there was no evidence of any bullet jacketing and the fragments had a granular border.

"Armor-Piercing" Handgun Ammunition: KTW and Its Legacy

In the 1960s, KTW ammunition, a form of "armor-piercing" handgun ammunition intended for police use, was introduced. It was subsequently banned in some localities because of its potential to perforate bullet-proof vests worn by police. The cartridge was loaded with a light-green Teflon-coated tungsten alloy or steel bullet with a copper half jacket on its base. This jacket, rather than the bullet proper, is gripped by the lands and grooves. Thus, rifling marks will be present only on this jacket and not on the bullet.

If it is fired through a body, there is the potential for this jacket to separate from the rest of the bullet and be deposited in the body.[9] The author is unaware of any homicides committed with this ammunition. This ammunition has not been available for decades. Its value now is in its collectability.

Because of the KTW controversy, a whole mythology has arisen about "armor-piercing" handgun ammunition in relationship to "bullet proof" vests, i.e., soft body armor worn by police. A number of vapid public statements and proposed laws concerning ammunition allegedly of this type has emanated from government officials. The only handgun ammunition currently manufactured in the United States that will routinely defeat the soft body armor worn by police is in the possession of the military. To prevent its getting into civilian hands, the military has made an agreement with Federal law enforcement agencies not to issue this 9 mm ammunition to troops unless they are going into combat.

If one wishes to defeat the soft body armor worn by most police, there is no need to resort to the procurement of exotic handgun ammunition. Most centerfire rifle cartridges will defeat this armor. Soft body armor used by police is intended to protect them from handgun bullets not rifle bullets. These vests are composed of multiple layers of bullet-retardant material such as Kevlar®. The number of plies of this material in a vest determines the ability of the vest to stop a handgun bullet. Vests are rated as to their ability to stop bullets of various calibers. Thus, one vest may be rated as sufficient to stop bullets from .22 LR to .38 Special, while another vest may be capable of stopping bullets up to .357 Magnum. Consequently, a vest will stop a bullet only as long as it does not exceed the capability of the vest. While increasing the number of layers of material increases the ability of the vest to stop bullets of increasing lethality, it also has the effect of making the vest heavier and more bulky, thus making it uncomfortable for the individual. After a certain point, a vest may become so uncomfortable that it is no longer worn, defeating its purpose. Because of this, police agencies and individuals end up making a compromise between the degree of protection sought and what an individual will wear. Thus, to defeat soft body armor, one only has to use a caliber of weapon beyond the capability of the vest.

Handgun Shot Cartridges

Handgun cartridges loaded with lead shot are available in various calibers, e.g., .22 Long Rifle, .38/.357. This ammunition, often called "birdshot" or "snakeshot," is used to kill small game — usually varmints — or snakes at close range. The rimfire versions of these cartridges have been discussed in Chapter 6. Blount (CCI) manufactures centerfire handgun shot cartridges in four calibers: 9 mm, .38/.357 Magnum, .44 Magnum, and .45 ACP. The first three of these cartridges are loaded with a plastic capsule, closed at its tip and sealed at its base with a plastic wad (Figure 10.17A). The 9-mm cartridge contains 64 gr. of #11 pellets; the .38/.357 109 gr. of #9 pellets; the .44, 140 gr. of #9 pellets and the .45 117 gr. of #9 shot. The plastic cylinder was an opaque yellow until 1975, when it was changed to a transparent blue. On firing, the plastic cylinder fragments; at close range, it can produce small cuts on the skin adjacent to the entrance (Figure 10.17B). The fragments of plastic can be found embedded in the skin adjacent to the entrance and in the wound proper. The .45 ACP does not have a plastic capsule. The muzzle velocity of the pellets ranges from 1000 to 1450 ft/sec.

Plastic Training Ammunition

A number of European countries manufacture military blanks and training ammunition whose cartridge cases and "bullets" are made of plastic. The blanks can be identified easily by the "breaking points" or serrated lines on the nose of the cartridge (Figure 10.18). These blanks are typically color-coded as to caliber.

In plastic training ammunition, the plastic bullet is integral with the plastic case (Figure 10.19). On firing, the plastic bullet breaks free of the case. The rifle projectiles have a muzzle velocity of 1280 m/sec with a maximum range of 300 m.

Figure 10.17 (A) .38/.357 Speer shot cartridge; (B) gunshot wound of arm from .38 shot cartridge. Arrows indicate marks from plastic casing.

Figure 10.18 Plastic blank with breaking points on top.

Figure 10.19 Plastic training round. Arrow indicates where bullet breaks free from case.

Although plastic blank and training ammunition are rarely encountered in the United States, there is a form of plastic ammunition manufactured domestically. This ammunition, manufactured by Speer, consists of a reusable red plastic case and a black cylindrical plastic bullet that uses a large pistol primer as the sole propellant. Muzzle velocity of the plastic bullet is approximately 500 ft/sec. This ammunition is intended for indoor use at close range. Test firings with the .38/.357 version of this plastic cartridge on cadavers at ranges varying from contact to 20 ft showed that the plastic bullets were incapable of penetrating the skin, let alone the body.[9] The wound inflicted, which was limited to the skin, consisted of a superficial, circular laceration with a diameter approximately the same as that of the bullet. Although incapable of penetrating the body, this ammunition probably can cause severe injury to the eye.

Flechettes

During the Vietnam war, the United States military used ammunition loaded with steel flechettes. A flechette is a small arrow-shaped projectile with a metal tail fin. It is made in both 8- and 13-gr. form. The 8-gr. flechette, which is the more common type, measures 1 mm in diameter by approximately 2.7 cm in length. Flechettes were fired from 90-mm recoilless rifles, 90-mm guns, the 105-mm howitzer, and the 2.75-in. air-to-ground rocket. The 90-mm gun fired from 4100 to 5600 8-gr. steel flechettes per round. These flechettes were driven at sufficient velocity for them to perforate steel helmets. Entrance wounds in the skin may have an X shape due to the tail fin.

12-Gauge shotgun shells loaded with flechettes were manufactured for military use. These rounds have hulls of either Federal or Western manufacture. The Federal round contains 25 flechettes; the Western round 20. The tips of the flechettes are exposed in the Federal rounds but are concealed in the Western by a crimped mouth. The Winchester shells are packed in military cardboard boxes of 10 shells each. The boxes are labeled "18.5-mm Flechette Plastic Case" and state that the shells should be fired in cylinder bore guns only. The 20 flechettes in each round weigh 7.3 gr. each and are packed in a plastic cup with granulated white polyethylene (Figure 10.20). A metal disk lies at the base of the cup. The shell is sealed with a pie crimp. Small quantities of shotgun shells loaded with flechettes appear to have been manufactured for civilian use by one or more small ammunition companies.

Rubber and Plastic Bullets

Rubber and plastic missiles have been used extensively by both British and Israeli authorities in riot control. They are intended to incapacitate by inflicting painful and superficial injuries without killing or serious injury. They are supposed to be fired at ranges no less than 30 to 70 meters, depending on the missile, with fire directed at the lower extremities.

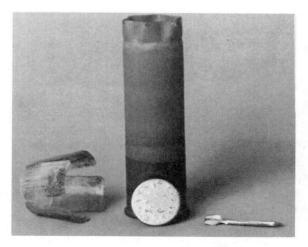

Figure 10.20   12-gauge flechette round.

Rubber bullets, introduced by the British in Northern Ireland in 1970, were bluntnosed, bullet-shaped missiles measuring 15 cm long, 3.5 cm in diameter and weighing 135 to 140 g. They were fired from weapons originally designed to fire tear gas. Muzzle velocity was 73 m/s; muzzle kinetic energy 401.7 J. Miller reported on 90 individuals injured by these missiles of whom one died and 17 had permanent disabilities or deformities.[20] To decrease the incidence of serious injuries, rubber bullets were replaced with plastic (polyvinyl chloride) bullets measuring 10 × 3.7 CM; weighing 135 g and having a muzzle velocity of 71 m/s and kinetic energy of 325.1 J. Even then deaths occurred, Touquet and Challoner reporting 17 deaths.[21]

Rubber and plastic bullets used by the Israelis are smaller and faster but have considerably less kinetic energy. Four types of rubber bullets have or are being used.[22] Two are spherical in configuration and measure 1.8 cm in diameter; two cylindrical, measuring 1.8 cm in diameter by 1.8 cm long. One of the spherical forms and one of the cylindrical are plain rubber. The other two are steel with a thick rubber shell. The pure rubber bullets weigh 8.3 g with a muzzle velocity of 75–100 m/s and kinetic energy of 23.3 to 41.5 J. The rubber coated steel bullets weigh 15.4 g with a muzzle velocity of 100 m/s and kinetic energy of 77 J. Rubber bullets are fired from a metallic canister that is mounted on the muzzle of either an M-16 or Galeil rifle. The cannister can hold up to 15 rubber bullets.

The Israeli plastic bullet is a 0.85 g, caliber 5.56-mm, bullet-shaped missile that is loaded in a 5.56 × 45 cartridge. The bullet is composed of polyvinyl chloride and metallic fragments. Muzzle velocity is 1250 m/s; muzzle kinetic energy 663.7 J.

Hiss et al. reported 17 deaths from Israeli rubber and plastic bullets.[22] Ten died from rubber bullets; seven from plastic bullets. In nine of the ten cases involving rubber bullets, the rubber coating was separate from the steel core. Six of the cases involved penetrating wounds of the head; one of the thoracic wall. In three instances, there was no penetration of the body but there was brain injury (two cases) or spinal cord injury (one case). The entrance wounds were described as "lacerations of varying size and shape." They ranged in size from 0.5 × 0.4 to 7.6 × 4.2 cm. In the seven cases involving plastic bullets, three penetrated the head and four the trunk. The entrance wounds resembled conventional small caliber bullet wounds with abrasion rings.

Blank Cartridge Injuries

A blank is a cartridge containing powder but no bullets or pellets. It is intended to produce noise. Blanks are generally loaded with ultra-fast burning powder that detonates rather than burns. The case itself may appear like any other case in this caliber or may have a rosette crimped end. The wad can cause injury to a person immediately in front of the gun. If the wad is removed and a bullet is substituted, pressure generated by the ultra-fast burning powder will explode the gun.

A number of European countries have manufactured blanks whose cartridge case and "bullet" are made of plastic. The blanks can be identified easily by breaking points or serrated lines on the nose of the cartridge.

Injuries from blank cartridges are rare in civilian life.[23-24] They are more commonly encountered in the military, where there is extensive use of blanks in training.[25] Thus, it is not surprising that most civilian physicians are unaware of the severe wounds blanks can cause – even fewer physicians realize that these cartridges can cause death. Gonzales et al. described the death of a 14-year-old boy shot with a pistol loaded with a .32 blank.[23] The weapon was held in contact with the skin of the left fifth intercostal space adjacent to the sternum. The blank perforated the chest wall and the right ventricle of the heart.

While serving in the military, the author had occasion to review a death from a rifle blank. A 22-year-old black male was dead on arrival at a dispensary in Germany with a blank gunshot wound of the chest. Inspection of the body revealed a circular wound of entry of the left chest in the second interspace, 5 cm from the midline. The wound measured 15 mm in diameter and was surrounded by a 75 mm area of powder blackening. Subsequent autopsy revealed a fracture of the third costal cartilage and adjacent lateral half of the sternum. There was an irregular laceration of the anterior wall of the right ventricle, the interventricular septum, and the aortic valve. A bilateral hemothorax and hemopericardium were present. The weapon involved in this incident was an M-1 rifle (caliber .30–06) loaded with a blank training round. The nature of the wound suggested either a loose or a near-contact wound.

In the civilian population, blank cartridge injuries and death are extremely rare. It is unlikely for a civilian forensic pathologist to see one in a lifetime. Injuries in the civilian population are most commonly due to blank pistol cartridges rather than rifle cartridges. Most modern blank pistol cartridges are loaded with smokeless powder. Black powder .22's and .32's are still encountered. The type of powder is important in that smokeless powder has a greater wounding capacity than black powder.

Shepard conducted a number of tests on dogs using .38 caliber blanks.[25] At a range of one (1) inch, he produced subdural and cortical hemorrhages in the head, penetration of the skin and pleura with laceration of the lung in the thorax, and penetration of the skin and peritoneum with lacerations of the liver in the abdomen. At 12 in., although there was injury to the skin, the pleura and peritoneum were intact. Tests with .22 Short blanks at a range of one (1) inch failed to produce either skin penetration or internal injuries.

The author conducted a number of experiments on cadavers to determine the wounding capacity of blank pistol cartridges. The first test was conducted with .38 Special smokeless blanks. Test firings were conducted on human thighs, using a Smith & Wesson revolver with a 6-in. barrel and firing at ranges from six (6) inches to contact. From a range of greater than 1 in. up to 6 in., focal accumulations of largely unburnt powder and shredded wad were deposited on the skin. The skin underlying the deposits was abraded. There was no powder blackening of the skin. At the one inch (1) range, a faint gray halo of soot, one inch (1) wide, enclosed a deposit of unburnt powder averaging 3/4 in. in diameter. An underlying 1/4 in. long × 1/2 in. deep laceration extended into the subcutaneous tissue.

Contact firings produced two different types of wounds in the thighs. In the first type, there was a 1/2 in.-diameter circular wound of entrance in the skin, surrounded by a faint gray sooty halo, 1/2 in. wide. A 3-in.-deep by 2-in.-wide cavity was present in the underlying muscle of the thigh. In the second type of wound, the entrance was irregular, measuring 1 1/2 × 3/4 in. with no detectable blackening of the wound edges. The underlying cavity in the muscle was 3 1/2 in. deep × 2 1/2 in. wide. Careful examination of these wound cavities revealed small shreds of wad and unburnt powder grains.

Contact test firings were also conducted on the head. These tests produced stellate wounds of the scalp up to 1 × 3/4 in. with no observable blackening. No fractures or injuries to the skull were produced. Deposited on the external table of the skull was a circular deposit of unburnt powder and shredded wad, averaging 1/2 in. in diameter.

Contact wounds of the thorax were of two types. When the muzzle of the gun was pressed firmly into the intercostal space, there was complete perforation of the anterior chest wall. Unburnt flakes of powder were deposited on the skin around the entrance wound. There was no powder blackening. When the muzzle overlaid a rib, there were no penetrating wounds, only a focal accumulation of powder with loss of the underlying superficial skin. When these areas were incised, however, there were comminuted fractures of the underlying rib with laceration of the parietal pleura. If the lungs had been expanded at the time of firing, lacerations of the parenchyma from the fractured rib would have been produced.

Contact test firings of the anterior abdominal wall produced circular perforating wounds with laceration of the underlying small bowel. Again, there was no evidence of blackening of the skin.

Test firings with .22-caliber smokeless blanks were of a limited nature. The weapon used had a 4-in. barrel. All test firings were contact and occurred in the intercostal spaces of the chest. These blanks produced perforating wounds of the chest wall.

A final series of tests were conducted with the M-9 military .45-caliber blank. This blank is loaded with smokeless powder. Contact firings of the thigh produced irregular entrance wounds of the skin, slightly larger (1 1/4 × 1 1/4 in.) than those produced by the .38 Special. Again, there was no observable blackening of the skin. The underlying cavity measured 4 × 3 in. Careful examination of this cavity revealed a small area of blackening on the surface of the femur and a few remnants of shredded wad. Both these elements were relatively inconspicuous.

Based on the experiments, we can conclude that contact wounds with pistol blanks are without doubt **potentially** lethal as such wounds can cause perforation of chest and abdomen. Close range non-contact wounds with pistol blanks probably would not produce significant internal injuries, though injury to the skin would be produced.

Electrical Guns

The 1970s saw the introduction of the first electrical gun — the Taser. The Taser is a device that uses electrical current to immobilize victims without killing them.[26] Superficially resembling a flashlight, it has a gray plastic body in which there is a flashlight bulb and lens. Each cassette contains two barbs connected to the case by approximately 18 ft of wire. The weapon is aimed and fired by pointing the flashlight and pressing the trigger. This procedure allows a spark to ignite the cassette, propelling the barbs out of the weapon at about a 15-degree angle of divergence. If the barbs lodge in either the skin or the clothing, continued pressure on the trigger delivers current and voltage down the wire. A current of 60 Mamps is driven at 50,000 V. This current causes depolarization of the muscle cells, leading to widespread contraction and immobilization. Current can be delivered continuously for approximately 20 min. While the weapon is supposed to be nonlethal, death can result by continuous deliverance of the current with respiratory paralysis, from an arrhythmia in an individual with heart disease, or from direct production of a ventricular arrhythmia due to the current inadvertently affecting the polarization — depolarization cycle of the heart at a critical point. This last possibility is fairly unlikely.

Interchangeability of Ammunition in Weapons

Recovery of a bullet of a particular caliber from a body does not necessarily indicate that the weapon used to fire this missile was of the same caliber as the cartridge in which the bullet was loaded. Certain weapons will chamber and fire ammunition of a caliber different from that for which they are chambered. Some automatic pistols are capable of firing revolver ammunition, and some revolvers can fire automatic ammunition. The .32-caliber revolver is well known for its ability to chamber and fire the semi-rimmed .32 ACP automatic cartridge (Figure 10.21). The .38-caliber Enfield revolver, chambered for the .38 Smith & Wesson cartridge, will accept and fire 9-mm Luger ammunition. Less well known is the fact that many .32 automatic pistols will chamber and fire the .32 Smith & Wesson Short revolver cartridge as well as feed the revolver ammunition from a clip and function the mechanism for at least three or four rounds without jamming. .32 Cartridges have been fired in .38 revolvers by being wrapped in tape so that they completely occupy the larger chamber. 9-mm Parabellum cartridges can be chambered and fired in .40 S&W pistols. The emerging bullet will begin to yaw widely immediately on exiting the barrel.

In theory, a .38 Special revolver should not be able to chamber and fire a .38 Smith & Wesson cartridge, as the latter cartridge case has a greater diameter than the former. However, a significant number of .38 Special revolvers have oversized chambers and will accept .38 Smith & Wesson cartridges.

During World War II, large numbers of revolvers were manufactured in the United States for Great Britain. These were chambered for the .38 Smith & Wesson cartridge. Since then, many of these revolvers have been brought back to the United States and rechambered for the .38 Special cartridge. These weapons will chamber and fire both cartridges.

All .357 Magnum revolvers will, of course, fire the .38 Special cartridge, as the Magnum cartridge is nothing but an elongated .38 Special. Some people erroneously believe that firing a .38 Special cartridge in a .357

Figure 10.21 .32 revolver loaded with a .32 S & W Short revolver cartridge and a .32 ACP automatic pistol cartridge (arrow).

Magnum revolver, increases the velocity and ballistics of the .38 Special cartridge. This, of course, does not occur.

The Astra, Model 400, is chambered for the 9-mm Bayard cartridge, which is not readily available in the United States. This particular weapon will chamber and fire the .38 Super cartridge reliably and the 9-mm Luger cartridge unreliably as well as single-fire the .380 ACP cartridge. In the last case, the cartridge case usually bursts. The .32 ACP cartridge can be single-fed and fired in a .380 ACP automatic pistol. The cases rupture, however.

Mention should be made of adapters (Figure 10.22). These permit firing of a cartridge in a weapon not chambered for it by the use of a device that fits in the weapon's chamber and will accept a different caliber cartridge. Adapters permit the use of .22 rimfire ammunition in .22-caliber centerfire rifles as well as .32 ACP and .30 Carbine ammunition in high-velocity .30-caliber centerfire rifles. Adapters have been made to permit firing a handgun cartridge from a shotgun and a .410 shotgun cartridge in a 12-gauge shotgun.

Ruger manufactures a line of single-shot revolvers that have interchangeable cylinders. Thus, one weapon will fire .38 Special and .357 Magnum ammunition in one cylinder and 9-mm Luger in another interchangeable cylinder. Another weapon fires .45 ACP in one cylinder and .45 Colt in a second. A number of firearms companies manufacture .22 rimfire revolvers with two interchangeable cylinders — one for .22 Short, Long, and Long Rifle cartridges and the other for the .22 Magnum cartridge.

Pistol bullets can be loaded in rifle cartridges. Thus, in one case seen by the author an individual was fatally wounded with a 7.62-Luger bullet loaded in a .30 carbine cartridge case. It is also possible to load .32 ACP bullets in any of the .30 centerfire cartridges. The .32 ACP cartridge in turn may be reloaded with a single 00 Buck pellet (0.33 in. diameter) rather than a bullet.

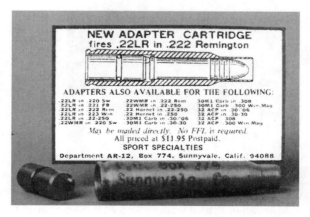

Figure 10.22   Adapter for firing .22 Long Rifle ammunition in .223 rifle.

Rifles have been and still are being chambered for certain handgun cartridges. Rifles are available in calibers .38 Special, .357 Magnum, 9-mm Parabellum, and .44 Magnum.

Specialized single-shot handguns chambered for rifle cartridges have been and still are manufactured. The Thompson-Contender, which features interchangeable barrels, can be obtained in calibers .223 Remington, .25–35 Winchester, and .30–30 Winchester, for example.

Markings and Foreign Material on Bullets

Bullets may carry materials from an intermediary target into a body as well as material from a body out with the exiting bullet.[27-28] Thus, examination of a bullet recovered from a body may reveal particles of glass, wood, or paint as well as fragments of the deceased's clothing. In one case, an individual shot himself while lying next to his wife. The bullet passed through his body, entering his wife's, where it was subsequently recovered. Tissue of his blood type, which was different from that of his wife's, was recovered from the tip of the bullet.

In passing through a target prior to entering a body, a bullet may have the pattern of the target impressed on its tip. Thus, one occasionally recovers lead bullets with the weave pattern of the clothing on the tip. Bullets, lead or jacketed, can have the grid pattern of a wire screen impressed on the tip if they perforate a screen.

Sometimes in passing through a target the bullet may pick up material that is not immediately visible. Thus, a bullet suspected of having passed through a screen and recovered from a body had a slight area of discoloration of the tip. On examination by scanning electron microscopy with x-ray probe (SEM–EDX), the smear was revealed to be aluminum from the screen.

On exiting a body a bullet may carry away fragments of tissue, bone, or even clothing overlying the exit site. The case that comes to mind was a 17-year-old male shot three times by a police officer.[27] All the bullets exited. One inflicted the fatal wound, two passed through bone, with the third bullet passing through only muscle. Three bullets were recovered at the scene — one from under where the body lay. In a civil case filed against the police, it was contended that the bullet recovered from under the body inflicted the fatal wound and was fired as the deceased lay helpless on the ground. When the author examined the other two bullets, he found fragments of white glistening material embedded in the tips at the point of junction of the lead core with the copper jacket. Analysis by SEM–EDX and light microscopy revealed this material to be bone. Since only two bullets passed through bone, one of these two bullets was the fatal bullet and the bullet recovered from under the body was not the fatal one.

Figure 10.23 Bullet with imprint of lettering from back of watch case.

Two cases with unusual marks on a bullet should be mentioned. The first involved a woman accidentally shot when the .25 automatic she was carrying fell to the ground and discharged. Etched on the jacket of the recovered full metal-jacketed bullet was the partial print of the woman. She apparently had handled the cartridge at one time, and the moisture and salt in her perspiration had corroded the jacket, with the resultant production of the partial print. In the second case, a bullet perforated the wrist of a woman, impacting the back of the case of a wrist watch that she was wearing. Examination of the bullet revealed mirror image impressions of inscribed lettering from the back of the watch (Figure 10.23).

Effect of Environmental Temperature on Bullet Velocity

Environmental temperature can significantly effect the velocity of a bullet. In tests conducted by the military using M-16 rifles, two rifles, having a rifling twist of 1:12, lost 167 ft/sec and 109 ft/sec, respectively, in muzzle velocity when the environmental temperature was decreased from 70°F to 0°F.[29] Table 10.3 shows the results of the experiment with the two rifles at different temperatures.

Table 10.3   Effect of Temperature on Bullet Velocity (weapons used, M-16 rifles)

Temperature (°F)	Weapon 1 Muzzle Velocity (ft/sec)	Weapon 2 Muzzle Velocity (ft/sec)
−65	2983	3031
−30	3011	3078
0	3039	3144
70	3206	3253
125	3219	3281

References

1. Powley, K. D., Dahlstrom, D. B., Atkins, V. J., and Fackler. M. L. Velocity necessary for a BB to penetrate the eye: an experimental study using pig's eyes. *Wound Ballistics Review* (1997) 3(1):10–12.

2. Smith, W. H. B. *Gas, Air and Spring Guns of the World*. Harrisburg, PA: Military Service Publishing Company, 1957.

3. Beyer, J. C. (ed). *Wound Ballistics*. Washington, D.C.: Office of the Surgeon General, Department of the Army, 1962.

4. Lawrence, H. S. Fatal non-powder firearm wounds: case report and review of the literature. *Ped.* 85(2):177–181, 1990.

5. Bond, S. J., Schnier, G. C., and Miller, F. B. Air-powered guns: too much firepower to be a toy. *J. Trauma* (1996)41(4):674–678.

6. Koffler, B. B. Zip guns and crude conversions — identifying characteristics and problems. *J. Crim. Law, Criminol. Police Sci.* 60(4): 520–531, 1969. Part II, 61: 115–125, 1970.

7. Book, R. G. and Botha, J. B. Zulu zip-guns and an unusual murder. *Amer. J. Forensic Med. Path.* 15(4):319–324, 1994.

8. Weedn, V. W. and Mittleman, R. E. Stud guns revisited: report of a suicide and literature review. *J. Forensic Sci.* 29(2):670–678, 1984

9. DiMaio, V. J. M. and Spitz, W U. Variations in wounding due to unusual firearms and recently available ammunition. *J. Forensic Sci.* 17:377–386, 1972.

10. Betz, P., Pankratz, H., Penning, R., and Eisenmenger, W. Homicide with a captive bolt pistol. *Amer. J. Forensic Med. Path.* 14(1):54–57, 1993.

11. Frost, R. E. A suicidal wound inflicted by a "Power Head". *J. Forensic Sci.* (1994) 39(5):1321–1324.

12. Personal communication with K. De Alwis and B. H. Win.

13. Thompson, R. L., Gluba, B. M., and Johnson, A. C. Forensic science problems associated with the accelerator® cartridge. *J. Forensic Sci.* 29(1):162–168, 1984.

14. Timperman, J. and Cnops, L. Tandem bullet in the head in a case of suicide. *Med. Sci.* 15(4): 280–283, 1975.

15. Mollan, R. A. B. and Beavis, V. A curious gunshot injury. *Br. J. Accident Surg.* 9(4): 327–328, 1978.

16. Tate, L. G., DiMaio, V. J. M., and Davis, J. H. Rebirth of exploding ammunition: a report of six human fatalities. *J. Forensic Sci.* 26(4) 636–644, 1981.

17. Lantz, P. E., Stone, R. S., Broudy, D. and Morgan, T. M. Terminal ballistics of the 9 mm with Action Safety Bullet or Blitz-Action Trauma (BAT) ammunition. *J. Forensic Sci.* 39(3):612–623, 1994.

18. Archer, D. H. R. (ed). *Jane's Infantry Weapons* — 1977. Jane's Yearbooks. London: Paulton House, 1977.

19. Kaplan, J., Fossum, R., and Di Maio, V. J. M. Centerfire frangible ammunition: wounding potential and other forensic concerns. *Amer. J. Forensic Med. Path.* (in press.)

20. Miller, R., Rutherford, W. H., Johnston, S., and Malhotra, V. J Injuries caused by rubber bullets: a report on 90 patients. *Br. J. Surg.* (1975) 62:480–486.

21. Touquet, R. and Challoner, T. Plastic bullets in Northern Ireland. *BMJ* (1990) 301:1053.

22. Hiss, J., Hellman, F. N., and Kahana, T. Rubber and plastic ammunition lethal injuries: the Israeli experience. *Med. Sci. Law* (1997) 37(2):139–144.

23. Gonzales, T. A., Vance, M., Helpern, M., Umberger, C.J. "Legal Medicine," in *Pathology and Toxicology*, 2nd ed. New York: Appleton-Century-Crofts 1954.

24. Rothschild, M. A., Karger, B., Strauch, H., and Joachim, H. Fatal wounds to the thorax caused by gunshots from blank cartridges. *Int. J. Legal Med.* (1998) 111(2):78–81.

25. Shepard, G. H. Blank cartridge wounds. Clinical and experimental studies. *J. Trauma* 9(2): 157–166, 1969.

26. Wright, R. K. Injuries caused by electrical guns. *News and Views in Forensic Pathology.* 6:2–3, 1978.

27. DiMaio, V. J. M., Dana, S. E., Taylor, W. E. and Ondrusek, J. Use of scanning electron microscopy and energy dispersive x-ray analysis (SEM-EDX) in identification of foreign material on bullets, *J. Forensic Sci.*, 32(1):38–47, 1987.

28. Petraco, N. and De Forest, P. R. Trajectory reconstructions. I: trace evidence in flight. *J. Forensic Sci.*, 35(6):1284–1296, 1990.

29. Piddington, M. J. Comparison of the exterior ballistics of the M-193 projectile when launched from 1:12 in. and 1:14 in. twist M-16A1 rifles. *Ballistics Research Lab. Report* 1943, October 1968.

X-Rays

11

X-rays are invaluable in the evaluation of gunshot wounds. They should be taken in all gunshot wound cases, especially those in which there appears to be an exit wound.

X-rays are useful for a variety of reasons:

1. To see whether the bullet or any part of it is still in the body.
2. To locate the bullet.
3. To locate for retrieval small fragments deposited in the body by a bullet that has exited.
4. To identify the type of ammunition or weapon used prior to autopsy or to make such an identification if it cannot be made at autopsy.
5. To document the path of the bullet.

Using x-rays to locate a bullet will save valuable time at autopsy whether one is dealing with a routine or a special situation. In instances of bullet emboli, x-rays are invaluable in locating the bullet. Hours of tedious dissection can be saved. X-rays are also helpful in instances where a bullet track abruptly ends in muscle and no missile is present at the end of the track. Theoretically, one should have a hemorrhagic track from the entrance to the site where the bullet finally lodges. However, in some instances — especially with small-caliber bullets such as the .22 rimfire — the last 3 to 4 in. of the track, if it is in skeletal muscle, may be free from hemorrhage and virtually unidentifiable because the bullet has slipped in between and along fascial planes. Such an occurrence is seen most commonly in the arm and thigh.

X-rays should be performed in all cases where a bullet exits, because an "exit wound" does not necessarily indicate that the bullet did indeed exit. Occasionally an exiting bullet will have enough energy to create a defect in the skin but will rebound back into the body. This may be due either to the elastic nature of the skin or to resistance from overlying clothing. The "exit"

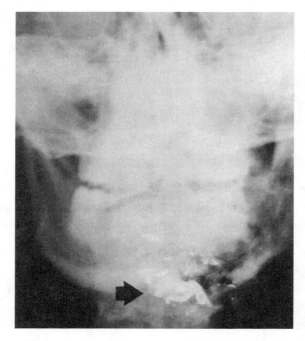

Figure 11.1   Copper jacket retained in jaw. Lead core exited.

can also be due to a fragment of bone being propelled through the skin ahead of the missile, with the bullet itself remaining in the body.

A special situation can arise with partial metal-jacketed bullets. Here separation of the jacket and the core can occur as the missile moves through the body. The lead core may exit while the jacket remains (Figure 11.1). The core is of no use for purposes of bullet comparison. Only the jacket possesses individual rifling characteristics. At autopsy, if one is unaware that the jacket is present in the body and that it was the core that exited rather than the whole bullet, the jacket can readily be missed. This is especially true if the jacket lodges in the muscle adjacent to the exit. To compound the problem, the core may be recovered at the scene by the police and then be mistaken for the complete bullet. The medical examiner may be informed that the "bullet" was recovered. Facilitating the misidentification of a lead core as a bullet is the fact that the core may have very faint "rifling" marks impressed on it through the jacket. These marks, however, are class characteristics, not individual characteristics; thus, ballistic comparison is not possible.

An artifact seen on the lead core of Remington .38 and .357 partial metal-jacketed bullets of older manufacture can be mistaken for rifling marks. As these bullets were assembled, they underwent a mechanical process by which the lead core was inserted into the jacket, resulting in six land- and groove-like marks being impressed on the core. These marks differ from lands and grooves in that they are vertical rather than canted as one would expect in rifling marks.

Although in most instances the lead core exits and the jacket remains, sometimes the opposite situation occurs, with the jacket exiting the body.

Sometimes, the jacket and core will separate in the body, but neither will exit. The forensic pathologist may recover the core with "rifling" on it and assume it to be the complete bullet. They may then inadvertently leave the jacket in the body or discard it with the viscera. Such mistakes can be prevented by an x-ray of the body, which will reveal whether separation of the core and jacket has occurred. With an x-ray, it is very easy to distinguish between the core and jacket by the different densities (Figure 11.2).

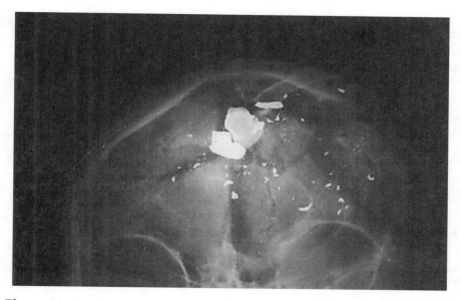

Figure 11.2 .357 Magnum bullet with separation of core and jacket. The less dense copper jacketing appears grey; the denser core, below the jacket, white.

The introduction of Silvertip® pistol ammunition by Winchester has complicated the whole process of detecting bullet jackets by x-ray. In some calibers of Silvertip® ammunition, the jacket is aluminum instead of copper alloy. In such cases, if separation of the jacket and lead core occurs in the body, the jacket may not be seen on routine x-rays because it is aluminum (see Figure 10.10). The recovered bullet core will show the impressed marks of the lands and grooves. Ballistic comparison cannot be made, however, as these are only class characteristics.

In through-and-through gunshot wounds, small fragments of metal from the missile may be deposited along the wound track or in bone perforated by the bullet. These fragments are readily missed at autopsy, especially if only two or three are present. It may be important, however, to recover such fragments as they can be analyzed by scanning electron microscope–energy dispersive x-ray (SEM-EDX) to determine the trace metals present. If the fragments are large enough, they can be submitted for quantitative compositional analysis by inductively coupled plasma atomic emission spectroscopy. A comparison can then be made with a bullet recovered at the scene and suspected to be the lethal missile. The trace metal content of these fragments may also be compared with bullets in a box of cartridges that is thought to have been the source of the fatal cartridge. Although no one can testify absolutely that a fragment came from a particular bullet or box of ammunition, one can testify that the fragment and the other ammunition are identical in all measurable properties. If the combination of trace metals is very rare, one can say that the probability of the bullet coming from another source is extremely small.

X-rays may give a pathologist an idea of what type of weapon or ammunition they are dealing with before the autopsy. Thus, the pathologist can recognize partial metal-jacketed pistol bullets, Glazer rounds, pistol shot cartridges etc. (Figure 11.3). X-rays of shotgun wounds may reveal a slug or buckshot rather than birdshot. Complete absence of a missile on total body x-ray (thus excluding embolization) and lack of an exit wound would suggest a blank cartridge.

In x-rays of through-and-through gunshot wounds, the presence of small fragments of metal along the wound track virtually rules out full metal-jacketed ammunition, such as may be used in a semi-automatic pistol. The reverse is not true, however; absence of lead on x-ray does not necessarily rule out a lead bullet. In rare instances, involving full metal-jacketed centerfire rifle bullets, a few small, dust-like fragments of lead may be seen on x-ray if the bullet perforates bone.

One of the most characteristic x-rays and one that will indicate the type of weapon and ammunition used is that seen from centerfire rifles firing hunting ammunition. In such a case, one will see a "lead snowstorm" [Figure 11.4]. In high-quality x-rays, the majority of the fragments visualized have a fine "dust-like" quality. Such a picture rules out full metal-jacketed rifle ammunition or a shotgun slug. The autopsy examination of the organs themselves cannot rule out these other forms of ammunition, as both produce internal injuries similar to if not identical to those from centerfire rifle hunting ammunition. High-velocity semi-jacketed pistol bullets (almost exclusively the .357 Magnum) may deposit fragments of bullet core as they travel through the body. This is especially true of .357 Magnum wounds of

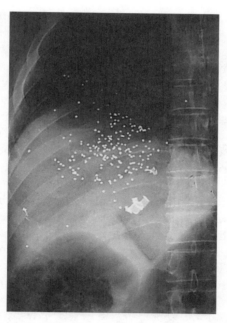

Figure 11.3 Gunshot wound of chest due to .38 Special Glazer round. Note numerous shot and copper jacket.

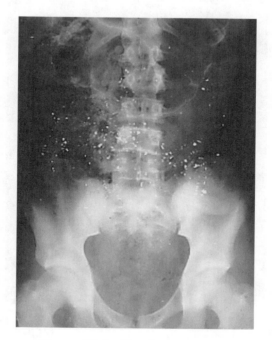

Figure 11.4 "Lead snowstorm."

the head (Figure 11.5). This picture may initially be confused with that of a "lead snowstorm" from a rifle bullet. Examination of the x-ray, however, will show that these fragments are larger, coarser and significantly fewer in number than those seen in the "lead snowstorm".

Routine x-rays in deaths from gunshot wound may reveal old bullets, pellets, or bullet fragments unrelated to the victim's death. There is usually no problem distinguishing them from new bullets when they are recovered, as the old bullets are encapsulated in fibrous scar tissue. These bullets usually have a black color as a result of oxidation. Black discoloration can occur in a new bullet, however, if the bullet is exposed to the contents of the gastrointestinal tract.

In one case that initially puzzled the author, an individual was shot in the left upper arm with a single 00 buckshot pellet. The pellet passed through the soft tissue of the upper arm, entering the left chest cavity between the fifth and sixth ribs. The pellet perforated the left lung, coming to rest in the musculature of the back adjacent to the spinal column. A routine chest x-ray, however, revealed two "pellets," the second of which was embedded in the

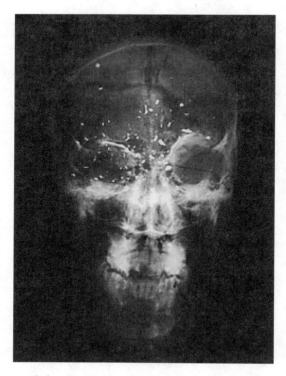

Figure 11.5 Partial fragmentation of lead core of .357 Magnum bullet that penetrated skull. The fragments are larger and fewer in number than those from a centerfire rifle bullet.

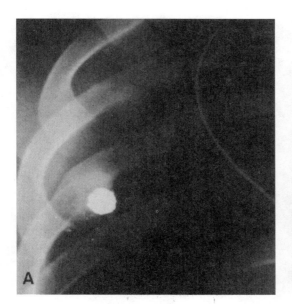
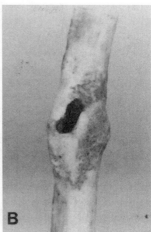

Figure 11.6 (A) Old .22-caliber bullet embedded in rib. Note callus formation on x-ray. (B) Rib with callous. The defect was from where the bullet was recovered.

fifth rib, adjacent to the wound track (Figure 11.6A). On recovery of the "pellet," it was found to be a deformed .22 Long Rifle bullet. Re-examination of the x-ray and rib showed a bony callus, indicating that the bullet had been lodged in the bone for a considerable amount of time (Figure 11.6B). In fact, the deceased had been shot almost exactly one year earlier by the same perpetrator.

In gunshot wounds of the skull, a large fragment of lead may be deposited between the scalp and the outer table of the skull at the entrance site. This piece of lead is sheared off the bullet as it enters. With lead .32 revolver bullets and less commonly with .38 bullets, this fragment often has a "C" or comma-shaped configuration (Figure 11.7). Rarely, the tip of the jacket of a full metal jacketed bullet is so deposited.

X-rays may also show evidence of internal ricochet. This is manifested by a trail of small lead fragments which doubles back on itself.

Less information can be learned by x-ray in the case of shotgun wounds. Fiber shotgun wads may on rare occasions be seen on x-ray. These fiber wads appear as faint opaque circles, resulting from lead deposits on the edge of the wad picked up from the barrel as the wad moved down it (Figure 11.8).

In shotgun wounds in charred bodies, the range at which the individual was shot is often an important question. Determination of range cannot be made from the spread of the pellets on x-rays, however. A contact wound of

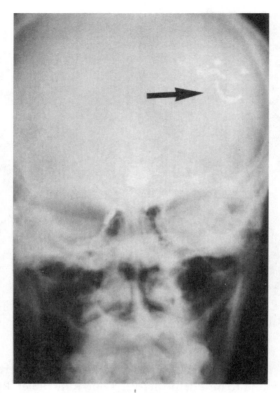

Figure 11.7   "C"-shaped fragment of lead under the scalp at entrance site.

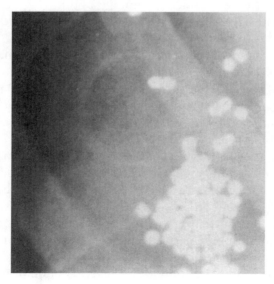

Figure 11.8   Shotgun wad outlined by thin coat of lead.

the chest can produce an x-ray picture identical to that in an individual shot at 10 ft. This is due to the "billiard ball" effect.[1] Pellets entering the body in a mass strike one another, dispersing at random angles throughout the tissue.

In "explosive" contact shotgun wounds of the head with birdshot, virtually all pellets may exit. This situation has caused confusion when no x-rays were taken of the head and the pathologist was unable to locate any pellets at autopsy. The pathologist then doubted the hypothesis that the individual had died of a shotgun wound. An x-ray in such cases should reveal at least a few pellets.

Winchester manufactures a .25-caliber cartridge loaded with a 42.6-gr lead bullet having a hollow-point filled with a #4 steel birdshot pellet.[2] On striking bone, the lead bullet tends to deform and is easily mistaken for a .22 Long Rifle bullet. The steel ball usually pops out and can be seen next to the bullet, thus presenting a very characteristic x-ray picture (Figure 11.9).

X-rays have some limitations. The exact caliber of a bullet cannot be determined with certainty by use of an x-ray. This is due to magnification of the bullet image depending on its distance from the source of x-ray. Bullets close to the origin of x-rays will appear larger and have fuzzier margins than those close to the film. Approximate caliber estimations can, of course, be made, and certain calibers can be ruled out.

X-rays in gunshot wound cases may show artifacts that can be misconstrued as bullets. The "stem" of a zipper often has the appearance of a slightly mushroomed bullet (Figure 11.10). The dislodged crown from a tooth may appear as a flattened bullet (Figure 11.11). In some cases, bullets carry fragments of an intermediary target into the body and these can be visualized on x-rays. Examples would be links of a necklace or wrist chain, links from a zipper or wire screen.

X-rays should always be taken while the deceased is fully clothed. This practice will reveal bullets that exited the body and are retained in the cloth-

Figure 11.9 Hollow-point .25 ACP bullet recovered from head showing extrusion of steel pellet.

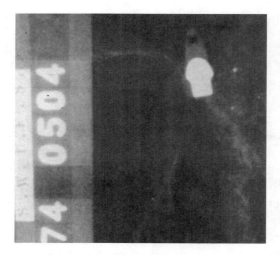

Figure 11.10 Zipper.

ing. In a case seen by the author, the bullet exited the right chest, impacting the inner surface of the front of a suit jacket the deceased was wearing, and then, having lost all its velocity, fell into the inside coat pocket. There was a hole in the bottom of the pocket, however, and the bullet fell through into the lining. This bullet would not have been recovered, if it had not been seen on a routine x-ray of the body.

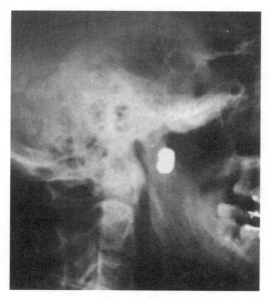

Figure 11.11 Aspirated gold cap of tooth.

References

1. Breitenecker, R. Shotgun wound patterns. *Am. J. Clin. Pathol.* 52:269–285, 1969.
2. Rao, V. J., May, C. L., and Di Maio, V. J. M. The behavior of the expanding point .25 ACP ammunition in the human body. *Am. J. Forensic Med. Pathol.* 5(1):37–39, 1984.

Detection of Gunshot Residues

12

The ability to determine whether an individual has fired a firearm is of great significance in the investigation of both homicides and suicides. Thus, over the years a number of tests have been developed in an attempt to fill this need. The first such test was the "paraffin test" also known as the "Dermal Nitrate" or "diphenylamine test."[1] It was introduced in the United States in 1933 by Teodoro Gonzalez of the Criminal Identification Laboratory, Mexico City police headquarters. In this test, the hands were coated with a layer of paraffin. After cooling, the casts were removed and treated with an acid solution of diphenylamine, a reagent used to detect nitrates and nitrites that originate from gunpowder and may be deposited on the skin after firing a weapon. A positive test was indicated by the presence of blue flecks in the paraffin. Although this test may give positive results on the hands of individuals who fired weapons, it also gives positive results on the hands of individuals who have not fired weapons because of the widespread distribution of nitrates and nitrites in our environment. The paraffin test is in fact nonspecific and is of no use scientifically.

In 1959, Harrison and Gilroy introduced a qualitative colormetric chemical test to detect the presence of barium, antimony, and lead on the hands of individuals who fired firearms.[2] These metals, which originate from the primer of a cartridge on discharge of a weapon, are deposited on the back of the firing hand as discrete particulate matter (Figure 12.1). In revolvers these metallic particles come primarily from the cylinder-barrel gap, and in automatic pistols from the ejection port. The technique developed by Harrison and Gilroy was intended as a relatively simple inexpensive test for detection of these residues. In the test a square of white cotton cloth was moistened with hydrochloric acid and then used to swab the hand. The swab was treated with triphenylmethylarsonium iodide for the detection of

Figure 12.1 Gas cloud containing primer residue flowing backward onto back of firing hand.

antimony and sodium rhodizonate for the detection of barium and lead. The limited sensitivity of this test prevented its widespread adoption.

Methods of Analyzing Gunshot Residues

By the mid-1980s, there were three generally accepted methods of analyzing for gunshot residues: neutron activation, flameless atomic absorption spectrometry (FAAS), and scanning electron microscope–energy dispersive x-ray spectrometry (SEM–EDX).[3-6] All three methods were based on the detection of metallic elements (principally barium, antimony, and lead) originating in primers and deposited on the back of the hand firing the weapon. Although all three compounds were found in the primers of virtually all centerfire cartridges at that time, this was not necessarily the case in rimfire primers. Thus, until the mid-1980s, Remington rimfire cartridges contained only lead in their primers whereas they now contain lead and barium. CCI and Winchester rimfire ammunition contain lead and barium; Federal, lead, barium, and antimony.

In the mid-1990s, centerfire cartridges free of all three metallic elements were introduced for use in indoor ranges by American ammunition manufacturers. In Europe, Sintox had been manufacturing such ammunition since the 1980s. Analysis of primer residue reveals the presence of strontium in CCI lead-free ammunition, potassium in Winchester's, calcium and silicon in Federal's, and titanium and zinc in Sintox.[7-8] In the case of CCI ammunition, the bullets have a lead core encased on all surfaces by a thick coat of electroplated copper. Remington ammunition is loaded with a full metal-jacketed bullet whose base is plugged with a copper disk, preventing vaporization of lead from the lead core. Winchester loads bullets with a copper jacket and a tin core; Federal a zinc core and copper jacketing.

By the 1990s, neutron activation had been discarded as a method of analysis. This was due not only to limitations in analytical capabilities (it can analyze for antimony and barium but not lead and, thus, had to be used in combination with FAAS) but, principally, because of the need for access to a nuclear reactor to perform tests.

Flameless Atomic Absorption Spectrometry (FAAS)

Use of FAAS techniques for detection and quantitation of gunshot residues is very popular in crime laboratories in the United States because of a combination of ease of analysis, adequate sensitivity and low cost. FAAS will detect antimony, barium, and lead from the primer as well as copper vaporized from either the cartridge case or the bullet jacketing.

In this method of analysis, four cotton swabs moistened with either nitric or hydrochloric acid are used to swab the palms and backs of the hands (Figure 12.2) in order to recover the metallic components of the primer. A fifth swab is moistened with the acid and acts as a control. The cotton-tipped swabs should have a plastic shaft as wood shafts may contain barium and, thus, theoretically, could contaminate the swab. Based on the distribution and amounts of antimony, barium, and lead detected on the four surfaces of the hands, one may conclude that the deposits are or are not consistent with gunshot residue and are or are not consistent with firing a weapon.

Typically, when one fires a gun and residue is deposited on the hand, it is on the back of the firing hand. Detection of primer residue on the palms of the hands, instead of on the back of the suspected firing hand, is suggestive of a defensive gesture rather than of firing a gun. It can also be due to handling a gun coated with firearms residue. In suicides with handguns, primer residue on the palm may be due to cradling the gun with this hand at the time of firing.

With rifles and shotguns, residue is virtually never detected on the firing hand using FAAS. Residue is often detected, however, on the non-firing hand that has been used to steady the muzzle against the body. The residue is detected more commonly on the back rather than on the palm. Occasionally, only high levels of lead are detected on the non-firing hand. It is hypothesized that the absence of antimony and barium is due to the fact that only small quantities of these elements are used in the primer and that they precipitate out inside the long barrel before they have a chance to exit in elevated levels.

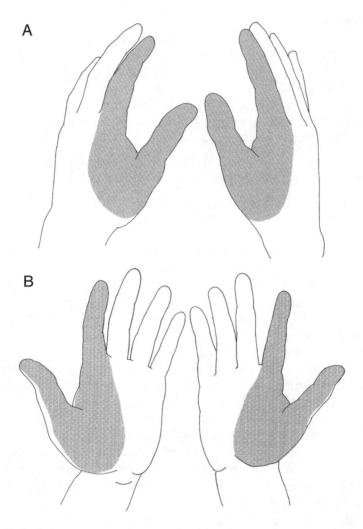

Figure 12.2 (A) Area to swab on back of hands; (B) Area to swab on palm of hands.

In the author's laboratory, when FAAS was used, levels of antimony, barium, and lead were considered significant only when they were above 35 ng for antimony, 150 ng for barium, and 800 ng for lead. For centerfire weapons, a hand washing was generally considered positive (consistent with gunshot residue) when all these three elements were present, and at least the lead was elevated. Marked elevation of barium alone may be due to the presence of soil rich in barium.

To correctly interpret the significance, if any, of a positive test result, one must take into account the surface area of the hand that is positive (left palm, right back, etc.); the quantity of metals deposited on the different areas, the nature of the weapon and, in self-inflicted wounds, the nature and location of the wound.

The classical picture of an individual who has fired a handgun is a positive test result on the back of the firing hand and negative results on the other surfaces of the hands. If an individual, instead of firing the weapon, put their hand up in a defensive gesture, with their palm toward the weapon at the time of discharge, elevated levels of primer residue will be present on the palm and sometimes on the back of the hand. In the latter case, primer residue on the back of the hand occurs when the whole hand is engulfed in a cloud of vaporized primer residue. The levels of metal on the back of the hand will be lower than those on the palm.

The following are actual cases from the author's laboratory. They represent a fair cross-section of the type of cases that are encountered.

Case 1. Hand washings in this case showed no evidence of gunshot residue. This is as it should be, as the individual was a young male dying during an episode of diabetic ketoacidosis.

Hand Area	Antimony (ng)	Barium (ng)	Lead (ng)
Right back	2.0	86	8
Left back	1.2	4	25
Right palm	0.4	0	16
Left palm	1.6	33	50

Case 2. This case was also negative for firearm residues. The individual died of stab wounds. The markedly elevated levels of barium present on the back and palms of the hands were due to contamination, probably by soil, which is very rich in barium in some areas of the country. The levels of lead and antimony were in background concentrations not consistent with the gunshot residue.

Hand Area	Antimony (ng)	Barium (ng)	Lead (ng)
Right back	2.4	390	58
Left back	0.8	1,387	159
Right palm	0	826	168
Left palm	0	1,409	478

Case 3. This test was interpreted as positive for gunshot residue on the back of the deceased's right hand. The deceased shot himself in the head with a .38 Special revolver, using the right hand.

Hand Area	Antimony (ng)	Barium (ng)	Lead (ng)
Right back	78	212	1,537
Left back	12	75	345
Right palm	5	90	210
Left palm	21	79	320

Case 4. This individual shot himself in the mouth with a .38 Special revolver. At the scene, the deceased's left hand was around the barrel. Hand washings were positive for primer residue on the back of the right hand and thus were consistent with the individual having used this hand to fire the weapon. Markedly elevated levels of primer residue were also present on the back and palm of the left hand. This hand was used to hold the muzzle in the mouth.

Hand Area	Antimony (ng)	Barium (ng)	Lead (ng)
Right back	81	232	975
Left back	250	635	67,292
Right palm	5	21	190
Left palm	193	804	45,360

Case 5. This is a case of an individual who shot himself in the right temple with a .410 shotgun. The deceased used his left hand to hold the muzzle of the weapon against his head. The right hand, which was used to fire the weapon, not unexpectedly with this type of weapon, is negative. The back of the left hand shows elevated levels of primer residue.

Hand Area	Antimony (ng)	Barium (ng)	Lead (ng)
Right back	1.6	202	210
Left back	98.8	233	3,738
Right palm	6.8	112	840
Left palm	12.0	152	344

Case 6. This is an example of an individual trying to ward off his attacker. There were significant levels of antimony, barium, and lead on the palm of the right hand.

Hand Area	Antimony (ng)	Barium (ng)	Lead (ng)
Right back	10.4	102	344
Left back	22.8	92	705
Right palm	54.8	301	1,999
Left palm	12.4	58	722

Case 7. This is a variation on Case 6. Significantly elevated levels of primer residue were present on the palms of the hands. The backs of the hands show elevated levels of lead and, in the case of the right hand, antimony. In this case the hands were probably outstretched toward the weapon and were enveloped by a cloud of residue, thus accounting for the elevated levels of lead on the back of the hands.

Hand Area	Antimony (ng)	Barium (ng)	Lead (ng)
Right back	81.2	30	3,166
Left back	18.2	5	1,646
Right palm	262.8	416	9,273
Left palm	148	349	2,931

Case 8. This is an example of a lead cloud from a high-velocity bullet that has passed through an object with resultant pulverization of the lead core, production of a lead cloud, and coating of the individual who was in the vicinity of the lead cloud. The deceased was shot through a car door with a high-velocity hunting bullet. Lead levels are markedly elevated. Barium levels are negative, with antimony levels elevated. The elevated antimony may have resulted because antimony is used to harden lead.

Hand Area	Antimony (ng)	Barium (ng)	Lead (ng)
Right back	149.2	92	10,054
Left back	57.2	0	2,646
Right palm	52.4	0	3,561
Left palm	75.2	52	4,880

The difficulty with FAAS analysis is that one can never be absolutely sure that one is dealing with firearms' residues. FAAS is a bulk, elemental analytical method involving measurement of the total quantity of metallic residues removed. One cannot distinguish the source of the metals. In addition, this technique has a high percentage of false negatives. Stone found that of individuals who committed suicide with centerfire revolvers, in only 50% of the cases were handwashings positive for gunshot residues.[9] In cases where a semi-automatic pistol was used, this figure dropped down to 32%. For .22 rimfire revolvers, the figure was 23%. These figures are in agreement with the authors experience. This illustrates the fact that a negative test for gunshot residue is meaningless. It does not prove that an individual did not fire a weapon.

In living individuals, as the time interval between firing and the taking of samples increases, there is a rapid loss of the residue from the hands. This can be produced not only by washing the hands but just by rubbing them against materials. In living individuals, the analysis is virtually always negative when the time interval is greater than 2 to 3 hours.

A positive test for gunshot residues on the hands can result from handling a weapon that has been recently discharged. The residue will of course be deposited on the palms rather than the backs of the hands. In a limited study (66 tests) of this phenomena conducted by Stone, 43% of individuals picking up a recently discharged revolver tested positive for gunshot residues. In the case of autoloading pistols, 29% of individuals were found to have metallic residues detected on the hands.[9]

Scanning Microscope-Energy Dispersive X-ray Spectrometery (SEM-EDX)

The third method of analysis employs a SEM-EDX capability.[5,6] Gunshot residue particles are removed from the hand using adhesive lifts. The material removed is scanned with the SEM for gunshot residue particles. These consist of discrete micrometer-sized particles, often of a characteristic shape. The X-ray analysis capability is used to identify the chemical elements in each of the particles.

Automated (computer-controlled) SEM-EDX analysis involves the automated scanning of lifts for particles possessing certain physical characteristics, e.g., size. The particles are then analyzed by EDX.[6] Particles of lead-antimony-barium (Pb–Sb–Ba) and antimony-barium (Sb–Ba) composition are considered characteristic of gunshot residue while other particles, containing various other combinations of these elements, are consistent but not unique. Based on testing, it has been found that in individuals who have fired handguns, 90% of the time residue will be detectable; for rifles and shotguns, 50%.[5] In long arms, rifles accounted for the majority of negative results. In the case of lead-free Sintox ammunition, the gunshot residue particles are spheroidal in shape, consisting mainly of titanium and zinc.[8]

Because particles can be identified absolutely as gunshot residue by SEM-EDX, this analysis is not as time-dependent as FAAS and neutron activation analysis. Analysis on the hands of firers by SEM has been positive up to 12 hours after they fired the weapon.[5] Recent testing comparing the efficacy of FAAS and automated SEM-EDX in screening living individuals suspected of having fired a gun revealed positive results in 3.9% by FAAS and 31.6% by SEM-EDX.*

The traditional weaknesses of SEM-EDX were the labor intensive nature of the analysis and the inability to quantitate. One could state absolutely that gunshot residue was present but not quantitate it as in FAAS so as to conclude that the distribution of the particles is consistent with firing a gun rather than a defensive gesture. Automation allows multiple unattended (automated) analyses, thereby permitting analyses of greater numbers of cases. This eliminates the labor intensive problem. If one standardizes the search parameters and the area searched on each lift, then one can express the number of gunshot reside particles per unit of area, permitting comparison of the concentration of particles on the different surfaces of the hands (palms and backs). This may possibly give one the ability to say if the distribution of residue is or is not consistent with firing a gun. (See Addendum at end of chapter.)

Trace Metal Detection Technique (TMDT)

Some police agencies, in an attempt to link a gun with an individual, use TMDT. These tests depend on the detection of trace metals left on the hand as a result of handling a gun. The metal forms characteristic color complexes with a reagent sprayed on the hand. Different metals produce different colors. The pattern and color produced depend on the shape and metal content of the weapon. Whether the pattern and color are present depends on how long the weapon was held and whether the individual was sweating. As sweating increases, the pattern and color increase in prominence. The initial TMDT involved the use of 0.2% 8-hydroxyquinoline solution with viewing the hand for color patterns under ultraviolet light. Positive results were obtained for 36 to 48 hr after handling metal. A new reagent, 2-nitroso-1-naphthol, does not require viewing under ultraviolet light.[10] Metallic patterns using this reagent last only 4 hr or less. The problems inherent with TMDT are its lack of specificity and in the case of the original reagent the long time period during which trace metal can be detected. Only rarely in actual practice is the characteristic pattern of a weapon produced on the hand, e.g., emblems or designs. More often, one has only a poorly defined area of color change. The trace metal that produced this color change could have come not only from a gun but an iron railing, a tire iron, and so forth. If the original reagent is used, the individual could have handled a metal object other than the weapon as long as 1 to 2 days previously. Thus, in actual practice this test is more subjective than objective.

---

* Personal communication: James D. Garcia.

Gunshot Wounds Through Clothing

In gunshot wound cases, examination of the clothing is often as important as examination of the body. The interposing of clothing between the muzzle of the gun and the skin can alter the appearance of close-range gunshot wounds of the body. Clothing can prevent soot or powder, either completely or in part, from reaching the skin as well as producing a redistribution of this powder and soot. In hard contact wounds of the body, where soot and powder ordinarily would be driven completely into the wound track, clothing can cause dispersion of soot and powder among the layers of clothing or onto the skin surrounding the entrance, thus altering the appearance of the wound from that of a hard contact wound to that of a loose contact wound [Figure 12.3]. With near-contact wounds, the clothing may absorb soot that would ordinarily be deposited on the skin as well as preventing or decreasing searing of the skin by hot gases.

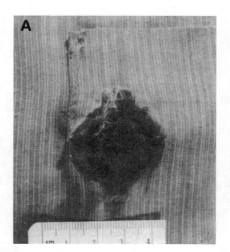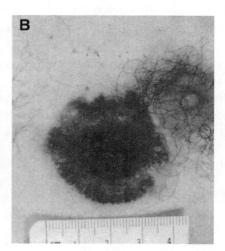

Figure 12.3 Contact wound of body through two layers of cloth. Note the appearance of the wound in chest, which simulates a loose contact.

Complete absorption of the soot and powder by clothing can occur in what ordinarily would be called an intermediate range wound. The resultant absence of powder tattooing on the skin results in an intermediate-range wound having the appearance of a distant wound.

Whether powder perforates clothing to mark the skin depends on the nature of the material, the number of layers of clothing, and the physical form of the powder. Ball powder can readily perforate one and even two layers of cloth to produce tattooing of the underlying skin. Under unusual circumstances, it will perforate three layers. It usually cannot penetrate four layers. Flake powder, on the other hand, usually does not perforate even one layer of cloth unless the range is extremely close.

In intermediate-range wounds involving clothed areas, apparent absence of powder on the outside of the clothing can be associated with dense powder tattooing of the underlying skin when the type of powder is ball powder (Figure 12.4). Ball powder, because of its shape, readily perforates the weave of the cloth, producing powder tattooing of the skin. Although powder may seem to be absent on the outside of the shirt with the naked eye, use of the dissecting microscope will reveal occasional balls of powder caught in the weave of the material. If for some reason the clothing has been separated from the body and the clothing is examined by one individual and the body

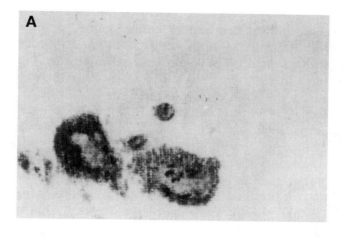

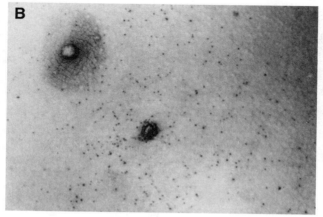

Figure 12.4 Intermediate-range gunshot wound of chest from .22 Magnum revolver. Note the absence of powder on the outside of the clothing with powder tattooing of the underlying skin.

by another, different conclusions may be reached as to the range from which the individual was shot.

In view of these facts, one can see why examination of the clothing is part of the autopsy. This examination should be conducted not only with the naked eye but with the dissecting microscope. The presence of one or two grains of powder on clothing does not necessarily mean that the deceased was shot at close range. Powder grains can travel as far as 20 ft from muzzle to clothing.

In addition to aiding in range determination, clothing may give an idea as to the position of the deceased at the time they were shot by correlating the holes in the clothing with the entrance and exit wounds in the body.

Just as the powder gases produce alterations in the wounds on the body, so will they alter the appearance of bullet holes in the clothing. In contact wounds through clothing, depending on the type of fabric and the amount of gas produced, tearing and/or melting of the material can occur. This is true whether the garment is hanging loose or pulled tightly against the skin. Contact wounds in cloth composed of cotton or a cotton mixture with medium and large-caliber weapons (.38 Special and above), usually result in tears with a cruciform appearance (Figure 12.5). Contact wounds in 100% synthetic material (nylon, triacetate, etc.) result not in tears but in "burn holes." The heat of the gases causes the material to melt producing large circular holes, usually with scalloped margins (Figure 12.5).

A contact shot in cotton material using a 4-in. barrel .38 Special revolver, firing a semi-jacketed, hollow-point bullet, resulted in a 9 × 8 cm (maximum

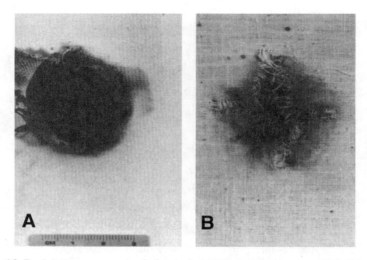

Figure 12.5 (a) Contact wound through 100% synthetic material; (b) stellate-shaped defect through 100% cotton material.

dimensions) cruciform tear in the material. Similar shots with 100% synthetic materials resulted in roughly circular holes 4 to 5.5 cm in diameter whose edges were scalloped.

With large- and medium-caliber weapons, tears in material may occur not only at contact range but at near-contact range. Thus, tests with the aforementioned weapon using 158-gr. roundnose ammunition resulted in tears of the cloth occurring with shots up to 0.5 cm from muzzle to target.

Ammunition that produces a small amount of gas, such as the .22 rimfire cartridge, tends to produce either a single tear or an incomplete cruciform tear in cotton material. In synthetics .22 Long Rifle ammunition produces burn holes averaging 10 mm in diameter.

Some of the older forensic literature mentions that clothing can be ignited by close-range firing. This refers to black powder cartridges, however. Black powder emerging from the barrel is often still burning. It can land on clothing, continue to burn, and ignite the clothing. This does not occur with smokeless powder.

Occasionally, a pillow is used to muffle a gunshot. If the weapon is a revolver, in addition to a blackened seared entrance hole, one can see a linear, an "L" or a "V" shaped blackened zone of seared material on the pillow where it was wrapped around the cylinder of the gun (see Figure 4.10). This mark is due to soot and hot gases that have escaped from the cylinder gap of the gun. Measurement of the distance between this mark and the entrance hole will give one an idea of the barrel length of the weapon (see Figure 4.11). If 100% synthetic material overlaps the cylinder gap, the gases may burn completely through the material.

"Bullet wipe" is a gray to black rim around an entrance hole in clothing. It is seen around holes made by both lead and full metal-jacketed bullets. It is not, as some people contend, lead wiped off the bullet but is principally soot. Lubricant and small amounts of metallic elements from the primer, cartridge case, and bullet may also be present in the bullet wipe.

As a bullet moves down the barrel of a gun, it is coated with soot, lubricant, and the previously mentioned metallic elements. In addition, the bullet may pick up debris left in the barrel by prior discharge of the weapon. Unburnt grains of powder may become adherent to a bullet, especially its base. The bullet carries all this material on itself to the target. As it passes through the clothing, it "wipes off" this material, producing the bullet wipe. If one thoroughly cleans the interior of a barrel until there is no material left in it and then fires a bullet down the barrel, this bullet on striking cloth will produce a light gray sometimes almost imperceptible bullet wipe. As more and more rounds of ammunition are discharged down the barrel, the bullet wipes produced will become increasingly darker in color until finally the color will stabilize as a dark black. If a bullet goes through multiple layers of cloth, bullet wipe may be present only around the defect in the cloth that was perforated first. Bullet wipe is seen in microscopic sections of entrance wounds as small particulate deposits of amorphous black material along the wound path. It is often mistakenly interpreted as "powder" and erroneously construed as evidence of a close range wound.

Careful examination of both sides of a bullet hole in clothing, using a dissecting microscope, may suggest the direction in which the bullet was moving by which way the fibers are bent. It should be realized that not all fibers are bent in the direction of the path of the bullet, and in fact some fibers may point in the opposite direction.

Deposition of fragments of tissue on the inner surface of clothing around a bullet hole strongly suggests that it is an exit. In the case of wounds due to centerfire rifles, and rarely with handguns, tissue may also be blown out the entrance, and deposited on the inner surface of the cloth around the entrance. This is a result of positive pressure waves generated in the temporary cavity formed by the bullet. The amount of such tissue is significantly less than that deposited adjacent to the exit.

Analytical Examination of Clothing for Range Determination

Although in many cases soot and powder grains are readily seen on the clothing, thus indicating a close-range shot, on occasion examination with the naked eye and the dissection microscope is insufficient. The powder may have fallen and/or bounced off, or one is at the extreme range at which powder exiting a barrel will have sufficient velocity to embed itself in the material. In such situations and in instances where an exact determination of the range may be necessary, rather than just saying it is close-range, an analytical examination of the clothing is desirable.[11] To make such determinations, Crime Laboratories use the Modified Griess test for nitrites and the Sodium Rhodizonate test for lead residues.[12-13]

The Modified Greiss Test

The Modified Greiss test is the evolutionary end product of the Walker test. This latter test was developed to detect nitrite compounds produced by the burning of smokeless powder (cellulose nitrate). The Walker test documents the presence of nitrites as well as showing the size, configuration and density of the pattern on clothing or other objects. A firearms examiner can then attempt to duplicate this pattern by firing the same weapon and type of ammunition, at know distances, at the same type of material. This procedure will give the examiner an approximation of the range at which the individual was shot. The test involves desensitizing glossy, photographic paper in a hypobath, washing and drying it, immersing it in a 5% solution of sulfanilic acid; drying it, dipping the paper in a 0.5% solution of alpha-naphthylamine in methyl alcohol, drying the paper, placing the clothing to be examined on the paper, placing a layer of cloth moistened with 20% acetic acid over the clothing to be examined, and pressing down on this cloth with a warm iron for 5 to 10 min. The paper is removed and washed in hot water and methyl alcohol. When nitrites are present, they will appear as orange-red spots on the paper which when retained constitutes a permanent record of the presence and distribution of the nitrite compounds.

Because alpha-naphthylamine was identified as a carcinogen, Watson introduced a variation on this test using Marshall's Reagent.[15] The test then became known as the Griess Test. Subsequently, Marshall's Reagent was also found to be carcinogenic and was replaced by alpha-naphthol or naphthoresorcinol. The former chemical will cause the nitrites to appear orange; the latter will make them appear yellow. This new test is the Modified Griess Test.[12] Alpha-naphthol is the chemical currently used as the orange color is brighter. The Modified Griess Test, as was true of the other nitrite tests, will not interfere with subsequent lead tests using Sodium Rhodizonate, though the opposite is not so.

The Modified Griess test is specific for nitrites and thus, in theory, will not react with unburnt powder grains. Since these grains are usually coated with nitrite compound from burning of other powder grains, this is more theoretical than actual.

The Sodium Rhodizonate Test

The Sodium Rhodizonate test, long used as a spot test for lead and barium, constituted one portion of the Harrison and Gilroy test for the detection of gunshot residue on the hands.[2] It is now used by firearms examiners for the detection of lead residue around an entrance.[13] This lead is principally from the primer though some of it originates from the bullet and lead residue deposited in the barrel from previous discharges of the gun. In a modification proposed by Bashinski et al., the material to be tested is pre-treated with 10% acetic acid.[16] This step improves the sensitivity of the test. The material is then sprayed with sodium rhodizonate followed by pH 2.8 tartaric acid buffer. Lead becomes visible as a bright pink reaction; barium has an orange color. Unlike the Modified Griess test for nitrites, the pattern of lead produced cannot be used to make exact range determinations. All that one can say is that the weapon was close enough to deposit lead on the article examined. Test firings can then determine the maximum range out to which the lead is deposited. If one has a hole and is not sure if it was due to a bullet, a sodium rhodizonate test can be done in order to see if there is lead on the margins of the defect. A positive test can be obtained even with full metal-jacketed bullets as these bullets may be coated with lead from the primer, the lead core or from deposits in the barrel. The Sodium Rhodizononate test is always performed after the Griess test as it may interfere with the latter test. The reverse is not true.

Negative Griess or Sodium Rhodizononate tests do not necessarily mean that the gun was not fired at close range as the gunshot residue could have been lost prior to the test.

EDX for Examination of Clothes

A less commonly used method of examining clothing in order to make range determination involves the use of energy dispersive x-ray (EDX). The edges of the entrance hole are analyzed for the presence of antimony, barium, lead, and copper. Multiple readings are taken at varying distances from this hole. Thus, readings will be taken at 1, 2, 3, etc., inches from the 12 o'clock position of the hole, followed by additional readings taken in a similar manner from the 3, 6, and 9 o'clock positions. The distribution of the metallic residue around the entrance hole can thus be mapped out in a semi-quantitative manner. This pattern can be duplicated on identical cloth, with the same weapon and type of ammunition. This procedure gives one an approximation of the range at which the wound was inflicted. Identical cloth must be used as differences in cloth can produce marked differences in the deposition of the metals. Use of the EDX has the advantage that it is nondestructive and extremely rapid with no preparation of the garment necessary. If desired, after examination with EDX, the garment can be submitted for analysis by the Modified Griess and/or the Sodium Rhodizonate test.

When rimfire ammunition containing only lead in the primer was fired at cloth, it was observed that one may detect antimony, barium, and lead. The source of the antimony and barium were deposits of antimony and barium in the bore of the weapon caused by previous firing of other rimfire ammunition that had these metals in their primers.

Range Determination in Decomposed Bodies

Determination as to whether a gunshot wound in a decomposing body is either close-range or distant can be difficult for a number of reasons. First are the changes of decomposition itself. Decomposition results in a blackish discoloration of the skin and subcutaneous tissue, which can either simulate or conceal soot. There is slippage of the epidermis, which can produce complete loss of powder tattooing and soot. Blood around the wound clots and dries out. Fragments of this desiccated blood can simulate partly burnt powder fragments.

In addition to the changes of decomposition, insect activity can obliterate as well as simulate wounds. Maggots and beetles are attracted to injury sites where blood is present. They can completely obliterate the entrance in the skin and thus any evidence of soot or powder. Insects can burrow into the skin, producing circular defects resembling gunshot entrance wounds. If there is subsequent drying of the edges, this may simulate the blackening and searing of a contact wound from a small caliber weapon (Figure 12.6).

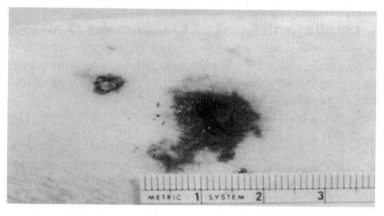

Figure 12.6 Hole in skin from insect burrowing. Note drying of edges which simulates contact wound.

Although nothing can be done if insects have obliterated a wound, it is possible to differentiate close-range versus distant wounds, provided that one has adequate instrumentation. In all decomposing bodies, the suspected wound should be examined *in situ* with the dissecting microscope for the presence of soot and powder. It should then be excised and the underlying subcutaneous tissue examined for soot and powder as well. In many instances, one cannot say with certainty whether soot is present. If one sees unburned powder grains, one will know that one is dealing with a close-range wound. As mentioned, fragmented, dried-out, desiccated blood can simulate partly burnt grains of powder. The suspected material can be submitted for analysis by thin-layer chromatography. This latter method can differentiate single-from double-base powder as well.[17]

After examination with the dissecting microscope, the wound can then be examined by EDX or SEM–EDX. Here one is looking for vaporized metal from the primer, cartridge case, and bullet deposited on the skin. Low levels of lead at an entrance are not significant in range determination, as the lead may have "wiped off" the bullet as it punched its way through the skin. This lead is either from the bullet itself or the primer residue that coats the fired bullet as it moves down the barrel.

Extremely high counts of lead found by EDX indicate close-range firing. The significance of specific levels or counts of lead depends on the time of counting and machine used and have to be worked out for each machine. Detection of either antimony or barium in significant levels of EDX indicates a close-range wound, as they are from the primer compounds. In addition, zinc and copper may be vaporized from the cartridge case; if this occurs in high enough concentrations, it will indicate close-range wounds. One has to have a control sample from the adjacent skin to see what is the normal background for the previously mentioned metals detected.

In contact wounds from shotguns and rifles, only lead may be detected by EDX at the wound entrance. The other metallic elements of the primer may not reach the entrance site in high enough concentrations to be detected by this method of analysis.

After initial examination of a wound by EDX, the wound can be split down the center and the interior re-examined with a dissecting microscope for powder and soot. Examination of the wound track by EDX should be carried out as the original EDX analysis detected trace metals deposited on the skin rather than in the wound track. Again, the presence of extremely high levels of lead or the presence of antimony and barium by EDX indicates that a wound is close-range.

Determination that a defect in a body is a pseudo-gunshot wound caused by an insect, is usually made by examining the wound and attempting to follow its bullet track. Usually, the insect burrows down only to the subcutaneous tissue and it is obvious that one is dealing with an insect defect. These alleged gunshot wounds can also be examined by SEM-EDX.

Addendum

Use of automated SEM-EDX in suicides is probably not justified as it is more costly than FAAS and does not offer any significant advantage. Analysis by the author of 100 suicides using SEM-EDX revealed that no specific particles were identified on the hands in 47% of cases involving .357 Magnums; 47% of .38 Specials; 85% of .22's; 38% of .380's, and 25% of 9 mm's. Based on indentification of specific particles, their number and their distribution on the hands, positive tests consistent with firing a gun were present only in 27 to 33% of cases involving .357 Magnum's; 33 to 37% of .38 Special cases; 5% of .22's; 8% of .380's, and 8 to 25% of 9 mm's.

References

1. Cowman, M. E. and Purdon, P. L. A study of the "paraffin test." *J. Forensic Sci.* 12(1): 19–35, 1967.

2. Harrison, H. C. and Gilroy, R. Firearms discharge residues. *J. Forensic Sci.* 4(2): 184–199, 1959.

3. Krishnan, S. S. Detection of gunshot residue on the hands by neutron activation and atomic absorption analysis. *J. Forensic Sci.* 19(4): 789–797, 1974.

4. Stone, I. C. and Petty, C. S. Examination of gunshot residues. *J. Forensic Sci.* 19(4): 784–788, 1974.

5. Wolten, G. M., Nesbitt, Calloway, A. R., Loper, G. L., and Jones, P. F. Particles analysis for the detection of gunshot residue (I–III). *J. Forensic Sci.* 24(2): 409–422, 423–430, 1979; 24(4): 864–869, 1979.

6. Germani, M. S. Evaluation of instrumental parameters for automated scanning electron microscopy/gunshot residue particle analysis. *J. Forensic Sci.* 36(2):331–342, 1991.

7. Haag, L. C. American lead-free 9 mm-P cartridges. *AFTE Journal* 27(2):142–147. 1995.

8. Gunaratnam, L. and Himberg, K. The identification of gunshot residue particles from lead-free Sintox ammunition. *J. Forensic Sci.* 39(2):532–536. 1994.

9. Stone, I. C. Characteristics of firearms and gunshot wounds as markers of suicide. *Amer. J. Forensic Med. and Path.* 13(4):275–280, 1992.

10. Kokocinski, C. W., Brundate, D. J., and Nicol, J. D. A study of the use of 2-nitro-1 naphthol as a trace metal detection reagent. *J. Forensic Sci.* 25(4): 810–814, 1980.

11. Dillon, J. H. A protocol for gunshot residue examinations in muzzle-to-target distance determinations. *AFTE Journal.* 22(3):257–274, 1990.

12. Dillon, J. H. The Modified Griess Test: A chemical specific chromophoric test for nitrite compounds in gunshot residue. *AFTE Journal.* 22(3):243–250, 1990.

13. Dillon, J. H. The Sodium Rhodizonate Test: A chemically specific chromophoric test for lead in gunshot residue. *AFTE Journal.* 22(3):251–256, 1990.

14. Walker, J. T. Bullet holes and chemical residues in shooting cases. *J. Crime. Law Criminol.* 31:497, 1940.

15. Watson, D. J. Nitrites examination in propellant powder residue. *AFTE J.* 2(1): 32, 1979.

16. Bashinski, J. S., David, J. E., and Young, C. Detection of lead in gunshot residues on targets using the sodium rhodizonate test. *AFTE J.* 6(4): 5–6, 1974.

17. Peak, S. A. A thin-layer chromatographic procedure for confirming the presence and identity of smokeless powder flakes. *J. Forensic Sci.* 25(3): 679–681, 1980.

Correct Handling of Deaths from Firearms

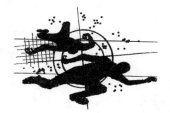

The correct handling of a death from gunshot wounds begins at the scene. Here valuable evidence on the body can be lost or altered and bogus evidence may be inadvertently introduced through mishandling of the body.

Before a body is touched, let alone examined, its position and appearance should be documented photographically and diagrammatically. The most important rule at the scene is to handle the body as little as possible so as not to dislodge trace evidence that may be clinging to garments or to the body surface. Hands should never be pried open, and fingerprints should never be taken at the scene. Prying the fingers apart may dislodge material such as fibers, hair, or gunpowder. Fingerprint ink can either mimic or obscure powder soot as well as introducing contaminating materials that may render subsequent examination of the hands for primer residues of questionable validity. Manipulation of the hands is of even greater potential danger if it is done by a police officer who, theoretically, can transfer primer residues from his hands to those of the deceased. After all, as part of the job, the officer handles and fires weapons, thus putting them in an environment where hands may be contaminated with primer residues.

Before transportation of the body to the morgue, paper bags should be placed over the hands to prevent loss of trace evidence. Paper bags should be used rather than plastic, because condensation will form in the bags if the body is refrigerated. This can wash away primer residues and make fingerprinting more difficult. Some authorities claim that it is possible for the hands to be contaminated by barium from the paper bags, thus rendering analysis for this metal by flameless atomic absorption spectrophotometry (FAAS) invalid. In the author's experience, this has never happened.

Once the paper bags are securely placed around the hands, the body should be wrapped in a white sheet or placed in a clean transport bag. This

347

is done to prevent loss of trace evidence from the body. It also avoids transference of bogus evidence from the transport vehicle enroute to the morgue, as such a vehicle has probably transported numerous other bodies previously.

On arrival at the morgue, the body should be logged in as to the deceased's name, the date and time of arrival, who transported it, and who received it. A case number should be assigned. At the time of the autopsy, an identification photo should be taken with the case number prominently displayed in the identification photo.

If the deceased did not die immediately after being shot and was transported to a hospital, a number of surgical and medical procedures may have been carried out. Because of this, complete medical records of the deceased from the time of admission to the death should be obtained before the autopsy. All hospitals in the area served by the medical examiner system should be informed that in all medical examiner cases, no tubing should ever be removed from the body after death, e.g., endotracheal tubes, intravenous lines, or Foley catheters. Injection sites should be circled in ink by the hospital staff to indicate that they are of therapeutic origin and did not antedate hospitalization. Thoracotomy, laparotomy, and surgical stab wounds should be labeled or described in the medical records. If death occurs within a few hours after hospitalization, paper bags should be placed on the hands, just as if the death had occurred at the scene. The body and any clothing worn by the deceased should be transferred to the medical examiner's office. All medical records detailing the procedures performed should accompany the body. Any blood obtained on admission to the hospital should be obtained for toxicology. Admission blood obtained for transfusion purposes in trauma cases often is saved for one to two weeks in the hospital blood bank. The blood bank should be queried for retained initial blood samples.

Before examination by the forensic pathologist, the body should not be undressed, washed, embalmed, or fingerprinted. Examination of the clothing is as much a part of the forensic autopsy as examination of the body. Embalming can induce artifacts, change the character of wounds, and make toxicological analyses impossible or extremely difficult. The best example of an artifact created by embalming is shown in Figure 13.1 The deceased was a young child who was allegedly accidentally shot by the father at a distance of 10 feet. The Justice of the Peace who initially handled the case saw no reason for an autopsy and had the body embalmed. When he changed his mind and the body was subsequently examined, there appeared to be a muzzle imprint in the left upper chest. This was in fact the outline of an embalming button that was used to "seal" the distant wound of entrance. During embalming, the tissue swelled around the button, producing the mark.

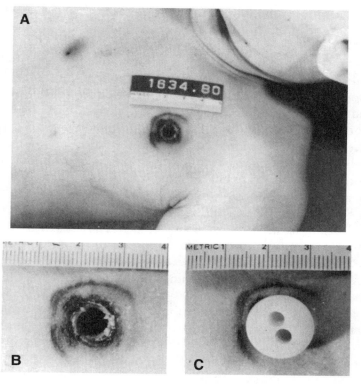

Figure 13.1 (A) Gunshot wound of left upper lateral chest; (B) circular mark around defect, suggestive of muzzle imprint; (C) embalming button in place, acting as causative factor for "imprint."

After receipt of a body, the pathologist should have x-rays taken. X-rays should be taken in all gunshot wound cases whether the missile is believed to be in the body or to have exited. The clothing should not ordinarily be removed before x-ray. On occasion, bullets have exited the body and become lodged in or among the clothing. In one case the bullet exited the right chest and fell into the inside pocket of a jacket. A hole was present in the bottom of the pocket, and the bullet then fell into the lining. It would not have been found had x-ray not revealed it to be in the clothing.

The next step is to recover any primer residue from the hands. This can be done by the use of swabs or lifts. At the same time, the hands should be examined for the presence of trace evidence, e.g., powder grains, fibers, hair, etc. Trace evidence should be retained and placed in properly labeled containers. Powder and soot may be found on the hand if the deceased had tried to reach for the weapon or had their hand around the weapon at the time of discharge. Fingernails may be clipped and retained at this time if indicated.

After this procedure, fingerprints may be taken. It is suggested that at least two sets of prints be made, one for the police and the other for the autopsy file. In homicides, palm prints should also be taken.

Next, the body is examined with the clothing still on it. Attention is paid as to whether the defects in the clothing correspond in location to wounds in the body. The clothing should be examined for the presence of powder, soot, and other trace evidence. Following this, the clothing is removed and laid out on a clean, dry surface. The clothing should not be cut from the body except under very unusual circumstances.

The body is then examined without the clothing and without cleaning. One should search for trace evidence, powder grains, and soot. One may want to take photographs of the uncleaned wounds at this time.

The body is then cleaned and re-examined for any other wounds that may have been concealed by dried blood. Photographs of the cleaned wounds may then be taken. The prosector should go back to the clothing and again correlate the observed entrances and exits with defects in the clothing. They should re-examine defects in the clothing for the presence of powder or soot. The use of a dissecting microscope is strongly recommended.

Photographing of the wounds on the body is recommended. At least two photographs of each entrance wound should be taken. One should be a placement shot showing where the wound is in relationship to other body landmarks. The second should be a close-up showing the appearance of the wound. Most individuals take a third shot between the two extremes. It is helpful if there is a scale and the number of the case in the photograph.

Each wound should be examined, and notes should be taken as to its exact location and appearance. Pertinent negatives should be noted. It is strongly recommended that the wounds be examined with a dissecting microscope. If there is any question as to range which cannot be settled at this time, the wound should be excised and retained for analysis by scanning electron microscope-energy dispersive x-ray (SEM-EDX) or energy dispersive x-ray (EDX). In routine gunshot wounds, it is not necessary to excise and retain entrance and exit sites. Microscopic sections of the entrance and exit do not ordinarily contribute any information that cannot be gained by examination with the naked eye or with a dissecting microscope. In some cases, microscopic sections may be misleading, especially to the novice.

If powder, polyethylene filler, or fragments of the bullet are on the surface of the body, these should be retained and submitted with the bullet or pellets to the crime lab.

In homicide cases, a complete autopsy involving the head, chest, and abdominal cavities should be performed. All viscera should be removed and examined. The track of the bullet should be followed and the point it lodges or exits measured in relationship to the entrance. If it is still present in the body, the bullet should be recovered. In shotgun cases, it is not necessary to recover all pellets but only a representative sample. Wadding should always be recovered. Wounds ordinarily should not be probed as they can create false wound tracks, distort a wound, or dislodge a missile.

In all gunshot wound cases, blood, vitreous, urine, and bile, should be retained. In cases, of advanced decomposition where these materials are not present, muscle (from the thigh, preferably) should be retained. These materials can be used for toxicological or serological purposes.

The Autopsy Report

In preparing an autopsy report in a death caused by gunshot wounds, it is always best to group the description of wounds in one area labeled "Evidence of Injury," rather than scattering this information throughout the protocol. Thus, when a bullet entering the left chest perforates the left lung, the heart, the right lung, and exits the back, one should have all this information in one area of the autopsy report rather than scattering it among the External Examination and the description of the individual internal organs. Once the description of the injury to the organ has been made in this section, there is no need to redescribe the injury in the area of the report devoted to the organs.

Each entrance wound should be given an arbitrary number for reference purposes. A wound should be fully described as to location, appearance, path of the missile, injuries produced and site of lodgement or exit before description of the next bullet wound is given. There is no necessity to assign a number to an exit. This latter practice is often very confusing to the subsequent readers of the autopsy report.

The first information to be noted in the autopsy report is the location of the entrance wound. The wound should be located in terms of its general geographic area, e.g., the left upper chest, followed by its distance from either the top of the head or the soles of the feet; the distance from the right or left of the midline; and most importantly its relationship and distance from a local landmark such as the nipple.

Measurements as to location may be in either the English or the metric system. Since most lay people in the U.S. do not understand the metric system, and the majority of people who will see a forensic autopsy report are lay people, the English system is preferable. Describing a gunshot wound in relation to a local landmark is usually of greater value than locating the wound from the top of the head or so many centimeters or inches to the right or left of the midline. It is easier to visualize the location of a gunshot wound of the left chest as being "one inch above the level of the nipples" and "one inch medial to a vertical plane through the left nipple," rather than "20 inches below the top of the head" and "three inches to the left of the midline." The value in using local landmarks becomes obvious if one considers the location of a wound 20 inches below the head in a six foot 11 in. basketball player compared to a five foot secretary. This does not, however, remove one's responsibility for locating the entrance from the top of the head and to the right or left of the midline.

After the entrance wound is located, the size, shape, and characteristics of this wound should be given. In contradiction to the suggestion that measurements locating the wounds on the outside of the body should be in the English system, measurements of the wound itself should be in the metric system for greater accuracy. Use of the English system of measurement, with its confusing mixture of sixteenths, eighths, and tenths of an inch, often results in errors or misconceptions as to the size and configuration of a wound. While the use of the metric system may be confusing to the lay public, the value of its simplicity and accuracy outweighs this consideration in this situation. The presence or absence of an abrasion ring, its symmetry, and its width should be described. The presence or absence of soot and powder should be noted in all cases. When soot is present, the configuration of the deposit along with its size and density should be described. Searing of the edges of the wound or adjacent skin should be noted and described in detail. When powder tattoo patterns are present, the maximum dimensions of the pattern and its density should be described. In measuring the pattern, occasional stray tattoo marks from the main powder tattoo pattern should be ignored. Unburned or partially burned grains of powder may be recovered. If so, an attempt should be made to identify them as flake, ball, or cylindrical powder. Grains should be retained for identification by a firearms examiner if the prosecutor is unsure of the type of powder present or wishes independent confirmation. The relationship of the bullet entrance hole to the distribution of the tattooing around it should be described.

Description of the abrasion ring or zone of searing around the entrance can be done by relating the appearance of these wound characteristics to the face of a clock whose center is the center of the bullet hole. Thus an eccentric abrasion ring may be said to average one (1)-mm wide, except from the 3 to 6 o'clock positions, where it averages three (3)-mm wide.

In contact wounds, if a muzzle imprint is present, the imprint should be described fully. If the weapon that is alleged to have produced the wound is available, comparison should be made of the muzzle end of the weapon with the imprint. It must be realized that the size of the imprint on the skin may be twice the actual dimensions of the muzzle.

After the external appearance of the wound is described, the path of the missile through the body should be given. The organs injured and the amount of blood present in the body cavities should be noted. The point where the bullet either lodges or exits the body should be described. It is helpful to describe the point of lodgement or the point of exit in relation to the wound of entrance, e.g., "three (3) in. below the level of the wound of entrance, one (1) in. to the left of the posterior midline." This description often aids one in visualizing the trajectory of the bullet through the body. A brief sentence about the overall direction of the bullet as it passes through the body is often helpful to an individual who has to read the autopsy protocol. Thus, the bullet may be said to have traveled from "front to back, downward and from right to left." The prosector should try to avoid terms, such as "medial," "dorsal," "ventral," "superior," or "inferior" in describing the bullet trajectory, since most lay people are unfamiliar with this terminology and forensic autopsies are more often read by lay persons than by physicians.

Exact calculation of the angle that the bullet traveled through the body is not possible and is often misleading. At the time of autopsy, the body is in an unnatural position, e.g., flat on its back and not upright. Calculations of the angle fail to take into account movement of the thorax, diaphragm, and internal viscera during the normal processes of breathing; distention of viscera by fluid, air, or food; the effects of gravity on the position of the internal viscera; and bending and twisting of the body at the time of bullet impact.

When a bullet is recovered from a body, removal should be done with the fingers, not with an instrument. Using instruments to recover a bullet can result in scratching of the surface and interference with ballistic comparison. If a bullet is recovered, it should be described briefly in the autopsy protocol. The general appearance of the bullet, i.e., deformed, un-deformed, lead, jacketed, or partial metal-jacketed; and the approximate caliber (if known) should be stated. The prosector should then mark the bullet with initials or numbers so that they can identify it later. This marking should never be inscribed on the side of the bullet, as it would obliterate rifling marks. Any inscription should be put on either the tip or the base of the bullet. After the bullet is inscribed, it should be placed in an envelope. The envelope should be labeled, at a minimum, with the name of the deceased, the autopsy number, the date of autopsy, what was recovered, where it was recovered, and the inscription put on the bullet. The prosector should then sign their name under this information. The envelope should be kept in a secure place. At the appropriate time, it should be turned over to a representative of the Criminal Investigation Laboratory or the police. At this time, a receipt for the bullet should be obtained as proof of maintenance of the chain of evidence. Occasionally, a cartridge case will be recovered from the clothing of the deceased; in such a case, the casing should be retained. It may be marked with a number or initials with these marks placed either in the mouth or near the mouth of the casing.

In the case of shotgun wounds, the size of the shotgun pellet pattern or the entrance hole (if the pellets have not "opened up") should be described in the autopsy report. With shotgun pellet patterns of the skin, just as in tattooing, one should ignore stray pellets and measure only the primary pattern. A representative number of pellets and all wadding (if any) should be recovered.

After the first gunshot wound is described, the process should then be repeated for any other gunshot wounds. Each description should be complete in itself from entrance to either recovery of the bullet or exit. There is no need to re-describe the injuries in areas of the report devoted to the individual organs.

After the description of the gunshot wounds, there should be a description of the clothing in regard to defects produced by entering and exiting bullets. These defects should be located at least in a general way. It should be noted whether powder or soot is present around these defects. Examination of the clothing with a dissecting microscope is strongly recommended. One should note whether the defects correspond to the wounds. The clothing should be air-dried, packaged in paper (not plastic), and either released to the police agency or sent on to the crime lab for further examination.

Appendix B may be consulted for a more general approach to the forensic autopsy as well as how it may be presented.

Suicide by Firearms

The most common method of committing suicide in the United States is by shooting. Approximately 65% of men committing suicide use firearms, with the remainder of the deaths almost equally divided between drug overdoses and hanging. Traditionally, the preferred method used by women was an overdose of drugs. Since the mid-1980s, however, use of firearms has become the most popular method of suicide in women.[1] In 1970, in the United States, 30% of women shot themselves and 48% took an overdose of drugs; by 1990, the percentages were 42% and 36%, respectively. In a study of 698 consecutive male suicides in San Antonio, Texas, 71.5% used a firearm, 13.8% hung themselves, 6.5% overdosed on drugs, and 8.2% used other means.[2] Of 221 consecutive female suicides, 49.3% used firearms, 31.7% drugs, 10.4% hanging, and 8.6% other means.

In regard to choice of weapons, handguns are used more often than rifles or shotguns. There is a difference in firearm use based on sex as demonstrated by the San Antonio study where 73% of men used handguns, compared to 92% of women.

While most suicidal gunshot wounds are contact wounds, a small (1 to 3%) but significant number are of intermediate range (Figure 14.1). Occasionally, one encounters a distant wound. The latter situation was illustrated by an individual brought to the Bexar County Medical Examiner's Office with a self-inflicted intraoral gunshot wound. At autopsy, the bullet was seen to have entered the dorsal surface of the tongue, traveled straight backward into the vertebral column severing the cord. There was no soot, powder tattooing, or powder on the face, in the mouth, or on the posterior pharynx. Powder tattooing was present on the inner aspect of the wrists, however. The weapon was a 2 in. barrel .38 Special revolver. Testing of this weapon and the ammunition in it revealed that powder tattooing extended out to 12 to 18 inches. The deceased held the weapon at arms length, opened her mouth and discharged the weapon, firing a bullet into her mouth. The range was

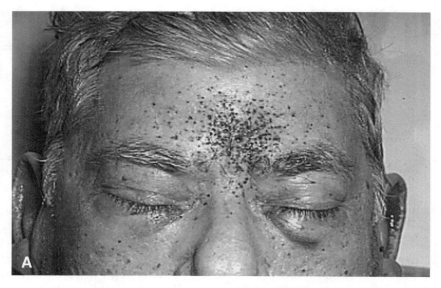

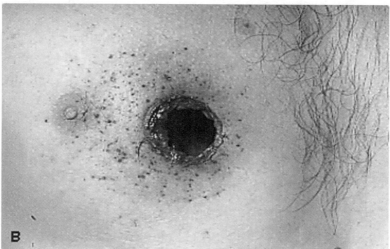

Figure 14.1   Self-inflicted intermediate-range gunshots with powder tattooing around the entrances. **(A)** Entrance of forehead from handgun. **(B)** Entrance of chest from sawed-off 12-gauge shotgun.

too great for powder tattooing of the face. Powder escaping out the cylinder gap produced the tattooing of her wrists.

Most people who commit suicide with a firearm, like suicide victims in general, do not leave a note; notes are only left in approximately 25% of all suicides. Therefore, the absence of a note does not indicate that a death was not a suicide.

In firearm deaths, the individual may attempt to make the suicide appear to be an accident. This generally takes two forms. The first of these is the "gun cleaning accident." The individual is found dead of a gunshot wound with gun cleaning equipment neatly laid out beside them. The proof that one is dealing with a suicide and not an accident is usually the nature of the wound — contact. An individual does not place a gun against the head or chest and then pull the trigger in an attempt to clean the weapon. The author has never seen a death caused by a self-inflicted wound incurred while "cleaning" a weapon that he believed to truly be an accident.

The second way an individual may attempt to make a suicide appear as an accident is the "hunting accident." Here the individual goes hunting and is subsequently found dead of a gunshot wound. Again, the nature of the wound (contact) will indicate that one is dealing with a suicide.

Self-inflicted wounds to the chest and abdomen from rifles and shotguns in individuals standing at the time they shoot themselves often have a characteristic trajectory that acts as confirmatory evidence that one is dealing with a suicide. The individual intending suicide braces the butt of the gun against the ground. They then lean over the weapon, holding the muzzle against the chest or abdomen with the left hand and reaching with the right for the trigger (if right-handed). In order to reach the trigger, the individual unconsciously rotates the body counter-clockwise. Thus, the bullet or pellets will follow a right-to-left path through the body because of this rotation. Because the victim is "hunched" over the gun, the trajectory of the bullet or pellets is downward and not the upward path one would expect. Thus, the trajectory of the bullet or pellets through the body will be downward and right to left. If the individual uses the left hand to fire the weapon, grasping the muzzle with the right hand, they will rotate the body clockwise, and the path of the bullet or pellets, while still downward, will be from left to right. As virtually all hunting is done with long arms, the trajectory of the bullet and pellets through the body is important in "hunting accident" cases.

Suicides Due to Handguns

The location of the self-inflicted wound varies depending on the type of the weapon, the sex of the victim, and whether the victim is right- or left-handed. In individuals who shoot themselves with handguns, the most common sites for the entrance wound are the head (81%), the chest (17%), and the abdomen (2%), in that order (Table 14.1). There is some difference by sex (Table 14.1) in that a smaller percentage of women (72%) shoot themselves in the head than do men (83.5%).

Table 14.1   Sites of Suicidal Handgun Wounds

Site	Males		Females		Combined Total
	Number	Percent	Number	Percent	
Head	304	(83.5%)	72	(72%)	376 (81%)
Chest	58	(15.9%)	22	(22%)	80 (17%)
Abdomen	2	(0.6%)	6	(6%)	8 (2%)
Total	364	(100%)	100	(100%)	464 (100%)

When individuals shoot themselves, they do not necessarily hold the weapon the same way they would if they were firing the weapon at a target. Commonly, they will hold a handgun with the fingers wrapped around the back of the butt, using the thumb to depress the trigger, firing the weapon (Figure 14.2). In gunshot wounds under the chin, they may hold the weapon "correctly", but bend their forearm upwards and backwards such that the gun is upside down when they fire it (Figure 14.3).

Some individuals will steady a gun against the body, by grasping the barrel with the non-firing hand (Figure 14.2). In the case of contact wounds of the head, and less commonly the trunk, soot may be deposited on the thumb, index finger, and connecting web of skin of the steadying hand due to blowback of gases from the muzzle (Figure 14.4A). In the case of a revolver, soot may be deposited on the palm from cylinder gap (Figure 14.4B). The location of the soot on the palm is influenced by the barrel length and where the gun is held. With two-inch barrel weapons, the soot is in the midpalm; with four-inch barrels, toward the ulnar aspect of the palm. In rare instances, the blast of gases from the cylinder gap is so strong as to lacerate the skin of

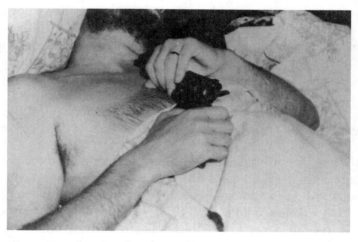

Figure 14.2   Note deceased's left hand around barrel of gun and use of thumb to fire weapon.

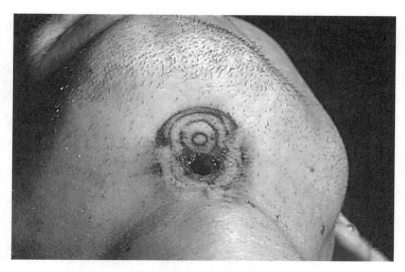

Figure 14.3 Contact wound under chin from pistol held inverted at time of firing. Upside-down muzzle imprint. Front-sight at 6 o'clock.

the palm (Figure 14.5). In two cases seen by the author, the individual committing suicide wore a glove on the hand used to grasp the cylinder, apparently so as not to burn their hand. Even if there is no visible powder or soot deposition on the hand, analysis for primer residues is often positive.

Occasionally, an individual steadying the barrel with their non-firing hand, inadvertently places part of the hand over the muzzle. This has lead to individuals shooting themself through the hand. In one case, the muzzle was held tightly against the palm of the hand, which was against the forehead. On discharge, the emerging hot gases, soot and powder perforated the palm

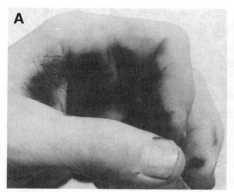
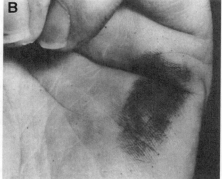

Figure 14.4 (A) Soot deposited on radial aspect and edge of palm of hand; (B) soot deposited on ulnar aspect of palm of hand.

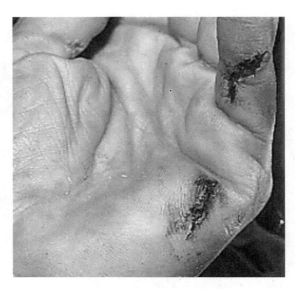

Figure 14.5 Lacerations of palm and fifth finger from gas escaping from cylinder gap of .357 Magnum revolver. Hand was around cylinder at time of discharge.

producing a wound of the forehead that had all the characteristics of a primary contact wound (Figure 14.6).

In the head, the most common site for a handgun entrance wound is the temple. Although most right-handed individuals shoot themselves in the right temple and left-handed individuals in the left temple, this pattern is not absolute. In a study by Stone of 125 right-handed individuals who shot themselves in the temple, seven (5.6%) shot themselves in the left temple.[3]

With handguns, after the temple, the most common sites in the head, in decreasing order of occurrence, are the mouth, the underside of the chin, and the forehead. There are people, however, who will be different and shoot themselves on the top of the head, in the ear, in the eye, etc. The author has seen a number of unquestionable cases of suicide in which individuals have shot themselves in the back of the head. These have occurred not only with handguns but also with rifles and shotguns (Figures 14.7 and 14.8). In another unusual case, the entrance wound was on the side of the chest, in the mid-axillary line. Thus, the fact that a wound is in an unusual location does not necessarily mean that it cannot be self-inflicted, though it is wise to always start with the presumption that such a case is a homicide.

As previously noted, with handguns, the sex of the victim appears to play a part in determining where they shoot themselves. In a study by the author (Table 14.1), while 83.5% of the men shot themselves in the head, only 72% of the women did. Stone, in a study of 703 male and 192 female suicides

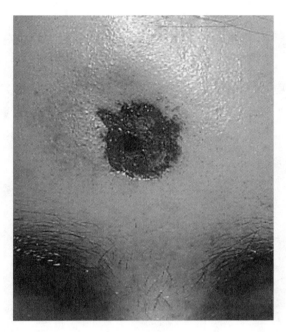

Figure 14.6 Apparent "contact" wound of forehead. In actuality, muzzle was in contact with palm which was against forehead.

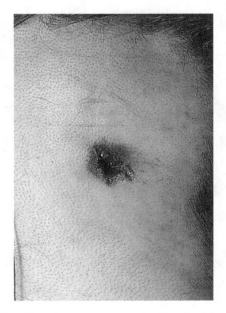

Figure 14.7 Self-inflicted contact wound of back of head from handgun.

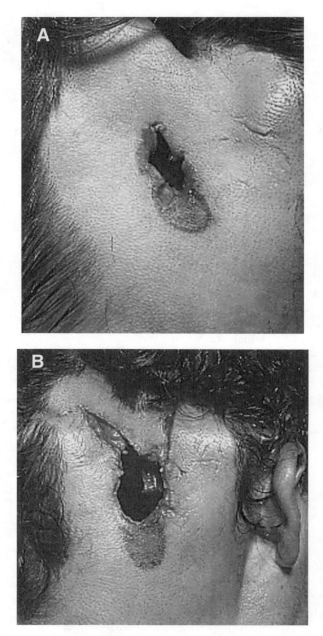

Figure 14.8 Self-inflicted gunshot wounds on back of head from (**A**) rifle (note imprint of magazine below entrance) and (**B**) shotgun.

using handguns, reported virtually the same incidence, 84% for males and 68% for females.[3]

Suicides Due to Long Arms

In suicides with long arms (rifles and shotguns), just as with handguns, the preferred sites are the head, chest, and abdomen, in that order. There is, however, very little difference in the percentage of head wounds between the sexes (Table 14.2). Thus, 69% of the men and 65% of the women had entrance wounds of the head.[3] The percentage of people shooting themselves in the head with rifles and shotguns is not as great as with handguns. This may be due to the fearsome reputation of these weapons. People do not mind shooting themselves in the head but do not want to "blow their head off."

Table 14.2   Sites of Suicidal Long Arm Wounds[a]

Site	Males		Females		Combined Total
	Number	Percent	Number	Percent	
Head	194	(69%)	15	(65%)	209 (69%)
Chest	83	(29%)	4	(17%)	87 (28%)
Abdomen	5	(2%)	4	(17%)	9 (3%)
Total	282	(100%)	23	(99%)	305 (100%)

[a]   Based on data from Stone, 1992.

In deaths involving centerfire rifles, most wounds of the head are in the mouth or temple. A study of 46 suicidal centerfire rifle wounds of the head revealed the location of the entrance, in decreasing frequency, was the mouth (41.3%), the temple (26.1%), underside of the chin (15.2%), the forehead (13%), and other (4.4%).[2] A study of 89 contact shotgun wounds of the head by Harruff found a similar distribution with the most common site of entrance the mouth (62%), followed by the temple (15%), and the submental region (13%).[4] While the vast majority of individuals who shot themselves in the temple with a centerfire rifle shoot themselves in the right temple compared to the left (11 to 1), in the case of shotguns, the difference as to which temple is selected is significantly less (7 to 4).[2] For both rifles and shotguns, most right handed individuals who shot themselves in the right temple use the left hand to steady the barrel.

Some individuals construct devices to shoot themselves at a distance or in unusual areas of the body. These devices may be as simple as clamping a gun to a chair and running a string through a pulley to the trigger, to elaborate devices employing electric motors and timers. An example of the former was a high-school student who shot himself in the back with a 12-gauge shotgun by wedging the gun partly under a mattress and inserting a baton in the trigger guard. While lying on his stomach, he used his feet to push the baton against the trigger, thus firing the gun.

In deaths due to long arms, just as in those with handguns, one should examine the hands for the presence of soot as well as test for primer residues. If soot is present, it will be on the hand used to steady the muzzle against the body and is due to blowback from the muzzle. The area involved is the thumb, index finger, and connecting web of skin. The presence of visible soot on the hands is relatively uncommon, in comparison to handguns. Very rarely, there may be tattooing due to blowback of powder from the muzzle (Figure 14.9). In two instances seen by the author, in holding the muzzle against the body, the web of skin between the index finger and thumb was inadvertently interposed between the muzzle and the target. This resulted in a tangential wound of the edge of the palm and searing of the skin. Even if there is no visible evidence of soot or powder, gunshot residue tests should be performed.

Suicides in General

Suicides in which multiple gunshot wounds are present are uncommon, but not rare. These wounds may involve only one area, e.g., the head, or multiple areas, such as the head and chest. Multiple gunshot wounds confined exclusively to the head are the least common, whereas those of the chest are the most common. A lack of knowledge of anatomy, flinching at the time the trigger is pulled, defective ammunition, ammunition of the wrong caliber, or just missing a vital organ, account for such multiple wounds. Occasionally, individuals have shot themselves simultaneously in the head with two different weapons (Figure 14.10).

Wounds that may appear to be fatal on initial examination may not be so on autopsy. Thus, in an individual who shot himself four times in the chest and once in the head with a .22-caliber pistol, one would assume that the head wound was the fatal shot. However, the autopsy revealed that the bullet flattened out against the frontal bone, and death was due to one of the four gunshot wounds of the chest, with one bullet going through the heart.

The largest number of gunshot wounds in a suicide that the author is aware of is nine.[5] The weapon was a nine-shot .22-caliber revolver. All nine bullets entered the chest, with one perforating a vital organ, the left lung, causing massive hemorrhage, hemothorax, and death.

Occasionally an individual will use two totally different methods in an attempt to commit suicide. Thus, one finds individuals dead of a gunshot

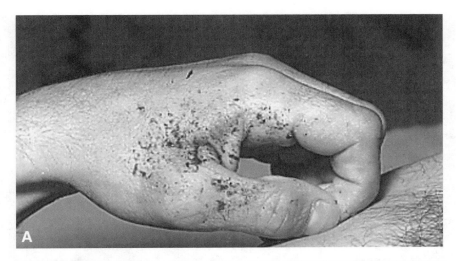

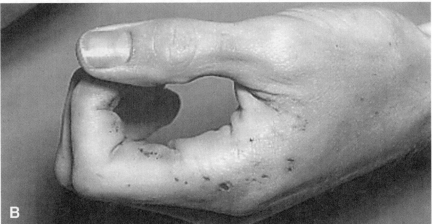

Figure 14.9 Powder tattooing of edge of palm from blowback of powder from muzzle of (**A**) shotgun and (**B**) rifle

wound with potentially lethal levels of drugs. Apparently the drugs do not work fast enough and the individual decides to shoot himself. Another individual shot herself twice in the chest with a .22 rifle. Only one bullet entered the chest cavity piercing the left lung, producing internal hemorrhage. This apparently was not quick enough as the woman, then cut her wrists with a broken bottle. Another individual, wishing to make absolutely sure he would die, placed a noose around his neck, tied one end to a support, and then shot himself in the head. The bullet itself would have been fatal, but as he collapsed, he suspended himself by the neck. If he had survived any length of time from the gunshot wound, he would have died of hanging.

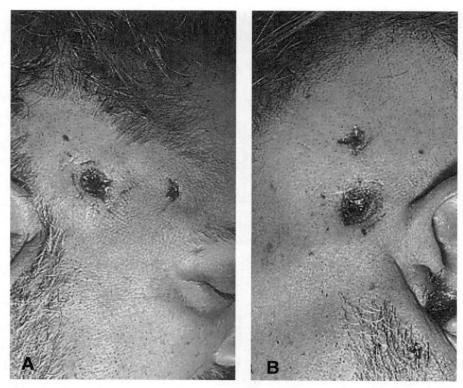

Figure 14.10 Simultaneously inflicted perforating gunshot wounds of head from two .25 ACP automatic pistols. Entrances of right (**A**) and left (**B**) temples with muzzle imprints and exits of bullets from other side.

The most unusual case of this kind the author has seen was a young woman who shot herself in the chest with a revolver while standing at the end of a pier. She was seen to collapse immediately after the discharge of the weapon, with the gun falling onto the pier, and the woman tumbling backward into the harbor. The body was recovered a few hours later. At autopsy, she was found to have a through-and-through gunshot wound of the left breast. The bullet did not enter the chest cavity and did not injure any major blood vessel. The cause of death was drowning.

Most people who shoot themselves do so in private. Exceptions are numerous, however. Individuals have shot themselves in front of friends, spouses, relatives, and even crowds. The place chosen for the suicide may be quite bizarre. Individuals have shot themselves while driving, in police cars, and on television. One individual climbed into the trunk of his car, closed it, and then shot himself with a shotgun.

Sometimes the fatal bullet will exit the victim and either re-enter another area of the body or strike another individual. In one case, an individual shot himself in the head while holding his other arm across his head, almost as if covering his ear. The bullet entered one temple, exited the other, and then lodged in the upraised arm. Another individual shot himself while lying in bed with the bullet exiting and striking his wife.

Suicide is not acceptable in American society, and thus there is often strenuous objection to the ruling of a death as suicide. The objections can vary from the naive "he wouldn't do such a thing" to a sophisticated and complicated explanation for why a weapon "accidentally" discharged. These objections can be motivated by guilt, religious belief, social pressure, or avarice.

Individuals may contest the ruling of suicide by stating that the deceased, though previously depressed, had recently been happy. In fact, it is not uncommon for individuals who have decided to commit suicide to show an elevation in mood before the suicide. After all, they have solved their problems—they are going to kill themselves.

Movement of Firearms at the Scene

In a study of 574 gunshot suicides in which the body was not transported from the scene, Garavaglia and Talkington found that the gun was moved in 96 instances (16.7%) before a representative of the Medical Examiners Office arrived. In 39% of the cases a family member or friend moved the gun; in 37% the police; 7% emergency medical technicians; 2% witnesses, and in 15% of the cases, it was not known who moved the gun.[6]

Guns Found in the Hand

Garavaglia and Talkington studied 498 cases of suicide from gunshot wounds — 365 from handguns and 133 from long arms — to determine in how many cases the weapon remained in the hand and what factors, if any, predisposed to this.[6] They found that in 24.1% (120) of the 498 cases, the gun was in the hand; in 69% (344) on or touching the body or within one foot of it, and in 7% (34) of the cases greater than a foot away. Of the 34 guns more than a foot from the body, four (4) were long guns (3% of all long guns) and 30 handguns (8% of all handguns).

In the case of the 365 handgun suicides, in 25.7% (94) of the cases, the gun was in the hand. By this is meant that at least one finger was in the trigger guard or the hands were found loosely gripping the barrel or grip. It was not considered in the hand if the gun appeared to have just simply fallen on the hand or vice versa. In 22 (23.4%) of these 94 cases (6% of all the handgun cases), the deceased shot themselves while standing and collapsed to the ground still holding the weapon.

In the case of long arms, in 19.5% (26) of the 133 cases, the gun was found in the hand, usually the left hand around the barrel. In 6 (23.1%) of the 26 cases (4.5% of the 133 cases), the deceased shot themselves while standing and collapsed to the ground still holding the weapon.

The sex of the deceased, the location of the wound, and the caliber of the gun were not significant in determining if a gun would stay in the hand. In contrast, the position of the deceased at the time they shot themselves was. Of the 498 cases, 249 (50%) individuals were sitting or lying down when they shot themselves; 249 (50%) standing. Of the 120 individuals found with the gun in the hand, 76.6% (92) were sitting or lying down when they shot themselves; 23.3% (28) standing.

Occasionally, one finds yellow to orange-brown areas of discoloration of the skin of the palm and/or fingers of a hand in which a gun was found (Figure 14.11). These are iron deposits in the epidermis due to "rusting" of the iron of the barrel or frame by water and salt in perspiration. This stain will not wipe away. The fact that this material is iron has been confirmed by energy dispersive x-ray and special stains for iron.[7] The exact time that the weapon has to rest in the hand for this phenomena to occur is not known but appears to be a few hours at least.

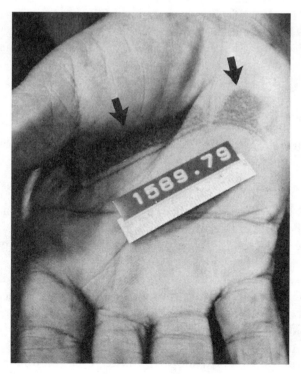

Figure 14.11   Discoloration of palm from deposits of iron.

Backspatter (Blowback) on the Hands of Shooters in Cases of Suicide

Articles and lecturers commonly make mention of the deposition of high-velocity blood droplets (backspatter) on the back of the hand used to fire a handgun in cases of suicide. Such a spray may in fact be present not only on the hand firing the gun, but also on the back of the hand used to steady the muzzle (Figure 14.12).

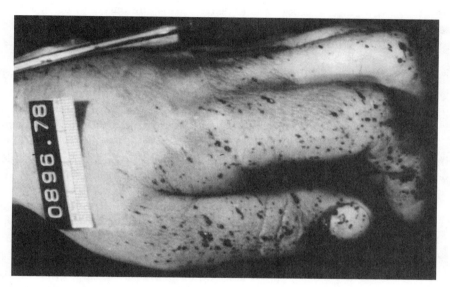

Figure 14.12   Spray of blood on hand used to steady muzzle of weapon.

Betz et al. studied 103 suicidal contact wounds: 18 from revolvers; 52 from pistols; 22 from a rifle or shotgun and 11 cases where the weapon was unknown.[8] In 32% of the 103 cases, blood spatter was present on the shooting hand by naked eye examination. More specifically blood spatter was present in 33% of the cases involving revolvers; 35% pistols; 27% rifles and shotguns and 27% of the cases where the weapon was unknown. All the wounds due to the handguns involved the head and neck. In 6 of the 22 cases involving rifles and shotguns, the wounds were in the chest. In none of the 6 cases was backspatter found. If one considers only the 16 cases of rifle and shotgun wounds where the wound was of the head or neck then the incidence of backspatter is 37.5%.

Betz et al. also noted that as the caliber of the pistols increased so did the frequency of visible backspatter.[8] Thus, while 35% of all pistols (calibers .25ACP to 9 mm) were associated with backspatter, 50% of the 9 mm cases (the largest caliber) were positive. The small number of revolver cases prevented any analysis.

Backspatter (Blowback) on Weapons in Cases of Contact Wounds

In addition to examining the hands for blood, if possible, one should examine the gun for the presence of blood or tissue. Examination for blood should be both visual and chemical. Blood is more often detected on the outside of the muzzle than inside the barrel. In a study of 653 revolvers, 242 pistols, 181 shotguns, and 124 rifles used in suicides, blood was detected on the barrel 74% of the time for revolvers, 76% for pistols, 85% for shotguns, and 81% for rifles.[3] In contrast, blood was detected inside the barrel in 53% of the revolvers, 57% of pistols, 72% of shotguns and 58% of rifles. The presence of blood inside the barrel of a gun indicates that the weapon was within a few inches of the body at the time of discharge. Absence of blood on or in the barrel does not preclude a close range or contact wound. Thus, no blood was found either on the outside or inside of the barrel in 24% of the suicides using a revolver and 23% using a pistol.

Blood may be detected in the barrel even after the weapon has been discharged. In a study of 25 revolvers and 36 pistols, in 40% of revolvers and in 42% of pistols, blood was detected after one test firing.[3] More remarkable was the fact that blood was still detected in 16% of revolvers and 25% of pistols after a second shot was fired.

"Russian Roulette"

No discourse on suicides would be complete without discussing "Russian roulette." Obviously, all such cases involve a revolver. In the author's opinion, the majority of such deaths are suicides. When an individual puts a weapon to his head that he knows to be loaded, and pulls the trigger, the ensuing death is a suicide until proven otherwise. Virtually, the only exceptions to this, i.e., when such a death might be ruled an accident are: when it occurs in a situation in which there are multiple participants in the "game" and the weapon is being passed around among the participants; when it is done to impress a friend, a family member or a member of the opposite sex of how "macho" the shooter is. Usually in these cases, a high blood alcohol or drug level will be found in the deceased.

Rarely, an individual will shoot themselves in the head with an auto-loading pistol under circumstances such that the author feels that the death is accidental. These individuals are usually young, and/or intoxicated and are "showing-off" in front of friends or relatives. In virtually all instances, the individual was apparently not knowledgeable about pistols. They thought that removing the magazine from a pistol unloaded it. They were not aware of the possibility of a residual round in the chamber. Some pistols have magazine disconnectors such that when the magazine is removed the gun will not fire. It is possible to remove this disconnector in some pistols and this is occasionally done.

Accidental Deaths from Firearms

In order to decide whether a death from gunshot wound is an accident, one should know the circumstances leading up to and surrounding the death: who was present, the findings at the scene, the type of weapon, the result of an examination of the weapon by a firearms examiner, the findings at autopsy, and the results of the toxicology study.

The number of deaths in the U.S. from accidental gunshot wounds has steadily declined since 1970. In 1970, there were 2406 such cases; in 1992, 1409.[1] Even this number may be too high as suicides are not uncommonly labeled as accidents. This misclassification may result from a multitude of reasons: lack of knowledge concerning weapons or the circumstances surrounding the death, naivete, an attempt to "make things easier" for a surviving spouse or family, etc. Misclassification of suicides as accidents is more common in coroner systems than medical examiner systems.

It is the opinion of the author that, if an individual is holding a weapon and this weapon discharges killing another individual, this death should be classified as a homicide. This is true even if the individual who was holding the weapon alleges that they did not intend to kill the other individual. The decision as to intent is not for the medical examiner to make but is up to the Courts. Guns do not discharge by themselves while being held. Someone has to pull the trigger. A gun does not "magically" go off. The only exception to such a ruling of homicide would be if the individual holding the weapon was a very young child (? 8–9 years or younger) who did not realize the consequences of pulling the trigger. Unfortunately, in our society, "children" of 10, 11, and 12 yrs of age are committing murder for money, drugs, to gain a reputation, for gang initiation or out of plain "meanness." Twelve- and thirteen-year-old contract killers exist. Thus, one has to be very careful in classifying a death as an accident based on the shooter's age.

A firearms death should be labeled as an accident if the weapon falls to the ground and discharges. Such an accidental discharge is due to the design of the weapon or a defect in it.

Handguns that will discharge on dropping fall into five general categories:

1. Single-action revolvers
2. Old or cheaply made double-action revolvers
3. Derringers
4. Striker-operated automatics
5. Certain external hammer automatics

Single-action revolvers are involved in most instances of discharge of a dropped weapon.[9] Unlike double-action revolvers, the hammer of a single-action revolver must be cocked manually before pressure on the trigger will release the hammer. The firing pin in this weapon may be either integral with the hammer or in the frame separate from the hammer. Whatever the case, single-action revolvers have traditionally been dangerous in that, when the hammer is down, the firing pin projects through the breech face, resting on the primer of the cartridge aligned with the barrel. If the weapon is accidentally dropped and lands on the hammer, the force transmitted through the hammer to the firing pin and then to the primer may be sufficient to discharge the weapon. Because of this characteristic, single-action revolvers traditionally have been carried with the hammer down on an empty chamber.

Ruger is the major manufacturer of single-action revolvers. In 1973, because of the large numbers of accidents reported from the dropping of single-action weapons, the design of their weapons was changed so that a safety lever permits discharge only when the trigger is held all the way back. The operation of a safety lever will be discussed later in this chapter.

Most revolvers now manufactured are double-action. Well-made double-action revolvers are equipped with safety devices that prevent contact between the firing pin and the trigger if the weapon is dropped. Smith & Wesson revolvers are equipped with two safety systems: the rebound slide and the hammer block (Figure 14.13). The older of these systems, the rebound slide, was introduced in 1896 and modified in 1908. It prevents forward rotation of the hammer unless the trigger is held to the rear. In 1915, Smith & Wesson added a second safety system to this revolver, the hammer block. This is an L-shaped metal rod whose foot is automatically interposed between the hammer and the frame except when the trigger is held to the rear.

Colt double-action revolvers are equipped with a rebound lever and a hammer block (Figure 14.14). The hammer of a Colt revolver lies in a cut in the rebound lever. The hammer cannot rotate forward because of the metal of the lever. Only when the trigger is pulled and the rebound lever elevated out of the way can the hammer rotate forward to fire the weapon. The Colt hammer block system was introduced in 1905 and has been standard with all double-action Colt revolvers since 1910. Its action is identical to that of the hammer block in the Smith & Wesson revolver.

Ruger double-action revolvers, the new version of the Ruger single-action revolvers, and Charter Arms revolvers all are equipped with a device called a "safety lever" (Figure 14.15). In these weapons, the hammer rests against the steel frame above the firing pin. When the trigger is pulled, the safety lever rises, interposing itself between the firing pin and the hammer. When the hammer falls, it strikes the safety lever, which transmits the force to the firing pin, which in turn strikes the primer, firing the cartridge. When the

Figure 14.13 Smith & Wesson revolver with rebound slide (a) and (b) hammer block. (Reprinted with permission from the *Journal of Forensic Sciences*, 19(4), 1974. Copyright ASTM, 1916 Race Street, Philadelphia, Pennsylvania.)

trigger is released, the safety lever drops below the firing pin and the hammer again comes to rest against the frame. The safety lever is also present in Colt Mark III revolvers.

These safety systems are often not present in cheap double-action revolvers know as Saturday Night Specials. In these weapons, safety devices may vary from non-existent to excellent in concept but poor in execution. Some Saturday Night Special revolvers use a hammer block consisting of a thin steel wire. The metal of the hammer, however, may be so soft that a number of sharp blows to the hammer causes the wire to indent the soft metal of the frame of the weapon, thus permitting the hammer to strike the firing pin, discharging the weapon.

In derringers with external hammers, just as in single-action revolvers, the firing pin rests on the primer of the chambered round. Dropping a derringer on the hammer will cause it to discharge. This does not happen with the hammerless derringer manufactured by High-Standard.

With automatic pistols, the firing mechanism is of two possible designs: striker-operated or hammer-operated. The cheaper automatic pistols are

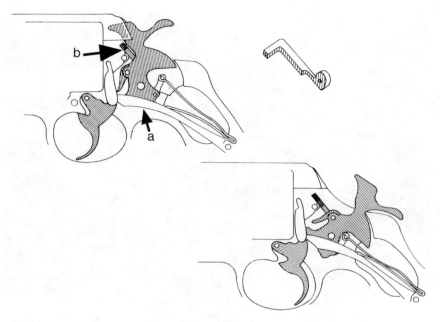

Figure 14.14 Colt revolver with **(a)** rebound lever and **(b)** hammer block.

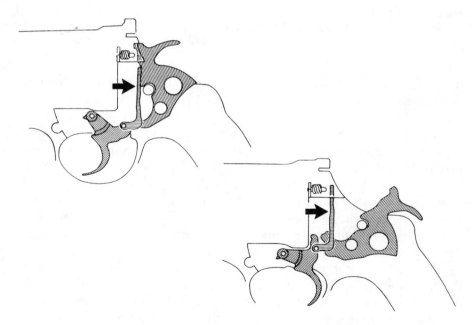

Figure 14.15 Revolver with safety lever.

usually striker-operated. Here a rod-like firing pin travels inside the breech block propelled by a coiled spring. When the weapon is cocked, the slide is pulled back and the striker is engaged by the sear and held in a rearward position. On pulling the trigger, the sear disengages the striker, and the spring drives it forward, firing the cartridge. With poorly made, cheap weapons, the internal tolerances of the parts may be such that if the weapon is dropped, the striker may jar loose from the sear, go forward, and fire the weapon.

Hammer-operated automatic pistols may have either an internal or an external hammer. For all practical purposes, accidental discharge of a dropped automatic pistol involves only external hammer weapons. Whether an automatic with an external hammer is safe or dangerous depends on the presence or absence of safety devices as well as the position of the hammer at the time of fall. Thus, both the Colt Model 1911A1 and the Browning Hi-Power are generally safe if dropped on their hammer when it is down. These weapons, at a minimum, are equipped with a "flying firing pin." The pin is shorter than the length it has to travel in the breech block. To propel the pin forward far enough to strike the primer, the hammer has to fall a great enough distance to impart sufficient inertia to the firing pin. If the hammer is down, a blow to it cannot be transmitted to the primer. If the weapon is at half cock when dropped, discharge can occur. The blow to the hammer, however, has to be sufficient to break off the half-cock notch or the tip of the sear engaging the notch. The forward travel of the hammer then may be sufficient to fire the weapon. If the weapon is at full cock and is dropped, it theoretically can discharge. Discharge is unlikely, however, because the force would have to be sufficient to break not only the full-cock notch but the half-cock notch. If only the full-cock notch was broken off, the half-cock notch would catch the hammer and the weapon would not discharge. The author is unaware of any Colt Model 1911A1 having discharged when dropped on a fully cocked hammer as long as the weapon had not been tampered with. Thus, weapons such as the Colt M1911A1 or Browning should be carried only with the hammer all the way down or at full cock.

There is one way a weapon such as the Colt M1911A1, theoretically, can discharge if dropped, even if the hammer is down. This occurs if the gun falls on its muzzle from a distance of 6 ft. or more. The inertia given to the firing pin by a fall of this height may be sufficient to discharge a primer. Since the gun would have fallen on its muzzle, the bullet would go into the floor or ground.

Some pistols, such as the Walther PPK are equipped with a hammer block that performs the same function as in a double-action revolver. Newer semi-automatic pistols designs e.g. the Sig-Sauers as well as modernized versions of traditional design pistols e.g. the Browning Hi-Power have a firing pin safety block that prevents the firing pin from moving forward unless the trigger is pulled. Thus, the weapon cannot fire if dropped.

Rifles and Shotguns

Just as for handguns, it is possible under certain circumstances for a rifle or shotgun to discharge when dropped. This can be due to the intrinsic design of the weapon, poor workmanship, alteration of internal parts or broken parts. With some bolt-action rifles, if (1) the trigger is held back as, (2) the action is opened, (3) a round is chambered, and (4) the action closed, while the rifle is not cocked, the firing pin is resting on the primer. If the rifle is then dropped a few feet, it may discharge. What the advantage is in carrying a rifle in this condition eludes the author.

Accidental discharges of rifles and shotguns are rare compared with discharge of handguns. In all alleged cases of accidental discharge of a long arm, as for a handgun, the weapon should be examined by an experienced firearms examiner for defects in design or construction, broken parts, or wear.

Occasionally an individual will put a loaded rifle or shotgun in the back of a vehicle. When they attempt to take it out, they grab it by the muzzle and pull it toward them. A projection in the vehicle may catch the trigger, discharging the weapon. This is an accidental death. One must be sure, however, that this is not a staged suicide.

Another category of death that may be considered accidental are "hunting accidents" in which one individual shoots another. One has to be careful that the death is not a homicide. Each case has to be examined individually and decided on its own merits. Personally, the author prefers to call these cases homicide and let the District Attorney or judicial system decide intent.

Slam-Fires

A slam-fire is the discharge of a firearm upon closing the action without the pulling of the trigger. They may be caused by a protruding or overly sensitive primer; a firing pin that protrudes because it is either stuck or failed to retract; a weak, broken or absent firing pin spring; inadequate headspace. Slam-fires are most commonly associated with self-loading military rifles in which civilian ammunition is being used as civilian primers are generally more sensitive to detonation than military primers. A protruding primer can cause a slam-fire from the closing bolt driving the primer cup against the anvil. A weak, broken or absent firing pin spring may fail to overcome the forward inertia imparted to the firing pin as the action closes. This permits the firing pin to impact the primer with sufficient force to discharge the primer.

References

1. U.S. Bureau of the Census, *Statistical Abstract of the U.S.:1995* (115th ed.). Washington, D.C. 1995.

2. Unpublished study by V. J. M. Di Maio.

3. Stone, I. C. Characteristics of firearms and gunshot wounds as markers of suicide. *Amer J. Forensic Med. Pathol.* 13:275–80, 1992.

4. Harruff, R. C. Comparison of contact shotgun wounds of the head produced by different gauge shotguns. *J. Forensic Sci.* 40(5):801–804, 1995.

5. Personal communication with J. Coe.

6. Garavaglia, J. and Talkington, W. *Amer J. Forensic Med. & Path.* (in press).

7. Norton, L. E., DiMaio, V. J. M., and Gilchrist, T. F. Iron staining of the hands in suicides with firearms. *J. Forensic Sci.* 24(3): 608–609, 1979.

8. Betz, P., Peschel, O., Stiefel, D., and Eisenmenger, W. Frequency of blood spatters on the shooting hand and of conjunctival petechiae following suicidal gunshot wounds to the head. *Forensic Sci. Intern* (1995):76:47–53.

9. DiMaio, V. J. M., and Jones, J. A. Deaths due to accidental discharge of a dropped handgun. *J. Forensic Sci.* 19(4): 759–767, 1974.

Appendix A

"Stopping Power" and Hollow-Point Pistol Ammunition: Myths and Facts

In the 1970s, a major controversy over the use of hollow-point handgun ammunition by police agencies erupted. The arguments against the use of this ammunition were generally emotional, with claims of "mutilating wounds" and organs reduced to "unidentifiable chopped meat." Most of the arguments heard for and against the use of hollow-point handgun ammunition were based on myths, false assumptions, and second-hand stories spread by both opponents and proponents of this type of ammunition.

From the introduction of the .38 Special cartridge in 1902 until the late 1970s, handguns chambered for this cartridge were used by most police agencies in the United States. The traditional .38 Special cartridge was loaded with a 158-gr., all-lead, round-nose bullet, propelled at velocities of 700 to 850 ft/sec. In the mid-1960s, many police organizations began to complain about this cartridge. They felt that this round did not have any "stopping power." They cited numerous instances in which officers, firing this cartridge in self-defense, were unable to stop their attacker before they injured the officer or an innocent bystander. What police agencies desired was a pistol cartridge that would stop a person "dead in his tracks." There is, of course, no such pistol cartridge and there never will be. "Stopping" an individual depends not only on the characteristics of a cartridge but also on the organ(s) injured, the severity of the wound(s) and the physiologic makeup of the person who is shot.

When a bullet strikes tissue, it produces injuries by two mechanisms: (1) directly crushing and shredding a wound track equal to the diameter of the bullet, and (2) creating a temporary cavity. These actions result in both anatomic and physiologic injuries that impair the function of the organs affected.

If a 9-mm hollow-point bullet expands (mushrooms) to 12 mm in passing through an organ, the amount of tissue crushed and shredded will,

379

theoretically, be greater than if the bullet did not expand or if it was a solid bullet. In reality, a solid or non-expanding bullet may produce equal if not more direct injury to tissue, if it tumbles after achieving penetration while the hollow-point doesn't. Solid bullets may even be more lethal than mushrooming bullets. As a general rule, mushrooming bullets do not penetrate as deeply as solid bullets because they mushroom. If the aorta, for example, is 14 inches from the skin surface and the mushrooming bullet stops after 12 inches of penetration but the solid bullet travels for 18 inches, then the solid bullet is more lethal than the hollow-point.

There is no objective proof that in real-life situations mushrooming of a bullet plays a significant role in increasing lethality or the "stopping power" of the bullet. This is because of the other factors that can also influence the amount of tissue destruction and incapacitation, e.g., the organ injured, the state of the organ at the time of impact (distended or collapsed), the stability of the bullet, and the emotional state of the victim, etc.

As a bullet moves through the body, not only does it directly injure tissue, it also creates a temporary cavity. The size of this cavity is directly related to the amount of kinetic energy lost by the bullet in the tissue. A hollow-point bullet should lose more kinetic energy in a vital organ than a non-expanding bullet. This is because as a hollow-point bullet travels through the tissue, it expands, creating greater resistance to its travel, decelerating more rapidly, and losing more kinetic energy than a solid bullet. As a result of this, the temporary cavity produced by the hollow-point bullet will be greater in size than that from a solid bullet. The key word in discussing cavity formation is "temporary." This cavity lasts only 5 to 10 msec before the tissue springs back into position as a result of the tissue's inherent elasticity and resiliency. In the case of handgun bullets, the size of the temporary cavities produced by hollow-point bullets versus non-deforming bullets is not significantly different so as to effect the severity of wounds. In other words, the temporary cavity phenomena is of little or no significance in wounding when dealing with handgun bullets.

Whether using either a hollow-point or a solid-lead handgun bullet to inflict a mortal injury, the bullet must strike a vital organ. Although hollow-point bullets, in comparison to traditional solid lead bullets, theoretically have a greater ability to kill by virtue of greater physiologic injury to an organ, such differences are only theoretical. An individual shot through the heart with a solid, round-nose bullet is just as likely to die as an individual shot through the heart with a hollow-point bullet. In the case of a gunshot wound of the lung, theoretically the hollow-point would be more likely to cause death. In reality, the speed at which a wounded individual is transported to the hospital is a greater determining factor as to whether the individual will live or die than the type of ammunition used.

More important than the theoretical concept of greater "stopping power," hollow-point ammunition does possess two virtues. The first is that such bullets tend to stay in the body. It is therefore unlikely that a bullet will exit and injure innocent bystanders. Second, hollow-point bullets tend to break up rather than ricochet if they strike hard objects. Again, this trait works to prevent injury to innocent bystanders.

There are a number of myths about hollow-point handgun ammunition which tend to impart a bad reputation to this type of ammunition. First, it should be said that hollow-point bullets do not mutilate organs or destroy them any more than their solid-nose, all-lead counterparts of the same caliber. The wounds in the skin, as well as those in the internal organs, are the same in appearance and extent for both types of ammunition. One cannot examine the wounds in a body and say that the individual was shot with a hollow-point rather than a solid-lead bullet. No organs are reduced to a "chopped meat" by a handgun bullet.

The second myth is that hollow-point handgun bullets fragment or "blow up" in the body. Fragments, both jacket and/or core, may break off a hollow-point bullet especially if it strikes a bone — but this breakup is not significant.

What is the origin of these myths? Part of the explanation is the normal exaggeration and distortion that occurs in stories when they are passed from person to person. Second is the fact that many people, with little or no experience with hollow-point handgun ammunition, do not let this inexperience stand in the way of their offering "expert" testimony on the topic. Third is the fact that some people confuse wounds caused by soft-point and hollow-point centerfire rifle bullets with those caused by handgun bullets. Individuals shot with soft-point or hollow-point rifle bullets show significantly more severe wounds than people wounded by handgun bullets—rifle bullets shed large numbers of fragment in the body. Confusion between handgun and centerfire rifle bullets or statements based on experience only in the military, where centerfire rifle bullets are the rule, may have caused the origin of some of these myths about hollow-point handgun bullets.

Is there any situation in which a hollow-point handgun bullet will invariably stop an individual "dead in his tracks"? Yes, if the bullet injures a vital area of the brain, the brain stem, or the cervical spinal cord. But any bullet, regardless of style or caliber, injuring these organs will cause instant incapacitation. It is the nature of the structure injured, not the nature of the bullet, that causes the incapacitation. Aside from areas in the central nervous system, while a bullet may produce rapid incapacitation, there is no guarantee that it will produce instant incapacitation. This is because in these other areas incapacitation is produced indirectly by depriving the brain of blood and oxygen. Since the brain can function for 10 to 15 seconds without oxygen, even if all blood is cut off by the wound, the individual can function for this time period. If the injury does not shut off the flow of blood to the brain completely, an individual will be capable of normal activity until they lose approximately 25% of their total blood volume. The amount of time necessary for this to happen can vary from a few seconds (plus the 10 to 15 second oxygen reserve of the brain), to minutes, to hours depending on the structures injured, compensatory mechanisms of the body and attempts to staunch the bleeding by the victim. The fact that an individual can be mortally wounded, yet still be capable of aggressive actions and a threat, sometimes for a prolonged amount of time, is not appreciated by the public whose concepts of shootings is derived from television and the movies. This is periodically manifested by outcries from the public and the news media against the police when an officer shoots a perpetrator multiple times.

While there are numerous cases where an individual has received a mortal wound and continued to function, there are also numerous cases where an individual collapsed immediately after receiving a non-lethal, even minor, wound. In these cases, the rapid incapacitation is due to psychological and physiological reactions to the trauma, specific to the victim, and not the nature of the wounds.

Appendix B

The Forensic Autopsy in Gunshot Wound Cases

The forensic autopsy differs from the hospital autopsy in its objectives and relevance. In addition to determining the cause of death, the forensic pathologist must establish the manner of death (natural, accidental, suicidal, homicidal or undetermined), the identity of the deceased if unknown, and the time of death or injury. The forensic autopsy may involve collection of evidence from the body, which can be used to either incriminate or exonerate an individual charged with a crime; determine that a crime had or had not been committed and provide clues towards a subject if it has.

Because of the possible medicolegal implications of forensic cases, not only do these determinations have to be made, but the findings or lack of findings must be documented. In many cases the cause and manner of death may be obvious. It is the documentation of the injuries or lack of them as well as the interpretation of how they occurred and the determination or exclusion of other contributory or causative factors that is important.

The forensic autopsy involves not only the physical examination of the body on the autopsy table, but consideration of other aspects that the general pathologist does not consider as part of the autopsy—the scene, the nature of the weapon (if any), clothing, toxicology, and the results of laboratory tests on evidence. The forensic autopsy begins at the scene. The pathologist should not perform a forensic autopsy unless they know the circumstances leading up to and surrounding the death. This is a very basic principle that is often violated. What would one think of a physician who examined a patient without asking what the patient's symptoms or complaints were? As in all examinations of patients, one must have a medical history. In the case of the forensic pathologist, the "patient" is unable to render this history. Therefore, the history must be obtained either by the medical examiner or police investigators. This history should be known prior to the autopsy.

The scene should be documented with diagrams or photographs, preferably both. Individuals should be interviewed, and a written report given to the pathologist before the autopsy. At the scene, the body should be handled as little as possible. It makes good television dramatics to poke and prod a body at the scene, but it does not make sense scientifically. At a homicide scene, there is often pressure to move the body—people are milling around, there is inadequate lighting, no instruments, and no running water. A body cannot adequately be examined under such conditions. What can be done, however, is to destroy evidence or introduce fallacious evidence. One can dislodge powder from the clothing, wipe away primer residue from the hands, contaminate the body with one's own hair or with the hair of the police officer assisting in turning, poking, and proding the body, and so forth.

In cases of violent death, paper bags should be secured about the hands prior to transport of the body so that no trace evidence will be lost. Plastic bags should not be used — with the body in a cooler, there will be condensation of water vapor on the hands (with possible loss of trace evidence) when it is moved back into a warm environment. Before transportation, the body should be wrapped in a clean, white sheet or placed in a clean body bag. A body should not be placed directly onto a cart in the back of an ambulance. Who knows what or who was lying on the cart prior to the body transport? Trace evidence from a prior body may be deposited on this body, or trace evidence from this body may be lost and subsequently transferred to another body.

At the morgue, the body should never be undressed before the medical examiner has seen it. This includes removing shoes and socks to place toe tags on the body. Rather than toe tags, the use of wrist identification bands such as those used in hospitals is recommended.

Examination of the clothing is as much a part of the autopsy as examination of the wounds. The clothing must be examined for bloodstains and trace evidence as well as to determine whether the wounds in the body correlate with the defects in the clothing. How would one know that the individual was not shot while nude or partially dressed and then dressed?

The body should never be embalmed before autopsy. Embalming ruins toxicologic analyses, changes the appearance of the wounds, and can induce artifacts. In homicides, suspicious deaths, and gun-shot related deaths, the body should never be fingerprinted prior to examination of the hands. In fingerprinting, the hands are pryed open and the fingers are inked. In the process, evidence can be lost and/or false evidence deposited. One can render tests for firearms' residue invalid in prying apart fingers and fingerprinting a body. When fingerprinting is subsequently done in homicides, it is recommended that palm prints also be taken.

In all gunshot deaths, x-rays should be taken. X-rays are especially important in cases in which the bullet appears to have exited. This is due to the fact that the bullet may not have exited but rather only a piece of the bullet or a piece of bone. With the semi-jacketed ammunition now in widespread use, it is not uncommon for the lead core to exit the body and for the jacket to remain. The core is usually of no interest forensically; it is the jacket that is important. The jacket may be retained beneath the skin adjacent to the exit site. It is very easy to miss the jacket at autopsy unless one knows that it is there by x-ray.

An identification photograph, with the case number included in the photograph, should be made after the body has been cleaned up and before the autopsy.

The Autopsy Report

The first part of the forensic autopsy is the **External Examination**. This should include: age, sex, race, physique, height, weight, and nourishment. Congenital malformations, if present, should be noted. Next, one should give a description of the clothing. This description initially does not need to be very detailed. A simple listing of the articles found or accompanying the body should be given, e.g., a short-sleeved white shirt unbuttoned down the front, a blood-stained white T-shirt, etc. If the case is a traumatic death with significant alterations of the garments as a result of trauma, the clothing will be described in further detail in another section of the autopsy. Following the description of the clothing, one should then describe as a minimum:

Degree and distribution of rigor and livor mortis.
Hair (length and color); facial hair; alopecia.
Appearance of the eyes; the eye color.
Any unusual appearance to the ears, nose, or face, e.g., congenital mal-
    formations, scarring, severe acne (excluded should be evidence of
    trauma, which will have its separate section).
Presence of teeth and/or dental plates.
Presence of vomitus in the nostrils or mouth.
Significant scars, tattoos, or moles.
External evidence of disease.
Old injuries.
Evidence of recent medical or surgical intervention.*
No recent injuries should be described in this section.

If there is injury to the body, it should now be described in the next section entitled **Evidence of Injury**. All recent injuries, whether minor or major, external or internal, should be described in this section. There is no

---

* One may want to put this material in a separate section entitled **Evidence of Medical/Surgical Intervention**.

need to repeat the description of these injuries in the subsequent **Internal Examination** section. If possible, the age of the lesions should be, at least, generally described.

There are many ways to handle the **Evidence of Injury** section. Excluding gunshot and stab wounds, it is easiest to group the injuries into two broad areas: the external evidence of injury and the internal evidence. Some people combine the two. They will describe the external evidence of injury to the head and then say, "Subsequent autopsy reveals..." and go on to describe the internal injuries of the head. They will then describe the external injuries of the trunk, followed by the internal injuries of the trunk.

Gunshot wounds represent a different situation. In gunshot wound cases, if at all possible, each individual wound should be described in its entirety (from entrance to exit or point of lodgement) before going on to the next wound. The entrance wounds should be assigned an arbitrary number (e.g., Gunshot Wound #1, #2, etc.) and then located on the body (in inches or centimeters) in relation to the top of the head or the sole of the foot and to the right or left of the midline. They should also be located (in inches or centimeters) in regard to a local landmark such as the nipple or the umbilicus. Describing a gunshot wound in relation to a local landmark is usually of greater value than locating the wound from the top of the head or so many centimeters or inches to the right or left of the midline. It is easier to visualize the location of a gunshot wound of the left chest as being "one inch above the level of the nipples" and "one inch medial to a vertical plane through the left nipple," rather than "20 inches below the top of the head" and "three inches to the left of the midline." The value in using local landmarks becomes obvious if one considers the location of a wound 20 inches below the head in a six foot 11 in. basketball player compared to a five foot secretary. This does not, however, remove one's responsibility for locating the entrance from the top of the head and to the right or left of the midline.

The features of a gunshot wound that make it an entrance wound and that define at what range it was inflicted i.e., the abrasion ring, soot, tattooing, etc., as well as the dimensions of these characteristics should be described. The author recommends that all measurements should be made using the metric system as this system is easier to use, more suitable for the measurements of small lesions, and less likely to result in inaccuracies. Pertinent negatives should be noted. Following this, the course of the bullet through the body should be described. All organs perforated or penetrated by the missile should be noted.

The location of the exit, if present, should be described, first in general terms e.g. the right lower lateral back and then either in relationship to the top of the head (or soles of the feet); or in relationship to the midline and the distance above or below the entrance. It is not useful and very confusing to give exit wounds numbers or letters.

If the bullet is recovered from the body, one should state where it was found; whether it is intact, deformed, or fragmented; whether the bullet is lead or jacketed; and the approximate caliber if known. A letter or number should be inscribed on the bullet and this information included in the autopsy report. The bullet then should be placed in an envelope with the name of the victim, the date, the case number, the location from which the bullet was recovered, the letter or number inscribed on it, and the name of the prosector. It goes without saying that all bullets should be recovered.

After describing the gunshot wound, one should then give an overall description of the missile path through the body in relation to the planes of the body. Thus, one will say, "The bullet traveled from back to front, left to right, and then sharply downward." Use of anatomical terminology such as dorsal, caudal etc. is not advisable as most individuals who will read a forensic autopsy are not physicians and will not understand these terms.

In cases where there are dozens of gunshot and/or fragment wounds, it may not be possible to handle each wound separately, and they may have to be handled in groups. This is of course how one handles shotgun pellet wounds. In the case of buckshot or pellet wounds, it is only necessary to recover a representative number of pellets. All wadding should be retained.

The last part of the **Evidence of Injury** section should concern the clothing. The location of defects due to bullets, pellets or knives, whether they correspond to the injuries or not and the presence of trace evidence, e.g., powder, soot, and car paint, should be described.

Following the section devoted to **Evidence of Injury** comes the **Internal Examination**. In this section, the major organ systems as well as the organ cavities are systematically described. The usual subdivisions of this section are:

Head
Body cavities
Neck
Respiratory system
Cardiovascular system
Gastrointestinal system
Biliary tract
Pancreas
Spleen
Adrenals
Urinary tract
Reproductive tract
Musculoskeletal system

In these sections, one gives organ weights (not necessary for adrenals and pancreas) as well as a brief description of the organs with pertinent negatives. With the pancreas, adrenals, and spleen, if there are no positive findings, use of the term "unremarkable" as the sole description is acceptable. Do not use the term "normal" as organs are rarely "normal," whatever that may mean.

The next section is **Microscopic Examination**. Microscopic slides are often not needed in forensic cases, especially in deaths from trauma. They should be made when indicated, however. Samples of tissue from all major organs should be saved for at least a year, preferably five years. In most gunshot wound cases, microscopic slides, including those of the wounds, are not necessary.

The next section is **Toxicology**. Here, the tests performed are listed; the tissue or fluid analyzed, the methods of analysis, e.g., gas chromatography and the results. In all autopsies, blood, urine, vitreous and bile, as a minimum, should be retained. These materials should be retained at least for a year after the case is completed.

Following Toxicology is **Findings**. List the major findings in order of importance. It is not necessary to list every minute or extraneous finding as is done in some hospital autopsy reports. This autopsy will most likely be seen by non-physicians. Having spent a half hour trying to explain acute passive congestion of the liver to a jury in a gunshot death, the author believes that inconsequential observations should not be listed in the Findings.

The last section is the **Opinion**. This should briefly describe the cause of death in as simple language as possible as well as stating the manner of death. This section is intended for the public and not for physicians. Thus, for example, one can say that the deceased "died of massive internal bleeding due to a gunshot wound of the aorta (the major blood vessel of the body)" or "... of a gunshot wound of the heart." Speculation about circumstances surrounding the death should be absent or kept to a minimum.

Following the autopsy, fingerprints, and in the case of homicides, palm-prints, should be taken if they have not already been.

Index